'Decisional privacy for a child, a multifaceted and presently poorly developed concept, is of critical importance in the evolution of parenting-related family law jurisprudence. This book offers real insight not presently elsewhere available. It is a must-read'.

The Honourable Justice Josh Wilson,
Federal Circuit and Family Court of Australia

'This book will appeal to those grappling with the tensions between children's rights, parental responsibilities and state duties in assessing children's best interests. Its innovative approach to decisional privacy will influence future best practice across the family justice community internationally'.

Professor Nicola Taylor, *Faculty of Law,*
University of Otago, New Zealand

Decisional Privacy and the Rights of the Child

Decisional privacy gives individuals the freedom to act and make decisions about how they live their lives, without unjustifiable interference from other individuals or the state. This book advances a theory of a child's right to decisional privacy. It draws on the framework of the United Nations Convention on the Rights of the Child and extends the work of respected children's rights scholars to address a significant gap in understanding the interconnections between privacy, family law and children's rights. It contextualises the theory through a case study: judicial proceedings concerning medical treatment for children experiencing gender dysphoria.

This work argues that recognising a substantive right to decisional privacy for children requires procedural rights that facilitate children's meaningful participation in decision-making about their best interests. It also argues that, as courts have increasingly encroached upon decision-making regarding children's medical treatment, they have denied the decisional privacy rights of transgender and gender diverse children.

This book will benefit researchers, students, judicial officers and practitioners in various jurisdictions worldwide grappling with the tensions between children's rights, parental responsibilities and state duties in relation to children's best interests, and with the challenge of better enabling and listening to children's voices in decision-making processes.

Georgina Dimopoulos is a socio-legal researcher and an Australian lawyer who has worked across the higher education sector, government, courts, commercial legal practice and community organisations. She holds a PhD from Melbourne Law School at the University of Melbourne and is experienced in legal and policy evaluation, and doctrinal, qualitative and empirical research, in the areas of family law and children's rights.

Routledge Research in Human Rights Law

Executive Clemency
Comparative and Empirical Perspectives
Edited by Daniel Pascoe and Andrew Novak

International Human Rights Law and Crimes Against Women in Turkey
Legislation on So-Called Honour Killings
Ayşe Güneş

Rights of the Child, Mothers and Sentencing
The Case of Kenya
Alice Wambui Macharia

Capturing Caste in Law
The Legal Regulation of Caste Discrimination
Annapurna Waughray

The Workings of Human Rights, Law, and Justice
A Journey from Nepal to Nobel Nominee
Surya P Subedi, QC

Civilian Drones, Visual Privacy and EU Human Rights Law
Girish Agarwal

International Human Rights Law and Destitution
An Economic, Social and Cultural Rights Perspective
Luke D. Graham

The European Convention of Human Rights Regime
Reform of Immigration and Minority Policies from Afar
Dia Anagnostou

Decisional Privacy and the Rights of the Child
Georgina Dimopoulos

For more information about this series, please visit: www.routledge.com/Routledge-Research-in-Human-Rights-Law/book-series/HUMRIGHTSLAW

Decisional Privacy and the Rights of the Child

Georgina Dimopoulos

Routledge
Taylor & Francis Group
LONDON AND NEW YORK

First published 2023
by Routledge
4 Park Square, Milton Park, Abingdon, Oxon OX14 4RN

and by Routledge
605 Third Avenue, New York, NY 10158

Routledge is an imprint of the Taylor & Francis Group, an informa business

British Library Cataloguing-in-Publication Data
A catalogue record for this book is available from the British Library

Library of Congress Cataloging-in-Publication Data
A catalog record has been requested for this book

ISBN: 978-1-032-12346-2 (hbk)
ISBN: 978-1-032-12348-6 (pbk)
ISBN: 978-1-003-22416-7 (ebk)

DOI: 10.4324/9781003224167

Typeset in Galliard
by Deanta Global Publishing Services, Chennai, India

For my children, Daria and Alec.

…For my children, Darin and Alec.

Contents

Acknowledgements

Just as 'it takes a village to raise a child', so too, in my experience, does it take a village to research and write a book. My heartfelt thanks go to Helen Rhoades and John Tobin for inspiring my passion for research in the areas of family law and children's rights. I also thank Andrew Roberts, Wendy Larcombe and Jenny Morgan for their support and guidance. John and Andy made my goal of completing the doctoral thesis from which this book derives a reality, and I thank John for his ongoing mentorship.

I thank Helen Stalford and Nicola Taylor, who examined my doctoral thesis, for their insightful comments and suggestions. I also thank Beate Rossler, Paul de Hert and Simona Giordano for the opportunity to discuss various ideas that form part of this book and for their constructive feedback on select chapters. Thank you to Nicola Jerkovic and Harrison Cant for their assistance with referencing, and to Alison Kirk, Anna Gallagher and Jayanthi Chander for their efficiency in seeing this book so smoothly through its various stages to completion.

I have been most fortunate to receive guidance and encouragement from a number of professional mentors over the years: the Honourable Justice Emilios Kyrou, Tony Kuhn, Mirko Bagaric, Timothy Marjoribanks, Amanda Scardamaglia and Rachel Carson. I thank them for their continuing counsel and their interest in, and support for, my career development.

Special thanks go to my husband, George, for his unwavering support, patience and encouragement, and to my mother, Stephanie, for always supporting, and reminding me of, my top priority: my family. My father, Nick, died a fortnight before I commenced the research for this book. I know how immensely proud he would be of it and of me. Most of all, I thank my children, Daria and Alec, for their unconditional love and for giving me the opportunity to see the world again through their eyes. They are, and always will be, my greatest achievement.

This book is based on the unpublished doctoral thesis, Georgina Dimopoulos, 'Children's Right to Decisional Privacy in Australian Family Law' (PhD Thesis, The University of Melbourne, 2020). The research for this book was supported by an Australian Government Research Training Program Scholarship and funding from Melbourne Law School, University of Melbourne. Parts of this book have been published previously and are reproduced with permission: Georgina Dimopoulos, 'A Theory of Children's Decisional Privacy' (2021) 41(3) *Legal*

Studies 430–53; Georgina Dimopoulos, 'Rethinking *Re Kelvin*: A Children's Rights Perspective on the "Greatest Advancement in Transgender Rights" for Australian Children' (2021) 44(2) *University of New South Wales Law Journal* 637–72; Georgina Dimopoulos and Michelle Taylor-Sands, '*Re Imogen*: The Role of the Family Court of Australia in Disputes over Gender Dysphoria Treatment' (2021) 39 (Suppl 1) *Monash Bioethics Review* S42–S66. Chapter 7 contains public sector information licensed under the Open Government Licence v3.0: *Bell and another v The Tavistock and Portman NHS Foundation Trust and others* [2021] EWCA Civ 1363; and *R (on the application of) Quincy Bell and A v Tavistock and Portman NHS Trust and others* [2020] EWHC 3274 (Admin).

Abbreviations

CRC	*United Nations Convention on the Rights of the Child* (1989)
CRC Committee	Committee on the Rights of the Child
ECHR	*European Convention for the Protection of Human Rights and Fundamental Freedoms* (1950)
TGD	transgender and gender diverse
UK	United Kingdom
UN	United Nations

Note on referencing style

This book is referenced in accordance with the *Australian Guide to Legal Citation* (4th edition). International treaties are cited only once in full.

A child-friendly summary

What this book is about

This book is about children having a right to take part in making decisions about things that matter to them, with help from their parents and other caregivers.

I say that it is important for children to take part in making decisions, because it can help them to decide how they would like to live and what kind of person they would like to be.

The important ideas of this book

I say that when adults make decisions about things that matter to children, they should understand four things:

1. Children do not always agree with their parents and other family members.
2. Children should take part in making decisions. How much children take part will depend on things like how old they are and how much they understand about the decision.
3. Children need help from their parents to make decisions. But as children get older and understand more, they can make some decisions on their own.
4. Children should be given a chance to tell adults what they think, in their own words. When a decision is made, adults should explain the decision to children in a way that they can understand.

What I hope adults learn from this book

I hope that this book helps adults who make decisions about things that matter to children to better listen to and hear what children have to say and what they think. This will help children to feel more included, and it will help adults to make better decisions.

Introduction

I.1 'It is my body, and only I have the right to decide what goes into it':[1] Enabling and listening to children's voices

This book begins with the voice of a young person,[2] as expressed in a letter to the Family Court of Australia:[3]

> [I]t frustrates me deeply that I have to go to court to be who I am. It frustrates me that anyone has to endure this. It shouldn't be the court's decision. It is my body, and only I have the right to decide what goes into it. It is acceptable for my family or the experienced doctors to advise me, but in the end, it should all be up to me. However, this right has been taken completely out of my hands.[4]

This is the voice of 'Jamie',[5] who in 2011 at the age of ten, became the youngest person in Australia to be granted approval by the Family Court to commence hormone treatment for gender dysphoria. Australia was, until quite recently, the only country in the world in which court authorisation was required for the medical treatment of gender dysphoria in children.[6]

1 'Jamie', letter to the Family Court of Australia, quoted in *Re Jamie* [2015] FamCA 455, [65].

2 Throughout this book, the terms 'child/children' and 'young person/young people' are used, rather than the composite phrases 'child or young person' and 'children and young people', for the purposes of consistency, save for where the semantic distinction is significant.

3 On 1 September 2021, the Family Court of Australia and the Federal Circuit Court of Australia came together under a unified administrative structure to become the Federal Circuit and Family Court of Australia. The judgments analysed in this book are those of the Family Court of Australia and its appellate division, the Full Court.

4 See n 1 above.

5 Section 121 of the *Family Law Act 1975* (Cth) ('*Family Law Act*') prohibits the publication of identifying details of proceedings. 'Jamie' is the pseudonym used in the judgments for the young person the subject of the various *Re Jamie* proceedings: see *Re Jamie (Special Medical Procedure)* [2011] FamCA 248; *Re Jamie* [2013] FamCAFC 110 ('*Jamie Appeal*'); *Re Jamie* [2015] FamCA 455.

6 Jacqueline K Hewitt et al, 'Hormone Treatment of Gender Identity Dysphoria in a Cohort of Children and Adolescents' (2012) 196(9) *Medical Journal of Australia* 578, 578.

DOI: 10.4324/9781003224167-1

Children's ability to participate meaningfully in decision-making processes, and adult decision-makers listening to and hearing children's voices, are persistent and ongoing areas of concern in a range of jurisdictions both within and beyond Australia. Often absent – and starkly so – from public discourse and debate are the voices of children themselves. Jamie's frustration and anguish at being deprived of the right to make decisions about her own body and identity, as articulated in her letter, highlight the perceived incursion by the Family Court on children's right to make decisions about their own medical treatment, and the active role that children should play, guided by their parents and other caregivers, in decision-making about matters that affect them.

Drawing on the legal and normative framework of the *United Nations Convention on the Rights of the Child 1989* ('CRC'),[7] and extending the work of respected children's rights scholars,[8] this book articulates a right that has not been theorised in any context or jurisdiction: a child's right to decisional privacy. Decisional privacy gives the individual the ability to make decisions that contribute to defining their[9] identity, without unjustifiable interference from other individuals or the state.[10] It offers the conditions to enable the individual to live autonomously, or to ask and answer the 'practical question'[11] of how they would like to live and what kind of person they would like to be.

This book presents a new conceptual model for enabling and listening to children's voices in decision-making processes. To illustrate how this model may apply in practice, it embeds a theoretical account of children's right to decisional privacy into one context – judicial proceedings concerning medical treatment

7 *United Nations Convention on the Rights of the Child*, opened for signature 20 November 1989, 1577 UNTS 3 (entered into force 2 September 1990) ('*CRC*').

8 See John Tobin, 'Judging the Judges: Are they Adopting the Rights Approach in Matters Involving Children?' (2009) 33(2) *Melbourne University Law Review* 579, 584–92 ('Judging the Judges'); Jane Fortin, 'Accommodating Children's Rights in a Post *Human Rights Act* Era' (2006) 69(3) *Modern Law Review* 299, 305; Helen Stalford and Kathryn Hollingsworth, 'Judging Children's Rights: Tendencies, Tensions, Constraints and Opportunities' in Helen Stalford, Kathryn Hollingsworth and Stephen Gilmore (eds), *Rewriting Children's Rights Judgments: From Academic Vision to New Practice* (Hart Publishing, 2017) 17, 18–21; Michael Freeman, 'The Value and Values of Children's Rights' in Antonella Invernizzi and Jane Williams (eds), *The Human Rights of Children: From Visions to Implementation* (Ashgate, 2011) 21, 33.

9 This book uses singular third person pronouns (they/them/their), rather than gendered pronouns, to be gender inclusive and to avoid assumptions regarding gender as a binary construct of male (he/him/his) and female (she/her/her): see John Gastil, 'Generic Pronouns and Sexist Language: The Oxymoronic Character of Masculine Generics' (1990) 23(11–12) *Sex Roles* 629; Anna Lindqvist, Emma Aurora Renström and Marie Gustafsson Sendén, 'Reducing A Male Bias in Language? Establishing the Efficiency of Three Different Gender-Fair Language Strategies' (2019) 81(1–2) *Sex Roles* 109.

10 Judith Wagner DeCew, *In Pursuit of Privacy: Law, Ethics and the Rise of Technology* (Cornell University Press, 1997) 77–8.

11 Beate Rossler, *The Value of Privacy* (Polity, 2005) 43.

for children experiencing gender dysphoria.[12] In so doing, the book addresses a significant gap in understanding the interconnections between privacy, family law and children's rights, which remain three dynamic, contested subjects of inquiry and debate.[13]

I.2 A new conceptual model of children's decisional privacy

Privacy, whilst still a much-contested concept,[14] has been understood as having three domains, which are based on a normative distinction between the 'public' and the 'private'. The implications of this distinction have been much-discussed and debated in feminist and family law scholarship,[15] but less so in relation to children.[16] The public/private dichotomy captures the idea that certain dimensions of life can be left to be shaped by the individual, free from intervention by the law and the state. Historically, the private has been equated with the domestic sphere, including intimate and family relationships, while the public has encompassed the realms of politics, market and power.[17] The *spatial* domain of privacy covers personal space and relationships, and selective access to certain physical areas like the home. The *informational* domain concerns issues of control of and access to information. It operates to protect individuals from the (mis)appropria-

12 This book uses the term 'experiencing' gender dysphoria, rather than 'diagnosed with' gender dysphoria, in recognition of the difference between the diagnosis of gender dysphoria as defined in the American Psychiatric Association's *Diagnostic and Statistical Manual of Mental Disorders: DSM-5* (American Psychiatric Association Publishing, 5th ed, 2013) and the use of the term 'gender dysphoria' to assess an individual's eligibility for transition-related care. Ashely has noted that the clinical requirement of diagnosis as a precondition to accessing such care 'can contribute to stigma and discrimination' towards transgender and gender diverse ('TGD') individuals: Florence Ashley, 'The Misuse of Gender Dysphoria: Toward Greater Conceptual Clarity in Transgender Health' (2019) 16(6) *Perspectives on Psychological Science* 1159, 1159.

13 In relation to the 'chaotic' nature of privacy as a concept, see, eg, Daniel Solove, 'A Taxonomy of Privacy' (2006) 154(3) *University of Pennsylvania Law Review* 477, 477; Hyman Gross, 'The Concept of Privacy' (1967) 42 *New York University Law Review* 34, 34–5; Judith Jarvis Thomson, 'The Right to Privacy' (1975) 4(4) *Philosophy and Public Affairs* 295, 295; Regarding the 'incoherence', 'anarchy' and 'chaos' of family law, see John Dewar, 'Family Law and its Discontents' (2000) 14(1) *International Journal of Law, Policy and the Family* 59, 79.

14 See Chapter 1 (Sections 1.2 and 1.3).

15 See, eg, Katherine O'Donovan, *Sexual Divisions in Law* (Weidenfeld and Nicolson, 1985); Eva Gamarnikow et al (eds), *The Public and the Private* (Heinemann, 1983); Carole Pateman, 'Feminist Critiques of the Public/Private Dichotomy' in Anne Phillips (ed), Fe*minism and Equality* (Basil Blackwell, 1987) 103; Michael Freeman, 'Towards A Critical Theory of Family Law' (1975) 38(1) *Current Legal Problems* 153.

16 Michael Freeman, 'The Human Rights of Children' (2010) 63(1) *Current Legal Problems* 1, 4 ('Human Rights of Children').

17 See Susan Boyd, 'Challenging the Public/Private Divide: An Overview' in Susan Boyd (ed), *Challenging the Public/Private Divide: Feminism, Law, and Public Policy* (University of Toronto Press, 1997) 3.

tion and (mis)use of their personal information. The focus of this book, privacy's *decisional* domain, protects an individual's ability to make their own decisions and to act and behave without unjustifiable interference from other individuals or the state, which contributes to defining their identity.[18]

Difficulties persist in recognising children as being able to enjoy these three dimensions of privacy. These difficulties emanate from the dominant conception of children in Western liberal societies as vulnerable, dependent on adults, and incapable of rational decision-making.[19] The law views childhood as 'a singular, fixed, and universal stage of life',[20] and constructs children as binary opposites to adults, or defines them as 'unrealised' adults who lack will and capacity.[21] Children are presumed to be dependent, irrational and incompetent; adults are presumed to be independent, rational and competent to determine and act in their own best interests.[22] According to O'Neill, the child's 'main remedy is to grow up'.[23] The facts of children's dependence on adults for their physical and cognitive development and for their various needs to be met,[24] and children's capacity to develop the ability to meet their own needs in the future,[25] mean that children prove a challenge to the task of conceptualising and theorising privacy. This book takes up that challenge by developing a children's rights approach to decisional privacy.

18 DeCew (n 10) 77–8. These three dimensions of privacy are discussed in Chapter 1 (Section 1.2).

19 See Chapter 1 (Section 1.4.1). See also Stalford and Hollingsworth (n 8) 31; Sheila Varadan, 'The Principle of Evolving Capacities under the UN Convention on the Rights of the Child' (2019) 27 *International Journal of Children's Rights* 306, 306–7; John Tobin, 'Courts and the Construction of Childhood: A New Way of Thinking' in Michael Freeman (ed), *Law and Childhood Studies: Current Legal Issues* (Oxford University Press, 2012) 55, 58–9; Michael Freeman, *The Rights and Wrongs of Children* (Frances Pinter, 1983) 7 ('*Rights and Wrongs*'); David Archard, *Children: Rights and Childhood* (Routledge, 2nd rev ed, 2004) 53–4.

20 Varadan (n 19) 307. See also John Tobin and Sheila Varadan, 'Article 5: The Right to Parental Direction and Guidance and Consistent with a Child's Evolving Capacities' in John Tobin (ed), *The UN Convention on the Rights of the Child: A Commentary* (Oxford University Press, 2019) 159, 182; Gerison Lansdown, *The Evolving Capacities of the Child* (UNICEF Innocenti Studies, 2005) 9–10, 22; Geraldine Van Bueren, *The International Law on the Rights of the Child* (Martinus Nijhoff, 1995) 50; Onora O'Neill, 'Children's Rights and Children's Lives' (1988) 98(3) *Ethics* 445, 462.

21 Barbara Bennett Woodhouse, 'Hatching the Egg: A Child-Centered Perspective on Parents' Rights' (1992) 14(6) *Cardozo Law Review* 1747, 1827.

22 Tobin and Varadan (n 20) 161; Freeman, 'Human Rights of Children' (n 16) 9; Nick Lee, *Childhood and Society: Growing Up In an Age of Uncertainty* (Maidenhead, 2001) 8; Stalford and Hollingsworth (n 8) 31.

23 O'Neill (n 20) 463.

24 Tobin and Varadan (n 20) 159.

25 Harry Brighouse, 'What Rights (If Any) Do Children Have?' in David Archard and Colin Macleod (eds), *The Moral and Political Status of Children* (Oxford University Press, 2002) 31, 40, 43.

I.2.1 The decisional privacy of children: Two new lenses for analysis

This book presents a novel approach to conceptualising privacy from two perspectives. The first is its focus upon the *decisional* dimension of privacy. In the United States, decisional privacy has found concrete expression in Supreme Court constitutional cases regarding family decision-making in matters such as reproductive control,[26] lifestyle[27] and schooling.[28] By contrast, privacy in Australian family law has been conceptualised through its informational dimension as the antithesis of publicity. Informational privacy protection for participants in family law proceedings manifests legislatively in the form of publication restrictions.[29] The emphasis is upon the need to shield family law litigants and their children from the perceived harms of unwanted media attention.[30] This book moves beyond a basic re-articulation of informational privacy, and information over which adults exercise control, to focus on the privacy of children's decision-making.

The second contribution of this book relates to its analytical focus within decisional privacy: *children*. Former Chief Justice of the Family Court of Australia, Diana Bryant, has described family law as 'an area which really intrudes into people's lives', in which judges 'make orders that tell people where they can and can't live, how often or if they will see their children at all'.[31] The advent of 'no fault' divorce with the enactment of the *Family Law Act 1975* (Cth) ('Family Law Act') was justified by legislators at the time as giving 'adult people … the credit and the dignity of being able to make decisions for themselves'.[32] In a submission to the Australian Law Reform Commission ('ALRC') inquiry into Australia's family law system, it was observed that:

> Children – their voices, fears, questions and interests – were largely absent from the debate on the Family Law Bill in the 1970s. Argument was very much centred around the process of divorce, and how it was experienced by the adult parties to the marriage, in isolation from their roles as parents. Sensibilities around children's views and voices (independent from those of their parents) … are relatively recent.[33]

26 See *Griswold v Connecticut*, 381 US 479 (1965); *Eisenstadt v Baird*, 405 US 438 (1972); *Roe v Wade* 410 US 113 (1973).
27 See *Loving v Virginia*, 388 US 1 (1967); *Stanley v Georgia*, 394 US 557 (1969).
28 See *Pierce v Society of Sisters*, 268 US 510 (1925).
29 See *Family Law Act* (n 5) s 121.
30 See Georgina Dimopoulos, '"Divorce with Dignity" as A Justification for Publication Restrictions on Proceedings under the *Family Law Act 1975* (Cth) in An Era of Litigant Self-Publication' (2019) 7(2) *Griffith Journal of Law and Human Dignity* 161.
31 Diana Bryant, quoted in 'Retiring Chief Justice Reflects on Thirteen Years in the Family Court', *The Law Report* (Australian Broadcasting Corporation Radio National, 19 September 2017) <www.abc.net.au/radionational/programs/lawreport/8956300>.
32 Commonwealth, *Parliamentary Debates*, Senate, 19 May 1975, 2419 (Kep Enderby).
33 Relationships Australia, Submission No 11 to Australian Law Reform Commission, *Review of the Family Law System – Issues Paper* (IP 48) (7 May 2018) 73.

These remarks reinforce the observation that children have been 'relegated to the shadows'[34] of privacy discourse in the area of family law. A troubling consequence of the focus on adults' privacy interests is that difficulties persist in recognising and protecting children's – as distinct from their parents' – decisional privacy interests. This book shifts the spotlight to children and their ability to enjoy and exercise their right to decisional privacy. In so doing, it contributes to multidisciplinary research on how children's rights theories operate in practice.

I.2.2 Bridging the gulf between children's rights theory and judicial decision-making

While children's rights research has operated as a 'driving force' for upgrading children's status in society,[35] Fortin has identified 'an unfortunate disjunction between theory and practice' in describing the approach of judges and legal practitioners to children's rights.[36] The theory of children's rights tends to be abstracted from day-to-day legal practice.[37] The role of the judiciary in protecting and advancing children's rights has been the subject of increasing scholarly attention in recent years.[38] Children's limited capacity to enjoy and assert their rights independently of adults, and their 'invisibility and vulnerability' under the law and 'lack of political voice', add weight to the perspective that judges 'step in where other adults (state authorities, parents, doctors) fail or disagree on how to give effect to children's rights'.[39] The ongoing difficulty, as Stalford, Hollingsworth and Gilmore have noted, lies in 'transposing rights from abstract expressions into meaningful, fruitful and enduring commitments by all of those

34 Alice Hearst, *Children and the Politics of Cultural Belonging* (Cambridge University Press, 2012) 14. See also Freeman, 'Human Rights of Children' (n 16) 5; Benjamin Shmueli and Ayelet Blecher-Prigat, 'Privacy for Children' (2011) 42 *Columbia Human Rights Law Review* 759, 762, 787.

35 Ann Quennerstedt, 'Children's Rights Research Moving into the Future – Challenges on the Way Forward' (2013) 21 *International Journal of Children's Rights* 233, 233.

36 Jane Fortin, *Children's Rights and the Developing Law* (Cambridge University Press, 3rd ed, 2009) 29 ('*Children's Rights*'). See also Helen Stalford, Kathryn Hollingsworth and Stephen Gilmore, 'Introducing *Children's Rights Judgments*' in Helen Stalford, Kathryn Hollingsworth and Stephen Gilmore (eds), *Rewriting Children's Rights Judgments: From Academic Vision to New Practice* (Hart Publishing, 2017) 1, 6 ('Introducing *Children's Rights Judgments*').

37 Stalford and Hollingsworth (n 8) 19.

38 See, eg, Aoife Nolan, *Children's Socio-Economic Rights, Democracy and the Courts* (Hart Publishing, 2011); John Eekelaar, 'The Role of the Best Interests Principle in Decisions Affecting Children and Decisions about Children' (2015) 23 *International Journal of Children's Rights* 3 ('Role of the Best Interests Principle'); Aoife Daly, *Children, Autonomy and the Courts: Beyond the Right to be Heard* (Brill, 2017); Jane Fortin, 'A Decade of the HRA and its Impact on Children's Rights' (2011) 41 *Family Law* 176.

39 Stalford and Hollingsworth (n 8) 21.

associated with the child'.[40] This view is reinforced by Ferguson, who has argued that an emphasis on children's rights is problematic because of the lack of a 'sufficiently workable child-centred conception of children's rights'.[41]

This book presents such a workable, child-centred model of a right to decisional privacy. It forges a dialogue between the practical (judicial decision-making) and the theoretical (academic research on children's rights) to enable them to influence and improve each other. It illustrates how a normative understanding of the meaning and value of a child's right to decisional privacy can be extended to inform judicial thinking about how this right may be incorporated into judicial reasoning. This book thus offers a 'testing ground'[42] for how and why academic research on children's rights is relevant to judges in their challenging, value-laden, invariably emotional day-to-day work. This is particularly important, given that court judgments often contain 'limited, often distinctly disempowering approaches to children's rights'.[43]

I.3 The central argument and its development

This book argues that recognising a substantive right to decisional privacy for children requires attendant procedural rights that facilitate children's meaningful participation in decision-making about their best interests. It also argues that, as courts have increasingly encroached upon decision-making in relation to medical treatment for children experiencing gender dysphoria, they have denied the decisional privacy rights of transgender and gender diverse ('TGD')[44] children. This argument is advanced through three stages: concept, method and practice.

I.3.1 Concept: Understanding the meaning and value of privacy

The first stage of the argument develops the concept of decisional privacy. It addresses the questions, 'what is privacy?' and 'why is privacy important?'[45] An important step in understanding what privacy 'is' is articulating why privacy is valuable. This book argues that privacy is valued as a prerequisite for achieving the Western liberal ideal of autonomy. Autonomy is understood to embrace both freedom *from* intervention by the state and others (negative freedom) and freedom *to* develop and pursue one's own life plan for self-fulfilment (posi-

40 Stalford, Hollingsworth and Gilmore, 'Introducing *Children's Rights Judgments*' (n 36) 7. See also Fortin, *Children's Rights* (n 36) 3–4.

41 Lucinda Ferguson, 'Not Merely Rights for Children but Children's Rights: The Theory Gap and the Assumption of the Importance of Children's Rights' (2013) 21 *International Journal of Children's Rights* 177, 182.

42 Stalford, Hollingsworth and Gilmore, 'Introducing *Children's Rights Judgments*' (n 36) 7.

43 Ibid 6.

44 This term is used throughout the book to capture the spectrum of gender identities of individuals who do not identify as cisgender.

45 See Chapter 1.

tive freedom).[46] It is submitted that privacy is important because it protects the diversity of personal choices, actions and ways of life, and provides the conditions or environment to enable individuals to live autonomously.[47] Put differently, individuals require decisional privacy to be able to experience autonomy.

The concept of privacy is more than the absence of unwarranted interference by the state or other individuals. Privacy rights, Feldman has observed, 'have extended beyond their original concern – threats to private space, particularly the home – to encompass personal security, self-fulfilment, and identity, including the organisation of family life and relationships'.[48] Privacy extends to the control that individuals, including children, have over their personal spaces and boundaries. It also captures individuals' capacity to define their relationships with others and to define themselves in relation to those others, including their families and communities.[49] Central to the ideas of control and capacity is the notion of autonomy. This notion does not sit well with conceptions of children as incapable of rational decision-making, vulnerable and dependent.[50] Such conceptions reflect the will or choice theory of rights, which conceptualises a right as 'the protected exercise of choice'[51] and so denies children the status of rights-bearers owing to their perceived incapacity and inability to exercise rational choice.[52]

The approach to children's decisional privacy advanced in this book is premised upon a competing theory of rights: the interest theory.[53] Under this theory,

46 See Robert Young, *Personal Autonomy: Beyond Negative and Positive Liberty* (Taylor & Francis, 2017). Cf Gerald McCallum, 'Negative and Positive Freedom' (1967) 76 *Philosophical Review* 312.

47 Helen Nissenbaum, *Privacy in Context: Technology, Policy, and the Integrity of Social Life* (Stanford Law Books, 2010) 82; James Griffin, *On Human Rights* (Oxford University Press, 2008) 223; Rossler, *The Value of Privacy* (n 11) 72–3; Fortin, *Children's Rights* (n 36) 19.

48 David Feldman, 'The Developing Scope of Article 8 of the European Convention on Human Rights' (1997) 3 *European Human Rights Law Review* 265, 266. See also John Tobin and Sarah M Field, 'Article 16: The Right to Protection of Privacy, Family, Home, Correspondence, Honour, and Reputation' in John Tobin (ed), *The UN Convention on the Rights of the Child: A Commentary* (Oxford University Press, 2019) 551, 560. Cf James Griffin, 'The Human Right to Privacy' (2007) 44 *San Diego Law Review* 697.

49 Tobin and Field (n 48) 599; Terri Dowty, 'Pixie-Dust and Privacy: What's Happening to Children's Rights in England?' (2008) 22 *Children and Society* 393, 397.

50 See Chapter 1 (Section 1.4.1).

51 Archard (n 19) 58.

52 See, eg, Brighouse (n 25) 45–6; James Griffin, 'Do Children Have Rights?' in David Archard and Colin Macleod (eds), *The Moral and Political Status of Children* (Oxford University Press, 2002) 19, 27; O'Neill (n 20) 462–3; Laura M Purdy, *In Their Best Interest? The Case Against Equal Rights for Children* (Cornell University Press, 1992).

53 See Joseph Raz, 'Legal Rights' (1984) 4(1) *Oxford Journal of Legal Studies* 1; Neil MacCormick, 'Children's Rights: A Test-Case' in Neil MacCormick (ed), *Legal Right and Social Democracy: Essays in Legal and Political Philosophy* (Clarendon Press, 1982) 154; Samantha Brennan, 'Children's Choices or Children's Interests: Which Do Their Rights Protect?' in David Archard and Colin Macloed (eds), *The Moral and Political Status of Children* (Oxford University Press, 2002) 53; Freeman, 'Human Rights of Children' (n 16) 21; Robert E Goodin and Diane Gibson, 'Rights, Young and Old' (1997) 17(2) *Oxford Journal of Legal*

children's entitlement to rights exists *irrespective* of their capacity to exercise those rights.[54] The interest theory understands a right as something that protects a sufficiently important interest and it imposes duties on others, the performance of which ensures that the rights-holder can enjoy that interest.[55] It is argued that children's evolving autonomy is the interest to be promoted by recognising and respecting children's right to decisional privacy.[56] This approach embraces an understanding of autonomy as a relational, evolving and gradual concept.[57] Understanding autonomy as evolving, rather than absolute, enables children to be treated as active subjects with agency, consistent with their evolving capacities, not as vulnerable objects of concern and protective adult intervention.[58] Further, it is submitted that the development and realisation of autonomy is a relational, gradual process: individuals learn to become, and to be, autonomous in and through social relations, including family relationships.[59] Parents are therefore

---

Studies 185; John Tobin, 'Justifying Children's Rights' (2013) 21 *International Journal of Children's Rights* 395, 403; Tom D Campbell, 'The Rights of the Minor: As Person, As Child, As Juvenile, As Future Adult' in Philip Alston, Stephen Parker and John Seymour (eds), *Children, Rights and the Law* (Clarendon Press, 1992) 1, 4–5.

54 Fortin, *Children's Rights* (n 36) 13; Tobin, 'Justifying Children's Rights' (n 53) 403; Campbell (n 53) 5.

55 See Raz, 'Legal Rights' (n 53) 5; MacCormick (n 53) 154; Joseph Raz, *The Morality of Freedom* (Oxford University Press, 1986) 165–92. These competing theories of rights – the interest theory, and the will or choice theory – are explained further in Chapter 1 (Section 1.4.2).

56 Fortin, *Children's Rights* (n 36) 20, 23; John Eekelaar, 'The Interests of the Child and the Child's Wishes: The Role of Dynamic Self-Determinism' (1994) 8(1) *International Journal of Law, Policy and the Family* 42, 53 ('Dynamic Self-Determinism').

57 See Chapter 1 (Section 1.4.3). See also Tobin, 'Justifying Children's Rights' (n 53) 424; John Christman, 'Relational Autonomy, Liberal Individualism, and the Social Constitution of Selves' (2004) 117(1/2) *Philosophical Studies* 143, 156; Jonathan Herring, *Relational Autonomy and Family Law* (Springer, 2014) 48–9 ('*Relational Autonomy*'); Jennifer Nedelsky, 'Reconceiving Autonomy: Sources, Thoughts and Possibilities' in Allan Hutchinson and Leslie Green (eds), *Law and the Community: The End of Individualism?* (Carswell, 1989) 219, 225 ('Reconceiving Autonomy'); Catriona MacKenzie and Natalie Stoljar (eds), *Relational Autonomy: Feminist Perspectives on Autonomy, Agency and the Social Self* (Oxford University Press, 2000); Jennifer Nedelsky, *Law's Relations: A Relational Theory of Self, Autonomy and Law* (Oxford University Press, 2011); Martha Minow and Mary Lyndon Shanley, 'Relational Rights and Responsibilities: Revisioning the Family in Liberal Political Theory and Law' (1996) 11 *Hypatia* 4.

58 John Tobin, 'Understanding Children's Rights: A Vision beyond Vulnerability' (2015) 84 *Nordic Journal of International Law* 155, 171 ('Understanding Children's Rights'); Tobin and Field (n 48) 559; Laura Lundy, John Tobin and Aisling Parkes, 'Article 12: The Right to Respect for the Views of the Child' in John Tobin (ed), *The UN Convention on the Rights of the Child: A Commentary* (Oxford University Press, 2019) 397, 397; Patrick Parkinson and Judy Cashmore, *The Voice of a Child in Family Law Disputes* (Oxford University Press, 2008) 7.

59 See, eg, Martha Albertson Fineman, *The Autonomy Myth: A Theory of Dependency* (The Free Press, 2004) 35; Herring, *Relational Autonomy* (n 57) 48–9; Nedelsky, 'Reconceiving Autonomy' (n 57) 225; John Eekelaar, 'Family Law and Legal Theory' in Elizabeth

both a source of and a potential threat to their children's autonomy.[60] Such a conceptualisation of autonomy responds to the criticisms that children are not, and cannot be, autonomous; and that, even if children are recognised as autonomous beings, they cannot in fact exercise that autonomy, because they lack the capacity to do so.

I.3.2 Method: A children's rights approach to decisional privacy

The second stage of the argument presents a children's rights approach to decisional privacy. A children's rights approach stands in contrast to the welfare model, which remains the dominant approach to determining children's best interests in proceedings under Part VII of the Family Law Act. In *Re Z*,[61] Fogarty J described the Family Law Act as 'a legislative code for the way in which the welfare of children who come within its ambit are to be protected'.[62] The principle of 'the best interests of the child' as 'the paramount consideration' underpins the welfare model of decision-making in Part VII proceedings.[63] The welfare model requires that parents act in the best interests of their children, and state intervention is justified by parents' failure to do so.[64] To the extent that the welfare model has shifted the sole focus away from parental and adult interests by emphasising children's best interests, it has been 'very beneficial for children'.[65] However, the 'dark side' of the welfare approach, according to Eekelaar, is that the obligation to promote and protect the child's best interests also involves adults exercising power to determine the content and nature of those interests.[66] The key feature of childhood as a 'legal' status, then, is adults' ability to exercise power to assess children's best interests and to 'impose a course of action' accordingly.[67] The idea of bestowing children with rights is seemingly at odds with the paternalism of the welfare model.

Brake and Lucinda Ferguson (eds), *Philosophical Foundations of Children's and Family Law* (Oxford University Press, 2018) 41, 52.

60 Nedelsky, 'Reconceiving Autonomy' (n 57) 235. The conception of autonomy as relational, gradual and evolving, and the family's role in children's development of autonomy, are developed in Chapter 1 (Sections 1.4.3 and 1.4.4).

61 (1996) 134 FLR 40.

62 Ibid 90.

63 See *Family Law Act* (n 5) ss 60CA, 67ZC.

64 See John Eekelaar, *Family Law and Personal Life* (Oxford University Press, 2007) 9–17 ('*Family Law and Personal Life*').

65 Ibid 159; Tobin, 'Understanding Children's Rights' (n 58) 181.

66 Eekelaar, *Family Law and Personal Life* (n 64) 13, 56. See also John Eekelaar, 'Families and Children: From Welfarism to Rights' in Christopher McCrudden and Gerald Chambers, *Individual Rights and Law in Britain* (Clarendon Press, 1994) 301; John Eekelaar, 'Personal Rights and Human Rights' in Peter Lodrup and Eva Modvar (eds), *Family Life and Human Rights: Papers Presented at the 11th World Conference of the International Society of Family Law* (Gyldendal, 2004) 183.

67 Eekelaar, 'Dynamic Self-Determinism' (n 56) 43.

To avoid the assertion that '"children's rights" is a slogan in search of a definition',[68] the approach to children's decisional privacy advocated in this book draws on the understanding and formulation of children's rights contained in the CRC. While the vision of children's rights promoted by this international convention remains subject to criticism,[69] the model and underlying values that the CRC embodies offer a sound basis for conceptualising children's decisional privacy. No explicit reference is made in the CRC to 'decisional privacy'. Article 16 protects the child against 'arbitrary or unlawful interference with [their] privacy, family, home or correspondence'. The concept of decisional privacy, as it is developed in this book, is more than a negative freedom or a protection against unjustifiable interference by the state or other individuals. It also serves a positive freedom: a child's ability to develop and pursue their own conception of the good life and to make choices that are consistent with that conception. This understanding of decisional privacy reinforces or facilitates a number of other rights under the CRC – notably, the child's right to express their views and to be heard (Article 12); to receive appropriate parental direction and guidance in the exercise of their rights, in a manner consistent with the child's evolving capacities (Article 5); to preservation of identity (Article 8); to protection of privacy (Article 16); and to freedom of expression (Article 13). Decisional privacy is a foundation for, or a precondition to, the exercise of these other CRC rights. Put differently, the fulfilment of these rights depends in part on the realisation of a child's right to decisional privacy. This is because children's rights are interdependent and interrelated,[70] and a sound theoretical framework for the analysis of children's decisional privacy must clearly articulate this interconnectedness.[71]

Expanding upon the important work of established children's rights scholars,[72] four fundamental principles of a children's rights approach to decisional privacy are proposed.[73] The first principle requires that children be recognised and

68 Hillary Rodham, 'Children under the Law' (1973) 43(4) *Harvard Educational Review* 487, 487.

69 For a sound discussion of such criticism, see Michael Freeman, 'Why It Remains Important to Take Children's Rights Seriously' (2007) 15 *International Journal of Children's Rights* 5 ('Why It Remains Important'). See also Priscilla Alderson, 'Common Criticisms of Children's Rights and 25 Years of the IJCR' in Michael Freeman (ed), *Children's Rights: New Issues, New Themes, New Perspectives* (Brill Nijhoff, 2018) 39; Fortin, *Children's Rights* (n 36) 45–6; Didier Reynaert, Maria Bouverne-De Bie and Stijn Vandevelde, 'Between "Believers" and "Opponents": Critical Discussions on Children's Rights' (2012) 20 *International Journal of Children's Rights* 155.

70 See John Tobin, 'Seeking to Persuade: A Constructive Approach to Human Rights Treaty Interpretation' (2010) 23(1) *Harvard Human Rights Journal* 1, 37–9 ('Seeking to Persuade'). See also Jonathan Todres, 'Children's Rights and Women's Rights: Interrelated and Interdependent' in Martin Ruck, Michele Peterson-Badali and Michael Freeman (eds), *Handbook of Children's Rights: Global and Multidisciplinary Perspectives* (Taylor & Francis, 2016) 21, 21; Freeman, 'Human Rights of Children' (n 16) 16.

71 A children's rights approach to decisional privacy is the focus of Chapter 2.

72 See n 8 above.

73 See Chapter 2 (Section 2.3).

respected as subjects with rights and interests that are *distinct* from those of their parents and other family members. Attaching decisional privacy to the family assumes that children's interests are subsumed within those of the family as a collective. It also assumes that parents will make decisions and act in their children's best interests.[74] Yet the hierarchical relationship – and attendant power imbalance – between parents and their children traditionally has been masked and reinforced on the basis of so-called 'non-intervention' by the state in the 'private' sphere of the family.[75] This principle disentangles the rights of children from those of their parents, with a view to countering the problematic notion of 'family privacy'[76] and examining how children's right to decisional privacy can be robustly protected.

The second principle is that children must play an active role, consistent with their evolving capacities, in decision-making about their best interests. The notion of evolving capacities, contained in Article 5 of the CRC, is a 'positive and enabling' one,[77] which is used to promote children's capacity for autonomy, or their actual autonomy, in the exercise of their rights.[78] The evolving capacities principle refers to 'processes of maturation and learning whereby children progressively acquire knowledge, competencies and understanding'.[79] It recognises that parental rights and power over the child diminish with the child's growing maturity. Understood thus, the principle of evolving capacities supports the right of all children, regardless of age, to experience increasing agency, autonomy and responsibility in the enjoyment and exercise of their rights as they develop and mature.[80]

The third principle is that children's relative vulnerability and immaturity require that parents provide children with 'appropriate direction and guidance'[81] in the exercise of their rights and to protect and enforce those rights. The emphasis must remain on *children's* right to receive appropriate direction and guidance

74 Suzanne A Kim, 'Reconstructing Family Privacy' (2006) 57(3) *Hastings Law Journal* 557, 595–6; Fortin, *Children's Rights* (n 36) 324.

75 Frances Olsen, 'The Family and the Market: A Study of Ideology and Legal Reform' (1983) 96(7) *Harvard Law Review* 1497, 1511, 1566. See also Martha Albertson Fineman, *The Neutered Mother, the Sexual Family, and Other Twentieth Century Tragedies* (Routledge, 2014) 187; Kim (n 74) 571; O'Donovan (n 15) 8.

76 See Chapter 1 (Section 1.4.4).

77 United Nations Committee on the Rights of the Child ('CRC Committee'), *General Comment No 7: Implementing Child Rights in Early Childhood*, UN Doc CRC/C/GC/7/Rev.1 (20 September 2006) [17] ('*General Comment No 7*'). See also CRC Committee, *General Comment No 20 (2016) on the Implementation of the Rights of the Child During Adolescence*, UN Doc CRC/C/GC/20 (6 December 2016) [18] ('*General Comment No 20*').

78 Varadan (n 19) 329, 331, 333.

79 CRC Committee, *General Comment No 7* (n 77) [17].

80 Tobin and Varadan (n 20) 177–8. See also CRC Committee, *General Comment No 12 (2009): The Right of the Child to be Heard*, UN Doc CRC/C/GC/12 (20 July 2009) [85].

81 *CRC*, art 5.

from their parents, rather than on *parents'* rights to non-interference by the state in the exercise of parental rights and responsibilities.[82]

The fourth fundamental principle of a children's rights approach to decisional privacy is children's meaningful participation in decision-making about their lives. Article 12(1) of the CRC gives children who are capable of forming a view the right to freely express their views in all matters affecting them, with those views being given due weight in accordance with the child's age and maturity. This principle emphasises the nexus between recognising children's substantive right to decisional privacy and giving children the opportunity to participate actively in decision-making processes. Affording children the right to express their views meaningfully, and giving them the opportunity to be heard, are the essence of children exercising their right to decisional privacy effectively.

A theory of children's right to decisional privacy undermines the traditional family unit insofar as it demands that children are not only seen, but also heard and listened to.[83] However, the model does not advocate that children can, and must, make all decisions in all matters affecting them. Two qualifications are imposed on the scope of children's right to decisional privacy. The first qualification is that the potential for parent–child conflict in the determination of a child's best interests must be understood through the perspective of relational autonomy.[84] The rights and interests of children and the rights and interests of their parents are inextricably interlinked.[85] Children's enjoyment of their right to decisional privacy will thus be interconnected and interdependent with the exercise of parental rights and responsibilities.[86] The second qualification derives from the principle of 'evolving capacities' in Article 5 of the CRC and the child's right to receive appropriate parental direction and guidance.[87] In practice, given children's lack of capacity to determine their best interests in relation to various matters, it is anticipated that parents will regularly make decisions on behalf of their children. However, it is argued that where a child is of sufficient understanding and maturity in relation to a matter, the child's views must be determinative of their best interests, even when they conflict with the views of the child's parents.[88]

82 Tobin and Varadan (n 20) 161.

83 Tobin, 'Justifying Children's Rights' (n 53) 429.

84 See Chapter 8 (Section 8.2).

85 Jonathan Herring, 'The Welfare Principle and the Rights of Parents' in Andrew Bainham, Shelley Day Sclater and Martin Richards (eds), *What is a Parent: A Socio-Legal Analysis* (Hart Publishing, 1999) 89, 89.

86 Tobin, 'Justifying Children's Rights' (n 53) 424.

87 See Chapter 8 (Section 8.3).

88 In support of this argument, see Tobin, 'Understanding Children's Rights' (n 58) 165, 180; Tobin, 'Justifying Children's Rights' (n 53) 428, 432; Eekelaar, 'Dynamic Self-Determinism' (n 56) 55; Laura Lundy, '"Voice" is Not Enough: Conceptualising Article 12 of the United Nations Convention on the Rights of the Child' (2007) 33(6) *British Educational Research Journal* 927; Daly (n 38) ch 6; John Seymour, *Children, Parents and the Courts: Legal Intervention in Family Life* (Federation Press, 2016) 101.

Within the conceptual framework of a child's right to decisional privacy, the focus narrows to court judgments. Features of a children's rights judgment are distinguished through four stages of the judicial decision-making process.[89] These features are consistent with, although differently calibrated to, the five 'primary characteristics' of a children's rights judgment presented by Hollingsworth and Stalford,[90] and the dimensions of a 'substantive rights approach' formulated by Tobin.[91] The first feature is selecting and framing: conceptualisation of the issues from the child's perspective and in terms of the child's rights. The second is court procedures that enable the child to participate meaningfully in the decision-making process. The third is reasoning and analysis: how the judge, having considered the evidence, analyses and justifies the resolution of the issues for determination in the proceedings. The fourth feature is communicating and enabling: a judgment that has the child as the focal point, enables the child to share their own voice and is written with the child (or children generally) as an audience. Together, these features of a children's rights judgment strive to make children's rights a 'way of thinking'[92] for judges in court proceedings. They suggest ways that judges might embrace a children's rights approach in their decision-making to make children more visible in the law.[93]

I.3.3 Practice: The case study of gender dysphoria proceedings

A theory of children's decisional privacy is attended by the challenge of filling an 'interpretive void' to determine its meaning and scope, which is 'ultimately an act of persuasion'.[94] This book constructs a conceptual framework for understanding and giving effect to children's right to decisional privacy, while being attuned to 'the diverse, overlapping, and potentially conflicting interests' of the 'interpretive community',[95] that is, those who have an interest in the meaning and value of this right in various contexts. The third stage of the central argument of this book applies the children's rights approach to decisional privacy and the elements of a children's rights judgment to a case study: judicial proceedings concerning medical treatment for children experiencing gender dysphoria.[96]

Decision-making about children's medical treatment has been described as 'a perennial problem in the evolution of medico-legal jurisprudence',[97] particularly

89 See Chapter 3 (Sections 3.2 to 3.5).
90 Kathrtyn Hollingsworth and Helen Stalford, 'Towards Children's Rights Judgments' in Helen Stalford, Kathryn Hollingsworth and Stephen Gilmore (eds), *Rewriting Children's Rights Judgments: From Academic Vision to New Practice* (Hart Publishing, 2017) 53.
91 Tobin, 'Judging the Judges' (n 8) 603–19.
92 Stalford, Hollingsworth and Gilmore, 'Introducing *Children's Rights Judgments*' (n 36) 31–2.
93 Hollingsworth and Stalford (n 90) 53.
94 Tobin, 'Seeking to Persuade' (n 70) 3–4.
95 Ibid 8–10.
96 See Part B (Chapters 4 to 7).
97 Robert Heywood, 'Parents and Medical Professionals: Conflict, Cooperation, and Best Interests' (2012) 20(1) *Medical Law Review* 29, 43.

given the flexibility and indeterminacy of the 'best interests' principle.[98] The Family Court of Australia has recognised that medical treatment decisions 'are likely to involve the intersection of a number of moral, ethical and clinical dilemmas and decisions for doctors as well as parents'.[99] The primary focus of this book is the welfare jurisdiction under section 67ZC of the Family Law Act and its exercise by the Family Court of Australia to authorise medical treatment for children experiencing gender dysphoria ('gender dysphoria proceedings'). Recent case law from England and Wales is also examined[100] to highlight an arguably concerning trend in both jurisdictions regarding the denial of TGD children's decision-making autonomy in relation to their bodies and identities. This case study is intended to demonstrate how the theory of children's right to decisional privacy might operate in one particular context. The theory could apply to a much wider range of areas that directly affect children's lives beyond family law and medical treatment, although a detailed examination of additional contexts lies beyond the scope of this book.[101]

Gender dysphoria involves a person experiencing a conflict between their self-perception of being female or male and their birth sex.[102] At the time of writing, diagnosis is governed by the fifth edition of the *Diagnostic and Statistical Manual of Mental Disorders* ('*DSM-5*'),[103] and the accepted medical treatment occurs in two stages. Stage one involves the administration of puberty-suppressant hormones, known as 'blockers'. Stage two involves gender-affirming hormone treatment through the administration of either testosterone or oestrogen to facilitate the adolescent's transition to the opposite sex.[104] Judges in Australia[105] and the

98 See, eg, Stephen Parker, 'The Best Interests of the Child: Principles and Problems' in Philip Alston (ed), *The Best Interests of the Child: Reconciling Culture and Human Rights* (Clarendon Press, 1994) 26; John Eekelaar, 'Beyond the Welfare Principle' (2002) 14(3) *Child and Family Law Quarterly* 237; Eekelaar, 'Role of the Best Interests Principle' (n 38); Helen Reece, 'The Paramountcy Principle: Consensus or Construct?' (1996) 49(1) *Current Legal Problems* 267; Raymie H Wayne, 'The Best Interests of the Child: A Silent Standard – Will You Know it When You Hear it?' (2008) 2(1) *Journal of Public Child Welfare* 33.

99 *Re Sean* (2010) 258 FLR 192, 206 [85] (Murphy J).

100 See *R (Bell) v Tavistock and Portman NHS Foundation Trust* [2020] EWHC 3274 (Admin) ('*Bell Judicial Review*'); *R (Bell) v Tavistock and Portman NHS Foundation Trust* [2021] EWCA Civ 1363 ('*Bell Appeal*').

101 For an illustration of how the theory may apply to private family law proceedings in England and Wales, see Georgina Dimopoulos, 'A Theory of Children's Decisional Privacy' (2021) 41(3) *Legal Studies* 430, 449–53.

102 Fiona Kelly, 'Treating the Transgendered Child: The Full Court's Decision in *Re Jamie*' (2014) 28(1) *Australian Journal of Family Law* 83, 83.

103 American Psychiatric Association, *Diagnostic and Statistical Manual of Mental Disorders: DSM-5* (American Psychiatric Association Publishing, 5th ed, 2013).

104 Eli Coleman et al, *Standards of Care for the Health of Transsexual, Transgender, and Gender-Nonconforming People* (World Professional Association for Transgender Health, 7th version, 2012) 18 <www.wpath.org/media/cms/Documents/SOC%20v7/SOC%20V7_English2012.pdf?%20t=1613669341>.

105 See *Re Lucas* [2016] FamCA 1129, [3] (Tree J); *Jamie Appeal* (n 5) [99] (Bryant CJ); *Re Brodie (Special Medical Procedure)* [2008] FamCA 334, [230] (Carter J).

United Kingdom ('UK')[106] have acknowledged that the diagnosis of children with gender dysphoria has grown significantly in recent years.

In Australia, post-separation parenting disputes, regarding parental responsibility for, and time with, children, comprise the majority of cases that are heard by courts exercising jurisdiction under Part VII of the Family Law Act. Gender dysphoria proceedings comprise but a narrow facet of the Family Court's jurisdiction. In England and Wales, courts have only relatively recently become involved in the medical treatment process for gender dysphoria, following a challenge to the practices of the Tavistock and Portman NHS Foundation Trust, through its Gender Identity Development Service, in prescribing puberty blockers to children with gender dysphoria.[107] However, gender dysphoria proceedings are a paradigm example of children's right to decisional privacy, for they are *literally* about children's autonomy, their ability to ask and answer the questions of how they would like to live and what kind of person they would like to be and their freedom to create their own 'authentic identity'.[108] Decisional privacy emphasises 'the privacy of the body', and there is a fundamental nexus between the body and identity which contributes to the 'societal coding and meaning' of decisional privacy.[109] As Rossler has explained:

> If one understands a person's self-determination and autonomy to consist in [their] right to be the (part-)author of [their] own biography, among other things this must mean that within very different social contexts the person can demand that [their] decisions and actions should be respected (in the sense that they are 'none of your business') both by social convention and state law.[110]

Gender dysphoria proceedings also expose the tensions between children's rights, parental responsibilities and the Family Court's duty to 'protect the rights of children and to promote their welfare',[111] which it is suggested lie at the core of understanding children's decisional privacy. Such proceedings raise – although do not necessarily answer – the challenging questions of *when* intervention by adults to limit a child's decision-making ability and choices can be justified and *who* is best-placed to protect the child's rights in this context.

Consistent with the dominant welfare model, the Family Law Act reflects the assumption that parents are in the optimal position to protect the interests

106 See *Bell Judicial Review* (n 100) [31] (Sharp P, Lewis LJ and Lieven J); *Bell Appeal* (n 100) [20] (Lord Burnett of Maldon CJ, Sir Geoffrey Vos MR and King LJ).
107 See *Bell Judicial Review* (n 100); *Bell Appeal* (n 100), which are the focus of Chapter 7.
108 Beate Rossler, 'Three Dimensions of Privacy' in Bart van der Sloot and Aviva de Groot (eds), *The Handbook of Privacy Studies: An Interdisciplinary Introduction* (Amsterdam University Press, 2018) 137, 138.
109 Ibid 137.
110 Ibid 138.
111 *Family Law Act* (n 5) s 43(1)(c).

of their children.[112] In Australia, it is generally within the bounds of 'parental responsibility'[113] for parents to be able to consent to medical treatment for and on behalf of their child. However, there are 'special medical procedures' which fall beyond that responsibility and must be authorised by the Family Court as part of its welfare jurisdiction under section 67ZC of the Family Law Act. Section 67ZC provides that, in addition to the jurisdiction under Part VII in relation to children, a court has jurisdiction to make orders relating to the welfare of children, having regard to the best interests of the child as the paramount consideration.[114]

The welfare jurisdiction under section 67ZC originally served to protect children whose interests might otherwise be eroded by the problematic liberal notion of 'family privacy'. However, as it has evolved and expanded to capture medical treatment for children experiencing gender dysphoria, the exercise of this 'protective' and 'paternalistic'[115] jurisdiction has challenged the role of the Family Court in relation to children's medical treatment. That role has swung the pendulum of decision-making authority away from parents and has denied TGD children decisional privacy in relation to their own bodies and identities. The Family Court has asked: 'How far, indeed, is the Court to intrude into the family unit and by what set of values should a Judge decide that he or she knows better than the parents what is best for their child?'[116] The Family Court's growing involvement in children's medical treatment reveals a judicial scepticism of 'unbridled parental autonomy',[117] but also an inability to embrace a paradigm that acknowledges and respects children as rights-holders.

A focus on court judgments

As a principle of judicial accountability, judges must give reasons for their decisions.[118] The High Court of Australia has held this obligation to be a feature of the administration of justice,[119] with published reasons susceptible to appeal and open to criticism and scrutiny by litigants, other judges, academics, the media and the broader community.[120] In 'controversial' cases attracting an expanded audience, judges are compelled to justify their reasoning and to articulate their

112 Fortin, *Children's Rights* (n 36) 22, 321, 739–40; Gerald Dworkin, 'Consent, Representation, and Proxy Consent' in Willard Gaylin and Ruth Macklin (eds), *Who Speaks for the Child: The Problems of Proxy Consent* (Plenum Press, 1982) 191, 204.

113 See *Family Law Act* (n 5) s 61B.

114 See Chapter 4 (Section 4.3).

115 *Re Alex* (2004) 180 FLR 89, 116 [154] (Nicholson CJ) ('*Re Alex*').

116 *Re a Teenager* (1988) 94 FLR 181, 212 (Cook J).

117 Tobin and Varadan (n 20) 174.

118 Michael Kirby, 'Judicial Accountability in Australia' (2005) 6(1) *Legal Ethics* 41, 46.

119 *Public Service Board (NSW) v Osmond* (1986) 159 CLR 656, 666 (Gibbs CJ); *Fleming v The Queen* (1998) 197 CLR 250, 260 (Gleeson CJ, McHugh, Gurnrnow, Kirby and Callinan JJ).

120 Kirby (n 118) 46; Kenneth Hayne, 'Letting Justice be Done Without the Heavens Falling' (2001) 27(1) *Monash University Law Review* 12, 19.

assumptions in such a way as to pre-empt and deflect criticism.[121] Gender dysphoria proceedings have tended to attract considerable public and media attention.[122]

The narratives of judgments in children's proceedings convey socio-cultural understandings of children, childhood, the parent–child relationship and the scope of state involvement in the private sphere of the family. The power of judgment writing lies in the scope of narratives to 'challenge and unsettle the legal status quo'[123] and to represent voices, perspectives and experiences that have been marginalised, omitted or ignored in the development of law and policy.

Two judgments of the Full Court of the Family Court of Australia ('Full Court') have been selected for analysis in this book. These judgments mark pivotal moments in the development and trajectory of the welfare jurisdiction under section 67ZC of the Family Law Act in relation to childhood gender dysphoria. Decided in 2013, *Re Jamie*[124] presented the first appellate opportunity to consider whether Family Court authorisation of medical treatment for children experiencing gender dysphoria should still be required – as a single judge of the Family Court had decided in 2004[125] – and whether the Family Court should still be involved in determining whether the child is competent to give informed consent to stage two treatment. *Re Kelvin*[126] provides a useful comparison with *Re Jamie*. At the time of writing, it remains the only other opportunity that the Full Court has had to examine these issues.

The judgment of the Court of Appeal of England and Wales in *R (Bell) v The Tavistock and Portman NHS Foundation Trust* ('*Bell*')[127] is also analysed from the perspective of children's right to decisional privacy to offer an important international perspective.[128] The analysis exposes cross-jurisdictional similarities in the conceptualisation of TGD children as uniquely vulnerable; a failure to conceptualise the issues in dispute as being about TGD children and their rights; and a reluctance to engage with children's rights in the court's reasoning and communication of the decision. While Australia has witnessed a gradual decline in court involvement in medical treatment for children experiencing gender dysphoria, the *Bell* proceedings suggest a troubling shift in the opposite direction.

121 Jonathan Montgomery, 'Rhetoric and "Welfare"' (1989) 9(3) *Oxford Journal of Legal Studies* 395, 397.

122 See *Re Kelvin* [2017] FamCAFC 258, [115] (Thackray, Strickland and Murphy JJ observing that 'this case, and other earlier cases involving Gender Dysphoria, have attracted widespread media attention') ('*Re Kelvin*'); *Bell Appeal* (n 100) [3] (Lord Burnett of Maldon CJ for the Court noting that '[t]he treatment of children for gender dysphoria is controversial' and raises 'not only clinical medical issues but also moral and ethical issues, all of which are the subject of intense professional and public debate').

123 Peter Brooks and Paul Gewirtz, *Law's Stories: Narrative and Rhetoric in the Law* (Yale University Press, 1996) 5.

124 *Jamie Appeal* (n 5). The judgment of the Full Court in *Re Jamie* is analysed in Chapter 5.

125 See *Re Alex* (n 115), discussed in Chapter 4 (Section 4.3.2.ii).

126 *Re Kelvin* (n 122). The judgment of the Full Court in *Re Kelvin* is analysed in Chapter 6.

127 *Bell Appeal* (n 100).

128 See Chapter 7.

The case study of this book exposes a fundamental question about medical treatment that, according to the High Court of England and Wales, 'goes to the heart of an individual's identity':[129] to what extent do TGD children have control over their own bodies and identities, if they require court approval to commence treatment for gender dysphoria? The interplay between the explicit legal questions for each court's determination and the broader question of children's rights makes these judgments ripe for analysis to contextualise the theory of children's decisional privacy.

I.4 The relevance and significance of children's right to decisional privacy in Australian family law

The central argument of this book, and the case study selected to illustrate the practical application and operation of the theory, are underpinned by the assumption that children's right to decisional privacy matters in Australian family law. It is therefore important to justify the relevance and significance of this right in decision-making under Part VII of the Family Law Act. Ferguson has asked, in more general terms, 'why should ... children's rights necessarily be better for children than regulating them through the notions of duties owed to them, or through the "welfare principle" and concomitant "best interests" assessment?'[130] The answer to this question has a doctrinal dimension and a philosophical one.

I.4.1 The best interests principle: A critical connector of children's rights and decisional privacy

From a doctrinal perspective, although Australia has ratified the CRC,[131] this international convention has not been incorporated into Australian law. Australia's ratification is nevertheless important. In *Minister for Immigration and Ethnic Affairs v Teoh*,[132] the High Court of Australia held that, in the event of an ambiguity in legislation, courts should favour a construction that accords with Australia's obligations under a treaty or international convention to which Australia is a party, because Parliament, *prima facie*, intends to give effect to Australia's obligations under international law.[133] The Full Court of the Family Court of Australia in *In Marriage of B*[134] said that the CRC must be given 'special significance' for the purpose of interpreting domestic law, given its almost

129 *Bell Judicial Review* (n 100) [134]; see also [148].
130 Ferguson (n 41) 189–90.
131 Australia ratified the CRC on 17 December 1990 and it came into force for Australia on 16 January 1991.
132 (1995) 183 CLR 273.
133 Ibid 287 (Mason CJ and Deane J).
134 (1997) 140 FLR 11.

universal acceptance and given that this convention 'is likely to be a fact or circumstance that the Court thinks is relevant in the absence of any inconsistent statutory provision'.[135]

The answer to the threshold question of why judges should 'take children's rights seriously'[136] in proceedings under Part VII of the Family Law Act derives, it is argued, from the 'paramountcy' principle[137] – the principle of 'the best interests of the child' as 'the paramount consideration'.[138] This principle is also enshrined in the CRC, although best interests are 'a primary' consideration.[139] Section 60CC of the Family Law Act lists the 'primary' and 'additional' considerations that the court must take into account in determining what is in a child's best interests.[140] While the Act does not explicitly require judges to consider the child's rights, or the child's privacy, in their decision-making under Part VII, the court has a wide discretion to take into account 'any other fact or circumstance that the court thinks is relevant' to the best interests assessment.[141] This provision arguably enables the judge to consider the model of children's rights under the CRC to determine the best interests of the child in each case.[142]

This argument is supported by an express legislative commitment to make the CRC relevant to judicial decision-making under Part VII of the Family Law Act,

135 Ibid 82 (Nicholson CJ, Fogarty and Lindenmayer JJ).

136 See Michael Freeman, 'Taking Children's Rights Seriously' (1987) 1(4) *Children and Society* 299; Michael Freeman, 'Taking Children's Rights More Seriously' (1992) 6(1) *International Journal of Law, Policy and the Family* 52; Freeman, 'Why It Remains Important' (n 69); Jane Fortin, 'Children's Rights: Are the Courts Now Taking Them More Seriously?' (2004) 15(2) *King's Law Journal* 253.

137 See Richard Chisholm, '"The Paramount Consideration": Children's Interests in Family Law' (2002) 16 *Australian Journal of Family Law* 87; Eekelaar, 'Beyond the Welfare Principle' (n 98); Jonathan Herring, 'Farewell Welfare?' (2005) 27(2) *Journal of Social Welfare and Family Law* 159; Robert van Krieken, 'The "Best Interests of the Child" and Parental Separation: On the "Civilizing" of Parents' (2005) 68(1) *Modern Law Review* 25.

138 *Family Law Act* (n 5) ss 60CA, 67ZC.

139 See Chapter 3 (Section 3.4.2).

140 *Family Law Act* (n 5) s 60CC(2), (3).

141 Ibid s 60CC(3)(m).

142 In support of this argument, see Hollingsworth and Stalford (n 90) 57–8, 66; Tobin, 'Judging the Judges' (n 8) 621 n 255; Stalford and Hollingsworth (n 8) 41. See also Fortin, *Children's Rights* (n 36) 40–1; John Eekelaar and John Tobin, 'Article 3: The Best Interests of the Child' in John Tobin (ed), *The UN Convention on the Rights of the Child: A Commentary* (Oxford University Press, 2019) 73, 87; CRC Committee, *General Comment No 14 (2013) on the Right of the Child to Have His or Her Best Interests Taken as a Primary Consideration (Art 3, Para 1)*, UN Doc CRC/C/GC/14 (29 May 2013) [6], [32]; Philip Alston and Bridget Gilmour-Walsh, *The Best Interests of the Child: Towards a Synthesis of Children's Rights and Cultural Values* (UNICEF Innocenti Studies, 1996) 9–10; Ursula Kilkelly, 'The Best Interests of the Child: A Gateway to Children's Rights?' in Elaine E Sutherland and Lesley-Anne Barnes Macfarlane (eds), *Implementing Article 3 of the United Nations Convention on the Rights of the Child: Best Interests, Welfare and Well-being* (Cambridge University Press, 2016) 51.

through the insertion of an 'additional object' into the objects of that Part.[143] The Family Court has described the objects as 'the core values of the legislation';[144] they 'provide the context' in which the primary and additional considerations 'are to be examined, weighed and applied' in determining the best interests of the child in each case.[145] The 'additional object' of Part VII is 'to give effect to the Convention on the Rights of the Child'.[146] Its purpose is to confirm, in cases of ambiguity, the obligation of decision-makers to interpret Part VII consistently with Australia's international obligations.[147] According to Parkinson, this makes the application of the CRC to proceedings under Part VII of the Family Law Act both 'uncertain and contentious'.[148] Accepting that the contents of the CRC 'are not enshrined as operative principles of law' in Australia and that 'the Convention is applicable only to the extent that it has been incorporated by specific provisions of the Family Law Act',[149] the additional object is nonetheless significant, for it embeds ideas about children's rights into the legislative framework of Part VII.

In the English case of *Nzolameso v City of Westminster*,[150] Baroness Hale of Richmond raised the 'interesting question', about which no argument was made before the UK Supreme Court, of whether, even where no right under the CRC is involved, 'welfare' in section 11 of the *Children Act 2004* (UK) should be interpreted consistently with the UK's obligations under Article 3 of the CRC.[151] Whilst a similar argument is yet to be raised in proceedings before the Australian family courts, it could well be made: that decision-making under Part VII of the Family Law Act, where the 'best interests of the child' are 'the paramount' consideration, requires that the child's other rights under the CRC be respected. Put differently, principles of 'internal system coherence' and 'external system coherence'[152] mean that a decision cannot be in a child's best interests where the outcome would infringe another right under the CRC.[153]

143 See *Family Law Act* (n 5) s 60B.

144 *Xiu v Hodges* [2019] FamCA 251, [37] (Bennett J).

145 *Goode v Goode* (2006) 206 FLR 212, 218 [10] (Bryant CJ, Finn and Boland JJ).

146 *Family Law Act* (n 5) s 60B(4). This provision came into force in 2012.

147 Explanatory Memorandum, Family Law Legislation Amendment (Family Violence and Other Measures) Bill 2011 (Cth) [23].

148 Patrick Parkinson, 'The Family Law Act and the UN Convention on Children's Rights: A New Focus on Children?', *Right Now* (online, 13 July 2012) <rightnow.org.au/opinion-3/the-family-law-act-and-the-un-convention-on-childrens-rights-a-new-focus-on-children/>. See also Michelle Fernando, 'Express Recognition of the UN Convention on the Rights of the Child in the Family Law Act: What Impact for Children's Participation?' (2012) 36(1) *University of New South Wales Law Journal* 88.

149 *Ralton v Ralton* [2017] FamCAFC 182, [18] (Bryant CJ, Strickland and Aldridge JJ). See also *Oram v Lambert* [2019] FamCAFC 4, 29 [156] (Ainslie-Wallace, Aldridge and Watts JJ).

150 [2015] UKSC 22.

151 Ibid [29].

152 Tobin, 'Seeking to Persuade' (n 70) 37–9.

153 See n 142 above.

I.4.2 Privacy as a value underpinning the Family Law Act

From a philosophical perspective, privacy is valuable not only for individuals (which is much-emphasised in justifications for its value)[154] but also for society more broadly.[155] Yet most discussions about decisional privacy – focusing on its value for adults – have conceptualised it as an *individual* interest rather than as a societal or state one.[156] The right to decisional privacy bears significance beyond the individuals who enjoy and exercise it, or alternatively, as the case study of gender dysphoria proceedings will illustrate, those who do not. Regan has suggested that

> [i]f privacy became less important to one individual in one particular context, or even to several individuals in several contexts, it would still be important as a value because it serves other crucial functions beyond those that it performs for a particular individual.[157]

Translating Regan's observation to the children's rights context, the value of recognising and respecting the decisional privacy of an individual child in one case before the Family Court, or a group of children, should not overlook the value of such recognition and respect for the dynamics of the relationship between parents, children and the state, and for the conceptualisation of children and childhood in society.

Taking a less myopic view of the value of children's decisional privacy – conceptualising it as valuable for not only the child as an individual – highlights its significance as a societal good and its 'common value' and 'public value'.[158] Decisional privacy promotes and enables the values of autonomy, freedom of expression and preservation of identity, which are vital for children's development and, by extension, to the development of liberal societies.[159] In denying children the opportunity to participate in decision-making processes, children are simultaneously denied the opportunity to develop the capacity to exercise their

154 See Chapter 1 (Section 1.3).

155 Nissenbaum (n 47) 86; Daniel Solove, *Understanding Privacy* (Harvard University Press, 2008) 98; Priscilla Regan, *Legislating Privacy: Technology, Social Values and Public Policy* (University of North Carolina Press, 1995) 212–14.

156 Regan (n 155) 214.

157 Ibid 221. See also Valerie Steeves, 'Reclaiming the Social Value of Privacy' in Ian Kerr, Valerie Steeves and Carole Lucock (eds), *Lessons from the Identity Trail: Anonymity, Privacy and Identity in a Networked Society* (Oxford University Press, 2009) 191, 193.

158 Regan (n 155) 213.

159 Lundy, Tobin and Parkes (n 58) 399. See also Jeremy Roche, 'Children: Rights, Participation and Citizenship' (1999) 6(4) *Childhood* 475; CRC Committee, *General Comment No 20* (n 77) [24].

autonomy[160] and so the argument becomes circular: children's perceived incapacity apparently justifies the failure to afford children decisional privacy.[161]

The public interest in promoting and protecting an understanding of children and the parent–child relationship that advances children's right to decisional privacy must be understood against the backdrop of the significant social role of family law. Family law allocates and enforces rights, duties and responsibilities on, and as between, parents, the family and the state.[162] Judicial enforcement of rights and allocation of responsibilities occurs through a multitude of discourses and conceptual understandings of children and childhood that change over time in response to changes in the socio-political climate, technology, policy, medicine and science, amongst many other factors.[163] As a public value, respecting children's decisional privacy necessarily limits state interference in decision-making in the 'private' sphere of the family.[164] That privacy is a value foundational to judicial decision-making in proceedings under the Family Law Act was identified by the ALRC in its inquiry into Australia's family law system:

> Many of the provisions of the Family Law Act as originally enacted, and as subsequently amended, illustrate how the objectives of informality, *privacy*, and respect for the dignity of separating couples were translated into legislation. They illustrate Parliament's intention to identify and treat family law as being different in character from other areas of civil law because of the emotional and financial consequences of relationship breakdown, and its public policy impacts on the wider society.[165]

Understanding privacy in Australian family law as a value underpinning the Family Law Act embraces the social importance of privacy. This is not to overlook or diminish the importance of privacy to individuals. But a children's rights approach understands the social value of privacy in this context as deriving from the role of adults to support and enable children to develop their capacity for autonomy. There is a public interest in reconceptualising children as rights-bearers and active subjects. To recognise and respect children's right to decisional privacy is to challenge the unhelpful – and arguably false – dichotomy between children's rights and best interests.[166] It is also to challenge the assumptions about children's dependence, incompetence, incapacity for rational decision-

160 Fortin, *Children's Rights* (n 36) 6.
161 Gerison Lansdown, 'International Developments in Children's Participation: Lessons and Challenges' in E Kay M Tisdall et al (eds), *Children, Young People and Social Inclusion: Participation for What?* (The Policy Press, 2006) 139, 140–1.
162 Alison Diduck, 'What is Family Law for?' (2011) 64(1) *Current Legal Problems* 287, 314.
163 Ibid.
164 Regan (n 155) 225–7.
165 ALRC, *Family Law for the Future – An Inquiry into the Family Law System* (Report No 135, March 2019) 357 [12.1] (emphasis added).
166 See Chapter 2 (Section 2.4.2).

making and vulnerability.[167] Reconceptualising the meaning and value of privacy in proceedings under Part VII of the Family Law Act as a social value – as *children's* right to *decisional* privacy – redefines the issue of children's participation in those proceedings and offers a stronger argument for enabling children to be more active participants in the determination of their own best interests.

I.5 The aims of this book

The most significant contribution that academic scholarship on children's rights can make, it is argued, is to promote self-awareness of *how* decisions for and about children are made; and to encourage dialogue about what decisional privacy for children means and why it is valuable. This book contributes to a rich body of socio-legal work that examines how, in various contexts, children's rights can and should be exercised within the dynamics of the family and in court processes. It strives to bring the theoretical and conceptual understanding of decisional privacy and the methodology of children's rights 'to bear on real life decision-making' in these contexts.[168]

Recognising and respecting children's right to participate in decision-making processes and to make decisions that might conflict with their parents' wishes remain significant unresolved challenges. These challenges are not unique to Australia, nor to the family law jurisdiction. They manifest in various jurisdictions worldwide. Children's activism in response to the effects of climate change, and the impacts of prolonged school closures and lockdowns in response to the COVID-19 pandemic, are but two pressing illustrations, at the time of writing, that underscore the importance of grappling with how to engage children more meaningfully in decision-making processes and how to better enable and listen to children's voices.

The conceptual model of children's right to decisional privacy developed in this book could apply to a range of areas beyond family law and medical treatment, including post-separation parenting disputes, child protection, child safety, education and youth justice. The aim is to present adult decision-makers with an opportunity to reflect upon how they make decisions for and about children, and how children can play a more meaningful role in those decision-making processes.

I.6 The structure of this book

I.6.1 Part A

Part A of this book (Chapters 1 to 3) lays the theoretical groundwork. It explains the notions of privacy, autonomy and children's rights, which form the conceptual foundation of the central argument. It also presents a children's rights

167 See Chapter 1 (Section 1.4.1).
168 Stalford and Hollingsworth (n 8) 21.

approach to decisional privacy and to re-reading judgments from a children's rights perspective.

Chapter 1 forges the nexus between privacy and autonomy, articulating how privacy enables and protects an autonomous way of life. It argues that the notion of autonomy sits uneasily with conceptions of children and childhood in Western liberal societies. It explains how a theory of children's right to decisional privacy draws on an interest theory of rights to bestow rights on children irrespective of their capacity to exercise those rights. This chapter also proposes a gradual, relational and evolving understanding of autonomy to overcome the criticism that children cannot exercise autonomy because they lack the capacity to do so.

Chapter 2 develops a children's rights approach to decisional privacy, situated within the formulation and understanding of children's rights contained in, and the values embraced by, the CRC. It builds on the significant work of children's rights scholars to present four fundamental principles of a children's rights approach: (i) children have rights and interests that are distinct from those of their parents and of the family as an entity; (ii) children must play an active role, consistent with their evolving capacities, in decision-making about their best interests; (iii) in light of their relative vulnerability and immaturity, children require appropriate direction and guidance from their parents to exercise, protect and enforce their rights; and (iv) children must meaningfully participate in decision-making about their lives. This chapter also highlights some factors that may constrain, or alternatively, encourage, judges to engage with children's rights in their decision-making.

Chapter 3 presents the key features of a children's rights judgment. It explains how a children's rights judgment can enhance the child's decisional privacy in court proceedings through four stages of the judicial decision-making process: (i) conceptualising the issues for determination from the child's perspective and in terms of the child's rights; (ii) court procedures that enable the child to participate meaningfully in the decision-making process; (iii) judicial reasoning and analysis of the issues that balance competing rights and interests; and (iv) a judgment that has the child as the focal point and is written with the child (or children generally) as an audience. Together, these features of a children's rights judgment strive to make children's rights a way of thinking for judges. They simultaneously serve to enable children to exercise their right to decisional privacy, as meaningful participation is vital to children's experience of autonomy.

I.6.2 Part B

Accepting that the theoretical underpinnings of children's rights are 'intimately connected' to their implementation in the law,[169] Part B (Chapters 4 to 8)

169 Ferguson (n 41) 182. See also Philip Veerman and Hephzibah Levine, 'Implementing Children's Rights on a Local Level: Narrowing the Gap Between Geneva and the Grassroots' (2000) 8 *International Journal of Children's Rights* 373; Quennerstedt (n 35).

contextualises children's right to decisional privacy by applying the theory developed in Part A, for illustrative purposes, to the case study of judicial proceedings concerning medical treatment for children experiencing gender dysphoria. The primary focus is the Australian family law context. A comparative analysis is also provided with the position in England and Wales.

Chapter 4 introduces the case study. It explains the nexus between children's right to decisional privacy and proceedings in the Family Court of Australia for the authorisation of medical treatment for children experiencing gender dysphoria, pursuant to the welfare jurisdiction under section 67ZC of the Family Law Act. Two factual issues that determine the Family Court's ability to exercise its welfare jurisdiction are discussed: the child's capacity to consent to treatment, and the subject matter of the application falling into the 'special medical procedure' category and so beyond the scope of parental responsibility to consent. The extension of the welfare jurisdiction to medical treatment for childhood gender dysphoria is examined through an overview of three significant court decisions. Finally, this chapter explains the role of courts in moderating the relationship between a child's decisional privacy and identity. This chapter provides the essential backdrop to the argument that, as courts have increasingly encroached upon decision-making in relation to TGD children's medical treatment, they have deprived those children of their decisional privacy rights.

Chapters 5 and 6 apply the children's rights approach to decisional privacy developed in Part A to critically analyse two judgments of the Full Court of the Family Court of Australia. The focus of Chapter 5 is the Full Court's judgment in the case of *Re Jamie*. It is argued that, through the conclusion in *Re Jamie* that the Family Court must determine the issue of the child's capacity to consent to stage two treatment for gender dysphoria, the Full Court denied decisional privacy to TGD children. This is notwithstanding the Full Court's efforts to engage with children's rights in its judgment.

Chapter 6 analyses the judgment of the Full Court in the case of *Re Kelvin*. Decided four years after *Re Jamie*, *Re Kelvin* provides a strong point of comparison and contrast of judicial approaches to children's right to decisional privacy in the context of medical treatment for gender dysphoria. This chapter challenges the alleged strides that the Full Court in *Re Kelvin* made in championing the rights of TGD children by removing the Family Court from the medical treatment process, save for circumstances of 'genuine dispute or controversy'.[170] It adopts the method of judgment re-writing to produce a child-friendly version of the Full Court's judgment. It is argued that the Full Court in *Re Kelvin* was not concerned with children's rights at all; rather, its decision was about the extent to which the Family Court should encroach on parents' ability (and responsibility) to make medical treatment decisions for and on behalf of their children.

170 *Re Kelvin* (n 122) [167] (Thackray, Strickland and Murphy JJ). See also [189] (Ainslie-Wallace and Ryan JJ).

Chapter 7 offers an important comparative dimension to the case study, analysing the judgment of the Court of Appeal of England and Wales in the case of *Bell*.[171] Three features of the Court of Appeal's judgment are examined to advance the argument that the decision is not a resounding victory for TGD children's rights: the Court's failure to conceptualise the issues as being about children and their rights, instead focusing on the appropriate 'gatekeeper' to gender dysphoria treatment; an evasive judicial approach that found it 'unnecessary'[172] to engage with rights-based arguments; and the missed opportunity to communicate the decision to children. However, it is argued that the Court of Appeal's judgment bears limited symbolic value for the ability of TGD children to exercise choice in discovering and preserving their gender identity without the need for court intervention.

Chapter 8 addresses the potential for intra-familial conflicts when a child's right to decisional privacy is recognised and respected. A children's rights approach anticipates the potential for such conflicts, given that it acknowledges children as subjects with rights and interests that are distinct from those of their parents. This chapter conceptualises the notion of 'conflict' in the family context using a relational approach to autonomy. It emphasises the influence of children's relationships with their parents and family members on children's ability to exercise and enjoy their right to decisional privacy. It also addresses the myth that respecting this right will grant children free rein in decision-making. Finally, this chapter articulates the social value of children's right to decisional privacy and proposes two interrelated processes for translating the theory developed in this book into policy and practice.

Recognising and respecting children's right to decisional privacy has significant implications not only for children themselves, but also for the dynamics and boundaries of the relationship between children, their parents and the state. The ultimate aim of this book is to stimulate dialogue and debate about whether, and if so how, the vision for a children's rights approach to judicial decision-making should be implemented to advance children's right to decisional privacy. Importantly, the new conceptual model presented can be accommodated within existing legal frameworks for determining children's best interests or welfare, so that children are not only seen, but also heard, and most importantly, listened to, in decision-making about matters that affect their identities and their lives.

171 *Bell Appeal* (n 100).
172 Ibid [90].

Part A

Privacy and children's rights

A theoretical perspective

1 The meaning and value of privacy

1.1 Introduction

Privacy has been labelled 'a concept in disarray',[1] 'infected with pernicious ambiguities'[2] and the 'Cheshire cat of values'.[3] The perceived 'chaos',[4] vagueness and confusion[5] shrouding privacy's content, value and function have led Thomson to suggest that 'the most striking thing about the right to privacy is that nobody seems to have any very clear idea what it is'.[6] This chapter articulates the meaning and value of the broad, contested notion of privacy. It first presents an overview of competing conceptions of privacy and lays the foundations for the argument that privacy serves the liberal ideal of autonomy. It then elaborates upon the value of privacy within the liberal democratic framework. It is submitted that privacy is instrumentally valuable as a condition that enables individuals to pursue their own conceptions of the good life. The crux of this framework is that individuals value privacy because they value autonomy; and autonomy can only be fully realised and experienced through the conditions of privacy.[7] Autonomy is understood to embrace both freedom *from* intervention by the state and others, and freedom *to* develop and pursue one's own life plan for self-fulfilment.

This chapter proposes that privacy enables autonomy through its three dimensions. The spatial dimension of privacy facilitates authentic behaviour

1 Daniel Solove, 'A Taxonomy of Privacy' (2006) 154(3) *University of Pennsylvania Law Review* 477, 477 ('Taxonomy of Privacy').

2 Hyman Gross, 'The Concept of Privacy' (1967) 42 *New York University Law Review* 34, 34–5.

3 Jonathan Franzen, *How to Be Alone: Essays* (Straus and Giroux, 2003) 42.

4 Julie Inness, *Privacy, Intimacy and Isolation* (Oxford University Press, 1992) 3, 8.

5 Alan Westin, *Privacy and Freedom* (Atheneum, 1967) 7; Judith Eichbaum, 'Towards an Autonomy-Based Theory of Constitutional Privacy: Beyond the Ideology of Familial Privacy' (1979) 14 *Harvard Civil Rights – Civil Liberties Law Review* 361, 361; David Lindsay, 'An Exploration of the Conceptual Basis of Privacy and the Implications for the Future of Australian Privacy Law' (2005) 29(1) *Melbourne University Law Review* 131, 135–8.

6 Judith Jarvis Thomson, 'The Right to Privacy' (1975) 4(4) *Philosophy and Public Affairs* 295, 295.

7 Beate Rossler, *The Value of Privacy* (Polity, 2005) 1, 75; Joseph Kupfer, 'Privacy, Autonomy and Self-Concept' (1987) 24(1) *American Philosophical Quarterly* 81, 81.

DOI: 10.4324/9781003224167-3

through the scope that it provides for self-reflection, self-invention and the possibility of intimate and family relationships. The informational dimension enables individuals to present themselves to others in different roles and in different ways, through selective, self-controlled information disclosure, thereby protecting the conditions for autonomy. Privacy's decisional dimension offers individuals the freedom to make important decisions about how they live their lives. The self-expression that decisional privacy enables gives individuals the independence to forge their identities and to define their values.

However, the notion of autonomy sits uneasily with conceptions of children and childhood in Western liberal societies, which emphasise children's vulnerability, immaturity and incapacity for rational decision-making, to justify the disparity in rights and responsibilities bestowed on children and adults respectively.[8] This chapter explains the significance of children's capacity (or lack thereof) for two competing theories of rights[9] – the interest theory, and the will or choice theory. It then articulates how a theory of children's decisional privacy draws on the interest theory to bestow rights on children irrespective of their capacity to exercise those rights. Acknowledging the perils inherent in the notion of 'family privacy' for children, it is argued that a gradual, relational and evolving understanding of autonomy overcomes the criticism that children cannot exercise autonomy because they lack the capacity to do so.

1.2 What is privacy?

The concept of privacy is conceived as an 'umbrella term' that serves a range of interests.[10] Some theories endeavour to explain privacy's meaning through a single

8 Helen Stalford and Kathryn Hollingsworth, 'Judging Children's Rights: Tendencies, Tensions, Constraints and Opportunities' in Helen Stalford, Kathryn Hollingsworth and Stephen Gilmore (eds), *Rewriting Children's Rights Judgments: From Academic Vision to New Practice* (Hart Publishing, 2017) 17, 31; Sheila Varadan, 'The Principle of Evolving Capacities under the UN Convention on the Rights of the Child' (2019) 27 *International Journal of Children's Rights* 306, 306–7; John Tobin, 'Courts and the Construction of Childhood: A New Way of Thinking' in Michael Freeman (ed), *Law and Childhood Studies: Current Legal Issues* (Oxford University Press, 2012) 55, 58–9; Michael Freeman, *The Rights and Wrongs of Children* (Frances Pinter, 1983) 7 ('*Rights and Wrongs*'); David Archard, *Children: Rights and Childhood* (Routledge, 3rd ed, 2014) 53–4 ('*Children*').

9 Cf Lucinda Ferguson, 'Not Merely Rights for Children But Children's Rights: The Theory Gap and the Assumption of the Importance of Children's Rights' (2013) 21 *International Journal of Children's Rights* 177, 179, 191–5 (arguing that both the interest theory and the will or choice theory 'fail as accounts of children's rights'). See also Samantha Brennan, 'Children's Choices or Children's Interests: Which Do Their Rights Protect?' in David Archard and Colin Macleod, *The Moral and Political Status of Children* (Oxford University Press, 2002) 53, 62.

10 See, eg, Judith Wagner DeCew, *In Pursuit of Privacy: Law, Ethics and the Rise of Technology* (Cornell University Press, 1997) 13; Solove, 'Taxonomy of Privacy' (n 1) 486; Daniel Solove, *Understanding Privacy* (Harvard University Press, 2008) 45; Annabelle Lever, *On Privacy* (Routledge, 2012) 4, 7.

defining feature. The most enduring and influential of these accounts include: the right to be let alone;[11] secrecy;[12] limited access to the self;[13] control over information;[14] intimacy;[15] and personhood.[16] More recent privacy law scholarship has emphasised theories that position social context as pivotal to understanding, defining and justifying privacy.[17]

A minority of scholars have argued against an independent right to privacy. The most noteworthy in this 'sceptical' or reductionist school is Judith Jarvis Thomson. Thomson has submitted that privacy is a 'cluster of rights' that 'derives' its value from other, 'more fundamental' rights or interests – particularly property rights and rights over the person – and so should be 'reduced' to these other rights.[18] Critics of Thomson's view emphasise that it is just as plausible that rights of ownership and rights to bodily security are 'derivative' from privacy rights, because privacy does in fact protect 'something unique' and it is intrinsically valuable.[19] That 'something unique' will be overlooked if privacy is held to have no distinct value of its own.

In conceptualising children's decisional privacy, to 'reduce' the notion of privacy to the 'more fundamental' rights to which Thomson refers – property rights and rights over the person – would generate both conceptual and practical difficulties in respecting decision-making by children. At the conceptual level, the doctrine of *patria potestas* (paternal power) in Roman law bestowed fathers with property-like rights of custody and control over their children. In doing so, this doctrine constructed social perceptions of the parent–child relationship as being

11 Samuel Warren and Louis Brandeis, 'The Right to Privacy' (1890) 4(5) *Harvard Law Review* 193, 193, 195 (citation omitted).

12 Sissela Bok, *Secrecy: On the Ethics of Concealment and Revelation* (Vintage Books, 1983) 11; Sidney Jourard, 'Some Psychological Aspects of Privacy' (1966) 31 *Law and Contemporary Problems* 307, 307.

13 Ruth Gavison, 'Privacy and the Limits of Law' (1980) 89(3) *Yale Law Journal* 421, 423; Gross (n 2) 35–6.

14 Westin (n 5) 7; Arthur Miller, *The Assault on Privacy: Computers, Data Banks and Dossiers* (University of Michigan Press, 1971) 25; Jerry Kang, 'Information Privacy in Cyberspace Transactions' (1998) 50(4) *Stanford Law Review* 1193, 1205; Charles Fried, 'Privacy' (1968) 77(3) *Yale Law Journal* 475, 482.

15 Inness (n 4) 56; Robert Gerstein, 'Intimacy and Privacy' in Ferdinand Schoeman (ed), *Philosophical Dimensions of Privacy: An Anthology* (Cambridge University Press, 1984) 265, 265, 270–71.

16 Stanley Benn, 'Privacy, Freedom and Respect for Persons' in Ferdinand Schoeman (ed), *Philosophical Dimensions of Privacy: An Anthology* (Cambridge University Press, 1984) 223, 228–9; Jeffrey Reiman, 'Privacy, Intimacy and Personhood' (1976) 6(1) *Philosophy and Public Affairs* 26, 37.

17 See Daniel Solove, 'Conceptualizing Privacy' (2002) 90(4) *California Law Review* 1088; Solove, 'Taxonomy of Privacy' (n 1); Helen Nissenbaum, *Privacy in Context: Technology, Policy, and the Integrity of Social Life* (Stanford Law Books, 2010).

18 Thomson (n 6) 306, 312–13.

19 See DeCew (n 10) 3, 29, citing William Parent, 'A New Definition of Privacy for the Law' (1983) 2(3) *Law and Philosophy* 305, 307; Thomas Scanlon, 'Thomson on Privacy' (1975) 4(4) *Philosophy and Public Affairs* 315; Reiman (n 16) 28.

akin to property ownership. The role of the child in society was predominantly to further the interests of the family as an entity, by maintaining the family's land-holding.[20] The progress of family law has been such that property norms regulating the relationship between parents and children have been displaced by an emphasis on children's best interests as the paramount consideration.[21] In contemporary liberal societies, parental rights are justified as existing 'for the benefit of the child',[22] and 'only so long as they are needed for the protection of the person and property of the child'.[23] For a concept of privacy to entertain the view that parents have property rights over their children would be fundamentally antithetical to the foundations of contemporary family law and the paramountcy of children's best interests.[24]

A related problem with Thomson's reductionist conception of privacy is that notions of 'ownership' over property and over the person are bound up with the notion of autonomy. If, as is argued below, the value of privacy inheres in upholding autonomy – the condition that enables individuals to pursue their own conceptions of the good life – then privacy is not derivative. Rather, privacy provides the preconditions required for individuals to consider their existence their own and to be able to meaningfully claim personal and property rights.[25] The theory of children's decisional privacy developed in this book is concerned with the *choices* that a child can make in relation to their possessions (property rights) and their body (rights over the person), consistent with the child's evolving capacities and guided by the child's parents. The ability to make such choices enables the child to answer the 'practical question'[26] of how they would like to live and what kind of person they would like to be. This question can only be answered if privacy is recognised as a distinct right or interest with unique value.

The liberal concept of privacy is constructed around three domains: spatial, informational and decisional.[27] These domains are predicated on an ideological separation of life into seemingly opposite spheres of 'private' and 'public' responsibilities and activities. The history of the 'private' as the sphere of the

20 John Eekelaar, 'The Emergence of Children's Rights' (1986) 6(2) *Oxford Journal of Legal Studies* 161, 162 ('Emergence of Children's Rights'); Barbara Bennett Woodhouse, 'Hatching the Egg: A Child-Centered Perspective on Parents' Rights' (1992) 14(6) *Cardozo Law Review* 1747, 1810–11; David Archard, 'Do Parents Own their Children?' (1993) 1 *International Journal of Children's Rights* 293.

21 Barbara Bennett Woodhouse, '"Who Owns the Child?" *Meyer* and *Pierce* and the Child as Property' (1992) 33 *William and Mary Law Review* 995, 1038–9 ('"Who Owns the Child?"').

22 *Gillick West Norfolk and Wisbech Area Health Authority* [1986] AC 112, 170 (Lord Fraser).

23 Ibid 183–4 (Lord Scarman).

24 Woodhouse, '"Who Owns the Child?"' (n 21) 1038-9. See *Children Act 1989* (UK), s 1(1), (3); *Family Law Act 1975* (Cth) ss 60CA, 67ZC.

25 Reiman (n 16) 43.

26 Rossler (n 7) 43.

27 DeCew (n 10) 75–8; Anita Allen, *Uneasy Access: Privacy for Women in a Free Society* (Rowman & Littlefield, 1988) 15; Rossler (n 7) 9; Kang (n 14) 1202–3.

family precedes liberalism, with its classic enunciation by Aristotle. The 'polis', a structured realm of political and civic activity, was strictly demarcated from the 'oikos', a private sphere attached to the home and the family.[28] The 'private' has been equated with the domestic realm and the home, comprising intimate and family relationships, while the 'public' has been used to capture the realms of politics and the market.[29] The public/private divide has long had a gendered, hierarchical aspect: the public considered the sphere of men, the private the sphere of women,[30] with children subordinate to adult decision-makers in each sphere. This normative distinction between 'public' and 'private' assumes the value of a distinct realm of non-intervention for the family and family members in their intimate and caretaking relationships.[31]

1.2.1 The spatial domain: The home as the locus of family life

The spatial domain of privacy recognises the sanctity of the home as a private or personal realm, where individuals can expect protection from arbitrary interference, intrusion and surveillance by the state or others.[32] On liberal accounts, the family is a symbol of private space; the home the localisation of the family's 'true private life',[33] valued as a secluded physical space for the possibility and realisation of both intimate and family relationships and individual solitude.[34] Spatial privacy facilitates authentic behaviour by offering scope for self-reflection and self-invention: the ability to withdraw from others gives individuals the freedom to define themselves.[35] However, as feminists have exposed, the spatial dimension of privacy has been used to legitimise violence against women and children in the home on the basis of 'non-intervention' in the family,[36] by viewing that violence as 'intimate' and non-systemic.[37] This is where spatial privacy poses a dilemma: it

28 See Arlene Saxonhouse, 'Classical Greek Conceptions of Public and Private' in Stanley Benn and Gerald Gaus (eds), *Public and Private in Social Life* (St Martin's Press, 1983) 363.

29 Susan Boyd, 'Challenging the Public/Private Divide: An Overview' in Susan Boyd (ed) *Challenging the Public/Private Divide: Feminism, Law, and Public Policy* (University of Toronto Press, 1997) 3, 8–10.

30 See Frances Olsen, 'The Family and the Market: A Study of Ideology and Legal Reform' (1983) 96(7) *Harvard Law Review* 1497, 1499–1501 ('The Family and the Market'); Boyd (n 29) 3.

31 Suzanne Kim, 'Reconstructing Family Privacy' (2006) 57(3) *Hastings Law Journal* 557, 581.

32 Rossler (n 7) 142–3, 152–3. See also *Semayne's Case*, 5 Co Rep 91, 195 (1604).

33 Rossler (n 7) 142.

34 Ibid 168.

35 Charles Fried, *An Anatomy of Values: Problems of Personal and Social Choice* (Harvard University Press, 1970) 143; Reiman (n 16) 40.

36 See Frances Olsen, 'The Myth of State Intervention in the Family' (1985) 18(4) *Michigan University Journal of Law Reform* 835.

37 Law reform campaigns, driven by the catchphrase, 'the personal is the political', have sought to shift or demolish the metaphorical boundaries around the family as a 'sacrosanct private sphere'. See, eg, Margaret Thornton, 'The Cartography of Public and Private' in Margaret

is fundamental to understandings of the family in contemporary liberal societies, yet bears the potential to foster and disguise situations that endanger individual family members, particularly women and children.[38]

1.2.2 The informational domain: Access to and control over information

The essence of the informational domain of privacy is 'who knows what about a person and how they know it'.[39] Informational privacy operates to protect individuals from actual and potential invasions of privacy through (mis) appropriation and (mis)use of information and it offers control in deciding who will access that information and for what purposes.[40] It thus contributes to a 'self-creative enterprise',[41] enabling individuals to present themselves to others in different roles and in different ways, through selective, self-controlled information disclosure.[42]

Consider the example of a family law litigant self-publishing details of their litigation on a social media platform. If that litigant has sought to restrict the disclosure of information posted, whether by having a 'private' account or limiting the 'friends' who can view their posts, then the subsequent sharing of that information by others beyond the audience intended would amount to a privacy violation, by fundamentally altering the conditions in which the litigant acts and makes choices.[43] This is known as 'context collapse'.[44] Privacy offers

---

Thornton (ed), *Public and Private: Feminist Legal Debates* (Oxford University Press, 1995) 2, 11; Katherine O'Donovan, 'Divisions and Dichotomies' in Katherine O'Donovan, *Sexual Divisions in Law* (Weidenfeld and Nicolson, 1985) 2, 8–11; Martha Albertson Fineman, 'What Place for Family Privacy?' (1999) 67 *George Washington Law Review* 1207, 1217; Barbara Bennett Woodhouse, 'The Dark Side of Family Privacy' (1999) 67 *George Washington Law Review* 1247, 1254–5 ('Dark Side'); Ruth Gavison, 'Feminism and the Public-Private Distinction' (1992) 45(1) *Stanford Law Review* 1, 14–18.

38 This tension between individual and group rights, with respect to the relationship between parents and children within the family, is discussed further in Section 1.4.4 below.

39 Rossler (n 7) 111.

40 Ibid 111–41; DeCew (n 10) 75–6; Nissenbaum (n 17).

41 Benn (n 16) 242.

42 Rossler (n 7) 108, 111; Kirsty Hughes, 'The Social Value of Privacy, the Value of Privacy to Society and Human Rights Discourse' in Dorota Mokrosinska and Beate Roessler (eds), *Social Dimensions of Privacy: Interdisciplinary Perspectives* (Cambridge University Press, 2015) 225, 226; Jeroen van den Hoven, 'Privacy and the Varieties of Informational Wrongdoing' in Richard Spinello and Herman Tavani (eds), *Readings in CyberEthics* (Jones & Bartlett, 2001) 488.

43 Reiman (n 16) 37.

44 See Jenny L Davis and Nathan Jurgenson, 'Context Collapse: Theorizing Context Collusions and Collisions' (2014) 17(4) *Information, Communication & Society* 476; Mark Tunick, *Balancing Privacy and Free Speech: Unwanted Attention in the Age of Social Media* (Routledge, 2014) 130.

individuals the capacity to 'compartmentalize information' about themselves.[45] The 'spreading of information beyond expected boundaries',[46] or a loss of control over what other people know about an individual and who has access to information about the individual, impairs the authenticity of that individual's self-determined and self-controlled behaviour, thus violating the conditions for autonomy. A violation of informational privacy can occur not only where previously concealed information is revealed, but also where information already made available is made more accessible.[47]

1.2.3 The decisional domain: Freedom for self-expression and decision-making

The decisional domain of privacy, which is the focus of this book, protects an individual's ability to make decisions which contribute to defining their identity and sense of self, free from the unwarranted interference of other individuals or the state.[48] It creates an area for the individual to develop 'plans of life',[49] facilitated by social relations of varying degrees of intimacy.[50] If autonomy lies in the individual being the 'author of [their] own biography', then the individual's life must be free from the 'interpretative sovereignty' of others – whether in the form of commentary, criticism, objections or influence – that may hamper the individual's decision-making, choices and behaviour.[51] Both negative comments and objections ('you shouldn't allow your children to walk to school by themselves at such a young age'), as well as approval and positive remarks ('your child is so polite!'), can amount to a violation of decisional privacy, as both might amount to unwelcome attention and interference in the seemingly 'private' matter of how a parent raises their child. A vital aspect of decisional privacy, drawn out by the case study in Part B of this book, is addressing the issues of to whom and how an individual should justify their decisions, actions and way of life.

1.3 Understanding the value of privacy

Pinpointing the value of privacy is vital to the task of conceptualising privacy; yet demonstrating that privacy is valuable can be difficult. The widespread disagreement about 'privacy' as a concept emanates from disagreements about

45 Tunick (n 44) 45; Edward Bloustein, 'Privacy as an Aspect of Human Dignity: An Answer to Dean Prosser' (1964) 39 *New York University Law Review* 962, 973.
46 Solove, 'Taxonomy of Privacy' (n 1) 535. See also Lior Jacob Strahilevitz, 'A Social Networks Theory of Privacy' (2005) 72(3) *University of Chicago Law Review* 919, 921.
47 Daniel Solove, *The Future of Reputation: Gossip, Rumor, and Privacy on the Internet* (Yale University Press, 2007) 170; Tunick (n 44) 151.
48 DeCew (n 10) 77–8; Rossler (n 7) 79–110.
49 John Rawls, *A Theory of Justice* (Harvard University Press, 1971) 407–15, §63.
50 Rossler (n 7) 1, 9–10, 75, 117; Inness (n 4) 92; DeCew (n 10) 69–70.
51 Rossler (n 7) 84, 88.

the values that privacy serves, and from different views on how those values are conceptualised. Consequentialist (or instrumentalist) theories on the one hand, and deontological (or intrinsic) theories on the other, differ in their answers to the question of why privacy is valued. Consequentialist approaches view privacy as instrumental to something else that is assumed or known to be valuable. The value of privacy lies, for instance, in its ability to foster intimate relationships;[52] to ensure individual autonomy;[53] to promote psychological well-being;[54] and to enable the effective functioning of democratic governments.[55] Privacy is worthy of protection for its beneficial consequences. By contrast, deontological approaches treat privacy as inherently or intrinsically valuable; privacy derives its value for what it 'is', rather than what it 'does'. The instrumental and intrinsic values of privacy are not necessarily mutually exclusive.

In this book, it is argued that privacy has an instrumental value and that it is valued as a prerequisite for the liberal ideal of autonomy. Privacy is normatively important because it protects the diversity of personal choices, actions and ways of life; it is a necessary condition of the development of an autonomous self. An individual is autonomous if they can ask what Rossler has coined the 'practical question'[56] and live accordingly. That question concerns 'how I want to live, what sort of person I want to be, and how I should best strive for my own good in my own way'.[57]

The essence of the concept of autonomy is the notion of an individual being able to live authentically, guided by desires, characteristics, values, conditions and considerations that are not externally imposed, but are self-determined and one's own.[58] As Ronald Dworkin has explained, autonomy 'allows us to lead our own lives rather than being led along them, so that each of us can be, to the extent a scheme of rights can make this possible, what he [sic] has made himself [sic]'.[59] To this end, privacy is valuable and necessary for both freedom *from* intervention by the state and other individuals; and freedom *to* forge a life plan and fulfil that plan in pursuit of a rewarding life.[60] There are two aspects of freedom. The negative aspect aligns with the Hobbesian definition of the absence

52 Gerstein (n 15) 265; Inness (n 4); Jeffrey Rosen, *The Unwanted Gaze: The Destruction of Privacy in America* (Vintage Books, 2001) 8.
53 Rossler (n 7) 1, 75; Kupfer (n 7) 81.
54 Westin (n 5) 35.
55 Gavison, 'Privacy and the Limits of Law' (n 13) 455; C Keith Boone, 'Privacy and Community' (1983) 9(1) *Social Theory and Practice* 1, 8; Solove, *Understanding Privacy* (n 10) 80.
56 Rossler (n 7) 43, 50–1.
57 Ibid 51.
58 John Christman and Joel Anderson, 'Introduction' in John Christman and Joel Anderson (eds), *Autonomy and the Challenges to Liberalism* (Cambridge University Press, 2005) 1, 3. See also Rossler (n 7) 53–60.
59 Ronald Dworkin, 'Autonomy and the Demented Self' (1986) 64 *Milbank Quarterly* 4, 8.
60 Rossler (n 7) 44.

of obstacles or interference.[61] The positive aspect of freedom is the conditions and capacity for autonomy, or the ability to 'will' and a sufficient range of options from which to choose. Privacy enables one aspect of freedom by addressing the other: it provides the conditions of negative freedom, within which an individual can exercise positive freedom.[62]

'Autonomy' and 'freedom' are sometimes used interchangeably, yet they are distinct values. Griffin distinguishes them thus: 'Autonomy is a feature of deliberation and decision; it has to do with deciding for oneself. [Freedom] is a feature of action; it concerns pursuing one's aims without interference.'[63] An individual requires freedom to be able to exercise autonomy, yet not every free action can be simultaneously labelled autonomous.[64] Hence a child may make a decision without independent thought and reflection, on the basis of conformity to the values of their parents (which could be the product of manipulation, indoctrination or domination), although that child might nonetheless be free to pursue those values as the child desires.[65] On this example, the child can be said to have freedom, but not autonomy. This nuance enlivens the practical question: an autonomous life is one in which an individual has an attitude to themselves, the opportunity to contemplate their desires and actions and to ask how they seek to live a rewarding, self-determined life: the individual's own conception of the good life.[66]

The capacity to understand what one considers to be the good life involves being able to both construct and act upon one's own set of values and life goals, which provide direction and scope for self-reflection.[67] Fulfilment of this liberal ideal of being able to lead an autonomous life depends on the conditions of, and on claims to, privacy.[68] Privacy thus 'substantialises' the freedoms protected in modern liberal societies, including autonomy, by securing the conditions that the individual needs to be able to exercise and enjoy those freedoms.[69] Each of privacy's three domains serves the ideal of autonomy in different ways. The spatial domain does so by regulating access to the individual; the informational domain does so by regulating the selective withholding and disclosure of information by, and about, the individual; and the decisional domain of privacy enables autonomy by protecting the individual's capacity to make decisions, behave, act

61 Thomas Hobbes, *Leviathan*, Crawford Brough Macpherson (ed) (Penguin, 1968) 261ff.

62 See also Catriona MacKenzie, 'Three Dimensions of Autonomy: A Relational Analysis' in Andrea Veltman and Mark Piper (eds), *Autonomy, Oppression and Gender* (Oxford University Press, 2014) 15.

63 James Griffin, *On Human Rights* (Oxford University Press, 2008) 226.

64 Ibid 150–1.

65 Ibid 151.

66 Rossler (n 7) 51–2.

67 Griffin (n 63) 32, 150; Eric Mitnick, *Rights, Groups, and Self-Invention: Group-Differentiated Rights in Liberal Theory* (Ashgate, 2006) 21.

68 See Nissenbaum (n 17) 82; Griffin (n 63) 223; Rossler (n 7) 72–3.

69 Rossler (n 7) 72, 81.

and pursue a way of life of their choosing. The essence of the privacy-autonomy nexus in liberal societies is that 'it is only through … "spaces" marked out by the borderline between private and public that the design, development and exercise of (certain aspects of) autonomy become possible'.[70]

The understanding of privacy's value just articulated aligns with the interpretation of the right to privacy in international human rights law. Article 16 of the CRC protects the child against 'arbitrary or unlawful interference with [their] privacy, family, home or correspondence'. International human rights jurisprudence has identified at least five discrete aspects of the right to privacy under Article 16, including physical and psychological integrity; decisional autonomy; personal identity; informational privacy; and spatial or physical privacy.[71] Similarly, the European Court of Human Rights ('ECtHR') has held that the 'right to respect for private and family life' under Article 8 of the *European Convention for the Protection of Human Rights and Fundamental Freedoms 1950* ('ECHR')[72] embraces all activities within the personal autonomy of an individual and 'covers the physical, moral and psychological integrity of a person … [and] can sometimes embrace aspects of an individual's physical and social identity'.[73] According to the ECtHR, the aim of the right under Article 8 of the ECHR is 'to ensure the development, without outside interference, of the personality of each individual'.[74] Article 8 has also been held to protect 'a right to identity and personal development, and the right to establish and develop relationships with other human beings and the outside world'.[75] These interpretations of the scope of Article 16 of the CRC and Article 8 of the ECHR reinforce the concept of

70 Ibid 73.

71 John Tobin and Sarah M Field, 'Article 16: The Right to Protection of Privacy, Family, Home, Correspondence, Honour, and Reputation' in John Tobin (ed), *The UN Convention on the Rights of the Child: A Commentary* (Oxford University Press, 2019) 551, 560–1. See also Manfred Nowak, *UN Covenant on Civil and Political Rights: CCPR Commentary* (NP Engel, 2005) 385–92.

72 *Convention for the Protection of Human Rights and Fundamental Freedoms*, opened for signature 4 November 1950, 213 UNTS 221 (entered into force 3 September 1953) ('*ECHR*'). Some scholars have argued that the term 'private life' under Article 8 of the ECHR and the term 'privacy' under Article 16 of the CRC 'basically mean the same thing': see Nowak (n 71) 385; David Harris et al, *Law of the European Convention on Human Rights* (Oxford University Press, 3rd ed, 2014) 305.

73 *Pretty v United Kingdom* (2002) 35 EHRR 1, [61]. See also *Georgel and Georgeta Stoicescu v Romania* [2011] ECHR 1193, [48]–[49]. For an overview of ECtHR jurisprudence on Art 8 of the ECHR, see Harris et al (n 72) ch 9; Bernadette Rainey, Elizabeth Wicks and Clare Ovey, *The European Convention on Human Rights* (Oxford University Press, 6th ed, 2014) ch 16.

74 *Botta v Italy* (1998) 26 EHRR 97, [32]; *Von Hannover v Germany (No 2)* [2012] ECHR 228, [95]. See also *Coereil and Aurik v The Netherlands*, Comm No 453/91 (9 December 1994) CCPR/C/52/D/453/1991, [10.2].

75 *Bensaid v United Kingdom* (2001) 33 EHRR 10, [47]. See also *Niemietz v Germany* (1993) 16 EHRR 97, [29].

autonomy as embracing personal self-determination and reflection about how an individual wishes to live their life.

1.4 Capacity, rights and the challenge of (re) conceptualising children's decisional privacy

It has been argued that

> children, as human beings, should, like adults, ... be free to lead their own lives according to their own conception of a good or worthwhile life, provided that this does not illegitimately restrict the liberty of others to do the same.[76]

However, the notion of autonomy in relation to children and their lives remains problematic. One obvious challenge to the justification for developing a theory of children's decisional privacy is that children are not, and cannot be, autonomous. Another challenge is that, even if children are recognised as autonomous beings, they cannot in fact exercise that autonomy, because they lack the capacity to do so. These challenges are addressed below.

1.4.1 The dominant Western conception of children and childhood

Childhood continues to be idealised in Western liberal societies and constructed as 'the "not-yet-ness" of adulthood'.[77] Pervasive in such idealisations are notions of the child as an innocent and vulnerable becoming, constantly threatened and in need of protection: from the perceived dangers of decision-making by those entrusted to act in the child's best interests (usually the child's parents), and also from the child's own behaviours and understandings.[78] Understanding children as 'vulnerable' in this context comprises children's exposure to the possibility of harm and their inability, or limited ability, to protect themselves from that harm.[79] This is reflected in the Preamble to the CRC, which provides that childhood is

76 Jane Fortin, *Children's Rights and the Developing Law* (Cambridge University Press, 3rd ed, 2009) 19, citing Richard Lindley, 'Teenagers and Other Children' in Geoffrey Scarre (ed), *Children, Parents and Politics* (Cambridge University Press, 1989) 75.

77 Archard, *Children* (n 8) 48.

78 See John Stuart Mill, *On Liberty*, Edward Alexander (ed) (Broadview Press, 1999) 52 ('Those who are still in a state to require being taken care of by others, must be protected against their own actions as well as against external injury').

79 John Tobin, 'Understanding Children's Rights: A Vision beyond Vulnerability' (2015) 84 *Nordic Journal of International Law* 155, 167 ('Understanding Children's Rights'). See also Doris Schroder and Eugenijus Gefenas, 'Vulnerability: Too Vague and Too Broad?' (2009) 18(2) *Cambridge Quarterly of Healthcare Ethics* 113, 117.

a period of 'special vulnerability during which children are in need of special protection'.[80]

The CRC assumes children's vulnerability to the risk of self-inflicted ('endogenous') harm and imposes obligations on adults to take measures to protect children against such risk.[81] This assumption is evident in Article 3(1) of the CRC, which permits state intervention in a child's life where necessary to protect the child's best interests, and in Article 5, which requires states to respect the rights, responsibilities and duties of parents to provide appropriate direction and guidance to children in the exercise of their rights. The desire to protect children from themselves is consistent with Freeman's notion of 'liberal paternalism'.[82] It is arguably justified by the reality that '[c]hildren do not always act in ways that are consistent with their best interests'.[83] In light of their perceived vulnerability, children are conceptualised as human beings who do not yet have the essential attributes of citizenship – including autonomy, reason and the capacity for self-determination – but who will develop these attributes in the future.[84]

However, characterising children as vulnerable comes with the attendant risks 'that they will be defined by their vulnerabilities'[85] and that adults will fail 'to appreciate the particular skills and talents ... that individual children have'.[86] These risks impede the recognition of children as capable of having and exercising decisional privacy rights. While the Preamble to the CRC stresses children's vulnerability and their need for 'special protection', the substantive text – in

80 See further discussion in Kirsten Sandberg, 'The Convention on the Rights of the Child and the Vulnerability of Children' (2015) 84(2) *Nordic Journal of International Law* 221. Cf Griffin (n 63) 85. Two other international instruments that acknowledge children as being in need of special protection are the *International Covenant on Civil and Political Rights*, opened for signature 16 December 1966, 999 UNTS 171 (entered into force 23 March 1976) art 24(1); and the *International Covenant on Economic, Social and Cultural Rights*, opened for signature 16 December 1966, 993 UNTS 3 (entered into force 3 January 1976) art 10(3).

81 Tobin, 'Understanding Children's Rights' (n 79) 164; John Tobin, 'Justifying Children's Rights' (2013) 21 *International Journal of Children's Rights* 395, 428–9.

82 Freeman, *Rights and Wrongs* (n 8) 54–60.

83 Tobin, 'Understanding Children's Rights' (n 79) 165. According to Gerald Dworkin, paternalism as a doctrine justifies 'interference with a person's liberty of action ... by reasons referring exclusively to the welfare, good, happiness, needs, interests or values of the person being coerced': see Gerald Dworkin, 'Paternalism' in Richard A Wasserstrom (ed), *Morality and the Law* (Wadsworth Publishing, 1971) 107, 108.

84 Barbara Arneil, 'Becoming Versus Being: A Critical Analysis of the Child in Liberal Theory' in David Archard and Colin Macleod (eds), *The Moral and Political Status of Children* (Oxford University Press, 2002) 70, 70–1. See also Michael Freeman, 'The Human Rights of Children' (2010) 63(1) *Current Legal Problems* 1, 9 ('Human Rights of Children').

85 Tobin, 'Understanding Children's Rights' (n 79) 157.

86 Jonathan Herring, 'Vulnerability, Children, and the Law' in Michael Freeman (ed), *Law and Childhood Studies* (Oxford University Press, 2012) 243, 249.

particular, the 'evolving capacities' principle[87] and children's right to express their views in all matters affecting them[88] – demands an understanding of children as 'active participant[s] in the promotion, protection and monitoring of their rights'.[89]

A children's rights approach to decisional privacy draws on these paradigms of children's evolving capacities and participation that underpin the CRC. Significantly, it does not deny that children are vulnerable. It accepts that vulnerability is a 'permanent and immutable feature of the human condition':[90] all human beings are vulnerable – adults and children alike – albeit to differing degrees.[91] While measures to protect children and their rights may be warranted in some circumstances, as Tobin has argued, '[c]hildren's vulnerabilities are not simply a basis for legitimising adult intervention in children's lives'.[92] A children's rights approach to decisional privacy requires that adults support and enable children to develop their decision-making capacities.[93]

1.4.2 The relevance of (in)capacity to competing theories of rights

The dividing line between childhood and adulthood as distinct life stages is arbitrarily fixed by age. Article 1 of the CRC defines a child, for the purposes of the convention, as 'every human being below the age of eighteen years unless under the law applicable to the child, majority is attained earlier'. The High Court of Australia has explained that:

> Children are presumed to be incompetent at birth and gradually to acquire legal competence for various purposes at different stages of their development until they reach the age of majority (eighteen), in which case they are presumed to have full legal capacity.[94]

87 *CRC*, art 5.
88 Ibid art 12.
89 CRC Committee, *General Comment No 7: Implementing Child Rights in Early Childhood*, UN Doc CRC/C/GC/7/Rev.1 (20 September 2006) [14].
90 Tobin, 'Understanding Children's Rights' (n 79) 161–2. See also Martha Albertson Fineman, 'The Vulnerable Subject: Anchoring Equality in the Human Condition' (2008) 20(1) *Yale Journal of Law and Feminism* 1, 10 ('The Vulnerable Subject').
91 Tobin, 'Understanding Children's Rights' (n 79) 157; Bryan S Turner, *Vulnerability and Human Rights* (Pennsylvania State University Press, 2006) 25–6; Fineman, 'The Vulnerable Subject' (n 90) 9–10; Martha Albertson Fineman, 'The Vulnerable Subject and the Responsive State' (2010) 60 *Emory Law Journal* 251, 255, 267; Herring, 'Vulnerability, Children, and the Law' (n 86) 253, 257; Martha Albertson Fineman, 'Equality, Autonomy, and the Vulnerable Subject in Law and Politics' in Martha Albertson Fineman and Anna Grear (eds), *Vulnerability: Reflections on a New Ethical Foundation for Law and Politics* (Ashgate, 2013) 13, 13.
92 Tobin, 'Understanding Children's Rights' (n 79) 177.
93 See Chapter 2 (Section 2.3.3).
94 *Re Woolley; Ex parte Applicants M276/2003* (2004) 225 CLR 1, 40 (McHugh J).

To deny children rights on the basis of age alone, in Archard's words, 'would be morally arbitrary and unjust'.[95] Something more than age is used to deprive children of rights-bearer status: capacity, or more accurately, a perceived connection between children's age and their attainment of a relevant capacity or competence.[96] The question of a child's capacity is fundamental to the conceptualisation of children's right to decisional privacy. It is important to distinguish between competence or capacity and rights. Children's actual or perceived lack of capacity provides a common justification for denying rights to children[97] and separates the interest theory of rights from the will or choice theory of rights.

The theory of children's decisional privacy developed in this book is premised upon an interest theory of rights,[98] under which all humans have rights in virtue of their shared humanity: 'the equal and inalienable rights of all members of the human family'.[99] The status of being a human being is enough to entitle a child to rights; capacity is irrelevant to that entitlement.[100] This is the preferred theory of rights under international human rights instruments, including the CRC, and it is endorsed by many scholars.[101] The interest theory understands a right as involving the protection of a sufficiently important interest and the imposition of duties on others, the performance of which ensures that the rights-holder can enjoy that interest. Children's evolving autonomy – their capacity for autonomy and in some cases, actual autonomy – is proposed here as the interest to be promoted by

95 Archard, *Children* (n 8) 85.

96 Ibid. See also Michael Freeman, *The Moral Status of Children: Essays on the Rights of the Child* (Kluwer Law International, 1997) 34–5 ('*Moral Status*'); Laurence D Houlgate, 'Children, Paternalism, and Rights to Liberty' in Onora O'Neill and William Ruddick (eds), *Having Children: Philosophical and Legal Reflections on Parenthood* (Oxford University Press, 1979) 274.

97 Tobin, 'Justifying Children's Rights' (n 81) 433.

98 See Joseph Raz, 'Legal Rights' (1984) 4(1) *Oxford Journal of Legal Studies* 1; Neil MacCormick, 'Children's Rights: A Test-Case' in Neil MacCormick (ed), *Legal Right and Social Democracy: Essays in Legal and Political Philosophy* (Clarendon Press, 1982) 154; Matthew H Kramer, 'Rights Without Trimmings' in Matthew H Kramer, Nigel Simmonds and Hillel Steiner (eds), *A Debate Over Rights: Philosophical Enquiries* (Clarendon Press, 1998) 7; Freeman, 'Human Rights of Children' (n 84) 21; Tobin, 'Justifying Children's Rights' (n 81) 403; Robert E Goodin and Diane Gibson, 'Rights, Young and Old' (1997) 17(2) *Oxford Journal of Legal Studies* 185.

99 *CRC*, Preamble.

100 Tobin, 'Justifying Children's Rights' (n 81) 403; Fortin (n 76) 13; Tom D Campbell, 'The Rights of the Minor: As Person, As Child, As Juvenile, As Future Adult' in Philip Alston, Stephen Parker and John Seymour (eds), *Children, Rights and the Law* (Clarendon Press, 1992) 1, 5. See also Freeman, 'Human Rights of Children' (n 84) 16; John Eekelaar, 'Personal Rights and Human Rights' in Peter Lodrup and Eva Modvar (eds), *Family Life and Human Rights: Papers Presented at the 11th World Conference of the International Society of Family Law* (Gyldendal, 2004) 183, 188; John Eekelaar, 'Invoking Human Rights' in Timothy Endicott, Joshua Getzler and Edwin Peel (eds), *Properties of Law: Essays in Honour of Jim Harris* (Oxford University Press, 2006) 336, 340.

101 See n 98 above.

recognising and respecting children's right to decisional privacy.[102] According to Tobin, '[c]hildren may lack capacity to exercise their rights but they do not lack interests, and it is their *interests*, not their *capacity*, which form the foundation of rights under an interest theory'.[103]

When rights depend on an individual possessing competency or capacity, they become 'exclusive and exclusionary',[104] which effectively denies children access to rights discourse and its attendant potential for accountability and empowerment.[105] However, that an individual must possess certain capacities, including the capacity to make rational choices, as a precondition to holding rights, has been pervasive in Western liberal philosophy. This understanding of rights is firmly rooted in notions of autonomy and reason in social contract theory.[106] The social contract theorists advanced the idea of a contract between citizen and state, based on the citizen's voluntary consent to be governed, with that notion of consent premised upon the citizen's ability to reason. Incapacity thus justified exclusion from the social contract. Yet the social contract theorists also envisioned a role for the child's parents and family in protecting the child.[107]

The view that a lack of capacity justifies a denial of rights forms the foundation of the will or choice theory of rights.[108] This theory conceptualises a right as 'the protected exercise of choice'[109] and denies children the status of rights-bearers owing to their perceived inability to exercise rational choice. Brighouse, a proponent of the will theory, has argued that '[t]he further an agent departs from the liberal model of the competent rational person, the less appropriate it seems to attribute rights'.[110] Thus, Brighouse considers that children should not be entitled to fundamental agency rights, because they are assumed to lack competency

102 This book acknowledges, but does not engage with, different approaches in the scholarship to determining the basis for justifying interests as rights: see, eg, Joseph Raz, *The Morality of Freedom* (Oxford University Press, 1986) 176–83 ('*Morality of Freedom*'); Griffin (n 63) 179–87; Charles R Beitz, *The Idea of Human Rights* (Oxford University Press, 2009) 109–10.

103 Tobin, 'Justifying Children's Rights' (n 81) 403.

104 Katherine Hunt Federle, 'Rights Flow Downhill' in Michael Freeman (ed), *Children's Rights: Progress and Perspectives* (Brill, 2011) 447, 448.

105 Tobin, 'Understanding Children's Rights' (n 79) 159–60.

106 Ibid 158.

107 John Locke, *Two Treatises of Government and a Letter Concerning Toleration*, (ed) Ian Shapiro (Yale University Press, 2003) 125, §61; Jean-Jacques Rousseau, *The Social Contract, Or Principles of Political Right*, (tr) Henry J Tozer (George Allen & Unwin, 1948) 101; Mill (n 78) 52.

108 See, eg, HLA Hart, 'Are There Any Natural Rights?' (1955) 64(2) *Philosophical Review* 175 ('Natural Rights'); Carl Wellman, *Real Rights* (Oxford University Press, 1995); Hillel Steiner, *An Essay on Rights* (Blackwell, 1994); L W Sumner, *The Moral Foundation of Rights* (Clarendon Press, 1987).

109 Archard, *Children* (n 8) 58.

110 Harry Brighouse, 'What Rights (If Any) Do Children Have?' in David Archard and Colin Macleod (eds), *The Moral and Political Status of Children* (Oxford University Press, 2002) 31, 31.

and so they depart from this liberal model of the 'competent rational person'.[111] Similarly, Griffin has claimed that infants cannot possess human rights because they are 'not normative agents',[112] while Hart has argued that '[i]f common usage sanctions talk of the rights of ... babies, it makes an idle use of the expression "a right"'.[113]

A diluted version of the will theory proposes a 'proxy' exercise of choice: children do have rights, but children's representatives (usually their parents) must make decisions on their behalf while children cannot exercise decision-making autonomy.[114] Where the child and their parents disagree about a matter, Gerald Dworkin has suggested that parents should choose for their children, 'not as they might want, but in terms of maximising [children's] interests that will make it possible for them to develop life plans of their own'.[115] The parental role, on Dworkin's view, is to maximise the child's *future* potential to exercise autonomy,[116] and what Rawls has called 'primary goods' such as 'liberty, health and opportunity'.[117]

The essence of such 'capacity scepticism'[118] is that for an individual to be a rights-holder presupposes capacities for rational choice, which children lack.[119] The assumption is that children do not appreciate the value of their choices and their ability to make those choices and so should be deprived of the ability to choose. In light of the dominant conception of children and childhood in Western liberal societies, the notion of autonomy sits 'uneasily with the reality

111 Ibid. Brighouse does, however, accept that children are entitled to 'welfare rights' (or economic and social rights), on the basis that such rights are consistent with an interest theory of rights. Yet Brighouse argues that children's agency rights are not compatible with the interest theory because children do not have the competency to know what is in their best interests, and so it is not in children's interests to have the agency to waive their welfare rights: at 38–9.

112 Griffin (n 63) 83. For a critique of Griffin's reliance on agency to justify human rights, see Tobin, 'Understanding Children's Rights' (n 79) 159–60; Tobin, 'Justifying Children's Rights' (n 81) 402–3; John Eekelaar, 'Naturalism or Pragmatism? Towards an Expansive View of Human Rights' (2011) 10(2) *Journal of Human Rights* 230, 234.

113 Hart, 'Natural Rights' (n 108) 181.

114 See HLA Hart, 'Bentham on Legal Rights' in Alfred W B Simpson (ed), *Oxford Essays in Jurisprudence (Second Series)* (Oxford University Press, 1973) 171, 184 n 86; Ferguson (n 9) 193–4; James G Dwyer, *The Relationship Rights of Children* (Cambridge University Press, 2006) 131.

115 Gerald Dworkin, 'Consent, Representation, and Proxy Consent' in Willard Gaylin and Ruth Macklin (eds), *Who Speaks for the Child: The Problems of Proxy Consent* (Plenum Press, 1982) 191, 205.

116 Ibid.

117 Rawls (n 49) 62.

118 Colin Macleod, 'Are Children's Rights Important?' in Elizabeth Brake and Lucinda Ferguson (eds), *Philosophical Foundations of Children's and Family Law* (Oxford University Press, 2018) 191, 200–1.

119 Freeman, *Rights and Wrongs* (n 8) 57.

of children's lives'.[120] An understanding of autonomy as gradual, evolving and relational enables children to be recognised as capable of having and exercising autonomy.

1.4.3 Autonomy as a gradual, evolving, relational concept

Classic definitions of autonomy within liberalism embrace the autonomous individual as 'a (part) author of [their] own life',[121] who has the 'capacity to choose [their] own roles and identities, and to rethink those choices'.[122] By virtue of a rich body of feminist scholarship[123] and children's rights scholarship,[124] the concept of autonomy is no longer wedded to the traditional liberal ideal of the rational, competent, independent adult who has the capacity to determine and act in their own best interests.[125] Rather, that concept now embraces relationality and acknowledges children's evolving capacities for decision-making.

Liberal discourse surrounding children and childhood has long emphasised the notion of development, or of 'becoming rather than being'.[126] However, as Julie Cohen has observed, '[a]utonomous adults do not spring full blown from the womb. Children and young adults must grow into their autonomy'.[127] A child's development of their various capacities – physical, cognitive, emotional, moral, social and spiritual – is not an 'instantaneous transformation'[128] from dependence to full autonomy when the child reaches the age of majority. The child's development is 'dynamic and interactional'[129] and takes 'an evolving,

120 John Tobin, 'Fixed Concepts but Changing Conceptions: Understanding the Relationship Between Children and Parents under the CRC' in Martin D Ruck, Michele Peterson-Badali and Michael Freeman (eds), *Handbook of Children's Rights: Global and Multidisciplinary Perspectives* (Taylor & Francis, 2016) 53, 55.

121 Raz, *Morality of Freedom* (n 102) 369.

122 Helen Reece, *Divorcing Responsibly* (Hart Publishing, 2003) 13. See also Ronald Dworkin (n 59) 8 ('autonomy makes each of us responsible for shaping his own life according to some coherent and distinctive sense of character, conviction, and interest').

123 See, eg, Katherine O'Donovan, *Sexual Divisions in Law* (Weidenfeld and Nicolson, 1985); Eva Gamarnikow et al (eds), *The Public and the Private* (Heinemann, 1983); Carole Pateman, 'Feminist Critiques of the Public/Private Dichotomy' in Anne Phillips (ed), *Feminism and Equality* (Basil Blackwell, 1987) 103; Margaret Thornton (ed), *Public and Private: Feminist Legal Debates* (Oxford University Press, 1995).

124 See, eg, Tobin, 'Understanding Children's Rights' (n 79) 161; Freeman, 'Human Rights of Children' (n 84); John Eekelaar, *Family Law and Personal Life* (Oxford University Press, 2007) ch 7.

125 Tobin, 'Understanding Children's Rights' (n 79) 161.

126 Sana Nakata, *Childhood Citizenship, Governance and Policy: The Politics of Becoming Adult* (Taylor & Francis, 2015) 165; Arneil (n 84) 70.

127 Julie Cohen, *Configuring the Networked Self* (Yale University Press, 2012) 113.

128 Robert Ludbrook, 'Children and the Political Process' (1996) 2(2) *Australian Journal of Human Rights* 278, 283.

129 Patrick Parkinson and Judy Cashmore, *The Voice of a Child in Family Law Disputes* (Oxford University Press, 2008) 4.

albeit not necessarily linear' course as the child ages.[130] When the realisation of autonomy is understood as a *gradual*, *evolving* process – that is, individuals learn to become, and to be, autonomous in and through social relations, including family relationships – then children can be understood as having the capacity for autonomy. As Hollingsworth and Stalford have explained, 'children have rights in the here and now *and* they are developing towards the acquisition of "full autonomy" … in adulthood'.[131] In light of the parental role to guide and direct children in the enjoyment of their rights, this gradual, evolving understanding of autonomy does not render the distinction between child and adult irrelevant or unimportant for the theory of children's decisional privacy.[132]

The *relationality* of autonomy is such that the good life does not simply involve the pursuit and promotion of one's own happiness, but also the fostering of relationships with others and the fulfilment of one's responsibilities.[133] Individuals are not completely free to live their lives however they wish. Relationships, responsibilities, moral duties and roles within the family and in society, influence and limit individuals' decisions and choices. In advancing the view that the value of privacy inheres in securing individual autonomy, a theory of children's decisional privacy does not presuppose *fully* autonomous individuals. Rather, autonomy is understood as a relational, socialised value. This understanding overcomes the objection that justifications for privacy which emphasise individual autonomy undermine respect for family relationships. The crux of such a criticism is that, if the value of privacy inheres in protecting individual autonomy, the family unit will be undermined because it promotes 'a conception of childhood that is severed from, and potentially antithetical, to the idea of the family'.[134] A

130 John Tobin and Sheila Varadan, 'Article 5: The Right to Parental Direction and Guidance and Consistent with a Child's Evolving Capacities' in John Tobin (ed), T*he UN Convention on the Rights of the Child: A Commentary* (Oxford University Press, 2019) 159, 172.

131 Kathryn Hollingsworth and Helen Stalford, 'Towards Children's Rights Judgments' in Helen Stalford, Kathryn Hollingsworth and Stephen Gilmore (eds), *Rewriting Children's Rights Judgments: From Academic Vision to New Practice* (Hart Publishing, 2017) 53, 73, citing Kathryn Hollingsworth, 'Theorising Children's Rights in Youth Justice: The Significance of Autonomy and Foundational Rights' (2013) 76(6) *Modern Law Review* 1046 (emphasis in original).

132 See Section 1.4.4 below.

133 See, eg, John Christman, 'Relational Autonomy, Liberal Individualism, and the Social Constitution of Selves' (2004) 117(1/2) *Philosophical Studies* 143, 156; Jonathan Herring, *Relational Autonomy and Family Law* (Springer, 2014) 48–9; Jennifer Nedelsky, 'Reconceiving Autonomy: Sources, Thoughts and Possibilities' in Allan Hutchinson and Leslie Green (eds), *Law and the Community: The End of Individualism?* (Carswell, 1989) 219, 225 ('Reconceiving Autonomy'); Catriona MacKenzie and Natalie Stoljar (eds), *Relational Autonomy: Feminist Perspectives on Autonomy, Agency and the Social Self* (Oxford University Press, 2000); Jennifer Nedelsky, *Law's Relations: A Relational Theory of Self, Autonomy and Law* (Oxford University Press, 2011); Martha Minow and Mary Lyndon Shanley, 'Relational Rights and Responsibilities: Revisioning the Family in Liberal Political Theory and Law' (1996) 11 *Hypatia* 4.

134 Tobin, 'Justifying Children's Rights' (n 81) 423.

relational approach accepts autonomy as an individual value; yet it also recognises that a child's sense of identity cannot be divorced from social context, including the role of the family in society and the complex nature of a child's relationships with their parents, siblings, caregivers and extended family.[135]

1.4.4 The family's role in children's development of autonomy

The gradual, evolving and relational approach to autonomy just articulated is particularly important in the context of the family, because socialisation within the family – through interactions between family members – offers the conditions that enable children to develop an understanding of themselves as autonomous individuals and as individuals who value autonomy.[136] The family provides a space for children to develop their identity and to learn and practise their autonomy.[137] Family informs a child's sense of identity at the most fundamental level, because that identity is deeply connected with the rights, interests and decisions of the child's parents or caregivers, who influence a child's development from infancy, through to adolescence and even adulthood.[138] The High Court of Australia has recognised that children's family relationships are vital to their identity formation, given that '[e]very child ... derives [their] own identity from the parents'.[139] Children develop their own sense of self by situating themselves within their family history and by participating in practices that are valued by their family. It is through their belonging to, and dependence on, their parents, families and communities, that children develop their autonomy.[140]

For children's rights and interests to be protected, these must be separable from the rights and interests of others, particularly parents.[141] Such a conceptual split might initially appear difficult to sustain, at least within a welfare or protectionist framework, in light of children's dependence on their parents and other adults for their needs to be met. The ability to choose between meaningful options is essential to autonomy: for if an individual has no options, or is unable

135 See Chapter 8 (Section 8.2).

136 Rossler (n 7) 167. See also David Oswell, *The Agency of Children: From Family to Global Human Rights* (Cambridge University Press, 2013) 91–8; Fortin (n 76) 89–90.

137 Mitnick (n 67) 80; Alice Hearst, *Children and the Politics of Cultural Belonging* (Cambridge University Press, 2012) 19; Oswell (n 136) 91–8.

138 Ibid. See also Jonathan Todres, 'Children's Rights and Women's Rights: Interrelated and Interdependent' in Martin D Ruck, Michele Peterson-Badali and Michael Freeman (eds), *Handbook of Children's Rights: Global and Multidisciplinary Perspectives* (Taylor & Francis, 2016) 21, 32.

139 *R v Cook; Ex parte C* (1985) 156 CLR 249, 258 (Brennan J).

140 See, eg, Mary Ann Glendon, *Rights Talk: The Impoverishment of Political Discourse* (Free Press, 1991) 130–6; Martha Minow, 'Rights for the Next Generation: A Feminist Approach to Children's Rights' (1986) 9 *Harvard Women's Law Journal* 1; Bruce C Hafen, 'Individualism and Autonomy in Family Law: The Waning of Belonging' (1991) *BYU Law Review* 1, 30–33.

141 Eekelaar, 'Emergence of Children's Rights' (n 20) 169. See Chapter 2 (Section 2.3.1).

to choose from those options, then that individual cannot be autonomous. But individual choice is both enabled and constrained by the context of family relationships. The parent–child relationship is a kind of intimate relationship that lacks the element of 'choice', in the sense that children cannot, and do not, 'choose' their parents. As Rossler has observed, 'the protection of privacy always has to do both with the protection *of* relations and *within* relations, protection *with* others and protection *from* others'.[142] Parents are a source of autonomy for their children, yet also a potential threat to that autonomy.[143] Attaching privacy to 'the family' as an entity is therefore problematic for children, given the power dynamics within families and power disparities between family members that the decisional domain of privacy embodies.[144]

Decisional family privacy, according to Allen, is

> a right of family members to be free from uninvited, unwarranted interference with the rearing, education, discipline, health, and custody decisions, made by family members (usually adults) on behalf of members of the same family (usually infants, children, teenagers, the elderly or the infirm).[145]

Such a 'hands off presumption' promotes the view that how parents raise and treat their children should be largely shielded from the law's purview.[146] As a result, children are 'doubly dependent': they are denied the status of rights-bearers and they simultaneously fall within the 'private' family sphere, 'with parents standing between them and the state'.[147] However, power, when understood in distributive terms – that is, parents have more power than, and power over, their children within the family unit – simplifies and overlooks the structural features of the parent–child relationship, such as the mediating and supporting role of social institutions, including the law, in perpetuating that power.[148]

The liberal concept of 'family privacy', buttressed by the public/private distinction,[149] understands privacy as protection against unwarranted state interference in the family; or as Dailey has suggested, 'the right of parents to exclude the state from intervening in decisions regarding their children'.[150] This concept assumes that the interests of children and those of their parents align and that parents will make decisions and act in their children's best interests.

142 Rossler (n 7) 192 (emphasis in original).
143 Nedelsky, 'Reconceiving Autonomy' (n 133) 235.
144 See DeCew (n 10) 77–8; Gavison, 'Privacy and the Limits of Law' (n 13) 448; Rossler (n 7) 84.
145 Allen (n 27) 115–16.
146 Fortin (n 76) 9; see also 321–4.
147 Ibid 9. See also Minow (n 140) 18.
148 Freeman, *Moral Status* (n 96) 74.
149 See Section 1.2 above.
150 Anne C Dailey, 'Constitutional Privacy and the Just Family' (1993) 67(4) *Tulane Law Review* 955, 985.

However, family privacy historically has failed to protect women and children, by endorsing hierarchical social roles within the family.[151] As Jean Cohen has explained:

> Insofar as privacy attached to the family, not to separate family members, and insofar as it was founded on the nature of the protected relationship, not on a conception of the autonomy ... of individuals, it meshed quite well with the prevailing conception of the natural family as hierarchical, heterosexual, patriarchal, and internally structured by relations of dependency of children on parents and wives on husbands.[152]

To claim that there exists a collective family interest or family values is to mask and reinforce power disparities between more powerful family members (usually men/fathers) over less powerful members (usually women/mothers and children).[153] References to the interests or values of 'the family', then, must be understood as interests or values determined by the more dominant family member(s). Ascribing rights to individuals within the family – and particularly to children – is antithetical to this traditional understanding of family privacy. The theory of children's right to decisional privacy developed in this book responds to the potential perils of family privacy. These dangers cannot be glossed over, given that debates in the privacy literature about the balance of power between parents, children and the state traditionally have overlooked the rights of children as distinct from their parents.

1.5 Conclusion

This chapter has articulated a conception of children's decisional privacy. It has proposed that privacy is valued because, in its absence, the notions of autonomy and individual freedom that are so fundamental to liberal societies could not be realised. A children's rights approach to decisional privacy is premised upon a relational, gradual and evolving understanding of autonomy and upon an interest theory of rights. It posits that children are entitled to rights regardless of their capacity to exercise those rights and also irrespective of their vulnerability and

151 Olsen, 'The Family and the Market' (n 30) 1511, 1566; see also Martha Albertson Fineman, *The Neutered Mother, the Sexual Family, and Other Twentieth Century Tragedies* (Routledge, 2014) 187; Kim (n 31) 571; Dailey (n 150) 985.

152 Jean L Cohen, 'Redescribing Privacy: Identity, Difference, and the Abortion Controversy' (1992) 3(1) *Columbia Journal of Gender and Law* 43, 60.

153 Olsen, 'The Family and the Market' (n 30) 1511, 1566. See also Woodhouse, 'Dark Side' (n 37) 1257; Dailey (n 150) 985; Vicki Coppock, '"Families" in "Crisis"?' in Phil Scraton (ed), *'Childhood' in 'Crisis'?* (UCL Press, 1997) 58, 59–64; Mitnick (n 67) 195–6; Allen (n 27) 115–16.

dependence on adults.[154] Bestowing children with a right to decisional privacy raises the spectre of disruption to the notion of family privacy as it has been conventionally understood in liberal philosophy. The next chapter presents four fundamental principles of a children's rights approach to decisional privacy, which acknowledge children's vulnerability, but also highlight children's evolving autonomy and demand children's participation in decision-making processes, consistent with their evolving capacities.

154 Freeman, 'Human Rights of Children' (n 84) 9–15; Tobin, 'Justifying Children's Rights' (n 81) 403.

2 A children's rights approach to decisional privacy

2.1 Introduction

This chapter situates children's decisional privacy and its value, as articulated in the previous chapter, in the context of children's rights. Building on the work of respected children's rights scholars,[1] it presents four fundamental principles of a rights-based approach to children's decisional privacy, which are situated within the formulation and understanding of children's rights contained in, and the values embraced by, the CRC. The first principle is that children are rights-bearing subjects with interests that are distinct from those of their parents and other family members. The second principle is that children must be able to exercise autonomy in the enjoyment of their rights, consistent with their evolving capacities. The third principle, which flows from the second, is that children's relative vulnerability and immaturity necessitate that parents provide appropriate direction and guidance to their children in the exercise of their rights. The fourth fundamental principle, and the most critical for children's ability to exercise their right to decisional privacy, is that children must participate meaningfully in decision-making about their lives.

The second part of this chapter identifies various factors that may influence judges' willingness and ability to engage with children's rights and to adopt such a framework in their decision-making.[2] These include each judge's personal values,

1 See John Tobin, 'Judging the Judges: Are they Adopting the Rights Approach in Matters involving Children?' (2009) 33(2) *Melbourne University Law Review* 579 ('Judging the Judges'); John Tobin, 'Courts and the Construction of Childhood: A New Way of Thinking' in Michael Freeman (ed), *Law and Childhood Studies: Current Legal Issues* (Oxford University Press, 2012) 55 ('Courts and the Construction of Childhood'); Helen Stalford, Kathryn Hollingsworth and Stephen Gilmore (eds), *Rewriting Children's Rights Judgments: From Academic Vision to New Practice* (Hart Publishing, 2017) ('*Rewriting Children's Rights Judgments*'); Barbara Bennett Woodhouse, 'The Courage of Innocence: Children as Heroes in the Struggle for Justice' (2009) *University of Illinois Law Review* 101; John Eekelaar, 'The Interests of the Child and the Child's Wishes: The Role of Dynamic Self-Determinism' (1994) 8(1) *International Journal of Law, Policy and the Family* 42 ('Dynamic Self-Determinism'); Michael Freeman, 'The Human Rights of Children' (2010) 63(1) *Current Legal Problems* 1 ('Human Rights of Children'); Aoife Daly, *Children, Autonomy and the Courts: Beyond the Right to be Heard* (Brill, 2017).

2 See Tobin, 'Judging the Judges' (n 1) 619–24; Helen Stalford and Kathryn Hollingsworth, 'Judging Children's Rights: Tendencies, Tensions, Constraints and Opportunities' in Helen

DOI: 10.4324/9781003224167-4

views and life experiences; how judges understand the relationship between children's best interests and children's rights; the role of the doctrine of precedent; judicial deference to the legislature for reform; and the parties' presentation of their case, which shapes the extent to which judges have the opportunity to engage with children's rights. This chapter and the next, which narrows the focus to court judgments, set the theoretical grounding for the case study in Part B of the book.[3] Establishing the fundamental principles of a children's rights approach and appreciating the 'empirical realities'[4] of judicial decision-making are intended to address the 'disjunction between theory and practice' in the context of children's rights.[5] A theory of children's decisional privacy, which may lack a 'clear and practical message' for judges and practitioners in their day-to-day work, becomes more relevant and useful when translated into principles to guide decision-makers.[6]

2.2 Children's rights: A still-contested notion

Childhood as a social identity is not merely a 'fact of human life' determined by biology,[7] but also a social construction shaped by cultural, historical and political influences, including law.[8] So, too, are 'rights' a social construct and a tool of power that can be used to challenge the *status quo* and shift children from the periphery of law and society to the centre – if not completely, then at least a little closer. Freeman has suggested that '[t]he language of rights can make visible what has for too long been suppressed. It can lead to different and new stories being heard in public'.[9] While it is beyond the scope of this book to explore and

Stalford, Kathryn Hollingsworth and Stephen Gilmore (eds), *Rewriting Children's Rights Judgments: From Academic Vision to New Practice* (Hart Publishing, 2017) 17, 40–50.

3 See Chapters 4 to 7, applying the theory of children's right to decisional privacy to judicial proceedings regarding medical treatment for children experiencing gender dysphoria.

4 Tobin, 'Judging the Judges' (n 1) 581.

5 Jane Fortin, *Children's Rights and the Developing Law* (Cambridge University Press, 3rd ed, 2009) 29 ('*Children's Rights*').

6 Ibid.

7 Barry Goldson, '"Childhood": An Introduction to Historical and Theoretical Analyses' in Phil Scraton (ed), *'Childhood' in 'Crisis'?* (UCL Press, 1997) 1, 2.

8 See Chapter 1 (Section 1.4.1). See also ibid 4–12; Allison James and Alan Prout, *Constructing and Reconstructing Childhood: Contemporary Issues in the Sociological Study of Childhood* (Falmer Press, 1990) 7–8; Lucinda Ferguson, 'Not Merely Rights for Children but Children's Rights: The Theory Gap and the Assumption of the Importance of Children's Rights' (2013) 21 *International Journal of Children's Rights* 177, 179 ('Not Merely Rights for Children'); Lucinda Ferguson, 'An Argument for Treating Children as a "Special Case"' in Elizabeth Brake and Lucinda Ferguson (eds), *Philosophical Foundations of Children's and Family Law* (Oxford University Press, 2018) 227, 235–7 ('Argument for Treating Children'). Cf John Tobin, 'Justifying Children's Rights' (2013) 21 *International Journal of Children's Rights* 395, 399–401; David Archard, *Children: Rights and Childhood* (Routledge, 2nd rev ed, 2004) 19–24, 27–36 ('*Children*'); Fortin, *Children's Rights* (n 5) 26.

9 Michael Freeman, 'Why It Remains Important to Take Children's Rights Seriously' (2007) 15 *International Journal of Children's Rights* 5, 6 ('Why It Remains Important'). See also Ferguson, 'Not Merely Rights for Children' (n 8) 183, citing Cass R Sunstein, 'On the Expressive Function of Law' (1996) 144(5) *University of Pennsylvania Law Review* 2021.

contribute to debates about the notion of 'children's rights',[10] it is important to offer an understanding of this concept and its content and scope.

The notion of children's rights captures a spectrum of civil, political, social, economic and cultural rights relating to childhood, which serve to enable children to 'thrive in the present and develop to their fullest potential in the future'.[11] Yet the content of 'children's rights' as a concept remains contested. The idea that children can claim, exercise and secure enjoyment of rights independently has not gained universal acceptance.[12] As Tobin has noted, notwithstanding 'widespread engagement' with children's rights in law, policy, research and advocacy, some consider that 'the idea of children's rights has "failed to secure a coherent … intellectual foundation"'.[13] Tobin has categorised the literature regarding the 'moral justification' for bestowing children with rights into 'three broad camps':[14] supporters of the idea of children's rights as a means of protecting children's dignity;[15] detractors of the idea of children's rights due to children's lack of capacity;[16] and those who oppose children's rights owing to, variously, concerns about the perceived potential for those rights to undermine the family structure[17] and the Western origins of human rights.[18]

10 See, eg, Ferguson, 'Not Merely Rights for Children' (n 8); Tobin, 'Justifying Children's Rights' (n 8); Colin Macleod, 'Are Children's Rights Important?' in Elizabeth Brake and Lucinda Ferguson (eds), *Philosophical Foundations of Children's and Family Law* (Oxford University Press, 2018) 191.

11 Stalford and Hollingsworth (n 2) 17.

12 Sheila Varadan, 'The Principle of Evolving Capacities under the UN Convention on the Rights of the Child' (2019) 27 *International Journal of Children's Rights* 306, 306.

13 Tobin, 'Justifying Children's Rights' (n 8) 395, citing Martha Minow, 'Whatever Happened to Children's Rights?' (1995) 80 *Minnesota Law Review* 267; Martin Guggenheim, *What's Wrong with Children's Rights* (Harvard University Press, 2005) ix.

14 Tobin, 'Justifying Children's Rights' (n 8) 396.

15 See, eg, Michael Freeman, 'Taking Children's Rights Seriously' (1987) 1(4) *Children and Society* 299; Michael Freeman, 'Taking Children's Rights More Seriously' (1992) 6(1) *International Journal of Law, Policy and the Family* 52, 55; Freeman, 'Human Rights of Children' (n 1) 16, 23, 44.

16 See Chapter 1 (Section 1.4.2). See also Guggenheim (n 13) 10, 13–14; Onora O'Neill, 'Children's Rights and Children's Lives' (1988) 98(3) *Ethics* 445; Harry Brighouse, 'What Rights (If Any) Do Children Have?' in David Archard and Colin Macleod (eds), *The Moral and Political Status of Children* (Oxford University Press, 2002) 31, 31.

17 See Chapter 8 (Section 8.3). See, eg, Bruce C Hafen and Jonathan O Hafen, 'Abandoning Children to Their Autonomy: The United Nations Convention on the Rights of the Child' (1996) 37(2) *Harvard International Law Journal* 449; Martha Minow and Mary Lyndon Shanley, 'Relational Rights and Responsibilities: Revisioning the Family in Liberal Political Theory and Law' (1996) 11 *Hypatia* 4, 18; Clare Huntington, 'Rights Myopia in Child Welfare' (2006) 53 *UCLA Law Review* 637, 664; Margaret O'Brien Steinfels, 'Children's Rights, Parental Rights, Family Privacy, and Family Autonomy' in Willard Gaylin and Ruth Macklin (eds), *Who Speaks for the Child: The Problems of Proxy Consent* (Plenum Press, 1982) 240.

18 Tobin, 'Justifying Children's Rights' (n 8) 418. See, eg, Erica Burman, 'Local, Global or Globalised? Child Development and International Child Rights Legislation' (1992) 3(1) *Childhood* 45; Sonia Harris-Short, 'International Human Rights Law: Imperialist, Inept and Ineffective? Cultural Relativism and the UN Convention on the Rights of the Child' (2003)

Scholars have broached the threshold question of whether the language of 'rights' for children is even appropriate,[19] or whether other frameworks or discourses, such as 'well-being',[20] 'ethic of care'[21] or 'capability',[22] might more accurately reflect the reality of children's lives, particularly their relative vulnerability to, and dependence on, adults.[23] Tobin has observed that the 'conceptual opposition' to children's rights largely reflects a preference for the will theory of rights;[24] a failure to read the text of the CRC; or a failure to appreciate the potential for alternative interpretations of the convention text that would respond to the concerns just outlined.[25]

A children's rights approach to decisional privacy embraces the understanding and formulation of children's rights contained in, and the values underpinning, the CRC. Acknowledging that the vision of children's rights promoted by the CRC remains subject to criticism,[26] the conception of children – vulnerable relative to adults, but having the evolving capacity for autonomy – provides the 'conceptual foundation' of children's rights under this international convention.[27] As Linde has noted, 'the CRC produces a very specific type of child subject that embodies certain contradictions, a child subject that is vulnerable, at risk, *and* rights-bearing'.[28] The CRC makes no explicit reference to 'decisional privacy'. Article 16(1) protects the child against 'arbitrary or unlawful interference with [their] privacy, family, home or correspondence'. The concept of decisional privacy embraces more than a negative freedom or protection against unjustifiable

---

25 *Human Rights Quarterly* 130; Brian Gran, *The Sociology of Children's Rights* (Polity Press, 2021) ch 6.

19 Ferguson, 'Not Merely Rights for Children' (n 8) 189–90; Carl Wellman, *The Proliferation of Rights: Moral Progress or Empty Rhetoric?* (Westview Press, 1999) 176–81.

20 See, eg, E Kay M Tisdall, 'Children's Wellbeing and Children's Rights in Tension?' (2015) 23 *International Journal of Children's Rights* 769; John Eekelaar, 'Beyond the Welfare Principle' (2002) 14(3) *Child and Family Law Quarterly* 237, 243–4.

21 See, eg, Fiona Kelly, 'Conceptualising the Child through an "Ethic of Care": Lessons for Family Law' (2005) 1(4) *International Journal of Law in Context* 375; Tom Cockburn, 'Children and the Feminist Ethic of Care' (2005) 12(1) *Childhood* 71.

22 See, eg, Martha Nussbaum, *Creating Capabilities: The Human Development Approach* (Belknap Press, 2011); Jérôme Ballet, Mario Biggeri and Flavio Comim, 'Children's Agency and the Capability Approach: A Conceptual Framework' in Mario Biggeri, Jérôme Ballet and Flavio Comim (eds), *Children and the Capability Approach* (Palgrave Macmillan, 2011) 22.

23 Stalford and Hollingsworth (n 2) 19.

24 See Chapter 1 (Section 1.4.2).

25 Tobin, 'Justifying Children's Rights' (n 8) 413.

26 See Freeman, 'Why It Remains Important' (n 9); Priscilla Alderson, 'Common Criticisms of Children's Rights and 25 Years of the IJCR' in Michael Freeman (ed), *Children's Rights: New Issues, New Themes, New Perspectives* (Brill, 2018) 39.

27 Tobin, 'Justifying Children's Rights' (n 8) 396. See also John Tobin, 'Introduction' in John Tobin (ed), *The UN Convention on the Rights of the Child: A Commentary* (Oxford University Press, 2019) 1, 1–2.

28 Robyn Linde, 'The Rights of Queer Children: The Denial of Children's Sexual Agency in the Convention on the Rights of the Child' (2019) 27(4) *International Journal of Children's Rights* 719, 729 (emphasis in original).

interference by the state or other individuals. It also serves a positive freedom: a child's ability to develop and pursue their own conception of the good life and to make choices that are consistent with that conception.[29] Accepting that children's rights are interdependent and interrelated,[30] this understanding of decisional privacy reinforces or facilitates a number of other convention rights.[31] These rights are drawn upon below to articulate four fundamental principles of a children's rights approach to decisional privacy.

2.3 The fundamental principles of a children's rights approach to decisional privacy

The theory of children's decisional privacy developed in this book builds upon the significant work of esteemed children's rights scholars, including Tobin, who has articulated a 'substantive' rights-based approach to judicial decision-making,[32] and Stalford, Hollingsworth and Gilmore, who consider how children's rights can be 'integrated into judicial reasoning' to increase children's 'visibility' in law through a 'children's rights' judgment.[33] The theory also embraces Eekelaar's notion of 'dynamic self-determinism', which seeks to reconcile the objective of furthering children's best interests with treating children as rights-bearers, by providing scope for the child (rather than adults alone) to determine the content of those interests.[34] Further, it overlaps with the work of Daly, who understands children's autonomy as relational[35] and detaches autonomy from children's capacity.[36] Children's right to decisional privacy also supports more broadly the views of scholars and children's rights advocates that emphasise children's resilience and evolving capacities.[37]

A children's rights approach to decisional privacy serves as an antidote to the dominant conception of children and childhood set out in the previous chapter:

29 See Chapter 1 (Section 1.3).

30 See John Tobin, 'Seeking to Persuade: A Constructive Approach to Human Rights Treaty Interpretation' (2010) 23(1) *Harvard Human Rights Journal* 1, 37–9 ('Seeking to Persuade'). See also Jonathan Todres, 'Children's Rights and Women's Rights: Interrelated and Interdependent' in Martin Ruck, Michele Peterson-Badali and Michael Freeman (eds), *Handbook of Children's Rights: Global and Multidisciplinary Perspectives* (Taylor & Francis, 2016) 21, 21; Freeman, 'Human Rights of Children' (n 1) 16.

31 See *CRC*, arts 3, 5, 8, 12 and 13(1).

32 See Tobin, 'Judging the Judges' (n 1); Tobin, 'Courts and the Construction of Childhood' (n 1).

33 See Stalford, Hollingsworth and Gilmore, *Rewriting Children's Rights Judgments* (n 1).

34 Eekelaar, 'Dynamic Self-Determinism' (n 1) 42.

35 Daly (n 1) 129–30.

36 Ibid ch 3.

37 See, eg, Woodhouse (n 1); Steven J Condly, 'Resilience in Children: A Review of the Literature with Implications for Education' (2006) 41(3) *Urban Education* 211; Staci M Zolkoski and Lyndal M Bullcock, 'Resilience in Children and Youth: A Review' (2012) 34(12) *Children and Youth Services Review* 2295; Varadan (n 12); Freeman, 'Human Rights of Children' (n 1).

the view that children are vulnerable, dependent on adults and incapable of rational decision-making.[38] It embraces the foundation or justification of human rights as moral rights, possessed by all humans by virtue of their shared humanity, not by virtue of reciprocity (that to give children rights requires that they also bear responsibilities) or capacity (the concept fundamental to the distinction between the will theory and the interest theory of rights).[39] A children's rights approach provides rhetorical and moral support for the proposition, recognised in the preamble to the CRC, that children need 'special safeguards and care'. Significantly, it also reconceptualises children as capable of making decisions consistent with their evolving capacities, who should be supported and guided in the exercise of their rights.

2.3.1 *Children are subjects with distinct rights and interests*

The first fundamental principle of a children's rights approach to decisional privacy responds to the hazards associated with liberal 'family privacy' discourse[40] by recognising that children have rights and interests that are *distinct* from those of their parents and of the family as an entity. This is an important conceptual recognition of the 'greater democratisation' of family relationships,[41] which displaces the presumption that the interests, values and identities of family members necessarily align within a cohesive, integrated unit. Baroness Hale of Richmond, former President of the Supreme Court of the UK, has explained that '[t]hose who do listen to children understand that they often have a point of view which is quite distinct from that of the person looking after them. They are quite capable of being moral actors in their own right'.[42] The CRC Committee similarly has emphasised that the CRC 'requires that children, including the very youngest children be respected as persons in their own right' and as 'active members of families, communities and societies with their own concerns, interests and points of view'.[43] This first feature does not discount the hierarchical relationship that exists between parents and their children. Yet it requires that, even within such an understanding of the parent–child relationship, children must be respected as active rights-bearing subjects with distinct rights and interests. They are more than simply as 'objects of concern' and protective intervention.[44]

38 See Chapter 1 (Section 1.4.1).
39 See Chapter 1 (Section 1.4.2).
40 See Chapter 1 (Section 1.4.4).
41 Patrick Parkinson and Judy Cashmore, *The Voice of a Child in Family Law Disputes* (Oxford University Press, 2008) 10.
42 *Re D (A Child) (Abduction: Rights of Custody)* [2007] 1 AC 619, 641 [57].
43 CRC Committee, *General Comment No 7: Implementing Child Rights in Early Childhood*, UN Doc CRC/C/GC/7/Rev.1 (20 September 2006) [5] ('*General Comment No 7*').
44 Parkinson and Cashmore (n 41) 7; Carol Smart, Amanda Wade and Bren Neale, 'Objects of Concern? Children and Divorce' (1999) 11(4) *Child and Family Law Quarterly* 365; John Tobin, 'Understanding Children's Rights: A Vision beyond Vulnerability' (2015) 84

2.3.2 *Children exercise autonomy consistent with their evolving capacities*

The second fundamental principle is that children must play an active role, consistent with their evolving capacities, in decision-making about their best interests.[45] Article 5 of the CRC underscores the importance of the child's family in providing 'appropriate direction and guidance' in the child's exercise of their rights, 'in a manner consistent with the evolving capacities of the child'. This notion of 'evolving capacities' importantly is a 'positive and enabling' one,[46] which supports the right of all children, regardless of age, to experience increasing agency, autonomy and responsibility in the enjoyment and exercise of their rights as they develop and mature.[47]

The evolving capacities principle also recognises that parental rights and power over the child diminish with the child's growing maturity. The CRC Committee has explained that Article 5 embodies the principle that parents 'have the responsibility to continually adjust the levels of support and guidance they offer to a child'.[48] These adjustments, according to the CRC Committee, take into consideration the child's 'interests and wishes' and the child's 'capacities for autonomous decision making and comprehension of [their] best interests'.[49] Whilst children are born dependent on adults, their various capacities evolve as they age. The expectation under the CRC is that, during this period of development, parents will give their child appropriate direction and guidance, consistent with the child's evolving capacities.[50] When applied in practice, the notion of evolving capacities envisions that a child may reach a level of understanding and maturity on a matter that is such as to obviate the need for parental guidance and direction. This means that the child's own views must be respected, even when

---

Nordic Journal of International Law 155, 171, 176 ('Understanding Children's Rights'); Stalford and Hollingsworth (n 2) 31; Tobin, 'Justifying Children's Rights' (n 8) 410; David Archard, 'Children, Adults, Best Interests and Rights' (2013) 13(1) *Medical Law International* 55, 59; John Tobin and Sheila Varadan, 'Article 5: The Right to Parental Direction and Guidance and Consistent with a Child's Evolving Capacities' in John Tobin (ed), *The UN Convention on the Rights of the Child: A Commentary* (Oxford University Press, 2019) 159, 172; Laura Lundy, John Tobin and Aisling Parkes, 'Article 12: The Right to Respect for the Views of the Child' in John Tobin (ed), *The UN Convention on the Rights of the Child: A Commentary* (Oxford University Press, 2019) 397, 397; Robyn Fitzgerald, 'How are Children Heard in Family Law Proceedings in Australia?' (2002) 6 *Southern Cross University Law Review* 177, 180, 193–4.

45 Tobin, 'Judging the Judges' (n 1) 591.

46 CRC Committee, *General Comment No 7* (n 43) [17]. See also CRC Committee, *General Comment No 20 (2016) on the Implementation of the Rights of the Child During Adolescence*, UN Doc CRC/C/GC/20 (6 December 2016) [18] ('*General Comment No 20*').

47 Tobin and Varadan (n 44) 178.

48 CRC Committee, *General Comment No 7* (n 43) [17].

49 Ibid.

50 Tobin and Varadan (n 44) 159–60. See also Eekelaar, 'Dynamic Self-Determinism' (n 1) 42.

they conflict with the views of the child's parents.[51] Or in Seymour's more blunt words, '[a]s a child matures, … parents must "back off"'.[52] The parent–child dialogue when a child reaches this level may shift from parental 'reminders and advice' to 'an exchange on an equal footing'.[53] Article 5 thus reconceptualises the parent–child relationship from one characterised by 'unbridled parental autonomy' to an 'interdependent' one.[54]

The principle of evolving capacities as a process of progressive acquisition of 'competencies, understanding and increasing levels of agency' that enable children 'to take responsibility and exercise their rights'[55] aligns with an understanding of autonomy as a relational, gradual and evolving concept.[56] Importantly, this second fundamental principle of a children's rights approach to decisional privacy does not permit children to be forced to make decisions where they are unwilling, or where they feel that they lack the competence, to do so.[57] To overestimate children's capacities and prematurely withdraw parental direction and guidance triggers the risk of exposing children to abuse, harm and exploitation.[58] Parents' primary responsibility for their child's upbringing and development is qualified by the requirement that the exercise of that responsibility is consistent with the best interests of the child and with the attainment of the child's rights.[59] This qualification leads to the third fundamental principle.

51 See Chapter 8 (Section 8.3.2).

52 John Seymour, *Children, Parents and the Courts: Legal Intervention in Family Life* (Federation Press, 2016) 101.

53 CRC Committee, *General Comment No 12 (2009): The Right of the Child to be Heard*, UN Doc CRC/C/GC/12 (20 July 2009) [84] ('*General Comment No 12*'); CRC Committee, *General Comment No 14: The Right of the Child to Have his or her Best Interests Taken as a Primary Consideration*, UN Doc CRC/C/GC/14 (29 May 2013) [44] ('*General Comment No 14*').

54 Tobin and Varadan (n 44) 173. See also Nicola Taylor, 'Parental Guidance in Support of Children's Participation Rights: The Interplay between Articles 5 and 12 in the Family Justice System' in Brian Sloan and Claire Fenton-Glynn (eds), *Parental Guidance, State Responsibility and Evolving Capacities: Article 5 of the United Nations Convention on the Rights of the Child* (Brill, 2021) 104, 107–8.

55 CRC Committee, *General Comment No 20* (n 46) [18].

56 See Chapter 1 (Section 1.4.3).

57 Gerison Lansdown, *The Evolving Capacities of the Child* (UNICEF Innocenti Studies, 2005) 4 ('*Evolving Capacities*'); Tobin and Varadan (n 44) 173.

58 Ibid. See also Lundy, Tobin and Parkes (n 44) 405.

59 *CRC*, art 18(1). Art 19(1) recognises that parents can exercise their rights in ways that are inconsistent with their parental responsibilities and with the objective of enabling children to realise their rights. See also Elaine Sutherland, 'The Enigma of Article 5 of the United Nations Convention on the Rights of the Child: Central or Peripheral?' in Brian Sloan and Claire Fenton-Glynn (eds), *Parental Guidance, State Responsibility and Evolving Capacities: Article 5 of the United Nations Convention on the Rights of the Child* (Brill, 2021) 13.

2.3.3 *Children require appropriate direction and guidance in the exercise of their rights*

Decisional privacy enables children to exercise autonomy in the enjoyment of their rights, consistent with their evolving capacities. But children's relative vulnerability and immaturity necessitate that parents provide their children with appropriate direction and guidance in the exercise of their rights, as well as means of protecting and upholding those rights.[60] Article 5 of the CRC strives for a 'delicate balance' between acknowledging children's evolving capacities, and recognising the role of parents in helping children to realise their rights as those capacities develop, without unjustified state intervention.[61] In doing so, it helps to establish the normative basis for moderating the trilateral relationship between children, their parents and the state. Critically, the focus must remain on the *child's* right to receive appropriate direction and guidance from their parents, to enable the child to enjoy their right to decisional privacy, rather than on *parents'* rights to non-interference by the state in the exercise of parental rights and responsibilities.[62] That parental power must be exercised for the *child's* benefit and not for the parents' benefit is reinforced by Article 18(1) of the CRC: the best interests of the child must be parents' 'basic concern'.

A relational approach to children's decisional privacy appreciates that children's rights and interests are intertwined with those of their parents and other family members.[63] As such, it may not always be easy to distinguish between parents' provision of appropriate direction and guidance to their child in the exercise of their rights and parents' manipulation of their child's exercise of those rights. Owing to the power imbalance inherent in the parent–child relationship, the potential for parents to influence their child's decision and the inherent difficulties in establishing whether, and if so, how, that decision has been so influenced, are live concerns.[64] A risk for the child in this context is that they will conform to

60 Tobin, 'Judging the Judges' (n 1) 586, citing Jane Fortin, 'Accommodating Children's Rights in a Post *Human Rights Act* Era' (2006) 69(3) *Modern Law Review* 299, 317–18 ('Accommodating Children's Rights').

61 Tobin and Varadan (n 44) 160.

62 Ibid 161; John Tobin and Sarah M Field, 'Article 16: The Right to Protection of Privacy, Family, Home, Correspondence, Honour, and Reputation' in John Tobin (ed), *The UN Convention on the Rights of the Child: A Commentary* (Oxford University Press, 2019) 551, 558–9.

63 See Chapter 1 (Section 1.4.4). See also Alice Hearst, *Children and the Politics of Cultural Belonging* (Cambridge University Press, 2012) 19; Martha Albertson Fineman, *The Autonomy Myth: A Theory of Dependency* (The New Press, 2004) 35.

64 Ferguson, 'Argument for Treating Children' (n 8) 244; Mianna Lotz, 'Parental Values and Children's Vulnerability' in Catriona Mackenzie, Wendy Rogers, and Susan Dodds (eds), *Vulnerability: New Essays in Ethics and Feminist Philosophy* (Oxford University Press, 2014) 242, 260–63; John Eekelaar and John Tobin, 'Article 3: The Best Interests of the Child' in John Tobin (ed), *The UN Convention on the Rights of the Child: A Commentary* (Oxford University Press, 2019) 73, 87. In the context of post-separation parenting proceedings, see Parkinson and Cashmore (n 41) 82–3, 89, 94–5, 120–22.

and internalise the values of their parents. These social conditions will thus diminish or deny the child's sense of individual choice and ability to exercise autonomy. Any assessment of a child's autonomous choice must be alive to the context of the child's family relationships, which may enable or constrain that choice. It is here that the 'best interests' or 'welfare' principle is critical:[65] parents would be expected to act in their child's best interests in assisting their child to enjoy their decisional privacy rights, by providing appropriate guidance and direction, consistent with the child's evolving capacities.

The notion of 'appropriate' direction and guidance may at first blush appear to impose a great burden on parents to provide the 'right' support for their children. Parents are effectively required to perform a 'trustee type role',[66] and to take positive steps to assist their child in developing the capacity for autonomy. A children's rights approach to decisional privacy proposes that parents have a broad degree of discretion in deciding how to offer appropriate direction and guidance to their child. However, as Lansdown has explained, parents do not have '*carte blanche* to provide whatever direction or guidance they happen to believe is suitable'.[67] Parental discretion is not unlimited; it is subject to two limitations. The first is that, for parental direction and guidance to be 'appropriate', it must be consistent with all other provisions of the CRC.[68] According to the CRC Committee, 'an adult's judgment of a child's best interests cannot override the obligation to respect all rights under the Convention'.[69]

The second limitation is that parental direction and guidance must be flexible enough to accommodate children's evolving 'interests and wishes' and their 'capacities for autonomous decision making and comprehension of [their] best interests'.[70] The role of parents is to help their children to develop the capacity for autonomy. The right to what Macleod has called 'an autonomy-facilitating

65 See *CRC*, art 3(1); *Family Law Act* 1975 (Cth) ss 60CA, 67ZC ('*Family Law Act*'); *Children Act 1989* (UK) s 1(1) ('*Children Act*').

66 Tobin and Field (n 62) 558. See also Daly (n 1) 82; Harry Brighouse and Adam Swift, 'Parents' Rights and the Value of the Family' (2006) 117(1) *Ethics* 80, 95–6; Didier Reynaert, Maria Bouverne-De Bie and Stijn Vandevelde, 'A Review of Children's Rights Literature since the Adoption of the United Nations Convention on the Rights of the Child' (2009) 16(4) *Childhood* 518, 525 (describing parental rights as 'functional rights' that 'serve the rights of children'); Samantha Brennan and Robert Noggle, 'The Moral Status of Children: Children's Rights, Parents' Rights and Family Justice' (1997) 23(1) *Social Theory and Practice* 1, 11–13 (referring to 'stewardship rights').

67 Lansdown, *Evolving Capacities* (n 57) 6. See also Tobin and Varadan (n 44) 162.

68 Tobin and Varadan (n 44) 172; CRC Committee, *General Comment No 8 (2006): The Right of the Child to Protection from Corporal Punishment and Other Cruel or Degrading Forms of Punishment*, UN Doc CRC/C/GC/8 (2 March 2007) [28].

69 CRC Committee, *General Comment No 14* (n 53) [4]. See also CRC Committee, *General Comment No 4: Adolescent Health and Development in the Context of the Convention on the Rights of the Child*, UN Doc CRC/GC/2003/4 (1 July 2003) [29]; CRC Committee, *General Comment No 15 (2013) on the Right of the Child to the Enjoyment of the Highest Attainable Standard of Health (Art 24)*, UN Doc CRC/C/GC/13 (17 April 2013) [31].

70 CRC Committee, *General Comment No 7* (n 43) [17].

upbringing' seeks to provide children with the skills, knowledge and experience required to live autonomously: to 'deliberat[e] about conceptions of the good and pursu[e] chosen life plans'.[71] The practical measures required of states to respect the child's right to receive appropriate parental direction and guidance, consistent with the child's evolving capacities, warrants further attention.[72] Parents could be provided with training and education by the state to support them in fulfilling their responsibilities, or legislative and policy measures could be implemented to regulate the effective protection and fulfilment of this right.

2.3.4 Children must meaningfully participate in decision-making about their lives

The final fundamental principle is a requirement that children meaningfully participate in decision-making about their lives. A theory of children's decisional privacy emphatically deletes the 'not' from the anachronistic adage, 'children should be seen and not heard'. Recognising children's *substantive* right to decisional privacy requires attendant *procedural* rights that facilitate children's participation in decision-making processes about matters that affect them.[73] It is argued that a failure to acknowledge these procedural rights renders children's right to decisional privacy ineffective, because it 'significantly condition[s]' children's 'options for action'.[74] Meaningful participation is thus critical to children's experience of autonomy. The CRC Committee has emphasised that the best interests principle in Article 3(1) of the CRC and the child's right to express their views and to be heard in Article 12 have 'complementary roles': the former 'aims to realize the child's best interests' and the latter 'provides the methodology' for hearing the child's views and the inclusion of those views in the assessment of the child's best interests.[75] The child's right under Article 12, together with the evolving capacities principle, have been said to acknowledge children 'as having agency and ... a voice that must be listened to'.[76]

Article 12(1) of the CRC gives children who are capable of forming a view the right to express their views freely in all matters affecting them, with those views being given due weight in accordance with the child's age and maturity. Some

71 Macleod (n 10) 198. See also Eamonn Callan, 'Autonomy, Child-Rearing, and Good Lives' in David Archard and Colin Macleod (eds), *The Moral and Political Status of Children* (Oxford University Press, 2002) 118; Peter G Brown, 'Human Independence and Parental Proxy Consent' in Willard Gaylin and Ruth Macklin (eds), *Who Speaks for the Child: The Problems of Proxy Consent* (Plenum Press, 1982) 209, 210–12.

72 See Tobin and Varadan (n 44) 184–5; Georgina Dimopoulos, 'A Theory of Children's Decisional Privacy' (2021) 41(3) *Legal Studies* 430, 443; John Eekelaar, 'Do Parents Know Best?' (2020) 28(3) *International Journal of Children's Rights* 613.

73 Larry Alexander, 'Are Procedural Rights Derivative Substantive Rights?' (1998) 17(1) *Law and Philosophy* 19, 42; Daly (n 1) 393–4; Freeman, 'Human Rights of Children' (n 1) 18.

74 Iris Young, *Inclusion and Democracy* (Oxford University Press, 2010) 145.

75 CRC Committee, *General Comment No 14* (n 53) [43].

76 Archard, *Children* (n 8) 58.

scholars have interpreted the two considerations identified in Article 12(1) – the child's age and maturity – as enabling 'adults to retain authority over children'[77] and denying children's citizenship.[78] An alternative interpretation of Article 12 is advanced here: that these two qualifiers assume that the weight to be afforded a child's views must increase as a child ages and matures,[79] requiring adults to 'cede their authority over children *and* actively facilitate their citizenship'.[80]

According to the CRC Committee, the notion of 'maturity' for the purposes of Article 12(1) 'refers to the ability to understand and assess the implications of a particular matter' and the child's capacity 'to express [their] views on issues in a reasonable and independent manner'.[81] The child's level of understanding in this context should be understood as a continuum rather than a 'binary'.[82] Significantly, 'understanding' does not equate to 'competency':[83] for the concepts to be equated would demand that children be unfairly held to adult standards for their views to be given due weight.

The right of participation embodied by Article 12 of the CRC is buttressed by the presumption that children are capable of expressing their views – and so it reverses the historical presumption of children's incompetence.[84] This right requires adult decision-makers to be aware that children can, and do, express their views in a range of ways, which might well be different from adult forms of expression.[85] As Lundy, Tobin and Parkes have suggested, 'the onus rests on adults to identify, encourage and value, rather than dismiss' the variety of ways that children express their views.[86] Article 12 thus elicits new ways of understanding children's participation, with the potential to make decision-making processes more inclusive and empowering for children.[87] The CRC Committee has

77 Ibid 66.

78 Brian Milne, 'Is "Participation" As It is Described by the United Nations Convention on the Rights of the Child (UNCRC) the Key to Children's Citizenship?' in Antonella Invernizzi and Brian Milne (eds), *Children's Citizenship: An Emergent Discourse on the Rights of the Child* (Kamla–Raj Enterprises, 2005) 31, 41.

79 Lundy, Tobin and Parkes (n 44) 409. See also Tobin and Varadan (n 44) 174; Lothar Krappman, 'The Weight of the Child's View (Article 12 of the UN Convention on the Rights of the Child)' (2010) 18 *International Journal of Children's Rights* 501, 505.

80 Tobin, 'Justifying Children's Rights' (n 8) 418.

81 CRC Committee, *General Comment No 12* (n 53) [30].

82 Lundy, Tobin and Parkes (n 44) 410, citing Parkinson and Cashmore (n 41) 4. See also Tobin and Varadan (n 44) 174.

83 Lundy, Tobin and Parkes (n 44) 410.

84 Ibid 400.

85 James Garbarino and Frances Stott, *What Children Can Tell Us: Eliciting, Interpreting, and Evaluating Critical Information from Children* (Jossey–Bass, 1992) 41.

86 Lundy, Tobin and Parkes (n 44) 400. See also CRC Committee, *General Comment No 12* (n 53) [20].

87 Tobin, 'Understanding Children's Rights' (n 44) 180; Nigel Thomas, 'Towards a Theory of Children's Participation' (2007) 15 *International Journal of Children's Rights* 199; Harry Shier, 'Pathways to Participation: Openings, Opportunities and Obligations' (2001) 15(2) *Children & Society* 107, 115; Kathryn Hollingsworth and Helen Stalford, 'Towards Chil-

described children's participation as involving 'ongoing processes, which include information-sharing and dialogue between children and adults based on mutual respect, and in which children can learn how their views and those of adults are taken into account and shape the outcome of such processes'.[88] Importantly, participation is a fluid process, rather than a singular event.[89] Its parameters are influenced by the child's age, capacities and the nature of the decision to be made.[90]

Article 12(2) of the CRC provides children with the opportunity to be heard in legal proceedings affecting them, either directly or through a representative or an appropriate body. The primary normative justification for participation in the legal process is its instrumental role in proper and accurate decisions and hence procedural fairness.[91] However, rights to participation and to be heard can also be justified on the ground that a person has a right to promote and defend their interests. In liberal societies that value autonomy, adults are generally taken to have primary responsibility for advancing and defending their own interests.[92] The image of children constructed is that they are unable to do so, such that children are denied participatory rights, or have those rights curtailed.

Judges arguably play a fundamental role in protecting and upholding children's rights and promoting children as active legal subjects.[93] The Family Court of Australia has observed that '[w]ithout their parents or the courts children have no effective means of enforcing any of their rights'.[94] Yet adults – whether they be judges or parents – who are willing to enable children's meaningful participation are not the only 'precondition' to effective participation by children in decision-making processes.[95] Other such preconditions include the provision

dren's Rights Judgments' in Helen Stalford, Kathryn Hollingsworth and Stephen Gilmore (eds), *Rewriting Children's Rights Judgments: From Academic Vision to New Practice* (Hart Publishing, 2017) 53, 67; Tobin, 'Justifying Children's Rights' (n 8) 430–2.

88 CRC Committee, *General Comment No 12* (n 53) [3]. See also Gary B Melton, 'Parents *and* Children: Legal Reform to Facilitate Children's Participation' (1999) 54(11) *American Psychologist* 935, 936.

89 Stephen Cobb, 'Seen but Not Heard?' [2015] *Family Law* 144, 152.

90 Parkinson and Cashmore (n 41) 19.

91 Denis J Galligan, *Due Process and Fair Procedures: A Study of Administrative Procedures* (Clarendon Press, 1996) 131–2.

92 Ibid 141, 158. See also Chapter 1 (Section 1.4.2).

93 Helen Stalford, Kathryn Hollingsworth and Stephen Gilmore, 'Introducing *Children's Rights Judgments*' in Helen Stalford, Kathryn Hollingsworth and Stephen Gilmore (eds), *Rewriting Children's Rights Judgments: From Academic Vision to New Practice* (Hart Publishing, 2017) 1, 5 ('Introducing *Children's Rights Judgments*'); Lundy, Tobin and Parkes (n 44) 402.

94 *W v G (No 1)* (2004) 35 Fam LR 417, 431 [117] (Carmody J).

95 Parkinson and Cashmore (n 41) 63. See also Gerison Lansdown, 'Children's Rights to Participation and Protection: A Critique' in Christopher Cloke and Murray Davies (eds), *Participation and Empowerment in Child Protection* (Pitman, 1995) 19; Phil Treseder, 'Involving and Empowering Children and Young People: Overcoming the Barriers' in Christopher Cloke and Murray Davies (eds), *Participation and Empowerment in Child Protection* (Pitman, 1995) 207.

of information that is appropriate for children's age and level of understanding; giving children a choice about whether, and if so, how, they will be involved in the decision-making process, which entails openness about the options for their involvement; 'scaffolding' or adult support to facilitate children's participation, which requires skills and resources to provide child-friendly processes; and a guarantee of confidentiality, such that children gain an understanding of, and trust in, how the information that they give may be used in the decision-making process.[96]

Collectively, the above four principles present a conceptual framework for analysing how children's right to decisional privacy should be recognised, interpreted and achieved. The value of this right lies in transforming children's status from 'passive recipients to … active agents',[97] by empowering and equipping children to participate in decision-making processes about matters that affect them, consistent with their evolving capacities. Children's exercise of their right to decisional privacy bears an instrumental role in their development of autonomy and capacity for independent decision-making.[98] It can also produce more well-informed and relevant decisions[99] and promote more effective policy-making on children's issues.[100] However, it would be naïve to suggest that all adult decision-makers, including judges, would be partial to embracing an understanding of children as 'active participant[s] in the promotion, protection and monitoring of their rights',[101] or that such a change in perspective would be possible in all contexts. The final part of this chapter discusses various factors that may inhibit judges from embracing, or alternatively, may encourage judges to embrace, a children's rights approach to decisional privacy in their decision-making.

2.4 Factors shaping judges' willingness and ability to engage with children's rights in their decision-making

A range of institutional, procedural, practical and personal factors – what Tobin has called 'empirical realities'[102] – constrain or embolden judges in their ability

96 Parkinson and Cashmore (n 41) 63–4.

97 Gerison Lansdown, 'The Realisation of Children's Participation Rights' in Barry Percy-Smith and Nigel Thomas (eds), *A Handbook of Children and Young People's Participation: Perspectives from Theory and Practice* (Routledge, 2009) 11, 13.

98 Lundy, Tobin and Parkes (n 44) 397, 399; Parkinson and Cashmore (n 41) 193–4; Leon Mann, Ros Harmoni and Colin Power, 'Adolescent Decision-Making: The Development of Competence' (1989) 12(6) *Journal of Adolescence* 265.

99 Rosemary Hunter, Mandy Burton and Liz Trinder, *Assessing Risk of Harm to Children and Parents in Private Law Children Cases* (Final Report, Ministry of Justice, June 2020) 97–9; *Karamalis v Karamalis* (2018) 57 Fam LR 588, 591 [16] (Bennett J); Parkinson and Cashmore (n 41) 191–2.

100 Lundy, Tobin and Parkes (n 44) 399. See also Jeremy Roche, 'Children: Rights, Participation and Citizenship' (1999) 6(4) *Childhood* 475; CRC Committee, *General Comment No 20* (n 46) [24].

101 CRC Committee, *General Comment No 7* (n 43) [14].

102 Tobin, 'Judging the Judges' (n 1) 581.

and motivation to adopt a children's rights approach to decisional privacy in their decision-making. Tobin has argued that there is 'a strong onus on proponents of a more active judicial approach' in the area of children's rights 'to recognise the extent of these potential obstacles and to articulate a coherent vision of how these might be overcome in order to facilitate more effective and systematic judicial involvement'.[103] Drawing upon examples from the case study of gender dysphoria proceedings,[104] five factors are explained below. The first two factors are 'individual', relating to the judge's personal experiences, values and characteristics.[105] The remaining three are 'structural' factors, concerning issues beyond the individual judge, such as procedural elements of the decision-making process and a court's place in the hierarchy or the constitutional order.[106] There are indeed many more such factors that may influence whether judges embrace a children's rights-based approach in their decision-making, although a discussion of these lies beyond the scope of this book.

Some factors will necessarily impair judges' willingness and ability to adopt a children's rights perspective, while others may in fact encourage such an approach. Or the operation of factors in combination may be in favour of children's rights decision-making in some cases, but prevent such an approach in others.[107] Much depends on context. These factors shape the proceedings themselves, including the nature and scope of the child's participation and representation of the child's views; the substance of the decision made, that is, whether the court's reasoning reflects a rights-based approach or a welfare approach; and they also shape the written judgment, including its length, tone, structure and audience.[108] Identifying the factors that impact upon judges in their day-to-day work, each factor's scope of influence and how the factors interact, facilitates the articulation of a clear path for how these factors can be accommodated or addressed to encourage a children's rights approach to judicial decision-making.

2.4.1 Judicial philosophy: The judge's own values and experiences

Judicial perspectives and approaches are influenced by both 'extralegal' constraints and context[109] and by the judge's own values, life experiences, personal characteristics and political leanings. This is to say, 'it matters who the judge is' in each case as to whether a children's rights approach is adopted.[110] Former Justice of the High Court of Australia, Michael Kirby, described the value-laden process of 'expressing the law' as follows:

103 Ibid.
104 See Part B (Chapters 4 to 7).
105 Stalford and Hollingsworth (n 2) 41.
106 Ibid.
107 Ibid.
108 Ibid 42.
109 Richard Posner, *How Judges Think* (Harvard University Press, 2010) 8.
110 Stalford and Hollingsworth (n 2) 48.

> Judges, like most mortals, have values. As judges, they have a vision of the Constitution and of society, its fairness and justice. Some are more concerned than others about protecting human rights and fundamental freedoms.[111]

In the Australian family law context, Chief Justices past and present have, through their extra-curial remarks, offered a glimpse into how their personal predilections and life experiences might colour their decision-making and their support for children's rights. Former Chief Justice Alastair Nicholson, a staunch advocate of children's rights, expressed the view that '[p]utting children first must be at the forefront of all of our thinking, and that includes legislators, the judiciary and especially parents'.[112] His successor, Chief Justice Diana Bryant, considered it 'really important … as a judge, to understand what your own prejudices and biases are'.[113] Her self-reflection and insights into her childhood and family life and her concession that a judge should understand 'what you might think yourself and mak[e] sure that you don't project that onto decisions that you are making',[114] are telling of the real influence that a judge's personal experiences can have on their judicial role. The current Chief Justice of the Federal Circuit and Family Court of Australia, Will Alstergren, has said that 'unacceptable delays' in Australia's family law system are 'what keeps me up at night' and 'we have got to have serious compassion' for litigants engaging with the system.[115] In this sense, judging is 'personal' as well as 'political': judges' personal characteristics, including their socio-cultural background, personality and their life and professional experiences, influence the task of judging.[116]

All aspects of the adjudicative process are influenced by the judge's own moral reasoning.[117] A judge whose moral reasoning is informed by a children's rights approach, shaped by the values underpinning the CRC, has the capacity to determine proceedings in a way that is consistent with the values underlying such an approach, even where there is no explicit legislative mandate to do so. The scope of a judge's ability to adopt a children's rights approach will

111 Michael Kirby, 'Judicial Dissent' (2005) 12 *James Cook University Law Review* 4, 5.

112 Alastair Nicholson, 'The Child's Rights Come First', *The Age* (online, 21 June 2003) <www.theage.com.au/national/the-childs-rights-come-first-20030621-gdvx3t.html>.

113 Diana Bryant, quoted in 'Retiring Chief Justice Reflects on Thirteen Years in the Family Court', *The Law Report* (Australian Broadcasting Corporation Radio National, 19 September 2017) <www.abc.net.au/radionational/programs/lawreport/8956300>.

114 Ibid.

115 Chief Justice Will Alstergren, quoted in Bianca Hall, '"It Keeps Me Up at Night": Chief Justice on Chronic Family Law Delays', *Sydney Morning Herald* (online, 3 November 2019) <www.smh.com.au/politics/federal/it-keeps-me-up-at-night-chief-justice-on-chronic-family-law-delays-20191101-p536lh.html>.

116 Posner (n 109) 369–70. See also Stalford, Hollingsworth and Gilmore, 'Introducing *Children's Rights Judgments*' (n 93) 3–4; Rachel J Cahill-O'Callaghan, 'The Influence of Personal Values on Legal Judgments' (2013) 40(4) *Journal of Law and Society* 596, 620.

117 See Jeremy Waldron, 'Judges as Moral Reasoners' (2009) 7(1) *International Journal of Constitutional Law* 2, 12; Ronald Dworkin, *Law's Empire* (Belknap Press, 1986) 238–58.

necessarily be constrained by the framework within which the decision-making occurs. This includes the doctrine of precedent and any relevant legislation pursuant to which the decision is made. Judges cannot simply 'drop inconvenient lines of precedent or modify propositions embodied in authoritative texts', or 'plant the flag' of their own moral convictions over existing legal frameworks and structures.[118] Yet the increasing influence of children's rights in public discourse gives judges who adopt such an approach the opportunity to be at 'the cutting edge' of interpretation.[119] More significantly, by embracing a children's rights model, judges have the potential to champion the decisional privacy rights of children and to show respect for them as active subjects with evolving capacities for decision-making.

The extent to which judges are willing and able to engage with understandings of children as rights-bearers is, as Ronald Dworkin has noted, 'grounded in [the judge's] own convictions'.[120] Two of the three judges of the Full Court of the Family Court of Australia who decided the case of *Re Jamie*[121] have made extra-curial remarks about the influence of human rights on decision-making about children. Strickland J foresaw that 'the language of human rights will increasingly permeate Australian decision making surrounding young people generally, and consent to medical treatment for young people specifically'.[122] Bryant CJ opined that, when given appropriate status, international human rights law has the inherent power to transform substantive and procedural rights in domestic law.[123] She argued that '[i]f children's ... rights are in issue, we should say so, rather than attempting, as I think we have done, to quietly subsume human rights considerations under the rubric of "best interests"'.[124] These remarks point to how judicial philosophy shapes understandings of the relationship between children's rights and children's best interests as another enabling or inhibiting factor.

2.4.2 Judges' understanding of the relationship between children's rights and children's best interests

Judges' own values – whilst most often unarticulated – insidiously influence all aspects of the adjudicatory process, from the framing of issues and the content of rights in question, to court processes, the balance achieved between competing

118 Waldron (n 117) 13; Dworkin (n 117) 211. See also Tobin, 'Judging the Judges' (n 1) 622.
119 Tobin, 'Judging the Judges' (n 1) 623; Dworkin (n 117) 88.
120 Dworkin (n 117) 88.
121 [2013] FamCAFC 110 ('*Jamie Appeal*'). This judgment is analysed in Chapter 5.
122 Steven Strickland, 'To Treat or Not to Treat: Legal Responses to Transgender Young People' (Conference Paper, Association of Family and Conciliation Courts Annual Conference, 28–31 May 2014) 80.
123 Diana Bryant, 'It's My Body, Isn't It? Children, Medical Treatment and Human Rights' (2009) 35(2) *Monash University Law Review* 193, 209 ('It's My Body').
124 Ibid 207.

rights and interests and the outcome of proceedings. Judicial value judgements lie at the core of perceived clashes of values.[125] The tension between the child's welfare and the child's rights arguably is driven by the 'best interests' or 'welfare' principle as 'the paramount consideration'.[126] Criticised by many scholars for its indeterminacy[127] and still 'profoundly contested in practice',[128] judges themselves have conceded the flexibility and discretion that underlie this principle.[129]

Colouring judicial reasoning in many family law proceedings is the inclination to dichotomise the child's rights and the child's best interests.[130] Fortin has described the interaction between the best interests test and the concept of children's rights as 'the elephant in the room'.[131] Both in conceptual and practical terms, two key commitments embraced by the *Family Law Act 1975* (Cth) – to promote the child's best interests or welfare;[132] and to enable the child to express their views on any matter affecting the child, giving those views due weight in accordance with the child's maturity and level of understanding[133] – appear to be opponents in a game of tug of war.[134] That is indeed how they have been understood by the Family Court of Australia. In *In Marriage of Harrison and Woollard*,[135] Fogarty and Kay JJ remarked that 'where a court is concerned with the welfare of a child no question of "self-determination" by a mature child can

125 Andrew Bainham, 'Can We Protect Children and Protect their Rights?' (2002) 32 *Family Law* 279, 279–80.
126 See *Family Law Act* (n 65) ss 60CA, 67ZC; *Children Act* (n 65) s 1(1).
127 See, eg, Stephen Parker, 'The Best Interests of the Child: Principles and Problems' in Philip Alston (ed), *The Best Interests of the Child: Reconciling Culture and Human Rights* (Clarendon Press, 1994) 26; David Archard and Marit Skivenes, 'Balancing a Child's Best Interests and a Child's Views' (2009) 17 *International Journal of Children s Rights* 1, 8; John Eekelaar, 'The Role of the Best Interests Principle in Decisions Affecting Children and Decisions about Children' (2015) 23 *International Journal of Children's Rights* 3; Eekelaar, 'Beyond the Welfare Principle' (n 20); Helen Reece, 'The Paramountcy Principle: Consensus or Construct?' (1996) 49(1) *Current Legal Problems* 267; Raymie H Wayne, 'The Best Interests of the Child: A Silent Standard – Will You Know it When You Hear it?' (2008) 2 *Journal of Public Child Welfare* 33; Jane Fortin, 'Children's Rights – Flattering to Deceive?' (2014) 26(1) *Child and Family Law Quarterly* 51, 59 ('Flattering to Deceive?').
128 Stalford and Hollingsworth (n 2) 33.
129 See, eg, *Dylan v Dylan* [2007] FamCA 842, [58]–[59] (Carmody J); *Secretary, Department of Health and Community Services v JWB & SMB* (1992) 175 CLR 218, 271 (Brennan J).
130 Archard and Skivenes (n 127) 2; Fortin, 'Accommodating Children's Rights' (n 60) 311.
131 Fortin, 'Flattering to Deceive?' (n 127) 63.
132 *Family Law Act* (n 65) ss 60CA, 67ZC(2).
133 Ibid s 60CC(3)(a).
134 Archard and Skivenes (n 127) 2. See also Parkinson and Cashmore (n 41) 40; Fortin, *Children's Rights* (n 5) 25; Felicity Kaganas and Alison Diduck, 'Incomplete Citizens: Changing Images of Post-Separation Children' (2004) 67(6) *Modern Law Review* 959, 972, 978.
135 (1995) 126 FLR 159.

arise'.[136] Likewise, the Full Court of the Family Court in *In Marriage of B*[137] described 'an inherent conflict between the child's best interests on the one side and self-determinism by the child on the other'.[138] The Full Court referred to 'the conflict ... involved when one is talking about the right of a child on the one hand and the overall responsibility of the Court to determine the issue in question having regard to that child's welfare or best interests on the other'.[139]

These judicial remarks are remnants of a welfare-based conception of the child's best interests. As Eekelaar and Tobin have explained, '[w]hereas the historical conception of the [best interests] principle was that a child should be seen but not heard, the rights-based conception ... presumes that children must be seen and heard'.[140] On a children's rights approach to decisional privacy, children's rights and the best interests principle are not at odds or mutually exclusive. Rather, the determination of the child's best interests must be informed by the child's other rights under the CRC, particularly the child's right under Article 12 to express their views.[141] The CRC Committee has said that:

> [a]ny decision that does not take into account the child's views or does not give their views due weight according to their age and maturity, does not respect the possibility for the child or children to influence the determination of their best interests.[142]

Another way of conceptualising the relationship between children's rights and children's best interests is to understand the best interests principle itself as a right of the child,[143] which detaches it from the paternalism of a welfare approach. Hollingsworth and Stalford have explained a rights-based approach to children's best interests as follows:

> Framing best interests as a right implies obligations and accountability for its fulfilment on the part of adults, and it also expresses the notion that it (whatever 'it' is determined to be in the specific context) is an interest that the

136 Ibid 173. See also *Brown v Pedersen* (1991) 105 FLR 83, 94 (Ellis, Nygh and Bell JJ) ('the difficulty with the use of the word "right" is that it detracts from the principle that the welfare of the child is the paramount consideration').
137 (1997) 140 FLR 11.
138 Ibid 89 (Nicholson CJ, Fogarty and Lindenmayer JJ).
139 Ibid. Courts in the UK have adopted a similar approach: see *Leeds Teaching Hospitals NHS Trust v A* [2003] EWHC 259 (QB) [55] (Dame Butler-Sloss P); *Mabon v Mabon* [2005] EWCA Civ 634, [28] (Thorpe LJ).
140 Eekelaar and Tobin (n 64) 85.
141 Tobin, 'Seeking to Persuade' (n 30) 37–9.
142 CRC Committee, *General Comment No 14* (n 53) [53].
143 Hollingsworth and Stalford (n 87) 64–5; Fortin, 'Accommodating Children's Rights' (n 60) 326; ibid [6(a)].

child plausibly claims rather than something imposed on the child by others (as is implied by welfare) or that can be waived by the actions of another.[144]

Accepting that the best interests test is 'by its very nature paternalistic and protective'[145] does not preclude judges from adopting a children's rights approach. Expression of the best interests principle as a right means that the child's best interests must be assessed, to the greatest extent possible, from the child's own perspective of their well-being.[146] Indeed, this may well encourage a 'more structured and analytical approach' to judicial decision-making in cases concerning children.[147]

2.4.3 *The doctrine of precedent*

Another possible curb on judges' enthusiasm for children's rights in their decision-making is the doctrine of precedent. Described as the 'hallmark'[148] and the 'cornerstone'[149] of the common law, this doctrine provides that the *ratio decidendi*, or the reasons for the decision of the judges in the majority, will bind lower courts in subsequent cases. The case study in Part B of this book will show that, in Australian gender dysphoria jurisprudence, binding precedent was a prominent factor that inhibited judges from removing the Family Court from the medical treatment process for children experiencing gender dysphoria.

However, precedent can be, in Posner's colourful language, a 'death grip' if judges ignore changed circumstances that make earlier decisions 'no longer a sound guide'.[150] The doctrine of precedent serves to enable judges to 'balance the need for continuity, consistency and predictability against the competing need for justice, flexibility and rationality'.[151] As Tobin has also argued, the importance of precedential constraints is 'often overstated'.[152] Judges retain considerable discretion, particularly in appellate courts where the best interests principle governs proceedings. In *Re Kelvin*,[153] submissions before the Full Court of the Family Court focused on the well-established principle that a later appellate court can depart from an earlier decision if that earlier decision can be said to be 'plainly

144 Hollingsworth and Stalford (n 87) 65.
145 Bryant, 'It's My Body' (n 123) 199, citing *Re Alex* (2004) 180 FLR 89, 116 [154] ('*Re Alex* (2004)').
146 John Eekelaar, *Family Law and Personal Life* (Oxford University Press, 2nd ed, 2017) 36; Eekelaar and Tobin (n 64) 92–3, 106.
147 Fortin, 'Accommodating Children's Rights' (n 60) 326.
148 Anthony Mason, 'The Use and Abuse of Precedent' (1988) 4 *Australian Bar Review* 93, 93 ('Use and Abuse').
149 Bruce V Harris, 'Final Appellate Courts Overruling Their Own "Wrong" Precedents: The Ongoing Search for Principle' (2002) 118(3) *Law Quarterly Review* 408, 412.
150 Posner (n 109) 111.
151 Mason, 'Use and Abuse' (n 148) 111.
152 Tobin, 'Judging the Judges' (n 1) 582.
153 [2017] FamCAFC 258 ('*Re Kelvin*'). This judgment is analysed in Chapter 6.

wrong'.[154] In holding it 'unnecessary and inappropriate'[155] to find that the earlier decision of *Re Jamie*[156] was plainly wrong, the majority reasoning in *Re Kelvin* suggests a judicial reluctance to overrule that earlier Full Court decision, 'to preserve the appearance of the law's continuity and stability'.[157] The majority in *Re Kelvin* instead preferred to distinguish *Re Jamie* on the basis of legally relevant factual differences between the two cases, relating to advances in medical science and the current state of medical knowledge.[158]

2.4.4 The separation of powers: Judicial deference to the legislature for reform

Whilst the doctrine of precedent constrains judges within the court hierarchy, constitutional constraints often generate judicial caution in making decisions that would affect parties beyond those in the case at hand, potentially exposing the judge to criticism that they have changed the law or policy.[159] Judicial deference to the legislature was evident from the strongly articulated dissatisfaction with the Full Court's decision in *Re Jamie*.[160] Some Family Court judges stressed the 'urgent need' for legislative intervention to 'undo the consequences' of *Re Jamie*.[161] Judges may adopt such 'language of deference' to avoid children's rights-based claims, where they consider that the legislature or the executive, rather than the judiciary, should determine the issue.[162] The decision of the Full Court in *Re Kelvin* shows that the courts do step in where the legislature fails to respond. Although the *Re Kelvin* decision, it is argued, was driven not by a desire to uphold children's rights, but by the court's desire for self-preservation, in light of a growing burden caused by the surge in gender dysphoria cases.[163]

154 Ibid [169] (Thackray, Strickland and Murphy JJ).
155 Ibid [171].
156 *Jamie Appeal* (n 121).
157 Posner (n 109) 45. See also Anthony Mason, 'Future Directions in Australian Law' (1987) 13(3) *Monash University Law Review* 149, 156; Michael Kirby, 'Precedent – Report on Australia' (Conference Paper, International Academy of Comparative Law Conference, 17 July 2006) 13–14; Mason, 'Use and Abuse' (n 148) 93.
158 *Re Kelvin* (n 153) [172], [174]–[175], [177] (Thackray, Strickland and Murphy JJ).
159 Stalford and Hollingsworth (n 2) 41.
160 See Chapter 6 (Section 6.2).
161 *Re Lucas* [2016] FamCA 1129, [73] (Tree J). See also *Re Martin* [2015] FamCA 1189, [27], [36], [38] (Bennett J); *Re Harley* [2016] FamCA 334, [42] (Bennett J); *Re Tahlia* [2017] FamCA 715, [4] (Bennett J).
162 Stalford and Hollingsworth (n 2) 44.
163 See Fiona Kelly, '"The Court Process is Slow but Biology is Fast": Assessing the Impact of the Family Court Approval Process on Transgender Children and their Families' (2016) 30(2) *Australian Journal of Family Law* 112, 120; Michelle Telfer, Michelle Tollit and Debi Feldman, 'Transformation of Health-Care and Legal Systems for the Transgender Population: The Need for Change in Australia' (2015) 51(11) *Journal of Paediatrics and Child Health* 1051, 1052; Miki Perkins, '"I Want Control Over My Body": Transgender Kids in Landmark Court Win', *The Age* (online, 30 November 2017) <www.theage.com

2.4.5 Parties' presentation of their case

The willingness and ability of judges to adopt a children's rights approach is also shaped by the way in which the parties present or frame their case.[164] Within an adversarial system, judges determine the issues put before them by the parties. The absence of submissions, evidence and argument in relation to children's rights may deny judges the opportunity to engage with this dimension of the proceedings and to determine the case within a children's rights framework.[165] In *Re Alex* (2009),[166] Bryant CJ devoted a section of the judgment to considering the various human rights instruments relevant to gender diverse individuals, even though no submissions had been directed to the Family Court on this issue.[167] In *Re Alex* (2004)[168] and *Re Jamie*,[169] the Family Court and the Full Court of the Family Court respectively discussed submissions that engaged rights under the CRC.

By and large, however, judges in gender dysphoria proceedings in Australia have not adopted the language of children's rights in their judgments. There is yet to be a 'paradigm shift' among the judiciary to make children's rights a 'way of thinking', rather than a mere 'formalised entitlement'.[170] This has been influenced in part by the failure of parties to raise children's rights arguments in their submissions. It is also notable that even independent children's lawyers appointed to represent the interests of children in gender dysphoria proceedings have tended not to espouse rights-based approaches. This enlivens a broader issue concerning the nature of children's representation in Australian family law, which lies beyond the scope of this book.[171] However, the finger cannot be pointed solely at the parties. Judges' own values, experiences and understandings of the rights-best interests nexus, as well as constraints imposed by the doctrine of precedent and

.au/national/victoria/i-want-control-over-my-body-transgender-kids-in-landmark-court-win-20171130-gzw6z4.html>.

164 Stalford and Hollingsworth (n 2) 44–5; Tobin, 'Judging the Judges' (n 1) 620.

165 Stalford and Hollingsworth (n 2) 33.

166 (2009) 248 FLR 312.

167 Ibid 353–5 [178]–[186].

168 *Re Alex* (2004) (n 145) [171]–[173], [220]–[224] (Nicholson CJ).

169 *Jamie Appeal* (n 121) [48], [64]–[65], [120]–[122] (Bryant CJ).

170 Stalford, Hollingsworth and Gilmore, 'Introducing *Children's Rights Judgments*' (n 93) 31–2.

171 See, eg, Geoff Monahan, 'Autonomy vs Beneficence: Ethics and the Representation of Children and Young People in Legal Proceedings' (2008) 8(2) *Queensland University of Technology Law and Justice Journal* 392; Rae Kaspiew et al, *Independent Children's Lawyers Study* (Final Report, 2nd ed, Australian Institute of Family Studies, June 2014); Nicola Ross, 'Images of Children: Agency, Art 12 and Models for Legal Representation' (2005) 19(2) *Australian Journal of Family Law* 94; Nicola Ross, 'Independent Children's Lawyers: Relational Approaches to Children's Representation' (2012) 26(3) *Australian Journal of Family Law* 214.

the separation of powers, may play a role in shaping whether, and if so, when and how, judges embrace children's rights in their decision-making.

2.5 Conclusion

The four fundamental principles of a children's rights approach to decisional privacy presented in this chapter account for the power disparities between children and their parents, and they recognise the vital role that family relationships – particularly the parent–child relationship – play in children's growth and development. Through a recognition of the child's evolving capacities and the requirement that parents appropriately direct and guide children in the exercise of their rights, the principles also strike a carefully-crafted balance between the need to protect children and to promote their capacity for autonomy. The most significant feature of a children's rights approach to decisional privacy is participation: ensuring that children are afforded procedural rights that enable them to express their views and to be heard, as a means of ensuring their substantive right to decisional privacy. The final part of this chapter outlined some practical influences on the willingness and ability of judges to adopt a children's rights perspective in their decision-making, drawing on examples from Australian gender dysphoria proceedings. The next chapter narrows the focus to the final product of the judicial decision-making process: the judgment. It presents the key features of a children's rights judgment and explains how, through four stages of the adjudicatory process, such a judgment can enable a child's right to decisional privacy.

3 Re-reading court judgments from a children's rights perspective

3.1 Introduction

Children's right to decisional privacy manifests in a practical sense in children's ability to participate, in a meaningful and active way, in decision-making about their welfare or best interests. At its most basic, facilitating children's participation in court proceedings requires modifications to court processes and procedures to make them more 'child-friendly' or child-inclusive. Potentially more unnerving is the attendant cultural shift that a children's rights approach demands in how children are conceptualised within their families, under the law and in society. The previous chapter presented four fundamental principles of a children's rights approach to decisional privacy. It also canvassed various factors that may influence judges' willingness and ability to adopt a children's rights approach in their decision-making. This chapter narrows the focus to court judgments. It presents a framework for re-reading judgments from a children's rights perspective and examines how some of the 'empirical realities'[1] that shape judicial decision-making might be addressed consistently with children's right to decisional privacy. The re-reading task provides an opportunity to 'reconceptualize the agenda for decision-makers'[2] and to bring the methodology of children's rights 'to bear on real life decision-making' in court proceedings.[3]

The features of a children's rights judgment are distinguished through four stages of the judicial decision-making process: selecting and framing the issues for determination from the child's perspective; court procedures that enable children's meaningful participation in proceedings; judicial reasoning that reconciles potentially competing rights and interests, using the CRC as a legal and

1 John Tobin, 'Judging the Judges: Are they Adopting the Rights Approach in Matters involving Children?' (2009) 33(2) *Melbourne University Law Review* 579, 581 ('Judging the Judges').

2 John Eekelaar and John Tobin, 'Article 3: The Best Interests of the Child' in John Tobin (ed), *The UN Convention on the Rights of the Child: A Commentary* (Oxford University Press, 2019) 73, 79.

3 Helen Stalford and Kathryn Hollingsworth, 'Judging Children's Rights: Tendencies, Tensions, Constraints and Opportunities' in Helen Stalford, Kathryn Hollingsworth and Stephen Gilmore (eds), *Rewriting Children's Rights Judgments: From Academic Vision to New Practice* (Hart Publishing, 2017) 17, 21 ('Judging Children's Rights').

DOI: 10.4324/9781003224167-5

normative framework; and communicating the court's decision in the form of a judgment that shares the child's own narrative and has children as a key audience. These features are consistent with, although differently calibrated to, the five 'primary characteristics' or 'markers' of a children's rights judgment presented by Hollingsworth and Stalford;[4] the guiding 'principles' for judges when drafting judgments for children outlined by Stalford and Hollingsworth;[5] and the dimensions of a 'substantive rights approach' formulated by Tobin.[6] These features of a children's rights judgment are not exhaustive or prescriptive; nor will they be appropriate in each case.[7] Judges' ability to implement them will be shaped by matters such as prevailing political agendas, the state of the law and developments in medical science, amongst other factors, at the time that the proceedings are heard.[8] The practical task of these features is to facilitate critical analyses of judgments in legal proceedings involving children, which 'pose … child-centered questions and move … closer to providing child-centered perspectives on the answers'.[9] The common thread that binds them is their contribution to enabling and listening to children's voices in court proceedings, as a key manifestation of children's ability to enjoy and exercise their right to decisional privacy.

3.2 Selecting and framing the issues 'through the eyes of children'[10]

The task of the judge who adopts a children's rights approach to decisional privacy is to frame the proceedings 'through the eyes of children'[11] and to 'conceptualise matters concerning children in terms of their rights'.[12] As Baroness Hale of Richmond observed in the case of *R (Williamson) v Secretary of State for Education and Employment*:

4 Kathryn Hollingsworth and Helen Stalford, 'Towards Children's Rights Judgments' in Helen Stalford, Kathryn Hollingsworth and Stephen Gilmore (eds), *Rewriting Children's Rights Judgments: From Academic Vision to New Practice* (Hart Publishing, 2017) 53, 53.

5 Helen Stalford and Kathryn Hollingsworth, '"This Case is about You and Your Future": Towards Judgments for Children' (2020) 83(5) *Modern Law Review* 1030, 1056–7 ('"This Case is about You"').

6 Tobin, 'Judging the Judges' (n 1) 603–19.

7 Hollingsworth and Stalford (n 4) 53; Stalford and Hollingsworth, '"This Case is about You"' (n 5) 1056.

8 Hollingsworth and Stalford (n 4) 53.

9 Barbara Bennett Woodhouse, 'Hatching the Egg: A Child-Centered Perspective on Parents' Rights' (1992) 14(6) *Cardozo Law Review* 1747, 1843.

10 *E v Chief Constable of the Royal Ulster Constabulary* [2009] 1 AC 536, [6] (Baroness Hale) ('*E v Chief Constable*').

11 Ibid.

12 Tobin, 'Judging the Judges' (n 1) 604–5.

> This is, and always has been, a case about children, their rights and the rights of their parents ... Yet there has been no one here ... to speak on behalf of the children ... The battle has been fought on ground selected by the adults.[13]

A children's rights judgment is one in which the judge centralises the child in framing the issues for determination. For a court to adopt a children's rights approach to decisional privacy, the issues must be conceptualised more broadly than simply a dispute between adults – such as a child's parents and treating medical practitioners – or between parents and the state. The child themselves must feature as the court's focal point. The court's assessment of a child's best interests or welfare includes a requirement to consider any views expressed by the child and to take those views into account in accordance with the child's maturity and level of understanding.[14] This factor, it is argued, requires the judge to conceptualise the issues for determination from the child's perspective.[15]

Additionally, the content of children's rights invoked by the judge must be imbued with an understanding of the lived experiences of the child who is the subject of proceedings. To be able to interpret the content of a right in such a way requires actual engagement with children's voices and desires, not simply adult assumptions about children's wishes and views.[16] Otherwise, there exists a real risk that adults will use talk of 'children's rights' as a proxy to speak on the child's behalf,[17] without representing the child's best interests, because those interests have not been informed adequately by the child. Woodhouse has labelled this 'asking "the child question"':

> how have children's experiences and values been left out of the law? How does the mismatch between children's experiences and law's assumptions and imposed structures serve the interests of those who hold power over children? In an ideal world, what would the life situation of children look like and how could law play a role in bringing this ideal world about?[18]

13 [2005] 2 FLR 374, [71]. See also *R (Kehoe) v Secretary of State for Work and Pensions* [2006] 1 AC 42, [49] (Baroness Hale) ('This is another case ... which has been presented to us largely as a case about adults' rights when in reality it is a case about children's rights'); *E v Chief Constable* (n 10) [6] (Baroness Hale) ('With the best will in the world, there is a tendency to see confrontations ... through adult eyes, and to forget these are not the eyes of children, who are simply the innocent victims of other people's quarrels').

14 See *Family Law Act 1975* (Cth) s 60CC(3)(a) ('*Family Law Act*'); *Children Act 1989* (UK) s 1(3)(a) ('*Children Act*'); *CRC*, art 12.

15 Eekelaar and Tobin (n 2) 106; Tobin, 'Judging the Judges' (n 1) 605; Rob George, *Ideas and Debates in Family Law* (Hart Publishing, 2012) 127.

16 Zach Meyers, 'Protecting "Innocence"? Deconstructing Legal Regulation of Child Sexuality' (2007) 27(1) *Australian Feminist Law Journal* 51, 52.

17 Woodhouse (n 9) 1820.

18 Ibid 1838 (citation omitted).

An aim of re-reading court judgments from a children's rights perspective, offered in Part B of this book, is to expose the disjunct that Woodhouse identifies between children's lived experiences and the law's assumptions about children's vulnerability and (in)capacity for rational decision-making about their best interests.

3.3 Child-friendly court procedures

A commitment to enabling and protecting children's right to decisional privacy – through which children can exercise and experience autonomy – also requires a commitment to ensuring the 'material and institutional circumstances' of autonomy.[19] These circumstances are the means by which children can actively and meaningfully participate in court proceedings[20] so that judges are able to reason from children's 'lived experiences rather than in abstract, categorical terms'.[21] Put differently, 'child-friendly' court procedures are a means of facilitating children's decision-making autonomy.[22] The second feature of a children's rights judgment, then, is 'adaptations to justice proceedings' that accommodate children's unique vulnerabilities and needs,[23] thereby enabling children to participate meaningfully in the decision-making process.[24]

Children's right to so participate manifests in Article 12(1) of the CRC, which gives children who are capable of forming a view the right to express their views freely in all matters affecting them, with those views being given due weight in accordance with the child's age and maturity; and pursuant to Article 12(2), which gives children the opportunity be heard in judicial and administrative proceedings affecting them, either directly or through a representative or appropriate

19 Joel Anderson and Axel Honneth, 'Autonomy, Vulnerability, Recognition, and Justice' in John Christman and Joel Anderson (eds), *Autonomy and the Challenges to Liberalism* (Cambridge University Press, 2005) 127, 129.

20 See *V v United Kingdom* (2000) 30 EHRR 121, [87] ('the procedures adopted must be conducive to active participation as opposed to passive presence').

21 Rosemary Hunter, 'More than Just A Different Face? Judicial Diversity and Decision-Making' (2015) 68(1) *Current Legal Problems* 119, 131.

22 Aoife Daly, *Children, Autonomy and the Courts: Beyond the Right to be Heard* (Brill, 2017) 31 ('*Children, Autonomy and Courts*'); *Mabon v Mabon* [2005] EWCA Civ 634, [26] (Thorpe LJ referring to 'a keener appreciation of the autonomy of the child and the child's consequential right to participate in decision making processes that fundamentally affect [their] family life').

23 Stalford and Hollingsworth, '"This Case is about You"' (n 5) 1031.

24 Michael Freeman, 'The Human Rights of Children' (2010) 63(1) *Current Legal Problems* 1, 18 ('Human Rights of Children'); Larry Alexander, 'Are Procedural Rights Derivative Substantive Rights?' (1998) 17(1) *Law and Philosophy* 19, 42; Patrick Parkinson and Judy Cashmore, *The Voice of a Child in Family Law Disputes* (Oxford University Press, 2008) 12; Jane Fortin, *Children's Rights and the Developing Law* (Cambridge University Press, 3rd ed, 2009) 234 ('*Children's Rights*'); Georgina Dimopoulos, 'A Theory of Children's Decisional Privacy' (2021) 41(3) *Legal Studies* 430, 452.

body. In *Duffy v Gomes*,[25] Judge Harman said that to be given 'life or meaning', the right under Article 12 of the CRC demands 'active engagement with the child – meeting them, explaining their options to them and giving them the opportunity to participate how and should they wish'.[26] Former President of the Family Division of the High Court of England and Wales, Sir James Munby, challenged judges to consider whether the approach to involving children in the family justice system 'accords with the demands of our international obligations' and 'how we can continue to justify it when so many of those who represent the voice of the child are pressing for change'.[27]

The issue of children's participation in family law decision-making remains highly contested. Commonly voiced concerns are that involving children may harm their well-being by putting them in the middle of parental conflict; and that children's voices might be used to enable 'irresponsible' adult decisions.[28] A related concern, noted above, is that 'children's rights' rhetoric may simply function as a vehicle for parental rights and interests.[29] Yet a considerable body of research in the family law context, both in Australia and overseas, has explained the value of children being afforded the opportunity to express their views and to have those views taken into account in decision-making about matters that affect them.[30] Children's participation in assessments of their best interests has been found to foster a sense of social and emotional empowerment, through an affirmation that children can, and do, play an active role in forging their life path.[31] Children themselves have emphasised the importance of 'having "someone" to

25 (2015) 52 Fam LR 562.
26 Ibid 582 [106].
27 Sir James Munby, 'Unheard Voices: the Involvement of Children and Vulnerable People in the Family Justice System' (Speech, Annual Lecture of The Wales Observatory on Human Rights of Children and Young People, Swansea University, 25 June 2015) 2.
28 Parkinson and Cashmore (n 24) 13–18, 114–15; Richard Chisholm, 'Children's Participation in Family Court Litigation' (1999) 13(3) *Australian Journal of Family Law* 197, 215–16.
29 See Martin Guggenheim, *What's Wrong with Children's Rights* (Harvard University Press, 2005) 143.
30 See, eg, Rachel Carson et al, *Children and Young People in Separated Families: Family Law System Experiences and Needs* (Final Report, Australian Institute of Family Studies, 2018) 30; Parkinson and Cashmore (n 24) 4–13; Australian Law Reform Commission ('ALRC'), *Family Law for the Future: An Inquiry into the Family Law System* (Final Report No 135, March 2019) 364 [12.28]; Judy Cashmore, 'Children's Participation in Family Law Decision-Making: Theoretical Approaches to Understanding Children's Views' (2011) 33(4) *Children and Youth Services Review* 515; Anne Graham and Robyn Fitzgerald, 'Taking Account of the "To and Fro" of Children's Experiences in Family Law' (2006) 31(2) *Children Australia* 30; Rachel Birnbaum, 'Views of the Child Reports: Hearing Directly from Children Involved in Post-Separation Disputes' (2017) 5(3) *Social Inclusion* 148; Rachel Birnbaum, Nicholas Bala and Francine Cyr, 'Children's Experiences with Family Justice Professionals in Ontario and Ohio' (2011) 25(3) *International Journal of Law, Policy and the Family* 398; Bren Neale, 'Dialogues with Children: Children, Divorce and Citizenship' (2002) 9(4) *Childhood* 455; Anne B Smith, Nicola J Taylor and Pauline Tapp, 'Rethinking Children's Involvement in Decision-Making After Parental Separation' (2003) 10(2) *Childhood* 201.
31 See, eg, Hollingsworth and Stalford (n 4) 67; Parkinson and Cashmore (n 24) 67–8.

listen to their views and then communicat[ing] those views so that they could inform the decision making in their case'.[32]

The corollary is that children feel persistently and consistently marginalised by the legal system. They perceive that adult participants in the legal process, including judges, do not listen to, take into consideration or care about their views. Research concerning children's experiences of participation in family law decision-making has exposed a gap between principle and policy on the one hand and practice on the other.[33] It has been found that 'too often the voices of children go unheard in the court process or are muted in various ways'.[34] Children and young people themselves have expressed a desire for 'a bigger voice more of the time' in family law decision-making processes that affect them.[35]

Children's effective participation in legal proceedings – both within and beyond the family law jurisdiction – is frustrated by the fact that the legal system is not designed for them. In Australia, while Part VII of the *Family Law Act 1975* (Cth) ('Family Law Act') posits children's best interests as 'the paramount consideration',[36] the procedures by which the court ascertains those best interests are skewed strongly in favour of the adults involved in the decision-making process.[37] Procedural, legal and practical barriers to children's participation in Part VII proceedings 'distort' the way that children's rights are 'argued, adjudicated and, ultimately, protected' by adult decision-makers.[38] While children can initiate parenting order proceedings on their own behalf, this rarely occurs.[39]

32 Carson et al (n 30) 44.

33 See, eg, Carson et al (n 30); Rae Kaspiew et al, *Independent Children's Lawyers Study* (Final Report, 2nd ed, Australian Institute of Family Studies, 2014); Parkinson and Cashmore (n 24) 4, 196–7; Stephanie Holt, 'A Voice or a Choice? Children's Views on Participating in Decisions about Post-Separation Contact with Domestically Abusive Fathers' (2018) 40(4) *Journal of Social Welfare and Family Law* 459.

34 Rosemary Hunter, Mandy Burton and Liz Trinder, *Assessing Risk of Harm to Children and Parents in Private Law Children Cases* (Final Report, Ministry of Justice, June 2020) 67.

35 Carson et al (n 30) 68, quoting Alana, aged 12–14 years. See also Parkinson and Cashmore (n 24) 73–5; Stalford and Hollingsworth, 'Judging Children's Rights' (n 3) 38; Megan M Gollop, Anne B Smith and Nicola J Taylor, 'Children's Involvement in Custody and Access Arrangements after Parental Separation' (2000) 12(4) *Child and Family Law Quarterly* 383; Harriet Bretherton, '"Because it's Me the Decisions Are About": Children's Experiences of Private Law Proceedings' (2002) 32(6) *Family Law* 450; Carol Smart and Bren Neale, '"It's My Life Too": Children's Perspectives on Post-Divorce Parenting' (2000) 30 *Family Law* 163.

36 See *Family Law Act* (n 14) ss 60CA, 67ZC.

37 Noel Semple, 'Whose Best Interests? Custody and Access Law and Procedure' (2010) 48(2) *Osgoode Hall Law Journal* 287, 289.

38 Stalford and Hollingsworth, 'Judging Children's Rights' (n 3) 37. See also ibid 289 (arguing that 'the *procedure* by which [custody and access] disputes are resolved primarily empowers the adult parties to the dispute' (emphasis in original)).

39 *Family Law Act* (n 14) s 65C(b). See, eg, *In Marriage of Pagliarella* (1993) 114 FLR 185; *Bondelmonte v Bondelmonte* [2016] FamCA 1145. See also Parkinson and Cashmore (n 24) 53–5.

Children cannot give evidence or be present in court during proceedings unless the court gives leave.[40]

Various provisions of Part VII of the Family Law Act also shape the extent to which children can participate by expressing their views. In determining what is in the child's best interests, the child's views are the first of the '[a]dditional considerations', qualified by the requirement that the court take into account any factors, such as the child's maturity or level of understanding, that the court thinks are relevant to the weight it should give to the child's views.[41] The court may inform itself of views expressed by a child by having regard to a family report;[42] by making an order for independent legal representation of the child's interests;[43] or 'by such other means as the court thinks appropriate'.[44] These provisions are counterbalanced by the requirement that nothing in Part VII of the Act 'permits the court or any other person to require the child to express [their] views in relation to any matter'.[45]

Similarly, in private family law proceedings in England and Wales, children 'commonly feel invisible to the court'.[46] Children's views are most often obtained through the preparation of a welfare report by the Children and Family Court Advisory and Support Service (Cafcass), Cafcass Cymru or a local authority social worker.[47] Where such a report is prepared, the relevant officer usually meets with the child to assess the child's views and convey those views to the court in the report.[48] A child can be made a party to proceedings,[49] although this is 'a step that will be taken only in cases which involve an issue of significant difficulty'.[50] Separate representation of the child through the appointment of a children's guardian is thus uncommon in practice.[51] The direct evidence of children is also

40 *Family Law Act* (n 14) s 100B(1), (2). See also Alastair Nicholson, 'Children and Children's Rights in the Context of Family Law' (Speech, LawAsia Conference, 21 June 2003) 3–4.
41 *Family Law Act* (n 14) s 60CC(3)(a).
42 Ibid s 62G.
43 Ibid s 68L.
44 Ibid s 60CD(2)(c).
45 Ibid s 60CE. In relation to children's expression of their views in Australian family law proceedings, see Parkinson and Cashmore (n 24) 68–70. See also, in relation to Article 12(1) of the CRC, Laura Lundy, John Tobin and Aisling Parkes, 'Article 12 The Right to Respect for the Views of the Child' in John Tobin (ed), *The UN Convention on the Rights of the Child: A Commentary* (Oxford University Press, 2019) 397, 405; CRC Committee, *General Comment No 12 (2009): The Right of the Child to be Heard*, UN Doc CRC/C/GC/12 (20 July 2009) [22] ('*General Comment No 12*').
46 Stalford and Hollingsworth, '"This Case is about You"' (n 5) 1055.
47 *Children Act* (n 14) s 7.
48 For concerns about the section 7 welfare report process, see Fortin, *Children's Rights* (n 24) 254–6; Gillian S MacDonald, 'Hearing Children's Voices? Including Children's Perspectives on Their Experiences of Domestic Violence in Welfare Reports Prepared for the English Courts in Private Family Law Proceedings' (2017) 65 *Child Abuse and Neglect* 1.
49 *Family Procedure Rules 2010* (UK), SI 2010/2955, r 16.2 ('*Family Procedure Rules*').
50 *Practice Direction 16A – Representation of Children*, [7.1].
51 *Family Procedure Rules* (n 49) r 16.4. See also Hunter, Burton and Trinder (n 34) 69–70.

'seldom heard or rarely available',[52] in light of a perceived presumption against children giving evidence in this context.[53] The practice of judges meeting with children is yet to be fully embraced and, in any event, cannot be used by judges as a means of obtaining evidence of the child's views and wishes.[54]

Such a 'cautious, protective approach'[55] to involving children in family law decision-making means that children's feelings and wishes are 'adult-filtered'[56] and their voices are marginalised and subject to 'interpretation by "experts"'.[57] The consequence is that children become 'the *object* but rarely the *subject* of family law decision-making',[58] as judicial interpretations of the facts and evidence are necessarily adult-centric. While this approach to children's participation 'does not ... mean that [children's] voices cannot be heard in the process of decision-making nor that their wishes are unimportant',[59] it does impact how the courts conceptualise children and their capacities for decision-making. Tobin has described children's 'objectification and silencing' as a 'classic exposition' of the welfare model, whereby adults conceptualise children as vulnerable and requiring assistance but ignore children's agency and evolving capacities.[60] From a decisional privacy perspective, the child's inability to be physically present in court during proceedings and to give evidence directly deprives the child of control over how they and their experiences are presented to the court.[61] This control lies in the ability or power[62] that a child has to exercise autonomy in

52 Vulnerable Witnesses and Children Working Group, *Report of the Vulnerable Witnesses and Children Working Group* (Final Report, February 2015) [5]. See also Family Justice Council, *Guidelines in relation to Children Giving Evidence in Family Proceedings* (December 2011).

53 *Re E (A Child)* [2016] EWCA Civ 473, [47], [56].

54 See Baroness Hale of Richmond, 'Children's Participation in Family Law Decision Making: Lessons from Abroad' (2006) 20(2) *Australian Journal of Family Law* 119 ('Children's Participation'); Family Justice Council, *Guidelines for Judges Meeting Children who are Subject to Family Proceedings* (April 2010) [5]; Daly, *Children, Autonomy and Courts* (n 22) 252–61.

55 Parkinson and Cashmore (n 24) 2. See also Felicity Bell, 'Barriers to Empowering Children in Private Family Law Proceedings' (2016) 30(3) *International Journal of Law, Policy and the Family* 225, 230; Rosemary Hunter, 'Close Encounters of a Judicial Kind: "Hearing" Children's "Voices" in Family Law Proceedings' (2007) 19(3) *Child and Family Law Quarterly* 283; E Kay M Tisdall and Fiona Morrison, 'Children's Participation in Court Proceedings when Parents Divorce or Separate: Legal Constructions and Lived Experiences' in Michael Freeman (ed), *Law and Childhood Studies: Current Legal Issues* (Oxford University Press, 2012) 156.

56 Stalford and Hollingsworth, '"This Case is about You"' (n 5) 1055.

57 Tobin, 'Judging the Judges' (n 1) 591. See also Kaspiew et al (n 33) 41, 135–7.

58 Robyn Fitzgerald and Anne Graham, 'The Changing Status of Children Within Family Law: From Vision to Reality?' (2011) 20(2) *Griffith Law Review* 421, 421 (emphasis in original).

59 Parkinson and Cashmore (n 24) 2.

60 John Tobin, 'Understanding Children's Rights: A Vision beyond Vulnerability' (2015) 84 *Nordic Journal of International Law* 155, 171.

61 Stalford and Hollingsworth, 'Judging Children's Rights' (n 3) 45.

62 See Lisa Austin, 'Enough About Me: Why Privacy is about Power, Not Consent (Or Harm)' in Austin Sarat (ed), *A World Without Privacy: What Law Can and Should Do?* (Cambridge University Press, 2015) 131, 178, 182.

choosing what to conceal or reveal about themselves to others. Such selective information disclosure in turn enables the child to develop and maintain their identity in different social contexts.[63]

A children's rights approach to decisional privacy embraces the notions of 'authentic' participation and children's 'inclusion', whereby the adult-centric system is modified to accommodate children's effective participation and values, rather than 'integration', which requires children to participate within pre-existing processes and structures.[64] The CRC Committee has emphasised that proceedings 'must be both accessible and child-appropriate', with a particular focus upon 'child-friendly information, adequate support for self-advocacy, appropriately trained staff, design of court rooms, clothing of judges and lawyers, sight screens and separate waiting rooms'.[65] A children's rights approach requires that court procedures are sufficiently 'child-friendly'.[66] Attention must be given to *all* features of court proceedings, including the giving of evidence and the physical layout of the courtroom.

The decisions of the Family Court of Australia in *Re Alex* (2004)[67] and *Re Alex* (2009)[68] offer pertinent illustrations of how a 'child-centric' understanding of court procedures can effectively provide for and respect the rights of the child who is the subject of proceedings.[69] In both *Re Alex* proceedings, the judge was prepared to have a private meeting with Alex.[70] This judicial willingness to

63 Ruth Gavison, 'Privacy and the Limits of Law' (1980) 89(3) *Yale Law Journal* 421, 450 (referring to this as 'control over "editing" one's self'). See also Hyman Gross, 'Privacy and Autonomy' in Joel Feinberg and Hyman Gross (eds), *Philosophy of Law* (Wadsworth, 1991) 340, 341; David Velleman, *How We Get Along* (Cambridge University Press, 2009) 67; Juha Raikka, 'Privacy and Self-Presentation' (2017) 23(2) *Res Publica* 213, 214.

64 Barry Percy-Smith and Karen Malone, 'Making Children's Participation in Neighbourhood Settings Relevant to the Everyday Lives of Young People' (2001) 42 *PLA Notes* 18, 18–19. See also Jaclyn Jean Jenkins, 'Listen to Me! Empowering Youth and Courts through Increased Youth Participation in Dependency Hearings' (2008) 46(1) *Family Court Review* 163; Aoife Daly, 'The Right of Children to be Heard in Civil Proceedings and the Emerging Law of the European Court of Human Rights' (2011) 15(3) *International Journal of Human Rights* 441; Jennifer E McIntosh, Diana Bryant and Kristen Murray, 'Evidence of a Different Nature: The Child-Responsive and Less Adversarial Initiatives of the Family Court of Australia' (2008) 46(1) *Family Court Review* 125.

65 CRC Committee, *General Comment No 12* (n 45) [34].

66 Dimopoulos (n 24) 452; Hollingsworth and Stalford (n 4) 76–7. See also Helen Stalford, Liam Cairns and Jeremy Marshall, 'Achieving Child Friendly Justice through Child Friendly Methods: Let's Start with the Right to Information' (2017) 5(3) *Social Inclusion* 207; Lundy, Tobin and Parkes (n 45) 401.

67 (2004) 180 FLR 89 ('*Re Alex* (2004)'). See Chapter 4 (Section 4.3.2.ii).

68 (2009) 248 FLR 312 ('*Re Alex* (2009)').

69 See Tobin, 'Judging the Judges' (n 1) 608–9.

70 *Re Alex* (2004) (n 67) 94 [17], 97–8 [41]–[43] (Nicholson CJ); *Re Alex* (2009) (n 68) 333 [99] (Bryant CJ). For perspectives on the practice of judges conducting interviews or meeting with children in chambers, see Hale, 'Children's Participation' (n 54); John Caldwell, 'Common Law Judges and Judicial Interviewing' (2011) 23(1) *Child and Family Law Quarterly* 41; Fiona E Raitt, 'Judicial Discretion and Methods of Ascertaining the Views

meet with Alex overcame the problem that, in most cases, the child in proceedings under the Family Law Act lacks the capacity to appoint a legal representative who acts solely on the child's instructions.[71] These meetings, parts of which remained confidential, enabled Alex to share his views and wishes directly with the judge who was deciding his case. They enabled the judge to see Alex as 'a real person, rather than as the object of other people's disputes or concerns'.[72] The initial *Re Alex* hearing was also conducted in an inquisitorial rather than an adversarial format. It 'took the form of an orderly discussion between witnesses and legal representatives' and the judge in a private conference room setting around a table, thereby facilitating a 'dialogue' between witnesses about each other's evidence.[73] The impact of these procedural modifications lay in their ability to promote Alex's participation and active involvement in the proceedings. They underscore the argument that participatory rights are essential if children are to enjoy and exercise their substantive right to decisional privacy.

In a number of subsequent gender dysphoria proceedings, judges have made an order permitting the young person in question to be present in court and/ or have given leave for an affidavit to be filed by the young person.[74] Whilst it is not possible to know how the hearings in these cases have been conducted, they do suggest that judges have substantial discretion in lowering the barriers to children's participation and to enabling children's views and wishes to contribute to the decision-making process.[75] The feasibility of implementing child-centric procedures within the institutional culture and structures of courts will be influenced heavily by resourcing considerations and constraints, as well as the proclivity of the individual judge to conduct proceedings in this way.[76]

---

of a Child' (2004) 16(2) *Child and Family Law Quarterly* 151; Michelle Fernando, 'What do Australian Family Law Judges Think About Meeting with Children?' (2012) 26(1) *Australian Journal of Family Law* 51; Parkinson and Cashmore (n 24) 55–8, 158–88; Fortin, *Children's Rights* (n 24) 281–4.

71 Tobin, 'Judging the Judges' (n 1) 608.

72 Hale, 'Children's Participation' (n 54) 124.

73 *Re Alex* (2004) (n 67) 98–9 [43] (Nicholson CJ).

74 See, eg, *Re Lucas* [2016] FamCA 1129, [7] (Tree J); *Re Rae* [2017] FamCA 958, [76] (Carew J); *Re Sam and Terry (Gender Dysphoria)* (2013) 49 Fam LR 417, 421 [11] (Murphy J); *Re Jamie* [2015] FamCA 455, [43]–[44] (Thornton J); *Re Leo* (2015) 52 Fam LR 533, 535 [6] (Rees J); *Re Cameron* [2015] FamCA 1113, [13] (Kent J); *Re Jordan* [2015] FamCA 175, [9] (Kent J); *Re Dylan* [2014] FamCA 969, [6] (Kent J); *Re Max* [2021] FamCA 290, [3] (Hartnett J).

75 Hollingsworth and Stalford (n 4) 78. See also Stalford and Hollingsworth, '"This Case is about You"' (n 5) 1033–5.

76 See Ruth Sinclair, 'Participation in Practice: Making it Meaningful, Effective and Sustainable' (2004) 18(2) *Children and Society* 106, 116; Daly, *Children, Autonomy and Courts* (n 22) 229–34 and ch 7; ALRC (n 30) 32 [1.8]; Parkinson and Cashmore (n 24) 219.

3.4 Using the CRC as a legal and normative framework for reasoning and analysis

The third stage of a children's rights judgment is judicial reasoning that: demonstrates substantive engagement with and an internally coherent application of the CRC; and balances the child's rights and best interests against the rights and interests of others. A children's rights approach to decisional privacy encourages judges to use the CRC as an express legal and normative framework to guide decision-making. Significantly, this international convention acknowledges children as rights-holders and shapers of their own development. By establishing children's right to express their views and to be heard in judicial proceedings affecting them (Article 12), the CRC moves beyond the confines of a welfarist or paternalistic approach to children's rights, which frames those rights in terms of protection from harm, abuse, neglect and exploitation.[77]

3.4.1 Substantive engagement with the CRC

While Australia has ratified the CRC, this international convention is not part of domestic law, as it has not been incorporated expressly by statute.[78] The UK has also ratified the CRC,[79] but only Scotland has sought to expressly incorporate it by statute.[80] Nonetheless, from a conceptual perspective, the values and model of children's rights underpinning the CRC can inform judicial decision-making by shaping the 'general intellectual environment'[81] in which judges contemplate their decision-making approach. From a doctrinal perspective, the 'best interests' or 'welfare' principle also arguably enables judges to take children's rights into account in their decision-making.[82]

Judicial references to the CRC in court judgments might, on their face, suggest that judges recognise children as rights-bearers and are keen to engage with children's rights in their interpretation and analysis of the issues for

77 Lundy, Tobin and Parkes (n 45) 398; Michael Freeman, 'Whither Children: Protection, Participation, Autonomy?' (1994) 22(3) *Manitoba Law Journal* 307, 319; Parkinson and Cashmore (n 24) 10–11.

78 See Introduction (Section I.4).

79 The UK ratified the CRC on 16 December 1991 and it came into force for the UK on 15 January 1992.

80 The United Nations Convention on the Rights of the Child (Incorporation) (Scotland) Bill was passed unanimously by the Scottish Parliament on 16 March 2021. A legal challenge was brought by the UK Government in relation to whether certain provisions were beyond the scope of legislative competence of the Scottish Parliament. The UK Supreme Court heard the matter in June 2021 and upheld the challenge: see *Reference by the Attorney General and the Advocate General for Scotland – United Nations Convention on the Rights of the Child (Incorporation) (Scotland) Bill* [2021] UKSC 42.

81 Ronald Dworkin, *Law's Empire* (Belknap Press, 1986) 88.

82 See Introduction (Section I.4.1).

determination.[83] Yet substantive engagement with children's rights requires more than token references to the CRC and an account of the rights that the judge considers are relevant to the proceedings. On Tobin's 'spectrum' of judicial approaches to matters concerning children's rights, only a 'substantive' rights approach exemplifies judicial decisions that are consistent with a children's rights model.[84] By contrast, 'invisible', 'incidental', 'selective', 'rhetorical' and 'superficial' rights approaches are said to 'overlook, marginalise or misappropriate' children's rights.[85] The presence or absence of references to the CRC in a judgment, and the means by which the convention is used to support or justify the court's reasoning in any particular case, will not necessarily be determinative of whether the judge has adopted a children's rights approach.

Put differently, the CRC is not the 'be all and end all of a children's rights judgment'.[86] Various other sources can and do shape judicial understandings of rights-based approaches to decision-making. Former Chief Justice of the Family Court of Australia, Diana Bryant, has suggested that a statutory human rights instrument in Australia would 'embolden' parties and lawyers in proceedings under Part VII of the Family Law Act to 'direct their submissions towards how particular rights, such as a child's right to autonomy, should be taken into account'.[87] Yet in the absence of a charter of human rights at the federal level in Australia,[88] the CRC remains the most promising legal tool for bestowing children with formal rights recognition – albeit indirectly, given that the CRC does not create legally enforceable rights for children in Australia.

3.4.2 Balancing competing rights and interests

Article 3(1) of the CRC provides that 'the best interests of the child shall be *a primary* consideration' in all actions concerning children. By contrast, Part VII of the Family Law Act requires the court to regard the child's best interests as *the paramount* consideration in deciding whether to make an order relating to the welfare of a child[89] or to make a particular parenting order in relation to

83 Hollingsworth and Stalford (n 4) 54; Stalford and Hollingsworth, 'Judging Children's Rights' (n 3) 24. See also Ton Liefaard and Jaap E Doek, 'Litigating the Rights of the Child: Taking Stock After 25 Years of the CRC' in Ton Liefaard and Jaap E Doek (eds), *Litigating the Rights of the Child: The UN Convention on the Rights of the Child in Domestic and International Jurisprudence* (Springer, 2015) 1, 1–2.

84 See Tobin, 'Judging the Judges' (n 1) 593–603.

85 Ibid 593.

86 Hollingsworth and Stalford (n 4) 58.

87 Diana Bryant, 'It's My Body, Isn't It? Children, Medical Treatment and Human Rights' (2009) 35(2) *Monash University Law Review* 193, 208.

88 At the time of writing, only Victoria, the Australian Capital Territory (ACT) and Queensland have adopted legislative charters of human rights: see *Charter of Human Rights and Responsibilities Act 2006* (Vic); *Human Rights Act 2004* (ACT); *Human Rights Act 2019* (Qld). Other States and Territories are yet to adopt a charter of human rights.

89 *Family Law Act* (n 14) s 67ZC.

a child.[90] The *Children Act 1989* (UK) provides in similar terms that when a court determines any question with respect to a child's upbringing, 'the child's welfare shall be the court's paramount consideration'.[91] This minor semantic distinction – 'a primary' versus 'the paramount' – is nonetheless an important one, which has received both scholarly and judicial attention.[92] This is because it influences the reasoning that the court adopts in resolving the issues, including how (potentially) competing rights and interests are weighed and balanced.[93]

The inclusion of best interests as 'a primary' consideration in the CRC recognises the potential for conflicts of rights to arise between children, their parents and other parties.[94] It also suggests that where such a conflict arises, the child's rights will not necessarily trump the rights of others. Judges of the Family Court of Australia have acknowledged that the child's best interests are 'the paramount but not sole determinant'.[95] Rather, a balancing exercise is involved between the rights and best interests of the child and the rights and interests of others, such as the child's parents, siblings, extended family members and treating medical practitioners. The court must acknowledge the relevance of these other rights and interests and engage in a meaningful discussion about how to reconcile them with those of the child.[96] As Eekelaar has observed, it might be 'easier and more comforting simply to say that we are all doing what we think is best for the child', which 'encourages a laziness and unwillingness to pay proper attention to all the interests that are at stake'.[97] To simply claim that a decision reached is in the 'best interests of the child', without according due attention to the other rights and interests involved, is unlikely to be a decision in the child's best interests.

90 Ibid s 60CA.
91 *Children Act* (n 14) s 1(1).
92 See, eg, *ZH (Tanzania) v Secretary of State for the Home Department* [2011] 2 AC 166; Stalford and Hollingsworth, 'Judging Children's Rights' (n 3) 35–6; Daly, *Children, Autonomy and Courts* (n 22) 7 n 31; Eekelaar and Tobin (n 2) 95–6.
93 Tobin, 'Judging the Judges' (n 1) 612.
94 Ibid 589.
95 *Aldridge v Keaton* (2009) 235 FLR 450, 469 [75] (Bryant CJ, Boland and Crisford JJ). See also *Lovine v Connor* [2011] FamCA 432, [33]–[35] (Mushin J) ('[b]est interests means "most important" as distinct from "sole"'); *Benson v Hughes* (1994) 123 FLR 175, 192 (Chisholm J) ('Where … there is some clear and important other conflicting interest, it seems that the law requires the court to take into account the child's welfare but balance it against the other interest or policy').
96 Jane Fortin, 'Accommodating Children's Rights in a Post *Human Rights Act* Era' (2006) 69(3) *Modern Law Review* 299, 306; Georgina Dimopoulos and Michelle Taylor-Sands, '*Re Imogen*: The Role of the Family Court of Australia in Disputes over Gender Dysphoria Treatment' (2020) 39 (Suppl 1) *Monash Bioethics Review* S42, S49–50; Stalford and Hollingsworth, '"This Case is about You"' (n 5) 1054.
97 John Eekelaar, 'Beyond the Welfare Principle' (2002) 14(3) *Child and Family Law Quarterly* 237, 248. See also Lucinda Ferguson, 'An Argument for Treating Children as a "Special Case"' in Elizabeth Brake and Lucinda Ferguson (eds), *Philosophical Foundations of Children's and Family Law* (Oxford University Press, 2018) 227, 227.

3.5 Communicating the court's decision: A judgment that 'makes sense to the person most closely affected'[98]

The final feature of a children's rights judgment focuses on the style in which the judgment is written and how it is communicated. Two key elements to communicating a children's rights judgment are proposed. First, the child must be the focal point and the judgment must share the child's own voice and narrative.[99] The second element is recognising children as one of the audiences.[100] This could be achieved through a judgment written using a structure and language appropriate for the age and developmental stage of the child(ren) the subject of proceedings, such as a letter,[101] or one that includes an abridged 'child-friendly' or 'plain English' version or summary that makes the complex factual and legal issues more concise and accessible.[102] To ensure that children with communication difficulties or those who cannot read can access the court's decision, the written judgment might be converted into an infographic, a cartoon or a video.[103]

The significance of judicial communication to children's decisional privacy rights derives from the argument that, unless children can experience the conditions under which their voice is expressed and heard – that is, unless the decision-making process is sufficiently 'child-friendly'[104] – then children's substantive right to decisional privacy will be ineffectual. This understanding of the value of court judgments to children's decisional privacy aligns with what Stalford and Hollingsworth have labelled the 'communicative' function of judgments that contemplate children as an audience.[105] Children's meaningful participation in proceedings, and effective judicial communication of the court's decision to children, are interconnected.[106] If ascertaining a child's views in proceedings is a 'two way street', as the Family Court of Australia has described it, then 'children should be accorded the respect of having the outcome notified to them in an appropriate manner'.[107] The 'best interests' or 'welfare' principle requires 'not just the elevation and consideration of children's best interests, but also a *process* by which such decisions may be justified and effectively communicated to children'.[108] A children's rights judgment is also a means by which children can

98 Hale, 'Children's Participation' (n 54) 119.
99 See Hollingsworth and Stalford (n 4) 79–81.
100 See ibid 82–4; Hale, 'Children's Participation' (n 54) 119.
101 See Section 3.5.2 below.
102 Hollingsworth and Stalford (n 4) 54; Stalford and Hollingsworth, '"This Case is about You"' (n 5) 1055–6.
103 Stalford and Hollingsworth, '"This Case is about You"' (n 5) 1056.
104 Hollingsworth and Stalford (n 4) 76–7. See also Stalford, Cairns and Marshall (n 66).
105 See Stalford and Hollingsworth, '"This Case is about You"' (n 5) 1046–50.
106 Ibid 1036.
107 *Karamalis v Karamalis* (2018) 57 Fam LR 588, 591 [16] (Bennett J).
108 Eekelaar and Tobin (n 2) 97. See also Stalford and Hollingsworth, '"This Case is about You"' (n 5) 1047, 1055.

exercise their right to freedom of expression in Article 13(1) of the CRC, which includes the freedom to *seek* and *receive* information.

However, it is important to acknowledge that a child-friendly judgment alone, without children's meaningful participation in the proceedings, may evoke scepticism from children that judicial attempts to reflect their lived experiences, views and wishes in the judgment are disingenuous, 'inauthentic' or 'tokenistic'.[109] The task of effective judicial communication must be 'more than a superficial exercise in rebranding' or simplifying language and judgment length.[110] The task requires genuine engagement with children and their views and wishes at all stages of the judicial decision-making process, which will be reflected in the judgment as the final product of that process.

3.5.1 Centralising the child in the judgment's narrative

Storytelling is vital to law. Garner has described judges as 'the custodians of the richest and most dramatic and poignant human stories'.[111] If judges are 'storytellers', then their written narratives are another form of adjudication.[112] The rhetorical choices reflected in a judgment – choices of facts, language, structure, length and style – form the 'art and craft' of judgment writing.[113] They seek to explain how and why the judge reached their conclusions on the issues in the case. According to Hollingsworth and Stalford, there is a particularly strong imperative to persuade through narrative in children's cases, given their often 'contentious, emotionally-charged, value-ridden and life-changing' nature.[114] The gravity of such judicial communication is magnified by the fact that a published judgment, as a publicly accessible narrative, is a textual means by which a child's identity can be shaped and constructed.[115] On a children's rights approach, the judicial construction of narrative and the judge's choice of language, tone and style should enliven the child's experiences, to persuade readers from the *child's* perspective. Yet the extent to which the judge in each case can produce a child-focused narrative will be influenced, in part, by the material tendered by the parties from and about the child.[116]

109 Stalford and Hollingsworth, '"This Case is about You"' (n 5) 1050.

110 Ibid 1057.

111 Helen Garner, quoted in Carolyn Ford, 'Getting to the Heart of the Matter', *Law Institute Journal* (3 September 2018) 83, 84.

112 Erika Rackley, 'The Art and Craft of Writing Judgments: Notes on the Feminist Judgment Project' in Rosemary Hunter, Clare McGlynn and Erica Rackley (eds), *Feminist Judgments: From Theory to Practice* (Hart Publishing, 2010) 44, 53; Woodhouse (n 9) 1835–6.

113 Rackley (n 112); Richard A Posner, 'Judges' Writing Styles (And Do They Matter?)' (1995) 62 *University of Chicago Law Review* 1421.

114 Hollingsworth and Stalford (n 4) 79. See also Dawn Watkins, 'Recovering the Lost Human Stories of Law: Finding Mrs Burns' (2013) 7(1) *Law and Humanities* 68.

115 Dawn Watkins, 'The Shaping and Misshaping of Identity through Legal Practice and Process: (Re)discovering Mr Kernott' (2014) 8(2) *Law and Humanities* 192, 192–3.

116 See Chapter 2 (Section 2.4.5).

As with any form of narration, there is no moral neutrality in the judgment writing process.[117] A children's rights approach is by no means naïve about the subtle ways in which the law stifles children's stories in developing its narrative. Various substantive and procedural legislative provisions governing family law proceedings frame the extent of children's participation in proceedings and the terms of that (very limited) participation.[118] The result, as Woodhouse has recognised, is that 'the stories framed by the legal rules bear little relation to children's reality'.[119] The facts of a case, which are subjective in the sense that they are the product of judicial selectivity and filtering,[120] embody the official (legal) story of the parties' experiences. The means by which the judge presents an account of the facts can develop a narrative that contextualises the child's life: a children's rights judgment tells *the child's* story.[121] It is through children's own voices woven into the narrative of a judgment – rather than adult interpretations of those voices – that conceptual and normative understandings of children and their lived experiences can be shaped and, in turn, influence beyond the judicial sphere.

The use of language to humanise the child is also a critical feature of a children's rights judgment.[122] Even a pseudonym – rather than a mere reference to 'the child' or 'the subject child' – provides validation of a child's lived experiences. It also draws attention to the reality that the category of 'child' is diverse and complex.[123] This language device simultaneously serves as a reminder to both the court and readers of the judgment that 'it is the life of a *real* child at stake'.[124] The nuanced choice of language is especially important in proceedings that are effectively 'test cases' exploring general legal principles. In such cases, both the court and readers of the judgment are liable to overlook the tangible, real impact that the decision will have on the child who is the subject of the proceedings, and on other children whose rights will be impacted.[125]

117 Peter Brooks, 'The Law as Narrative and Rhetoric' in Peter Brooks and Paul Gewirtz (eds), *Law's Stories: Narrative and Rhetoric in the Law* (Yale University Press, 1996) 14, 16.

118 See Section 3.3 above.

119 Woodhouse (n 9) 1836.

120 Jerome Frank, *Courts on Trial: Myth and Reality in American Justice* (Princeton University Press, 1950) 55; Graeme Austin, *Children: Stories the Law Tells* (Victoria University Press, 1994) 9.

121 Hollingsworth and Stalford (n 4) 79–80; Stalford and Hollingsworth, '"This Case is about You"' (n 5) 1048–9, 1054. See also Woodhouse (n 9) 1829–37; Gemma Edgar, '*Re Alex*/Real Alex: Transsexual Narratives and Their Possibilities for Resistance' (2005) 23(1) *Australian Feminist Law Journal* 79.

122 Hollingsworth and Stalford (n 4) 81; Stalford and Hollingsworth, '"This Case is about You"' (n 5) 1048.

123 Hollingsworth and Stalford (n 4) 79; Stalford and Hollingsworth, '"This Case is about You"' (n 5) 1056.

124 Hollingsworth and Stalford (n 4) 81 (emphasis in original).

125 Ibid.

3.5.2 *Recognising children as an audience of the judgment: Child-friendly writing*

The second element of communicating a children's rights judgment is ensuring that the judgment is conveyed effectively to the children themselves.[126] 'Child-friendly'[127] judgments should capture the features of a well-written judgment in that they should be 'concise, clear, interesting and accessible'.[128] Yet each judge has an 'audience' in mind when writing a judgment. This audience might differ depending on the jurisdiction, the nature of the proceedings and where the court is situated in the court hierarchy.[129] A children's rights judgment must be mindful of children as one of its audiences. It should tailor the structure, language and narrative to enable children – during their childhood – to access and understand the court's reasoning and decision.[130] Baroness Hale of Richmond, writing extra-curially, has remarked that 'we judges could make a start by producing a version of our decision which makes sense to the person most closely affected by it', that is, the child.[131] An assessment of how persuasive a judicial narrative is, however, is (almost) always made according to adult standards. There remains a tendency for adults to 'underestimate children's capacities',[132] including children's capacity to understand decisions made by courts about them and their lives. As a consequence, judgments in proceedings that are *about* children and their lives are 'usually impenetrable to the children directly affected by them'.[133]

The nature of the family law jurisdiction, being 'an area which really intrudes into people's lives',[134] imposes a great responsibility upon judges to explain the reasons for their decisions in a clear, sensitive and cogent manner. A children's rights judgment should advise the child, in age-appropriate language, of the court processes followed, including how the child's views have been taken into account in the determination of their best interests. Importantly, if the decision does not align with the child's views, the judgment should articulate the reasons for the

126 Ibid 79; Dimopoulos (n 24) 452–3.

127 But see Stalford and Hollingsworth, '"This Case is about You"' (n 5) 1032 (advocating for a shift in terminology from 'child friendly judgments' to 'judgments for children').

128 Rackley (n 112) 48; Stalford and Hollingsworth, '"This Case is about You"' (n 5) 1056.

129 Hollingsworth and Stalford (n 4) 82.

130 Ibid.

131 Hale (n 54) 119.

132 Parkinson and Cashmore (n 24) 4, 197. See also Freeman, 'Human Rights of Children' (n 24) 22; John Tobin and Sheila Varadan, 'Article 5: The Right to Parental Direction and Guidance and Consistent with a Child's Evolving Capacities' in John Tobin (ed), *The UN Convention on the Rights of the Child: A Commentary* (Oxford University Press, 2019) 159, 166; Chisholm (n 28) 217.

133 Stalford and Hollingsworth, '"This Case is about You"' (n 5) 1035.

134 Diana Bryant, quoted in 'Retiring Chief Justice Reflects on Thirteen Years in the Family Court', *The Law Report* (Australian Broadcasting Corporation Radio National, 19 September 2017) <www.abc.net.au/radionational/programs/lawreport/8956300>.

judge deciding contrary to those views.[135] As Baker J explained in *In Marriage of Harrison and Woollard*:[136]

> a child's wishes must not only be considered, but must be shown to have been considered, in the reasons for judgment of the trial judge. Furthermore, if the trial judge decides to reject the wishes of a child, then clear and cogent reasons for such a rejection must be given particularly if ... the separate representative submits that the court should give effect to such wishes ... The wishes of children should not be discounted simply because they are expressed by children.[137]

At the time of writing, just one published judgment in proceedings under Part VII of the Family Law Act, to the author's knowledge, has endeavoured to embrace this element of a children's rights judgment through a letter written by the judge to the children.[138] The judge ordered that the letter be provided to each child when they turned 14 years of age, in the context of counselling or therapy.[139] The judge suggested that enabling the children to find out the reasons for the orders made about them might be 'the final and ultimate manifestation of their participation' in the proceedings[140] and recognised that:

> traditional reasons for judgment are not usually written with the audience of the children in mind. The language and format of reasons are, more often than not, styled for an audience consisting of the parents, the lawyers involved in the case, and an appellate court.[141]

Another excellent example is the judgment in *A (Letter to a Young Person)*.[142] Mr Justice Jackson of the Family Division of the High Court of England and Wales published his decision in the form of a letter to the 14-year-old young person. This letter employed age-appropriate explanations of the law and the court's reasoning. It explained to the young person that Justice Jackson was writing to him

135 Lundy, Tobin and Parkes (n 45) 415.
136 (1995) 126 FLR 159.
137 Ibid 199.
138 See *Gaylard v Cain* [2012] FMCAfam 501 ('*Gaylard*').
139 Ibid [99]; Order of Altobelli FM in *Gaylard v Cain* (Federal Magistrates Court of Australia, WOC83/2011, 30 May 2011) [19].
140 *Gaylard* (n 138) [84] (Altobelli FM). See also [86]: 'If [the children's] right to be heard in proceedings relating to them is conceptualised into the perhaps more general right to participate in these proceedings, arguably the final act of participation will not occur until they have read and understood these reasons'.
141 Ibid [87].
142 [2017] EWFC 48 ('*A (Letter to a Young Person)*'). See also *Lancashire County Council v Mr A, Mr B, The Children* [2016] EWFC 9; and in the Scottish family law context, *Mr Patrick v Mrs Patrick* [2017] SC GLA 46.

because '[t]his case is about you and your future'.[143] However, uncertainty and inconsistency in judges' communication of their decisions to children and the rarity of child-friendly judgments 'risk reinforcing a relatively superficial, perhaps even sentimentalised engagement with the notion of child friendly justice'.[144] A potential antidote to this identified risk is recent reforms to Scottish law, which take this 'innovation in judicial writing'[145] a step further, by requiring courts that make orders in relation to parental responsibilities to ensure that such orders are 'explained to the child concerned in a way that the child can understand'.[146]

A practical challenge for judges in producing a child-friendly version of their judgments is the diversity that exists within the concept of 'children', not only in terms of their age, but also their various capacities. Writing a judgment for a 5-year-old is not the same as writing a judgment for a 15-year-old, or both, in proceedings involving or affecting children of various ages. In some cases, particularly post-separation parenting proceedings, judges will also need to be attuned to the 'ethical considerations' of 'what to tell the child and when'.[147] However, writing with not only the child (or children) who is (are) the subject of the proceedings in mind, but also children as a *collective* audience, contributes to fulfilling what Stalford and Hollingsworth have called the 'instructive' function of judgments for children.[148] This is a judicial commitment to ensuring that judgments can be understood by children 'as a wider community of legal citizens affected by the decision'.[149]

Child-friendly judgments are not merely a way to communicate more effectively to children affected by a judicial decision. Such judgments have 'a broader communicative value': they show and tell children and adults alike that 'the law recognises and treats [children] as rights-holders who are worthy of respect'.[150] From a practical perspective, it is suggested that the production of such a judgment would not be an onerous or resource-intensive task for judges. The issue would be largely one of conceptualisation: judges turning their minds to *children* as a primary audience for their judgments. This is particularly important in cases where the court's substantive determination regarding a child's best interests is at odds with the child's views of their own best interests. From a decisional privacy perspective, the court in these circumstances 'curtails the child's autonomy' and conveys 'a message that [the child's] version of the "good life" is not one to be respected'.[151] A child-friendly version of the judgment helps to develop or preserve the child's ability to see their life, choices and values as

143 *A (Letter to a Young Person)* (n 142).
144 Stalford and Hollingsworth, '"This Case is about You"' (n 5) 1031–2.
145 Hollingsworth and Stalford (n 4) 83.
146 See *Children (Scotland) Act* 1995 (Scot), s 11F(2).
147 Hollingsworth and Stalford (n 4) 84. This dilemma arose in *Gaylard* (n 138) [86]–[99].
148 Stalford and Hollingsworth, '"This Case is about You"' (n 5) 1052–3.
149 Ibid 1053. See also Chapter 7 (Section 7.4.3).
150 Hollingsworth and Stalford (n 4) 83.
151 Ibid.

'meaningful, worthwhile and valuable'.[152] It does so by explaining the decision to the child in a way that they can understand: including why the court made a decision contrary to the child's views. This is even where the court's decision might have limited the child's decisional privacy, in the sense of impairing the child's ability to pursue their own life plan.

Finally, it is important to consider the legal status of a child-friendly judgment. Adapting a judgment for children might be viewed as undermining its 'legal integrity' – a concern amplified if the judgment has 'precedential potential'.[153] The view taken here is that this concern should not be overstated. As Hollingsworth and Stalford have explained, such a judgment is not akin to a language translation, so it would not be an exact replica of the original decision.[154] Indeed, its purpose is to use age-appropriate language to communicate the decision to children, which will necessitate the use of different words in the same language. In the event of a contradiction between the child-friendly version and the original version of the judgment, it is 'highly unlikely' that a child-friendly judgment produced in addition to the original judgment would be binding in law.[155] Rather, the child-friendly version would sit above the court's main reasons for judgment.

3.6 Conclusion

This chapter has presented four means by which a theory of children's decisional privacy may be implemented by judges to improve children's experiences of participation in court proceedings. It has illuminated four stages of the adjudicatory process as a framework for re-reading court judgments, which suggest ways that judges may adopt a children's rights approach in their decision-making. These features of a children's rights judgment simultaneously serve to enable children to exercise their right to decisional privacy in the context of judicial proceedings. This is because, it is argued, for children's substantive right to decisional privacy to be effective, children require procedural rights to enable them to participate actively and meaningfully in decision-making processes. Meaningful participation is essential to children's experience of autonomy.

This chapter concludes Part A of the book. With the theoretical foundations of privacy and children's rights now established, Part B turns to the implementation and operation of children's right to decisional privacy in practice. Chapter 4 introduces the case study of judicial proceedings concerning medical treatment for children experiencing gender dysphoria.

152 Catriona MacKenzie, 'Three Dimensions of Autonomy: A Relational Analysis' in Andrea Veltman and Mark Piper (eds), *Autonomy, Oppression and Gender* (Oxford University Press, 2014) 15, 37. See also Anderson and Honneth (n 19) 135.

153 Stalford and Hollingsworth, '"This Case is about You"' (n 5) 1041.

154 Hollingsworth and Stalford (n 4) 83.

155 Ibid.

Part B

Children's right to decisional privacy in practice

4 Medical treatment for gender dysphoria as a 'special medical procedure'

4.1 Introduction

Part A of this book laid the theoretical groundwork. It explained the notions of privacy, autonomy and children's rights, which form the conceptual foundation of the argument that recognising a substantive right to decisional privacy for children requires attendant procedural rights that facilitate children's meaningful participation in decision-making about their best interests. It also articulated a children's rights approach to decisional privacy and to re-reading court judgments. Part B applies the theory developed in Part A to a case study: judicial proceedings concerning medical treatment for children experiencing gender dysphoria, focusing upon the Family Court of Australia's exercise of its welfare jurisdiction under section 67ZC of the *Family Law Act 1975* (Cth) ('Family Law Act') to authorise such treatment. It forges the nexus between gender dysphoria proceedings, children's identity and autonomy and children's right to decisional privacy.

Gender dysphoria involves a person experiencing a conflict or dissonance between their self-perception of being female or male and their natal or phenotypical body (their 'birth sex').[1] In simpler terms, children with gender dysphoria feel 'trapped' inside the wrong body.[2] At the time of writing, the diagnosis of gender dysphoria in Australia is governed by the fifth edition of the American Psychiatric Association's *Diagnostic and Statistical Manual of Mental Disorders* (DSM-5).[3] To be diagnosed with gender dysphoria, a child must experience a 'marked incongruence' between their expressed or experienced gender and their assigned gender based on their birth sex that persists for at least six months and causes 'clinically significant distress or impairment in social, school or other

1 Fiona Kelly, 'Treating the Transgendered Child: The Full Court's Decision in *Re Jamie*' (2014) 28(1) *Australian Journal of Family Law* 83, 83.

2 See, eg, *Re Alex* (2004) 180 FLR 89, 105–6 [97] (Nicholson CJ) ('*Re Alex* (2004)'); *Re Alex* (2009) 248 FLR 312, 315–16 [14] (Bryant CJ) ('*Re Alex* (2009)'); *Re O (Special Medical Procedure)* [2010] FamCA 1153, [62] (Dessau J).

3 American Psychiatric Association, *Diagnostic and Statistical Manual of Mental Disorders* (American Psychiatric Association Publishing, 5th ed, 2013).

DOI: 10.4324/9781003224167-7

important areas of functioning'.[4] Gender dysphoria must manifest in at least six of the eight ways outlined in the DSM-5. These include 'a strong desire to be of the other gender or an insistence that one is the other gender', 'a strong dislike of one's sexual anatomy' and 'a strong desire for the … sex characteristics that match one's experienced gender'.[5] Not all individuals who identify as transgender will exhibit gender dysphoria.[6]

In Australia, medical treatment for gender dysphoria in children and young people is informed by clinical treatment guidelines and standards of care. These include the Australian Standards of Care and Treatment Guidelines for Trans and Gender Diverse Children and Adolescents,[7] the World Professional Association for Transgender Health Standards of Care[8] and the Endocrine Society Clinical Practice Guideline.[9] These various standards and guidelines endorse a 'gender-affirming' model of care, which is considered to 'holistically attend … to transgender people's physical, mental, and social health needs and well-being while respectfully affirming their gender identity'.[10] The accepted medical treatment for gender dysphoria in children and young people occurs in two stages.[11] The first stage involves the administration of puberty-suppressant hormones, also referred to as 'blockers'. The second stage of treatment, which occurs when the young person is approximately 16 years of age, involves the administration of either testosterone or oestrogen to facilitate the young person's transition to their affirmed sex.

This chapter first explains the notion of 'parental responsibility'[12] in the context of consent to children's medical treatment. It then sets out the welfare jurisdiction under section 67ZC of the Family Law Act, which provides the legislative basis for the Family Court to grant or refuse permission for what have come to be known as 'special medical procedures'[13] for children. These procedures lie

4 Ibid 452.
5 Ibid.
6 Timothy F Murphy, 'Adolescents and Body Modification for Gender Identity Expression' (2019) 27(4) *Medical Law Review* 623, 624.
7 Michelle Telfer et al, *Australian Standards of Care and Treatment Guidelines for Trans and Gender Diverse Children and Adolescents* (version 1.3, Royal Children's Hospital, 2020) <www.rch.org.au/uploadedFiles/Main/Content/adolescent-medicine/australian-standards-of-care-and-treatment-guidelines-for-trans-and-gender-diverse-children-and-adolescents.pdf>.
8 Eli Coleman et al, *Standards of Care for the Health of Transsexual, Transgender, and Gender-Nonconforming People* (World Professional Association for Transgender Health, 7th version, 2012) 21 <www.wpath.org/media/cms/Documents/SOC%20v7/SOC%20V7_English2012.pdf?%20t=1613669341>.
9 Wylie C Hembree et al, 'Endocrine Treatment of Gender-Dysphoric/Gender-Incongruent Persons: An Endocrine Society Clinical Practice Guideline' (2017) 102(11) *Journal of Clinical Endocrinology & Metabolism* 3869.
10 Sari L Reisner, Asa Radix and Madeline B Deutsch, 'Integrated and Gender-Affirming Transgender Clinical Care and Research' (2016) 72(Supp 3) *Journal of Acquired Immune Deficiency Syndromes* S235, S238.
11 Coleman et al (n 8) 18.
12 *Family Law Act 1975* (Cth) s 61B ('*Family Law Act*').
13 The term 'special medical procedure' does not have a settled meaning or legislative definition. It was not used in the judgment of the High Court of Australia in *Secretary, Depart-*

beyond the scope of parental responsibility and require court authorisation. Two factual issues that determine the Family Court's ability to exercise its welfare jurisdiction are discussed: the child's capacity to consent to treatment, and the subject matter of the application falling into the special medical procedure category and so beyond the scope of parental responsibility to consent.

The extension of the welfare jurisdiction to medical treatment for childhood gender dysphoria is examined through an overview of three significant court decisions. The first is the decision of the High Court of Australia in *Secretary, Department of Health and Community Services v JWB & SMB* (*Marion's Case*),[14] which established the categories of special medical procedure that are presumptively beyond the scope of parental responsibility and for which parents must seek court authorisation. The second is the decision of *Re Alex* (2004),[15] which broadened the scope of special medical procedures to medical treatment for childhood gender dysphoria. The third is *Re Bernadette*,[16] in which it was unsuccessfully argued that *Re Alex* (2004) had been wrongly decided. The evolution of the welfare jurisdiction under section 67ZC of the Family Law Act exposes assumptions about children's incapacity and vulnerability. It also highlights judicial concerns about the potential for conflict between the child's best interests and parental interests. The final section of this chapter articulates the role of courts in moderating the relationship between a child's decisional privacy and identity. This chapter contextualises the argument, advanced in subsequent chapters, that as courts have increasingly encroached upon decision-making in relation to TGD children's medical treatment, they have deprived those children of their decisional privacy rights.

4.2 Parental responsibility to consent to children's medical treatment

Part VII of the Family Law Act recognises the primacy of the parental role in relation to children's best interests.[17] It embraces the assumption that 'parents are empowered at law to make decisions for the protection and benefit of the child'.[18] To this

---

ment of Health and Community Services v JWB & SMB (1992) 175 CLR 218 ('*Marion's Case*'), discussed in Section 4.3.2.i below. It is also not a term used in the Family Law Act. In *Re Jamie* [2013] FamCAFC 110 ('*Jamie Appeal*'), Finn J expressed reservations about 'the usefulness of the expression "special medical procedure"' and considered it preferable to refer to a 'medical procedure which requires court authorisation': at [153]. See also Diana Bryant, 'It's My Body, Isn't It? Children, Medical Treatment and Human Rights' (2009) 35(2) *Monash University Law Review* 193, 198 ('It's My Body').

14 *Marion's Case* (n 13).

15 *Re Alex* (2004) (n 2).

16 (2010) 244 FLR 242 ('*Re Bernadette*').

17 Jane Fortin, *Children's Rights and the Developing Law* (Cambridge University Press, 3rd ed, 2009) 22, 321, 739–40 ('*Children's Rights*'); Gerald Dworkin, 'Consent, Representation, and Proxy Consent' in Willard Gaylin and Ruth Macklin (eds), *Who Speaks for the Child: The Problems of Proxy Consent* (Plenum Press, 1982) 191, 204.

18 *Re Tahlia* [2017] FamCA 715, [35] (Bennett J) ('*Re Tahlia*').

extent, Part VII reflects a relational, rather than atomistic, approach to autonomy.[19] Australian family law and policy promote a view of children as requiring parental guidance for their development into autonomous individuals and interdependent members of society.[20] The Family Law Act requires courts exercising family law jurisdiction to have regard to 'the need to give the widest possible protection and assistance to the family as the natural and fundamental group unit of society, particularly while it is responsible for the care and education of dependent children'.[21] This objective emanates from the significance of the family in liberal societies as 'the traditional stronghold of private life'.[22] The objects and underlying principles of Part VII emphasise the benefit to children of the 'meaningful involvement' of both parents in their lives and the importance of children receiving 'adequate and proper parenting to help them achieve their full potential'.[23] The objects place correlative duties and responsibilities on parents regarding the 'care, welfare and development' of their children.[24] The principles that undergird these objects – subject to when it is or would be contrary to a child's best interests – refer to children's rights to 'know and be cared for by both their parents' and to 'spend time on a regular basis with, and communicate on a regular basis with, both their parents'.[25]

The 'bundle of rights'[26] that Part VII bestows on parents is defined in the Family Law Act as 'parental responsibility': 'all the duties, powers, responsibilities and authority which, by law, parents have in relation to children'.[27] Subject to any court order in force,[28] parental responsibility is assigned to each of the child's parents and persists until the child turns 18 years of age.[29] It has effect 'despite any changes in the nature of the relationships of the child's parents', such as through separation or re-partnering.[30] Parental responsibility is presumptively vested in each parent,[31] or it can be allocated by court order.[32] The Family Court has stated that it 'intervenes

19 See Chapter 1 (see Section 1.4.3) and Chapter 8 (Section 8.2).
20 This view is consistent with Article 18(1) of the CRC, which requires states to 'use their best efforts to ensure recognition of the principle that both parents have common responsibilities for the upbringing and development of the child'. Article 18(2) requires states to provide 'appropriate assistance to parents ... in the performance of their child-rearing responsibilities'. See also Article 29(1) of the CRC, which stipulates, relevantly, that the child's education (the right to which is provided in Article 28) shall be directed to (c) 'the development of respect for the child's parents' and (d) 'the preparation of the child for responsible life in a free society'.
21 *Family Law Act* (n 12) s 43(1)(b).
22 Beate Rossler, *The Value of Privacy* (Polity, 2005) 2–3.
23 *Family Law Act* (n 12) s 60B(1)(a), (c).
24 Ibid s 60B(1)(d).
25 Ibid s 60B(2)(a), (b).
26 *Re Lucy (Gender Dysphoria)* (2013) 286 FLR 327, 344 [82] (Murphy J).
27 *Family Law Act* (n 12) s 61B.
28 Ibid s 61C(3).
29 Ibid s 61C(1).
30 Ibid s 61C(2).
31 Ibid s 61C.
32 Ibid s 61D.

as little as possible and only to the extent that the welfare or interests of the child requires it'; it 'does its best to avoid needless interference with parental autonomy and responsibility'.[33] However, the Family Court has also acknowledged that 'parental responsibility is not absolute authority'.[34] It 'merely provides the time frame within which it can be assumed … that parents are empowered at law to make decisions for the protection and benefit of the child'.[35]

The essence of parental responsibility, according to the Family Court, is 'much more than exercising parental rights or power over children. It encompasses protecting and respecting the child's rights even where they collide with their parents' contrary views or conflicting interests'.[36] The legitimacy of parental rights, on this view, derives from parental responsibilities and duties to guide and aid children so that they may enjoy their rights effectively.[37] This concept of parental responsibility is consistent with the starting premise of the CRC, namely, that parents have 'both a presumptive entitlement *and* a responsibility' to determine the best interests of their child.[38] The 'default position', then, is that parents have a right and responsibility to decide upon medical treatment for their child who is not yet able to consent, 'reflected through the prism of … children's best interests'.[39] The Family Court has explained that '[w]here a decision falls properly within the ambit of parental responsibility, the authorisation or consent to a [medical] procedure is a parental decision'.[40] However, 'special medical procedures'[41] fall beyond that responsibility. They must be authorised by the Family Court pursuant to its welfare jurisdiction under section 67ZC of the Family Law Act.

4.3 The welfare jurisdiction under section 67ZC of the Family Law Act

Section 67ZC of the Family Law Act is the statutory basis for the Family Court of Australia's jurisdiction to grant or refuse permission for special medical procedures for children. It provides that, in addition to the jurisdiction under Part VII in relation to children, a court has jurisdiction to make orders relating to the

33 *W v R* (2006) 197 FLR 241, 247 [44] (Carmody J). See also *VR v RR* (2002) 167 FLR 385, 390 [30], 391 [36] (Kay, Coleman and Warnick JJ).
34 *Re Tahlia* (n 18) [35] (Bennett J).
35 Ibid.
36 *W v G (No 1)* (2004) 35 Fam LR 417, 430 [111] (Carmody J) ('*W v G (No 1)*').
37 Barbara Bennett Woodhouse, 'Hatching the Egg: A Child-Centered Perspective on Parents' Rights' (1992) 14(6) *Cardozo Law Review* 1747, 1819–20.
38 John Eekelaar and John Tobin, 'Article 3: The Best Interests of the Child' in John Tobin (ed), *The UN Convention on the Rights of the Child: A Commentary* (Oxford University Press, 2019) 73, 89 (emphasis in original).
39 *Re Kelvin* [2017] FamCAFC 258, [123] (Thackray, Strickland and Murphy JJ) ('*Re Kelvin*'). See also *Marion's Case* (n 13) 239–40.
40 *Re Sean* (2010) 258 FLR 192, 206 [84] (Murphy J) ('*Re Sean*').
41 See n 13 above.

welfare of children.[42] In deciding whether to make such an order, the court must regard the best interests of the child as the paramount consideration.[43] Akin, but not confined, to the historical *parens patriae* jurisdiction,[44] the welfare jurisdiction under section 67ZC has been concerned with identifying risks to children and preventing harm. Australian judges have described the welfare jurisdiction variously as 'designed to protect against risk' and not 'to supervise parents and guardians in the exercise of their rights and responsibilities',[45] yet also as 'essentially supervisory of parental responsibility'.[46] The Family Court has observed that the welfare power bestowed on it by section 67ZC is wide, as it allows for orders to be made requiring a parent to do any act necessary for the child's welfare.[47] The two factual issues that determine the Family Court's capacity to exercise the jurisdiction granted by section 67ZC are: whether the child is competent to consent to the medical treatment; and whether the subject matter of the application is a 'special medical procedure' to which a parent or guardian cannot consent.[48]

4.3.1 Children's capacity to consent to medical treatment

The question of capacity is fundamental to the conceptualisation of children's right to decisional privacy.[49] In the context of medical treatment, the law has approached this question in its favoured fashion as a 'binary choice':[50] either a child has the capacity to make an informed decision concerning their medical treatment or the child does not have such capacity. The assessment of a child's capacity to consent to medical treatment is commonly referred to as '*Gillick* competence'. The House of Lords in *Gillick v West Norfolk and Wisbech Area Health Authority* ('*Gillick*')[51] established the principle that a child will be found

42 *Family Law Act* (n 12) s 67ZC(1).
43 Ibid s 67ZC(2).
44 Explanatory Memorandum, Family Law Reform Bill 1994 (Cth) 71 [319]. See also *Jacks v Samson* (2008) 221 FLR 307, 353 [220] (Stevenson J). Cf *Re Z* (1996) 134 FLR 40, 45 [323] (Nicholson CJ and Frederico J).
45 *AMS v AIF* (1999) 199 CLR 160, 189 [87] (Gaudron J).
46 *Re Bernadette* (2011) 249 FLR 294, 304 [55] (Bryant CJ and Strickland J) ('*Bernadette Appeal*').
47 *W v G (No 1)* (n 36) 425 [59] (Carmody J). See also *L v T* (1999) 154 FLR 211, 225–6 [57] (Kay, Coleman and Brown JJ); *Re Kelvin* (n 39) [190] (Thackray, Strickland and Murphy JJ).
48 An additional factual issue is whether the child or young person is currently under a care order: see *Re Alex* (2004) (n 2) 116 [151] (Nicholson CJ). The High Court of Australia has held that the welfare jurisdiction conferred by section 67ZC of the Family Law Act is not at large; rather, it depends on another provision in Part VII of the Act creating a 'matter' to which the jurisdiction conferred by section 67ZC can attach: *Minister for Immigration and Multicultural and Indigenous Affairs v B* (2004) 219 CLR 365, 383–4 [23] (Gleeson CJ and McHugh J). Cf *Re Ash* [2021] FedCFamC1F 100, [60] (Wilson J).
49 See Chapter 1 (Section 1.4.2).
50 Patrick Parkinson and Judy Cashmore, *The Voice of a Child in Family Law Disputes* (Oxford University Press, 2008) 3.
51 [1986] AC 112.

to be competent to consent to medical treatment if the child has achieved 'a sufficient understanding and intelligence to enable [them] to understand fully what is proposed'.[52] Thus, parental rights will yield to the child's right to make their own decisions. As the Family Court of Australia has said, 'parental authority over a child wanes as [the child] grows older and marches inexorably towards majority'.[53] This approach accords with the second fundamental principle of a children's rights approach to decisional privacy, namely, that children exercise autonomy consistent with their evolving capacities.[54]

While the *Gillick* decision concerned contraceptive advice and treatment, the House of Lords did not limit the kinds of 'matters' that a child might be competent to decide to the facts of that case.[55] The principle that emerged from *Gillick* was expressly approved by the High Court of Australia in *Marion's Case*.[56] The notion of *Gillick* competence has been pivotal to all cases involving authorisation of medical treatment for gender dysphoria under section 67ZC of the Family Law Act. 'Almost inevitably' in gender dysphoria proceedings, the evidence before the Family Court has demonstrated the child's *Gillick* competence.[57] In the minority of cases where the child was found not to be *Gillick* competent, the Family Court held that the child's parents could consent to medical treatment on the child's behalf.[58]

The Family Court of Australia has forged a nexus between *Gillick* competence and autonomy, noting that '[w]hen a child of *Gillick* competency makes a decision in relation to [themselves], that child acts autonomously'.[59] A declaration of *Gillick* competence has been said to signify the child's 'attainment of autonomy in relation to medical treatment'.[60] Yet the Family Court has also held that an 'integral part' of its role is to protect the child's *future* autonomy and decision-making capacity: 'a child's right to later make for themselves important decisions including, crucially, the broader right to become the adult that [they] wish …'.[61] Two decisional privacy issues pertaining to the assessment of *Gillick* competence in the context of gender dysphoria treatment are examined below.

52 Ibid 188–9 (Lord Scarman).
53 *W v G (No 1)* (n 36) 430 [112] (Carmody J).
54 See Chapter 2 (Section 2.3.2).
55 *R (Bell) v The Tavistock and Portman NHS Foundation Trust* [2021] EWCA Civ 1363, [76] ('*Bell Appeal*').
56 *Marion's Case* (n 13) 237–8 (Mason CJ, Dawson, Toohey and Gaudron JJ holding that '[t]his approach, though lacking the certainty of a fixed age rule accords with experience and with psychology. It should be followed in this country as part of the common law'.).
57 *Re Lucas* [2016] FamCA 1129, [68] (Tree J).
58 See *Re Kelvin* (n 39) [51]–[52] (Thackray, Strickland and Murphy JJ).
59 *Re Tahlia* (n 18) [35] (Bennett J). See also *Re Harley* [2016] FamCA 334, [45] (Bennett J).
60 *Re Tahlia* (n 18) [37] (Bennett J).
61 *Re Sam and Terry (Gender Dysphoria)* (2013) 49 Fam LR 417, 429 [60] (Murphy J) ('*Re Sam*').

i. The standard of competence required

The standard of competence against which a child is assessed enlivens the notion of the child's 'evolving capacities',[62] which underpins the second fundamental principle of a children's rights approach to decisional privacy.[63] Children's various capacities – cognitive, emotional, social, cultural and physical – develop, not necessarily in a linear fashion, as children mature with age.[64] As these capacities evolve, so do children's 'knowledge, competencies and understanding' of their rights and how to make decisions for themselves.[65] The CRC Committee has explained that various factors affecting decision-making must be considered when determining the balance between respect for a child's evolving capacities and the appropriate level of protection for that child, including:

> the level of risk involved, the potential for exploitation, understanding of adolescent development, recognition that competence and understanding do not necessarily develop equally across all fields at the same pace and recognition of individual experience and capacity.[66]

The perpetual challenge, from a children's rights perspective, lies in determining when, how and by whom this balance should be achieved. Gender dysphoria proceedings arguably expose a conflict between 'the right to bodily integrity and self-determination versus parents' right to ensure that children are protected from harm and from making impetuous decisions inimical to their best interests'.[67] Jurisprudence in Australia and the UK has displayed considerable unease with the notion that TGD children are *Gillick* competent to consent to medical treatment for gender dysphoria. In *Re Alex* (2004), Nicholson CJ emphasised that there was:

> a considerable difference between a child or young person deciding to use contraceptives as in *Gillick* and a child or young person determining upon a course that will 'change' [their] sex. It is highly questionable whether a

62 *CRC*, art 5. See Aoife Daly, 'Assessing Children's Capacity: Reconceptualising our Understanding through the UN Convention on the Rights of the Child' (2020) 28(3) *International Journal of Children's Rights* 471.

63 See Chapter 2 (Section 2.3.2).

64 See Gerison Lansdown, *The Evolving Capacities of the Child* (UNICEF Innocenti Studies, 2005) 9–13; John Tobin and Sheila Varadan, 'Article 5: The Right to Parental Direction and Guidance and Consistent with a Child's Evolving Capacities' in John Tobin (ed), *The UN Convention on the Rights of the Child: A Commentary* (Oxford University Press, 2019) 159, 172.

65 CRC Committee, *General Comment No 7: Implementing Child Rights in Early Childhood*, UN Doc CRC/C/GC/7/Rev.1 (20 September 2006) [17].

66 CRC Committee, *General Comment No 20 (2016) on the Implementation of the Rights of the Child During Adolescence*, UN Doc CRC/C/GC/20 (6 December 2016) [20].

67 Bryant, 'It's My Body' (n 13) 195.

> 13-year-old could ever be regarded as having the capacity for the latter, and this situation may well continue until the young person reaches maturity.[68]

A higher threshold of capacity and understanding than adults is often required of children to afford them decision-making autonomy.[69] Some scholars have attempted to justify this differential treatment on the basis of children's 'autonomous trajectory' and 'stage of life', arguing that children have 'not yet reached the time in their life cycle when they are expected to make crucial choices that will define their identities'.[70] Adults are presumed to have the capacity to appreciate the consequences of their actions and decisions. They are thus free to act and make decisions that might nonetheless pose a risk to their interests.[71] On the other hand, it is presumed that 'often children do not choose well or wisely',[72] such that adults must act on behalf of children to protect their best interests.

In determining the standard of competence required, other scholars consider that society should adopt 'a sceptical approach to autonomy' in the context of children's decision-making.[73] On this view, courts can and should override children's decisions where those decisions are considered by the judge to be rash or unwise according to adult standards[74] or to protect children from making 'life-threatening mistakes'.[75] These observations suggest that, even when children reach the *Gillick* threshold, judges may be loath to decide contrary to the

68 *Re Alex* (2004) (n 2) 120 [173]. *Re Alex* (2004) is discussed at Section 4.3.2.ii below.

69 Michael Freeman, 'Rethinking *Gillick*' (2005) 13 *International Journal of Children's Rights* 201, 211. See also Andrew Franklin-Hall, 'On Becoming an Adult: Autonomy and the Moral Relevance of Life's Stages' (2013) 63(251) *The Philosophical Quarterly* 223, 242; Laura Lundy, John Tobin and Aisling Parkes, 'Article 12: The Right to Respect for the Views of the Child' in John Tobin (ed), *The UN Convention on the Rights of the Child: A Commentary* (Oxford University Press, 2019) 397, 410; Helen Stalford and Kathryn Hollingsworth, 'Judging Children's Rights: Tendencies, Tensions, Constraints and Opportunities' in Helen Stalford, Kathryn Hollingsworth and Stephen Gilmore (eds), *Rewriting Children's Rights Judgments: From Academic Vision to New Practice* (Hart Publishing, 2017) 17, 39; Tobin and Varadan (n 64) 174; Melinda Jones, 'Children's Health Rights and Gender Issues' in Jozef HHM Dorscheidt and Jaap E Doek (eds), *Children's Rights in Health Care* (Brill, 2018) 382, 416; Jamie Potter, 'Rewriting the Competency Rules for Children: Full Recognition of the Young Person as Rights-Bearer' (2006) 14(1) *Journal of Law and Medicine* 64.

70 Franklin-Hall (n 69) 240–1, 243.

71 John Tobin, 'Understanding Children's Rights: A Vision beyond Vulnerability' (2015) 84 *Nordic Journal of International Law* 155, 165; Ronald Dworkin. *Taking Rights Seriously* (Bloomsbury, rev ed, 1997) 228–9.

72 Carol Brennan, 'Children's Choices or Children's Interests: Which Do Their Rights Protect?' in David Archard and Colin Macleod (eds), *The Moral and Political Status of Children* (Oxford University Press, 2002) 53, 59. See also Parkinson and Cashmore (n 50) 84, 96; Fortin, *Children's Rights* (n 17) 73–4.

73 Margaret Brazier and Caroline Bridge, 'Coercion or Caring: Analysing Adolescent Autonomy' (1996) 16(1) *Legal Studies* 84, 109.

74 Ibid. See also *Re Alex* (2004) (n 2) 118 [168] (Nicholson CJ).

75 Fortin, *Children's Rights* (n 17) 29.

opinions and advice of the adults in the proceedings, particularly medical practitioners and parents.[76]

Adults can thus be seen to 'reify [children's] incapacity'[77] in their assessment of *Gillick* competence. They do so by failing to recognise that children's capacities evolve as they mature and develop or by unfairly holding children to adult standards of capacity. In this way, adults excuse their reluctance to respect children's decisional privacy rights by discounting children's experiences, needs and wishes. In light of little practical guidance,[78] some scholars have suggested that the application of *Gillick* can be used as a guise for paternalistic decision-making about children 'in the rhetoric of their rights'.[79] This is because the child's capacity is a matter of adult value judgements, which transfers agency from children to adults.[80]

For instance, an adult decision-maker may hold a child to be incompetent and so unable to give consent, simply because the child's views differ from what the decision-maker considers to be in the child's best interests. As Freeman has submitted, '[i]t is much easier to assume abilities and capacities are absent than to take cognisance of children's choices'.[81] It is here that judges must be cautious to distinguish between an assessment of the child's maturity and an evaluation of the

76 Jane Fortin, 'Accommodating Children's Rights in a Post *Human Rights Act* Era' (2006) 69(3) *Modern Law Review* 299, 323 ('Accommodating Children's Rights'). See also Jane Fortin 'Children's Rights: Are the Courts Now Taking Them More Seriously?' (2004) 15(2) *King's Law Journal* 253, 260–1; Stalford and Hollingsworth (n 69) 31; Sara Fovargue and Suzanne Ost, 'Does the Theoretical Framework Change the Legal End Result for Mature Minors Refusing Medical Treatment or Creating Self-Generated Pornography?' (2013) 13(1) *Medical Law International* 6, 8.

77 Woodhouse (n 37) 1829.

78 Fortin, *Children's Rights* (n 17) 94; Emma Cave, 'Goodbye *Gillick*? Identifying and Resolving Problems with the Concept of Child Competence' (2014) 34(1) *Legal Studies* 103, 109–10; Aoife Daly, *Children, Autonomy and the Courts: Beyond the Right to be Heard* (Brill, 2017) 167–71. Cf *Bell Appeal* (n 55), in which the Court of Appeal of England and Wales overturned the attempt of the High Court to offer such 'practical guidance', emphasising that '[i]t is a matter of clinical judgement, tailored to the patient in question, how to explain matters to ensure that the giving or refusal of consent is properly informed': at [81]; see also [64], [74]–[75]. The judgment of the Court of Appeal in *Bell* is analysed in Chapter 7.

79 John Tobin, 'Judging the Judges: Are they Adopting the Rights Approach in Matters involving Children?' (2009) 33(2) *Melbourne University Law Review* 579, 600. See also Freeman, 'Rethinking *Gillick*' (n 69) 206–8, 211–12.

80 Priscilla Alderson, 'Giving Children's Voices "Due Weight" in Medical Law' (2018) 26(1) *International Journal of Children's Rights* 16, 21; David Archard and Marit Skivenes, 'Balancing a Child's Best Interests and a Child's Views' (2009) 17(1) *International Journal of Children s Rights* 1, 10; Nigel Thomas and Claire O'Kane, 'When Children's Wishes and Feelings Clash with their "Best Interests"' (1998) 6(2) *International Journal of Children's Rights* 137, 150–1; Lothar Krappman, 'The Weight of the Child's View (Article 12 of the UN Convention on the Rights of the Child)' (2012) 18(4) *International Journal of Children's Rights* 501, 505; Fortin, 'Accommodating Children's Rights' (n 76) 318.

81 Michael Freeman, *The Moral Status of Children: Essays on the Rights of the Child* (Kluwer Law International, 1997) 37 ('*Moral Status*').

child's views. To conflate the two – capacity and opinion – might result in a finding that the child lacks capacity to make an informed decision, on the basis that the judge disagrees with the sagacity of the child's views and wishes.[82] The issue then becomes whether a child has 'any real rights if she must rely on others in this way to determine when she can make rights claims'.[83] The question in assessing *Gillick* competence should perhaps be reframed, as Zimmerman has suggested, as 'not so much a question as to whether a child should be recognized as having a capacity to give informed consent, but whether a person, who happens to be a child, bears such a capacity'.[84]

ii. Balancing the child's current views and wishes with the child's future autonomy

A children's rights approach to decisional privacy seeks to foster a child's current and future potential as a rights-bearing subject. To do so, it recognises that a child's decision-making autonomy might need to be limited if the child's exercise of that autonomy would irreparably impair their 'right to an open future'[85] or ability to live an autonomous life. Yet in focusing on the child's future potential, a children's rights approach does not overlook the child's current needs, attitudes, feelings and preferences.[86] This is because children are simultaneously recognised as beings *and* becomings.[87] Children's present status as human beings under international law entitles them to rights irrespective of their capacity and their vulnerability.[88] At a practical level, there is a tension between protecting children's future autonomy and listening to children's views and wishes in the present.

82 Archard and Skivenes (n 80) 10; Simona Giordano, 'Medical Treatment for Children with Gender Dysphoria: Conceptual and Ethical Issues' in Baudewijntje P C Kreukels, Thomas D Steensma and Annelou L C de Vries (eds), *Gender Dysphoria and Disorders of Sex Development: Progress in Care and Knowledge* (Springer, 2014) 205, 218.

83 Lucinda Ferguson, 'Not Merely Rights for Children but Children's Rights: The Theory Gap and the Assumption of the Importance of Children's Rights' (2013) 21 *International Journal of Children's Rights* 177, 192.

84 Nigel Zimmermann, '*Gillick* Competence: An Unnecessary Burden' (2019) 25(1) *The New Bioethics* 78, 88.

85 See, eg, Joel Feinberg, 'The Child's Right to an Open Future' in William Aitken and Hugh La Follette (eds), *Whose Child? Children's Rights, Parental Authority, and State Power* (Rowman and Littlefield, 1980) 124; Freeman, *Moral Status* (n 81) 39, 98; Michael Freeman, 'The Human Rights of Children' (2010) 63(1) *Current Legal Problems* 1, 25 ('Human Rights of Children'); Lucinda Ferguson, 'An Argument for Treating Children as a "Special Case"' in Elizabeth Brake and Lucinda Ferguson (eds), *Philosophical Foundations of Children's and Family Law* (Oxford University Press, 2018) 227, 240. Cf Claudia Mills, 'The Child's Right to an Open Future' (2003) 34(4) *Journal of Social Philosophy* 499.

86 Fortin, *Children's Rights* (n 17) 22.

87 Freeman, 'Human Rights of Children' (n 85) 13, 15, 19–20.

88 See Chapter 1 (Section 1.4.2) and Chapter 2 (Section 2.2).

MacCormick, a proponent of the interest theory of rights,[89] has explained that '[c]hildren are not always or even usually the best judges of what is good for them', such that they are more likely than adults to impair their future prospects by making imprudent choices in the short-term.[90] For children with gender dysphoria who seek medical treatment, arguments concerning their best interests have revolved around their capacity to make what some consider to be 'irreversible' decisions that will impact on their future choices and which they cannot fully understand at present.[91] In *R (Bell) v The Tavistock and Portman NHS Foundation Trust* ('*Bell*'),[92] the first claimant in proceedings before the High Court of England and Wales, who had undergone medical treatment for gender dysphoria, gave evidence that:

> I made a brash decision as a teenager, (as a lot of teenagers do) trying to find confidence and happiness, except now the rest of my life will be negatively affected. I cannot reverse any of the physical, mental or legal changes that I went through. Transition [to the opposite sex] was a very temporary, superficial fix for a very complex identity issue.[93]

The High Court in *Bell* endorsed this sentiment of 'brash' decision-making in finding that:

> For many children, certainly younger children, and some as young as 10 and just entering puberty, it will not be possible to conceptualise what not being able to give birth to children (or conceive children with their own sperm) would mean in adult life. Similarly, the meaning of sexual fulfilment, and what the implications of treatment may be for this in the future, will be impossible for many children to comprehend.[94]

The High Court also considered that the provision of additional, age-appropriate information would not be an adequate remedy, noting that '[t]here is no age appropriate way to explain to many of these children what losing their fertility or

89 See Chapter 1 (Section 1.4.2).

90 Neil MacCormick, 'Children's Rights: A Test-Case' in Neil MacCormick (ed), *Legal Right and Social Democracy: Essays in Legal and Political Philosophy* (Clarendon Press, 1982) 154, 166.

91 See, eg, Carrie Paechter, 'The Rights and Interests of Trans and Intersex Children: Considerations, Conflicts and Implications in relation to the UNCRC' (2021) 30(7) *Journal of Gender Studies* 844, 847; Brendan S Abel, 'Hormone Treatment of Children and Adolescents with Gender Dysphoria: An Ethical Analysis' (2014) 44 (Suppl 4) *Hastings Centre Report* S23.

92 [2020] EWHC 3274 (Admin).

93 Ibid [83].

94 Ibid [139].

full sexual function may mean to them in later years'.[95] According to Paechter, the troubling implication of this judicial approach is that

> the best interests of the trans child, in all cases, are best served by withholding treatment for as long as possible, without reference to any child's specific circumstances, and even when the child's own strongly expressed wishes are to have treatment.[96]

The tension between current wishes and future autonomy for children with gender dysphoria is magnified by the inherent difficulty in articulating the content of an 'open future'.[97] As Wilkinson has observed, 'it is hard to come up with a non-arbitrary way of individuating and counting options'.[98]

The future decision-making capacity of children experiencing gender dysphoria arguably is impaired by both *providing* treatment and by *withholding* treatment. For instance, the potential for gender-affirming hormones (stage two treatment) to cause permanent infertility clearly impacts their future reproductive choices;[99] yet significant problems for their physical and psychological health and well-being may arise from delaying treatment.[100] The approach of 'watching and waiting' can also impair a child's right to an open future, for 'the child's body may change

95 Ibid [144]. Such judicial unease over *Gillick* competence in relation to gender dysphoria treatment appears to have been driven, at least in part, by the perceived 'experimental' or 'innovative' nature of that treatment: see Michelle Taylor-Sands and Georgina Dimopoulos, 'Judicial Discomfort over "Innovative" Treatment for Adolescents with Gender Dysphoria' (2022) *Medical Law Review* fwac018; Bernadette Richards and Katrina Hutchinson, 'Consent to Innovative Treatment: No Need for a New Legal Test' (2016) 23(4) *Journal of Law and Medicine* 938, 938; Simona Giordano and Søren Holm, 'Is Puberty Delaying Treatment "Experimental Treatment"?' (2020) 21(2) *International Journal of Transgender Health* 113; Simona Giordano, Fae Garland and Søren Holm, 'Gender Dysphoria in Adolescents: Can Adolescents or Parents Give Valid Consent to Puberty Blockers?' (2021) 47(5) *Journal of Medical Ethics* 324; Monique Robles, 'The Bioethical Dilemma of Gender-Affirming Therapy in Children and Adolescents' (2021) 88(3) *The Linacre Quarterly* 259.

96 Paechter (n 91) 848.

97 See n 85 above.

98 Stephen Wilkinson, *Choosing Tomorrow's Children: The Ethics of Selective Reproduction* (Clarendon Press, 2010) 46.

99 Philip J Cheng et al, 'Fertility Concerns of the Transgender Patient' (2019) 8(3) *Translational Andrology and Urology* 209. For judicial acknowledgement of the impacts of stage two treatment on fertility, see, eg, *Re Kelvin* (n 39) [15] (Thackray, Strickland and Murphy JJ); *Re Imogen [No 6]* (2020) 61 Fam LR 344, 357–8 [64] (Watts J); *Re Jamie* [2015] FamCA 455, [79], [81] (Thornton J).

100 See, eg, Coleman et al (n 8) 21; Fiona Kelly, '"The Court Process Is Slow but Biology Is Fast": Assessing the Impact of the Family Court Approval Process on Transgender Children and their Families' (2016) 30(2) *Australian Journal of Family Law* 112, 123–5; *Re Jamie* [2011] FamCA 248, [5], [53], [111] (Dessau J). Delays have in some cases have resulted in the child's development of secondary sexual characteristics later requiring surgery: see *Re Alex* (2009) (n 2).

irreversibly' in the interim.[101] Indeed, as the Court of Appeal in *Bell* acknowledged, 'neither puberty suppression nor allowing puberty to occur can be regarded as a neutral act'.[102] Decision-making in relation to gender dysphoria treatment for children therefore exemplifies Giordano's observation that 'there is no such a thing as *no action* … any choice, including the choice not to intervene, is still *doing something*'.[103] A children's rights approach to decisional privacy requires adults to facilitate – rather than deny, on the basis of life stage alone – children's effective enjoyment of their decisional privacy rights, including the right to participate in decision-making that impacts their bodies and identities. As the CRC Committee has explained, the child need not have 'comprehensive knowledge of all aspects of the matter' affecting them to be able to express their views and to have those views taken into account in the decision-making process.[104]

4.3.2 'Special medical procedures' requiring court authorisation

The second factual issue that determines the Family Court's ability to exercise the jurisdiction bestowed by section 67ZC of the Family Law Act is whether the subject matter of the application is a 'special medical procedure' to which a parent or guardian cannot consent. The Family Court has emphasised that the kinds of medical treatment that may fall within its welfare jurisdiction under section 67ZC will be influenced by all the circumstances surrounding the treatment. In *Re Alex* (2004), Nicholson CJ held that '[t]he categories of cases in which the welfare jurisdiction properly ought to be invoked are not closed', particularly as 'the march of science overtakes the perimeters of the settled law'.[105] In *Re Jamie*, Bryant CJ stated that the mere 'possibility of different treatments' and 'different views about what treatment should be given' would not render the treatment a 'special medical procedure' solely on that basis.[106] However, her Honour agreed that 'the evolving state of medical knowledge' may well lead to cases that involve issues requiring court authorisation.[107] Reinforcing these views, a majority of the Full Court in *Re Kelvin* observed that:

> the types of medical treatment for which court authorisation is required are neither closed nor confined to sterilization of a child who is not, and never will be, *Gillick* competent. Rather, as a general rule, whether court

101 Paechter (n 91) 852.
102 *Bell Appeal* (n 55) [29]. See also ibid 848, 852; Kenneth J Zucker, 'Adolescents with Gender Dysphoria: Reflections on Some Contemporary Clinical and Research Issues' (2019) 48(7) *Archives of Sexual Behavior* 1983.
103 Giordano (n 82) 214 (emphasis in original).
104 CRC Committee, *General Comment No 12 (2009): The Right of the Child to be Heard*, UN Doc CRC/C/GC/12 (20 July 2009) [21].
105 *Re Alex* (2004) (n 2) 124 [198].
106 *Jamie Appeal* (n 13) [105].
107 Ibid [106].

authorisation is required will be dependent upon the entirety of the circumstances surrounding the particular treatment.[108]

The final part of this chapter presents three seminal cases that have shaped the exercise of the welfare jurisdiction under section 67ZC of the Family Law Act in the context of childhood gender dysphoria. The judgments below reflect a construction of childhood as 'essentially a protectionist experience'[109] and demonstrate that judges – rather than medical practitioners – have become the 'gatekeepers'[110] to treatment sought by children experiencing gender dysphoria.

i. Marion's Case: Delimiting the scope of the Family Court's welfare jurisdiction in special medical procedure cases

The decision of the High Court of Australia in *Marion's Case*[111] is the leading Australian authority on the scope of the welfare jurisdiction under section 67ZC of the Family Law Act. The proceedings arose from an application to the Family Court by the parents of a 14-year-old girl with severe intellectual disabilities. The parents sought an order authorising the performance of two medical procedures on their child;[112] and in the alternative, a declaration that it was lawful for the parents themselves to consent to the performance of the procedures.[113]

A majority of the High Court in *Marion's Case* identified a number of 'factors involved in a decision to authorize sterilization' of a child, which suggested that 'such a decision should not come within the ordinary scope of parental power to consent to medical treatment'.[114] The majority held that if a child was not *Gillick* competent, the child's parents could not consent where the proposed treatment was 'invasive', 'irreversible' and 'non-therapeutic', that is, not 'appropriately

108 *Re Kelvin* (n 39) [138] (Thackray, Strickland and Murphy JJ). See also *Re Sean* (n 40) 202 [65] (Murphy J noting that it was 'not possible, nor … desirable, to further define or list those procedures, treatments or the like which require court authorisation'); and in the UK, *AB v CD* [2021] EWHC 741 (Fam), [99] (Lieven J noting 'the need for caution in imposing blanket rules, even for the most difficult categories of case').

109 Freeman, *Moral Status* (n 81) 9.

110 See Catherine Downs and Stephen Whittle, 'Seeking a Gendered Adolescence: Legal and Ethical Problems of Puberty Suppression among Adolescents with Gender Dysphoria' in Eric Heinze (ed), *Of Innocence and Autonomy: Children, Sex and Human Rights* (Taylor & Francis, 2000) 195, 199; Jaye Cee Whitehead et al, 'Reluctant Gatekeepers: "Trans-Positive" Practitioners and the Social Construction of Sex and Gender' (2012) 21(4) *Journal of Gender Studies* 387.

111 *Marion's case* (n 13).

112 These procedures were a hysterectomy and an ovariectomy. The majority noted that the term 'sterilisation' was used throughout the High Court's judgment as 'a shorthand for these procedures in the particular circumstances': ibid 229 (Mason CJ, Dawson, Toohey and Gaudron JJ).

113 Ibid.

114 Ibid 249 (Mason CJ, Dawson, Toohey and Gaudron JJ).

carried out to treat some malfunction or disease'.[115] The majority held that Family Court authorisation was necessary for such treatment, pursuant to the welfare jurisdiction under section 67ZC of the Family Law Act, essentially as a 'procedural safeguard'.[116]

The majority further justified its decision to categorise sterilisation as a special case requiring court authorisation on the basis of the 'significant risk of making the wrong decision', either as to a child's present or future capacity to consent, or about the best interests of a child who cannot consent;[117] and the 'particularly grave' consequences of a wrong decision being made.[118] The majority considered that the complexity of the question of consent; the medical profession's key role in the decision to perform the medical procedure and in the procedure itself; and the potentially conflicting interests of the child, the child's parents and other family members; were factors contributing to the significant risk of a wrong decision being made.[119] In balancing the child's best interests with parental decision-making autonomy, the majority considered that there was 'less likelihood of (intentional or unintentional) abuse of the rights of children if an application to a court is mandatory, than if the decision in all cases could be made by a guardian alone'.[120]

The distinction between 'therapeutic' and 'non-therapeutic' treatment, drawn by the High Court majority in *Marion's Case*, is captured legislatively in the rule regarding 'medical procedure proceedings' in the *Federal Circuit and Family Court of Australia (Family Law) Rules 2021* (Cth). Rule 1.11 applies to applications 'for an order authorising a major medical procedure for a child that is not for the purpose of treating a bodily malfunction or disease'; or 'where there is a dispute about the *Gillick* competence of, or the diagnosis or treatment of a child for gender dysphoria'.[121] In such an application, evidence must be given, including from a medical, psychological or other relevant expert witness, to satisfy the court that the proposed medical procedure is in the child's best interests.[122] Of the nine matters that must be established by this evidence,[123] some directly bear upon the child's decisional privacy: whether a child who is capable of making an informed decision about the procedure agrees to the procedure;[124] whether a child who is currently incapable of making an informed decision about the procedure is likely 'to develop sufficiently to be able to make an informed decision within the time

115 Ibid 250.
116 Ibid 249.
117 Ibid 250.
118 Ibid.
119 Ibid 250–2.
120 Ibid 253.
121 *Federal Circuit and Family Court of Australia (Family Law) Rules 2021* (Cth) r 1.11(1) ('*FCFCA Rules*').
122 Ibid r 1.11(4), (5).
123 These matters are largely a codification of the matters listed in *Re Marion (No 2)* (1994) 17 Fam LR 336.
124 *FCFCA Rules* (n 121) r 1.11(5)(g).

in which the procedure should be carried out, or within the foreseeable future';[125] and whether the child's parents or carer agree to the procedure.[126]

ii. Gender dysphoria as a 'special medical procedure': The case of Re Alex (2004)

The decision of the Family Court of Australia in *Re Alex* (2004)[127] extended the category of 'special medical procedures' requiring court authorisation, as developed by the High Court in *Marion's Case* in relation to sterilisation, to the medical treatment of childhood gender dysphoria. A government department, as legal guardian of 13-year-old 'Alex',[128] applied to the Family Court for the authorisation of stage one and stage two treatment for Alex, who had been diagnosed with what was then known as 'gender identity disorder'.[129] This was a 'novel' application, being the first of its kind pursuant to section 67ZC of the Family Law Act.[130] The evidence did not establish that Alex was *Gillick* competent to consent to the proposed treatment.[131] However, it was common ground that Alex had 'a long-standing, unwavering and present identification as a male'.[132] There was 'uncontroverted' evidence that the proposed treatment was entirely consistent with Alex's wishes and that his best interests accorded with those wishes.[133]

Nicholson CJ concluded that both stage one and stage two treatment for childhood gender dysphoria amounted to a special medical procedure to which Alex's guardian could not consent.[134] His Honour held that, on the evidence, it could not be said that treatment for childhood gender dysphoria was 'to cure a disease or correct some malfunction'.[135] Further, he considered that there were 'significant risks' involved in 'embarking on a process that will alter a child or young person who presents as physically of one sex in the direction of the opposite sex, even where the court is not asked to authorise surgery'.[136]

125 Ibid r 1.11(5)(h).
126 Ibid r 1.11(5)(i).
127 *Re Alex* (2004) (n 2).
128 As he was anonymised in the judgment: see *Family Law Act* (n 12) s 121, which prohibits the publication of identifying details of proceedings.
129 As per the fourth edition of the *Diagnostic and Statistical Manual of Mental Disorders*: American Psychiatric Association, *Diagnostic and Statistical Manual of Mental Disorders: DSM-IV* (American Psychiatric Association Publishing, 4th ed, 1994).
130 *Re Alex* (2004) (n 2) 121 [180] (Nicholson CJ).
131 Ibid 118 [168].
132 Ibid 103 [80].
133 Ibid 119 [169].
134 Ibid 124 [196]. The two stages of treatment were treated as a 'single treatment plan': at 122–3 [188].
135 Ibid 124 [196].
136 Ibid.

Re Alex (2004), whilst not immune to criticism,[137] became the seminal judgment concerning the medical treatment of children experiencing gender dysphoria in Australia. The practical effect of this decision was to require parents of TGD children to cede their responsibility for medical treatment decision-making to the Family Court. Constrained by the precedent established in *Marion's Case*,[138] Nicholson CJ nonetheless endeavoured to move beyond the confines of what he described as a 'protective' and 'paternalistic' jurisdiction, accepting that 'in modern thinking about children and young people', the welfare jurisdiction under section 67ZC of the Family Law Act 'must be understood with regard to their rights'.[139]

iii. Re Bernadette: An unsuccessful attempt to reclaim decisional privacy for TGD children

Up until *Re Bernadette*,[140] applications to the Family Court for authorisation of medical treatment for children experiencing gender dysphoria had followed the approach in *Re Alex* (2004). *Re Bernadette* was the first in which the Family Court was asked to reconsider the issue of whether court authorisation was necessary. At the time of the hearing at first instance, Bernadette was 15 years of age. It was agreed that Bernadette was not *Gillick* competent to consent to the treatment herself. There was also no dispute about the proposed treatment or its appropriateness. Orders were made by consent, pursuant to section 67ZC of the Family Law Act, enabling Bernadette to commence stage one, and later stage two, treatment. However, Bernadette's parents sought that the Family Court determine a number of questions of law, which would apply to all future childhood gender dysphoria cases. One of these questions concerned, relevantly, whether the parent of a child with gender dysphoria has the authority to lawfully authorise stage one and/or stage two medical treatment without a court order.[141] As the parties were unable to settle terms of a stated case for referral to the Full Court for determination,[142] it remained for the trial judge, Collier J, to determine the issues.[143]

Bernadette's parents argued that *Re Alex* (2004) had been wrongly decided. They submitted that, had Nicholson CJ in that case had the benefit of evidence

137 See, eg, Rachael Wallbank, '*Re Kevin* in Perspective' (2004) 9(2) *Deakin Law Review* 461, 487–93; *Re Sam* (n 61) 433–4 [81]–[85] (Murphy J).
138 *Re Alex* (2004) (n 2) 116 [152] (Nicholson CJ). But see Wallbank (n 137) 489.
139 *Re Alex* (2004) (n 2) 116 [154].
140 *Re Bernadette* (n 16).
141 Ibid 243–5 [3]–[4] (Collier J).
142 See *Family Law Act* (n 12) s 94A(1).
143 Collier J was satisfied that he could do so by virtue of Part 10.3 of the *Family Law Rules 2004* (Cth): see *Re Bernadette* (n 16) 245 [10]. That Part enabled a party to apply for a decision on any issue, if the decision may: (a) dispose of all or part of the case; (b) make a trial unnecessary; (c) make a trial substantially shorter; or (d) save substantial costs.

and submissions that were now available to Collier J, then the judgment may have been different and 'the necessity for proceedings of this type ... may have been avoided, and may in future be avoided'.[144] Collier J in *Re Bernadette* was not satisfied on the evidence that there had been 'such a change in the state of medical knowledge' that would enable him to disregard the views of the High Court in *Marion's Case* and of Nicholson CJ in *Re Alex* (2004).[145] His Honour's stated concern was the risk of making the 'wrong decision', as referred to in both of those earlier authorities.[146]

Bernadette had turned 18 years of age by the time Collier J's reasons for judgment and final orders were published. The reasons exposed his Honour's immense anxiety at the prospect of making a decision that would impact on TGD children beyond Bernadette.[147] Collier J repeated 'to the point of boredom' that Bernadette's parents, who displayed their 'genuine concern and interest' in the difficulties experienced by other TGD children, sought findings that would have 'general application'.[148] His Honour considered it 'unsafe' to determine the questions raised 'as matters of general or theoretical application',[149] because the evidence was particular to the case of Bernadette. Collier J emphasised that 'it is not ... the function of the single judge to make what might be called "findings of general application for future use"'.[150] To do so in this case, it was said, could expose children to 'unwarranted risks'[151] and 'do a disservice to other persons contemplating treatment'.[152] On this issue, Collier J explained:

> To say as a rule of general application that parents could or could not authorise such treatment could mean that parents without the full understanding, that the parents in this case clearly have, could make a decision which was ill informed and may well have a disastrous long term affect [sic] on a child, either by permitting or denying the child access to treatment.[153]

Collier J concluded that it would not be in the best interests of every child experiencing gender dysphoria to enable parents or guardians to authorise medical treatment on their behalf. In reaching this conclusion, Collier J recognised the potential danger of relationships marked by a power imbalance, as that between parent and child.[154] His Honour was satisfied that, 'in the best interests of chil-

144 *Re Bernadette* (n 16) 245–6 [11] (Collier J).
145 Ibid 260 [123].
146 Ibid.
147 See Ibid 243 [1], 253 [63]–[65], 260 [124].
148 Ibid 253 [63]–[64].
149 Ibid [65].
150 Ibid [67].
151 Ibid 260 [126].
152 Ibid 253 [68].
153 Ibid.
154 See Chapter 1 (Section 1.4.4).

dren' (collectively), the Family Court must retain the power to authorise medical treatment in respect of a particular child and to determine on a case-by-case basis whether the child's parents could authorise that treatment.[155] An appeal by Bernadette's parents was dismissed.[156]

4.4 Judicial validation of gender identity

The final section of this chapter articulates the role of courts in moderating the relationship between a child's decisional privacy and identity. The negative feelings that children with gender dysphoria experience tend to emanate from a need to be 'validated' in their gender identity.[157] The Family Court of Australia has explained, summarising expert evidence in proceedings for the determination of a child's *Gillick* competence, that with such treatment:

> [t]he child ... comes to feel much more at ease with his body in terms of its appearance and functioning, as well as with his social identity. Other people will be much more likely to perceive him to be male, and will automatically treat him as such. This social validation further validates the child's sense of core gender identity ...[158]

This view supports the understanding of identity as having both an 'external' aspect (bodily appearance and functioning), as well as an 'internal' aspect (the features unique to the child's own sense of identity).[159] Children's right to decisional privacy facilitates or reinforces, amongst other rights, the right to preservation of identity under Article 8(1) of the CRC. The CRC Committee has not defined the term 'identity' in Article 8,[160] such that the term remains 'inherently fluid and ambiguous'.[161] However, Masson and Harrison have observed that '[m]any accounts of identity describe a complex constellation of inter-related aspects of identity which contribute to a sense of self, self-knowledge and self-awareness'.[162] Tobin and Todres, for instance, have described identity as a 'constellation of historical and evolving characteristics' that offer children an understanding of

155 *Re Bernadette* (n 16) 260 [126].
156 See *Bernadette Appeal* (n 46).
157 *Re Alex* (2004) (n 2) 106–7 [99].
158 *Re Desi* [2017] FamCA 203, [29] (Johnston J). See also *Re Anita* [2016] FamCA 1137, [30] (McClelland J); *Re Sage* [2017] FamCA 910, [38] (Johnston J); *Re Lincoln* [2016] FamCA 267, [26] (Stevenson J).
159 John Tobin and Jonathan Todres, 'Article 8: The Right to Preservation of a Child's Identity' in John Tobin (ed), *The UN Convention on the Rights of the Child: A Commentary* (Oxford University Press, 2019) 281, 294.
160 Ibid 292; Judith Masson and Christine Harrison, 'Identity: Mapping the Frontiers' in Nigel Lowe and Gillian Douglas (eds), *Families Across Frontiers* (Martinus Nijhoff, 1996) 277.
161 Alice Hearst, *Children and the Politics of Cultural Belonging* (Cambridge University Press, 2012) 19.
162 Masson and Harrison (n 160) 278.

'where they have come from, who they are, and the right to decide who they will become'.[163] The term 'identity' in the context of this CRC right can be understood as 'everything constituting the person's feeling of self and distinguishing the person from others'.[164] While not expressly mentioned in Article 8 of the CRC, the child's right to identity arguably embraces gender identity.[165] The European Court of Human Rights ('ECtHR') has recognised elements of identity as falling within the scope of Article 8 of the ECHR, which provides for the right to respect for private and family life.[166] It has held that this right includes the 'freedom to define [one's] gender identity, one of the most basic essentials of self-determination'.[167]

The right to preservation of identity under Article 8 of the CRC requires states to adopt effective measures to ensure that a child does not need to hide or suppress elements of their identity.[168] The Family Court of Australia has described the 'fundamental task' of the law, in a socio-legal context underpinned by a male/female gender binary, as being 'to assign individuals to one category or the other, including individuals whose characteristics are not uniformly those of one or other sex'.[169] Western cultural norms – which have both influenced and been influenced by the law's gender dualism[170] – for a long time made it generally unacceptable for people who did not fit neatly into the categories of male or female to 'come out' publicly as TGD.[171] For individuals with gender dysphoria

163 Tobin and Todres (n 159) 285.

164 Kirsten Sandberg, 'The Rights of LGBTI Children under the Convention on the Rights of the Child' (2015) 33(4) *Nordic Journal of Human Rights* 337, 343.

165 In support of this argument, see ibid 343–4; Jones (n 69) 389; Ana-Maria Bucataru, 'Using the Convention on the Rights of the Child to Project the Rights of the Transgender Children and Adolescents: The Context of Education and Transition' (2016) 3(1) *Queen Mary Human Rights Review* 59, 62–3; Phil CW Chan, 'No, It Is Not Just A Phase: An Adolescent's Right to Sexual Minority Identity under the United Nations Convention on the Rights of the Child' (2006) 10(2) *International Journal of Human Rights* 161.

166 See, eg, *Jaggi v Switzerland* (Application No 58757/00, 2006) [37]; *Bensaid v United Kingdom* (2001) 33 EHRR 10, [47].

167 *YY v Turkey* [2015] ECHR 257, [102]. See also *Van Kück v Germany* (2003) 37 EHRR 51, [73]; *Garçon & Nicot v France* [2017] ECHR 338, [95]; *SV v Italy* (Application No 55216/08, 2018) [56]–[58].

168 Tobin and Todres (n 159) 295–6.

169 *Kevin v Attorney-General (Cth)* (2001) 165 FLR 404, 473 [315] (Chisholm J). See also Laura Grenfell and Anne Hewitt, 'Gender Regulation: Restrictive, Facilitative or Transformative Laws?' (2012) 34(4) *Sydney Law Review* 761; Abigail W Lloyd, 'Defining the Human: Are Transgender People Strangers to the Law?' (2005) 20(1) *Berkeley Journal of Gender, Law & Justice* 150; Andrew Alston, 'Transgender Rights as Legal Rights' (1999) 7 *Canterbury Law Review* 329.

170 See Laura Grenfell, 'Making Sex: Law's Narratives of Sex, Gender and Identity' (2003) 23(1) *Legal Studies* 66.

171 Murphy (n 6) 624; P L Chau and Jonathan Herring, 'Defining, Assigning and Designing Sex' (2002) 16(3) *International Journal of Law, Policy and the Family* 327, 358. See also Anniken Sørlie, 'Legal Gender Meets Reality: A Socio-Legal Children's Perspective' (2015) 33(4) *Nordic Journal of Human Rights* 353, 354.

who do not seek medical treatment and 'just suffer out there',[172] this 'survival method' known as 'stealth' involves them living a public life in denial of their experience of gender diversity.[173] Such 'stealth' and 'subterfuge' clearly result in a violation of TGD people's decisional privacy rights, because those who 'choos[e] to live a false and secret existence in order to live free of physical harm and/or prejudice'[174] do not live an authentic life. Rather, their decisions, behaviour and choices, which contribute to defining their identity, are subject to interference (whether direct or indirect) by other individuals and the state.

The nature of a state's obligation to respect a child's right to preserve their identity pursuant to Article 8 of the CRC also requires the state 'to take reasonable measures to enable children not simply to preserve their identity in a historical sense, but to enable them to discover and develop their identity'.[175] This obligation extends to supporting and protecting the dynamic, evolving elements of a child's identity.[176] For children experiencing gender dysphoria to exercise their decisional privacy rights in this context involves having the freedom to eschew their birth sex and the associated predetermined gender practices and roles imposed by society and law, including by participating meaningfully in decision-making about their desired medical treatment. The corollary is that the need to obtain court authorisation to commence treatment deprives children with gender dysphoria of the ability to exercise, consistently with their evolving capacities, autonomy in asserting 'who they are' and exercising their right 'to decide who they will become'.[177] Court involvement in the medical treatment process has triggered both a literal and a figurative 'identity crisis' for TGD children. The critical question is whether these children can reconcile the person they take themselves to be, with the law's and society's expectations of who they are and who they ought to be.

4.5 Conclusion

This chapter has explained parental responsibility to consent to children's medical treatment and 'special medical procedures' which lie beyond the scope of that responsibility. Such procedures must be authorised by the Family Court pursuant to its welfare jurisdiction under section 67ZC of the Family Law Act. This chapter has also examined two factual issues that determine the exercise of the welfare jurisdiction in the medical treatment context, highlighting that children are often

172 *Re Brodie (Special Medical Procedure)* [2008] FamCA 334, [231] (Carter J).
173 Wallbank (n 137) 463. See, eg, *Re Alex* (2009) (n 2) 352 [174] (Bryant CJ noting that Alex was 'forced to resort to a degree of subterfuge to avoid having his biological gender revealed'.).
174 Wallbank (n 137) 463.
175 Tobin and Todres (n 159) 285. See also Maureen Carroll, 'Transgender Youth, Adolescent Decisionmaking, and *Roper v Simmons*' (2009) 56 *UCLA Law Review* 725.
176 Tobin and Todres (n 159) 293, 295.
177 Ibid 285.

held to a higher standard of competence than adults; and exposing a tension between respecting a child's current views and wishes and protecting the child's future decision-making autonomy. The three judgments discussed to illustrate the development of the welfare jurisdiction, including its extension to medical treatment for childhood gender dysphoria, reflect an uneasy recalibration of the respective responsibilities and duties of parents and the state in relation to children's medical treatment. They expose a judicial awareness of conflicts that are ripe to arise in some cases between the child's best interests and parental interests; as well as assumptions about children's perceived incapacity for rational decision-making and their vulnerability to harm at the hands of those adults tasked with acting in their best interests. The final part of this chapter has articulated the nexus between children's decisional privacy and right to identity under Article 8 of the CRC. The children's rights analysis of three appellate judgments in the ensuing chapters will illustrate that the law 'conditions the formation of certain types of identity', for it 'allows, permits, protects and provides; it also recognises, misrecognises and ignores identities'.[178]

178 Jill Marshall, *Human Rights Law and Personal Identity* (Routledge, 2014) 18, 19. See also Sørlie (n 171) 354–5; Eric Mitnick, *Rights, Groups, and Self-Invention: Group-Differentiated Rights in Liberal Theory* (Ashgate, 2006) 81.

5 'Harsh' but 'bound'

Re-reading the Full Court's judgment in *Re Jamie*

5.1 Introduction

The previous chapter provided the socio-historical context of the case study of this book. It traced the development of the Family Court of Australia's welfare jurisdiction under section 67ZC of the *Family Law Act 1975* (Cth) ('Family Law Act') in the context of special medical procedure applications, including its extension to medical treatment for childhood gender dysphoria. This chapter applies the concept of children's right to decisional privacy to analyse the judgment of the Full Court of the Family Court of Australia ('Full Court') in the case of *Re Jamie*.[1] The *Re Jamie* proceedings concerned the authorisation of stage one treatment (puberty blockers) and stage two treatment (gender-affirming hormones)[2] for 'Jamie',[3] who had been diagnosed with 'gender identity disorder'.[4] *Re Jamie* provided the first appellate opportunity to consider whether medical treatment for gender dysphoria was still a 'special medical procedure'[5] that attracted the Family Court's welfare jurisdiction under section 67ZC of the Family Law Act. In a judgment delivered in July 2013, the Full Court held that stage one treatment fell within the scope of parental responsibility to consent,[6] but that court authorisation remained appropriate for stage two treatment, unless the child was competent to consent to the treatment (that is, *Gillick* competent).[7]

1 [2013] FamCAFC 110 ('*Jamie Appeal*').
2 See Chapter 4 (Section 4.1).
3 The young person the subject of the *Re Jamie* proceedings is referred to in this chapter by her pseudonym, 'Jamie', which was adopted in the judgments. Section 121 of the *Family Law Act 1975* (Cth) ('*Family Law Act*') prohibits the publication of identifying details of proceedings.
4 As per the fourth edition of the *Diagnostic and Statistical Manual of Mental Disorders*: American Psychiatric Association, *Diagnostic and Statistical Manual of Mental Disorders: DSM-IV* (American Psychiatric Association Publishing, 4th ed, 1994) ('*DSM-IV*'). At the time of writing, the condition is known as 'gender dysphoria': see American Psychiatric Association, *Diagnostic and Statistical Manual of Mental Disorders: DSM-5* (American Psychiatric Association Publishing, 5th ed, 2013) ('*DSM-5*').
5 See Chapter 4 (Section 4.3.2).
6 *Jamie Appeal* (n 1) [106]–[108] (Bryant CJ), [179] (Finn J).
7 Ibid [129], [140] (Bryant CJ). See *Gillick v West Norfolk and Wisbech Area Health Authority* [1986] AC 112. On the issue of *Gillick* competence, see Chapter 4 (Section 4.3.1).

DOI: 10.4324/9781003224167-8

The Full Court concluded 'with some reluctance' that the nature of the stage two treatment required the Family Court to determine the question of *Gillick* competence.[8]

This chapter first offers a brief history of the *Re Jamie* proceedings. It then applies a children's rights approach to decisional privacy[9] to analyse the judgment of the Full Court. Four features of the judgment are examined: the Full Court's pathologisation of Jamie in its selection and framing of the issues; the 'selective' and 'rhetorical' approach to children's rights[10] adopted by the Court in its reasoning; Jamie's limited opportunity to put her views before the Court; and Jamie's objectification in the judgment, as well as the evident tension between Jamie's right to share information about her court experience and the stringent, legislatively mandated informational privacy protection for the proceedings. This analysis supports the argument that, through its conclusion that the Family Court must remain involved in decision-making regarding stage two treatment for gender dysphoria, the Full Court in *Re Jamie* violated the decisional privacy rights of Jamie and other TGD children seeking to access such treatment. It did so by impairing Jamie's ability to determine, consistently with her evolving capacities and with the direction and guidance of her parents, what she wanted to do to her own body, which adversely impacted Jamie's autonomy and identity formation.

5.2 The *Re Jamie* proceedings: A brief history

5.2.1 The initial Family Court proceedings

Jamie was almost 11 years old at the time of the initial Family Court proceedings.[11] She had been diagnosed by medical experts with 'gender identity disorder'.[12] Jamie's parents applied to the Family Court for the authorisation of stage one medical treatment for Jamie. This would involve the administration of puberty suppressant hormones ('puberty blockers') to suppress male puberty and additional treatment of oestrogen. Dessau J at first instance held that stage one treatment was in Jamie's best interests and made an order authorising Jamie's parents to consent to that treatment.[13] In relation to stage two treatment – which would involve the administration of oestrogen as the gender-affirming hormone – her Honour concluded that the two stages of treatment could be viewed as a single treatment plan. However, she held that the Family Court could not

8 Ibid [136]–[137] (Bryant CJ), [182], [186], [188] (Finn J), [192]–[196] (Strickland J).

9 The fundamental features of which were presented in Chapters 2 and 3.

10 John Tobin, 'Judging the Judges: Are they Adopting the Rights Approach in Matters involving Children?' (2009) 33(2) *Melbourne University Law Review* 579, 597–601 ('Judging the Judges').

11 *Re Jamie (Special Medical Procedure)* [2011] FamCA 248 ('*Jamie Stage One*').

12 See American Psychiatric Association, *DSM-IV* (n 4).

13 *Jamie Stage One* (n 11) [7] (Dessau J).

determine, when Jamie was only ten years old, what would be in her best interests in six years' time.[14] Authorisation of stage two treatment would thus require a further application to the Family Court. Dessau J acknowledged the decisional privacy implications of this decision for Jamie's parents, who were likely to view further court proceedings as a 'constraint on their freedom to determine, with Jamie, issues about which there has been a great deal of thinking, advice and soul-searching'.[15] Her Honour also noted the 'risk of uncertainty for Jamie at an age and stage when it may be beneficial for her to feel empowered to participate in these decisions outside the shadow of the court'.[16]

5.2.2 The Full Court appeal

Jamie's parents appealed the decision to the Full Court of the Family Court. They argued that treatment of gender dysphoria was not a 'special medical procedure' which displaced their parental responsibility to decide upon the appropriate treatment for their child (ground 1); and that Dessau J erred in concluding that stage two treatment should be the subject of a further application to the Family Court (ground 2).[17] Jamie's parents sought to distinguish cases of childhood gender dysphoria from the facts of *Secretary, Department of Health and Community Services v JWB & SMB* ('*Marion's Case*').[18] A majority of the High Court in *Marion's Case* held that sterilisation was a special medical procedure that displaced parental responsibility and required court authorisation, because it was 'invasive', 'irreversible' and 'non-therapeutic' (that is, not carried out 'to treat some malfunction or disease').[19] Other factors that contributed to its classification as a special medical procedure were the 'significant risk of making the wrong decision', either as to a child's present or future capacity to consent, or about the best interests of a child who cannot consent, and the 'particularly grave' consequences of a wrong decision being made.[20]

Jamie's parents argued that medical treatment for childhood gender dysphoria was not like sterilisation, because it was reversible; it was for therapeutic purposes, being a medically recognised, diagnosed psychiatric condition with well-recognised treatment strategies; and no one other than the child stood to benefit directly from the treatment.[21] Jamie's parents also argued that the need to apply to the court in a case where there was 'no controversy' between the parents, medical practitioners and the child, caused undue anxiety, delay and expense.[22]

14 Ibid [123]–[124], [130].
15 Ibid [129].
16 Ibid.
17 *Jamie Appeal* (n 1) [12]–[14] (Bryant CJ).
18 (1992) 175 CLR 218 ('*Marion's Case*'). See Chapter 4 (Section 4.3.2.i).
19 Ibid 250 (Mason CJ, Dawson, Toohey and Gaudron JJ).
20 Ibid.
21 *Jamie Appeal* (n 1) [23]–[27] (Bryant CJ).
22 Ibid [28].

The matters raised on appeal were not the subject of dispute at trial. They could only be agitated before the Full Court because they raised a point of law.[23] The Full Court granted leave to a public authority to intervene in the appeal.[24]

The primary question for the Full Court was whether two-stage treatment for gender dysphoria was a 'special medical procedure' for which consent was beyond the bounds of parental responsibility and required Family Court authorisation under section 67ZC of the Family Law Act.[25] The Full Court held that stage one treatment fell within the 'wide ambit of parental responsibility' that parents had when a child was not yet able to make their own medical treatment decisions.[26] Bryant CJ justified this conclusion on the basis of the 'evolving state of medical knowledge';[27] and the view that, in childhood gender dysphoria cases, it was unlikely that 'parental interests would be anything other than the welfare of the child (as opposed to having a collateral interest in having the treatment carried out)'.[28]

The Full Court distinguished stage one and stage two treatment, focusing on the reversibility and side effects of each stage, as well as the child's capacity to consent.[29] Bryant CJ held that court authorisation was appropriate for stage two treatment, unless the child had capacity to consent (that is, the child was *Gillick* competent).[30] Her Honour held that if the child was found to be *Gillick* competent, there was no role for the court at all.[31] On the more 'vexing' question of *who* should determine the question of *Gillick* competence – the child's medical practitioners or the Family Court – the Full Court concluded 'with some reluctance' that the nature of stage two treatment required the Court to determine that question.[32] Bryant CJ conceded that ongoing court involvement was 'harsh', but considered the Full Court 'bound by what the High Court said in *Marion's Case*'.[33]

23 Ibid [4].

24 This public authority was identified in the reasons of Dessau J as the Office of the Public Advocate: see *Jamie Stage One* (n 11). Leave was granted pursuant to section 92 of the *Family Law Act*, upon the conditions that the public authority was not permitted to call or tender any evidence in relation to the appeal; and was confined to making written and oral submissions in relation to the first ground of appeal: see *Re Jamie* (2012) 257 FLR 41 ('*Jamie Application to Intervene*').

25 *Jamie Appeal* (n 1) [5] (Bryant CJ), [170] (Finn J).

26 Ibid [106]–[108] (Bryant CJ), [179] (Finn J).

27 Ibid [106].

28 Ibid [107].

29 Ibid [111], [114] (Bryant CJ).

30 Ibid [129], [140].

31 Ibid [129].

32 Ibid [136]–[137] (Bryant CJ), [182], [186], [188] (Finn J), [192]–[196] (Strickland J).

33 Ibid [138].

5.2.3 Family Court authorisation of stage two treatment

In light of the Full Court's decision, Jamie's parents applied to the Family Court to determine whether Jamie, who was now 15 years of age, was able to consent to stage two treatment. Thornton J observed that there was no controversy about Jamie's diagnosis, her wishes or her competence to provide informed consent to the proposed treatment.[34] Jamie's parents and her treating medical practitioners supported the application. In holding that Jamie was *Gillick* competent, Thornton J found that she had demonstrated the 'intellectual capacity and sophistication to understand the information relevant to making the decision and to appreciate the potential consequences'.[35] Her Honour also noted that Jamie's 'clear' and unwavering views were illustrated by a letter she had written to the Court and her scrutiny of the evidence in support of the application.[36]

Having provided an overview of *what* the Family Court in the various *Re Jamie* proceedings decided, the focus now turns to *how* the Full Court in particular reached its conclusions. The next section analyses the Full Court's judgment from the perspective of Jamie's right to decisional privacy.

5.3 A children's rights analysis of the Full Court's judgment in *Re Jamie*

The judgment of the Full Court in *Re Jamie* arguably perpetuated the construction of children experiencing gender dysphoria as vulnerable 'becomings' in need of protection, who might be seen, and to a very limited extent heard, in court proceedings, but not listened to by adult decision-makers. The Full Court's substantive decision-making, together with procedural aspects of the proceedings, undermined Jamie's decision-making autonomy in relation to her body and identity. However, a 'general intellectual environment'[37] emerged from the Full Court's judgment of framing issues concerning TGD children seeking medical treatment in terms of their rights. The Full Court made an effort to engage with children's rights, discussing the submissions of the Australian Human Rights Commission ('AHRC'), as intervener in the appeal, which invoked various articles of the CRC. The ensuing sections articulate this argument through an analysis of four features of the Full Court's judgment.

34 *Re Jamie* [2015] FamCA 455, [3] (Thornton J) ('*Jamie Stage Two*').
35 Ibid [81].
36 Ibid [81]–[83].
37 Ronald Dworkin, *Law's Empire* (Belknap Press, 1986) 88; Tobin, 'Judging the Judges' (n 10) 583.

5.3.1 *Selecting and framing the 'potentially far reaching'*[38] *issues*

The Full Court in *Re Jamie* framed the issues for determination in a way that recognised the broader implications of the decision for other TGD children seeking access to medical treatment for gender dysphoria. However, it emphasised the rights of Jamie's parents, the responsibilities of medical practitioners and the importance of maintaining court involvement, over the rights of Jamie herself. For Jamie's proposed medical treatment to be considered 'therapeutic' (on the distinction between therapeutic and non-therapeutic treatment drawn in *Marion's Case*)[39] and hence within the bounds of parental responsibility to consent, Jamie's parents had to establish that Jamie suffered from a bodily 'malfunction or disease'.[40] The Full Court thus assigned Jamie the various identities of a child under a disability, who had a mental disorder and a psychological condition. The discursive power of such terms was to construct Jamie as having something 'wrong' with her.

i. *Recognising the potential impacts on TGD children beyond Jamie*

The scope of state intervention, through Family Court authorisation of special medical procedures for children, ultimately depends on what is considered to be the appropriate degree of paternalism required to promote children's rights. Freeman has argued that the rhetoric of children's rights has been 'couched predominantly in child-saving language, in terms of salvation'.[41] The Family Court's concern in gender dysphoria proceedings has been to protect the individual child the subject of the proceedings, with reservations expressed about expounding principles of general application that would affect TGD children more broadly. In *Re Bernadette*,[42] Collier J steadfastly refused to make a finding of 'general application for future use'.[43]

In *Re Jamie*, however, the Full Court acknowledged the significance of the appeal for not only Jamie, but for all TGD children in Australia. The Full Court noted that the 'potentially far reaching' issue agitated on appeal, regarding the characterisation of childhood gender dysphoria as a special medical procedure, raised the possibility of a 'significant change in the law' and the 'overturning of many cases',[44] including *Re Alex* (2004)[45] and *Re Bernadette*.[46] For this reason, three parties in addition to Jamie's parents (the appellants) were involved in the

38 *Jamie Application to Intervene* (n 24) 50 [45] (Bryant CJ, Finn and Strickland JJ).
39 See *Marion's Case* (n 18) 250 (Mason CJ, Dawson, Toohey and Gaudron JJ).
40 Ibid.
41 Michael Freeman, *The Moral Status of Children: Essays on the Rights of the Child* (Kluwer Law International, 1997) 84 ('*Moral Status*').
42 (2010) 44 FLR 242 ('*Re Bernadette*').
43 Ibid 253 [67] (Collier J). See Chapter 4 (Section 4.3.2.iii).
44 *Jamie Application to Intervene* (n 24) 49–50 [44]–[45] (Bryant CJ, Finn and Strickland JJ).
45 (2004) 180 FLR 89 ('*Re Alex* (2004)').
46 *Re Bernadette* (n 42).

hearing: an independent children's lawyer (ICL) appointed to represent Jamie's interests; and two interveners, the Office of the Public Advocate ('OPA') and the AHRC.[47] The Full Court's acknowledgement of the public policy ramifications of its decision raised the broader question for Jamie herself, and for the law, about how Jamie's identity 'should be defined and managed'.[48] How the Full Court perceived Jamie's predicament, and that of other TGD children seeking access to medical treatment for gender dysphoria, was necessarily influenced by how it constructed Jamie.

ii. Jamie as a child under a disability and suffering a mental illness

Jamie was almost 12 years of age at the time of the Full Court hearing and 13 years of age when the Full Court delivered its judgment. Throughout the judgment, the various judges of the Full Court referred to Jamie as a 'child'. The only references to 'young person' or 'young people' were in the context of discussing the submissions of the AHRC,[49] while the submissions of the OPA referred to 'differing professional opinions as to how a child or adolescent should be treated for gender identity disorder'.[50] Bryant CJ considered Jamie's age relevant to the child/young person nomenclature distinction, noting that while every case must be considered according to the level of maturity and understanding of the particular child, 16 is 'an age at which children are regarded, for some purposes, as persons capable of autonomous decision-making'.[51] An 'all-or-nothing' approach to children's autonomy is problematic from a children's rights perspective, for it overlooks the importance of the child's evolving capacities.[52] Assumptions cannot be made about a child's capacity solely on the basis of the child's biological age, given that various factors influence the development of children's capacities to form their own views.[53]

At first blush, the Full Court's choice of descriptor for Jamie – 'child' – might appear trivial to the proceedings. However, the judgment in *Re Alex* (2004)[54] provides a useful comparator. Alex was 13 years of age at the time of the initial application to the Family Court. Nicholson CJ made it clear that, while the Family Law Act and the relevant case law referred to 'a child', his Honour preferred to use the expression 'young person' when referring to Alex in the judgment,

47 *Jamie Appeal* (n 1) [6]–[7] (Bryant CJ).
48 *Kevin v Attorney-General (Cth)* (2001) 165 FLR 404, 425 [109] (Chisholm J).
49 *Jamie Appeal* (n 1) [49]–[50], [62]–[63], [84] (Bryant CJ).
50 Ibid [101(e)].
51 Ibid [130].
52 See Chapter 1 (Section 1.4.3) and Chapter 2 (Section 2.3.2).
53 CRC Committee, *General Comment No 12 (2009): The Right of the Child to be Heard*, UN Doc CRC/C/GC/12 (20 July 2009) [29] ('*General Comment No 12*'). See also Richard Chisholm, 'Children's Participation in Family Court Litigation' (1999) 13(3) *Australian Journal of Family Law* 197, 216.
54 *Re Alex* (2004) (n 45). See Chapter 4 (Section 4.3.2.ii).

having regard to Alex's age and maturity.[55] Nicholson CJ subsequently used the phrase 'child or young person' throughout the judgment, to emphasise what he considered to be an important distinction. Following the Full Court's decision in *Re Jamie*, the matter returned to the Family Court for an assessment of Jamie's *Gillick* competence to consent to stage two treatment. Thornton J described Jamie, who was 15 at the time of this hearing, as 'a young person in the transition phase from childhood to adulthood referred to in the *Gillick* case'.[56] Just as Nicholson CJ's conscious choice in *Re Alex* (2004) to refer to Alex as a 'young person' recognised the importance of the Family Court treating young people as subjects with rights, the Full Court's terminology in *Re Jamie* reflected the ingrained conceptualisation of children as vulnerable objects of concern.[57] As did the way in which the Full Court pathologised Jamie.

On appeal, the Full Court was asked to relate Jamie's condition to the factors devised by the High Court in *Marion's Case*, so that Jamie's parents could succeed in their claim. Jamie's parents argued that medical treatment for gender dysphoria in children was 'therapeutic' and so within the bounds of parental authority to consent. The argument that Jamie suffered from a 'bodily malfunction or disease'[58] warranting 'therapeutic' treatment contradicted the view that 'transgender is an expression of sexual identity that is part of the normal continuum of human diversity'.[59] As a consequence, Jamie was given labels that had the potential to harm the formation of her evolving identity, as well as the extent to which she could control her self-presentation.[60]

By virtue of her diagnosis, the Full Court placed Jamie in a 'group of persons generally referred to in current literature as … transgendered'.[61] Bryant CJ acknowledged that affixing the term 'disorder' to individuals who identify as

55 Ibid 94 [18] (Nicholson CJ). See also Family Law Council, *Involving and Representing Children in Family Law* (Discussion Paper, May 1995) 31 ('the word "child" is not entirely appropriate when applied to young persons approaching adulthood'); *Duffy v Gomes (No 2)* (2015) 299 FLR 108, 155 [72] (Judge Harman noting, in relation to young people aged 13 and 15 years: 'These young people – "children" being a somewhat erroneous term at their ages').

56 *Jamie Stage Two* (n 34) [82].

57 See Chapter 1 (Section 1.4.1). See also Carol Smart, Amanda Wade and Bren Neale, 'Objects of Concern? Children and Divorce' (1999) 11(4) *Child and Family Law Quarterly* 365; John Tobin, 'Understanding Children's Rights: A Vision beyond Vulnerability' (2015) 84 *Nordic Journal of International Law* 155, 171, 176.

58 *Jamie Appeal* (n 1) [32].

59 Melinda Jones, 'Children's Health Rights and Gender Issues' in Jozef HHM Dorscheidt and Jaap E Doek (eds), *Children's Rights in Health Care* (Brill, 2018) 382, 410.

60 See Chapter 4 (Section 4.4).

61 *Jamie Appeal* (n 1) [8] (Bryant CJ). Bryant CJ affirmed Jamie as belonging to this group by citing the *Sex Discrimination Amendment (Sexual Orientation, Gender Identity and Intersex Status) Act 2013* (Cth) and the *Australian Government Guidelines on the Recognition of Sex and Gender* (July 2013), which were said to indicate that TGD people are an 'identifiable group in our society' whose 'right to live as a member of the sex with which they feel compatible' should be respected: at [9]–[10].

transgender aroused 'discomfort'.[62] While her Honour did not need to determine the correctness of that characterisation, she remarked that:

> It may be that in time to come, transsexualism will no longer be described as a disorder, but for the time being, and for the foreseeable future, the weight of professional opinion is that it represents a particular category of pathology or mental illness.[63]

Bryant CJ framed the issue concerning the definition of 'gender identity disorder' in terms of the congruence between an individual's self-identity and physical self-representation, and society's expectations of 'normal' characteristics of male and female gender categories. Her Honour's view was that medical treatment for gender dysphoria 'is not … the alteration of an otherwise healthy body to accommodate a psychological imperative, but rather it is the alignment of the body with the person's self-identity'.[64] An effect of drawing a distinction between an individual's view of themselves and society's expectations of how a person 'should' be, is that a self-identity which departs from the 'normative' – that is, the expected physical characteristics of a particular gender – is considered abnormal.[65] Bryant CJ added that, '[o]nce it is accepted that there is no normative state, at least not in every person, then the absolute necessity of aligning the self-identity and the physical characteristics becomes apparent'.[66]

While there have been shifts over time in judicial language used to describe individuals who identify as transgender or gender diverse, the semantic effect of such labels as disorder, dysphoria and mental illness, is to continue to pathologise the child experiencing gender dysphoria.[67] The discursive power of such terms is to construct a TGD child as having something 'wrong' with them, which subsequently justifies both medical and state intervention. In this way, the law not only reflects the child's identity, but also contributes to its (re)production.

62 *Jamie Appeal* (n 1) [69]. See also *Re Alex* (2004) (n 45) 124 [197] (Nicholson CJ noting that 'Alex and other people who have longed for transition to the opposite sex may find it offensive to find the incompatibility between their sense of self and the sex of their body being categorised as a "disease" or a "malfunction"'; and questioning whether the condition with which Alex had been diagnosed was properly described as a 'disorder'. Nicholson CJ preferred to use the 'more accurate' expression 'dysphoria' throughout the judgment: at 92 [2]).

63 *Jamie Appeal* (n 1) [69].

64 Ibid [67].

65 Moira Gatens, 'Can Human Rights Accommodate Women's Rights? Towards an Embodied Account of Social Norms, Social Meaning, and Cultural Change' (2004) 3(3) *Contemporary Political Theory* 275, 280, 283–4.

66 *Jamie Appeal* (n 1) [68].

67 Fiona Kelly, 'Treating the Transgendered Child: The Full Court's Decision in *Re Jamie*' (2014) 28(1) *Australian Journal of Family Law* 83, 83 n 3. See also Diana Bryant, 'It's My Body, Isn't It'? Children, Medical Treatment and Human Rights' (2009) 35(2) *Monash University Law Review* 193, 209–10 ('It's My Body').

The perceived pathologisation of gender diversity, through the classification of gender dysphoria as a 'mental disorder' under the fifth edition of the *Diagnostic and Statistical Manual of Mental Disorders* ('*DSM-5*'),[68] remains a matter of controversy.[69] Scholars have argued that the 'transgender child' is a category constructed by medicine and law, which does not exist independently of medico-legal discourse;[70] and that the 'pathologisation' of TGD people has 'plagued' healthcare.[71] An alternative perspective is that the continued clinical classification of gender dysphoria may better facilitate access to specialist support for TGD children.[72]

In a media interview following the decision in *Re Alex* (2009),[73] Bryant CJ said that describing the medical intervention that Alex sought as 'treatment' when there was no physical illness or injury was 'just semantics'; and that it was 'overwhelming that these children feel they are in the wrong body'.[74] A children's rights approach to decisional privacy does not gloss over judicial terminology selection as 'just semantics'. Pathologising children who are the subject of gender dysphoria proceedings contributes to a violation of their decisional privacy rights. This is because these children are faced with an unenviable choice: to incorporate

68 American Psychiatric Association, *DSM-5* (n 4).

69 See, eg, David C Rettew, 'Apples to Committee Consensus: The Challenge of Gender Identity Classification' (2012) 59(3) *Journal of Homosexuality* 450; Roberto Vitelli, 'Gender Dysphoria in Adults and Adolescents as a Mental Disorder … But, What Is a Mental Disorder? A Phenomenological/Existential Analysis of a Puzzling Condition' in Beverly L Miller (ed), *Gender Identity: Disorders, Developmental Perspectives and Social Implications* (Nova Science Publishers, 2014) 55; Austin H Johnson, 'Rejecting, Reframing, and Reintroducing: Trans People's Strategic Engagement with the Medicalisation of Gender Dysphoria' (2019) 41(3) *Sociology of Health & Illness* 517, 531–2; Chris Dietz and Ruth Pearce, 'Depathologising Gender: Vulnerability in Trans Health Law' in Chris Dietz, Mitchell Travis and Michael Thomson (eds), *A Jurisprudence of the Body* (Palgrave Macmillan, 2020) 179.

70 Heather Brunskell-Evans, 'The Medico-Legal "Making" of "The Transgender Child"' (2019) 27(4) *Medical Law Review* 640. See also Jones (n 59) 394–6, 410–11; Simona Giordano, 'Medical Treatment for Children with Gender Dysphoria: Conceptual and Ethical Issues' in Baudewijntje P C Kreukels, Thomas D Steensma and Annelou LC de Vries (eds), *Gender Dysphoria and Disorders of Sex Development: Progress in Care and Knowledge* (Springer, 2014) 205, 220–1.

71 Florence Ashley, Colton M St Amand and G Nic Rider, 'The Continuum of Informed Consent Models in Transgender Health' (2021) 38(4) *Family Practice* 543, 543. See also Y Gavriel Ansara and Peter Hegarty, 'Cisgenderism in Psychology: Pathologising and Misgendering Children from 1999 to 2008' (2012) 3(2) *Psychology & Sexuality* 137, 138, 142.

72 Edmund Horowicz, 'Rethinking "Need" for Clinical Support in Transgender and Gender Non-Conforming Children without Clinical Classification: Learning from "the Paper I Almost Wrote"' (2021) 35(3) *Bioethics* 246. See also Johnson (n 69).

73 (2009) 248 FLR 312. This decision authorised stage three treatment (bilateral mastectomies) for Alex.

74 Diana Bryant, quoted in Karen Kissane, 'Young People, Big Decisions', *Sydney Morning Herald* (online, 4 May 2009) <www.smh.com.au/national/young-people-big-decisions-20090504-arxc.html>.

the label – suffering from a mental illness, a disorder, a psychological condition – with its negative connotations, into their self-presentation; or to change their self-presentation to reflect or refute that label. Both options have obvious adverse consequences for TGD children's ability to forge their identity and to live autonomously.

Decisional privacy, it has been argued, is valuable because it provides the conditions or environment that enable individuals to live autonomously.[75] In the case of children experiencing gender dysphoria, a right to decisional privacy serves to 'secure the possibility' for those children to pursue 'a self-determined, authentic life' and their 'individual practical identity'.[76] It offers them the ability to determine, consistently with their evolving capacities and with the direction and guidance of their parents, who they are and who they want to be in the future. The way in which the Full Court in *Re Jamie* constructed Jamie in its judgment had a 'constitutive' impact on Jamie herself, in the sense that Jamie became 'in the eyes of the law, and in the eyes of society, and perhaps even in her own eyes, "disabled"'.[77] In granting leave to the OPA to intervene in the appeal, the Full Court agreed with the OPA's submission that Jamie was a person under a 'disability', as defined in the relevant state legislation.[78] The OPA submitted that it had a series of statutory responsibilities regarding 'the welfare and interests, not just of children, not just of persons who are incompetent, but of, in this instance, children with a disability'.[79]

There is a marked and uncomfortable incongruence between the Full Court's acceptance in *Re Jamie* that Jamie had a 'mental disorder' and was a person under a 'disability', and the remarks of Nicholson CJ in *Re Alex* (2004). In the latter case, while Nicholson CJ permitted a representative of the OPA to observe the proceedings, his Honour explicitly noted that his approval 'was not because any of the parties or I construed that Alex has a disability'.[80] By contrast, the Full Court in *Re Jamie* held that there was scope for gender identity disorder to be categorised as a mental disorder within the fourth edition of the *Diagnostic and Statistical*

75 See Chapter 1 (Section 1.3).

76 Beate Rossler, 'Three Dimensions of Privacy' in Bart van der Sloot and Aviva de Groot (eds), *The Handbook of Privacy Studies: An Interdisciplinary Introduction* (Amsterdam University Press, 2018) 137, 138.

77 Eric Mitnick, *Rights, Groups, and Self-Invention: Group-Differentiated Rights in Liberal Theory* (Ashgate, 2006) 114.

78 Section 3 of the *Guardianship and Administration Act 1986* (Vic), in force at the time of the *Re Jamie* appeal, defined 'disability' in relation to a person as 'intellectual impairment, mental disorder, brain injury, physical disability or dementia'.

79 *Jamie Application to Intervene* (n 24) 46 [24] (Bryant CJ, Finn and Strickland JJ).

80 *Re Alex* (2004) (n 45) 94 [14]–[15]. Nicholson CJ justified the OPA's involvement in the proceedings on the basis that the OPA was also concerned with 'matters of this nature, particularly as they affect children and young people', such that it was 'in the interests of the broader community' for such an office to have the benefit of observing the proceedings.

Manual of Mental Disorders ('*DSM-4*')[81] and so to constitute a 'disability'.[82] The *DSM-5* was published two months before the Full Court delivered its reasons for judgment in *Re Jamie*. Bryant CJ in the judgment observed that the term 'gender identity disorder' in *DSM-4* had been replaced with the term 'gender dysphoria'. The latter term is intended to focus on 'dysphoria as the clinical problem, not identity per se', emphasising the distress for individuals that might accompany the incongruence between their experienced or expressed gender and their gender assigned at birth.[83] However, 'dysphoria' might still be an inapt descriptor.[84] In *Re Jamie*, Jamie had no unease about or dissatisfaction with her identity. She was not 'conflicted about her gender. As far as she is concerned, she is female. She does not want to have to continue living in a male body'.[85]

From a children's rights perspective, judicial choice of language to refer to children reflects society's values, such that 'changes in language, like changes in law, can also motivate changes in attitudes and behaviour'.[86] Word choice and language are telling of broader constructions and perceptions of children in society, of children's relationships with their parents and other adults, and the judicial and political willingness to view children as rights-bearers with distinct interests, views and wishes. The Full Court's labelling of Jamie in its judgment as a child (rather than a young person) under a disability, who was suffering from a mental disorder, enabled the Full Court to sustain the justification for the exercise of the welfare jurisdiction under section 67ZC of the Family Law Act in relation to gender dysphoria treatment: to protect a seemingly 'vulnerable' group of children who had something 'wrong' with them from harm.

iii. Relegating Jamie's rights: Emphasis on the scope of parental rights and responsibilities

Family law proceedings that invoke children's rights usually arise in the context of disputes between adults.[87] Most commonly, the dispute relates to whom children should live with and spend time with following their parents' separation. Another kind of dispute arises in medical treatment cases involving conflicts between

81 American Psychiatric Association, *DSM-IV* (n 4).

82 *Jamie Application to Intervene* (n 24) 50 [49]–[50] (Bryant CJ, Finn and Strickland JJ).

83 *Jamie Appeal* (n 1) [69] n 4 (Bryant CJ).

84 Rachael Wallbank, '*Re Kevin* in Perspective' (2004) 9(2) *Deakin Law Review* 461, 476.

85 See *Jamie Stage One* (n 11) [81] (Dessau J). Jamie's endocrinologist gave evidence that 'this patient is in no way uncertain': at [85].

86 Bernadette J Saunders, 'Words Matter: Textual Abuse of Childhood in the English-Speaking World, and the Role of Language in the Continuing Denial of Children's Rights' (2017) 25 *International Journal of Children's Rights* 519, 522, 526.

87 Helen Stalford, Kathryn Hollingsworth and Stephen Gilmore, 'Introducing *Children's Rights Judgments*' in Helen Stalford, Kathryn Hollingsworth and Stephen Gilmore (eds), *Rewriting Children's Rights Judgments: From Academic Vision to New Practice* (Hart Publishing, 2017) 1, 5 ('Introducing *Children's Rights Judgments*').

parents and their child's treating medical practitioners.[88] Notwithstanding that such proceedings clearly affect various rights of children, arguments tend to be either framed in terms of adults' rights or constructed in a paternalistic way, focusing on children's vulnerability and their need to be protected from harm.[89] As a result, the interests of the child or children the subject of proceedings are obfuscated by, or subsumed into, a discussion of the interests of adults.[90] The first fundamental principle of a children's rights approach aims to address this tendency, by requiring that children are understood as having rights and interests distinct from those of their parents and other caregivers.[91]

The Full Court in *Re Jamie* recognised that the interests of Jamie and other TGD young people were at stake;[92] yet it pursued the claims in relation to Jamie's best interests on adult terms. The 'main issue' on appeal was whether two-stage treatment for gender dysphoria in children was 'a medical procedure … for which consent lies outside the bounds of parental authority and requires the imprimatur of the court'.[93] The appeal thus centred on the scope of *parental* authority and the ambit of the Family Court's welfare jurisdiction under section 67ZC of the Family Law Act. Bryant CJ's framing of the impacts of gender dysphoria proceedings also attests to an adult-centric approach:

> It seems harsh to require *parents* to be subject to the expense of making an application to the court with the attendant expense, stress and possible delay when the doctors and parents are in agreement … .[94]

Absent from her Honour's statement was any express acknowledgement of the impacts of the proceedings on the child or young person seeking medical treatment. Finn J was equally unwilling to impose the costs and stress of further court proceedings, but did make reference to the impact of those proceedings upon 'the child', Jamie:

> I am extremely reluctant to impose upon *the child* and her parents the costs and stress of further court proceedings, particularly when the court

88 See, eg, Rob Heywood, 'Parents and Medical Professionals: Conflict, Cooperation, and Best Interests' (2012) 20(1) *Medical Law Review* 29; Margot Brazier, 'An Intractable Dispute: When Parents and Professionals Disagree' (2005) 13(3) *Medical Law Review* 412; Dominic Wilkinson and Julian Savulescu, *Ethics, Conflict and Medical Treatment for Children: From Disagreement to Dissensus* (Elsevier, 2019) 8–9.

89 Stalford, Hollingsworth and Gilmore, 'Introducing *Children's Rights Judgments*' (n 87) 5. Cf Tobin, 'Judging the Judges' (n 10) 605 (offering examples, from refugee law, custody disputes and sentencing decisions, where courts have conceptualised the issues in terms of the impact on a child's rights).

90 Stalford, Hollingsworth and Gilmore, 'Introducing *Children's Rights Judgments*' (n 87) 10.

91 See Chapter 2 (Section 2.3.1).

92 See Section 5.3.1.i above.

93 *Jamie Appeal* (n 1) [5] (Bryant CJ); see also [170] (Finn J).

94 Ibid [138] (emphasis added).

may ultimately reach the same decision which the child and her parents had already reached with the child's doctors.[95]

That the issues were conceptualised in this way – as being between the scope of parental rights and responsibilities and the Family Court's duty to protect children's best interests – is characteristic of most gender dysphoria judgments up to and including the Full Court's decision in *Re Jamie*. A notable exception is the judgment of Nicholson CJ in *Re Alex* (2004),[96] which offers an excellent example of a substantive approach to children's rights in the context of medical treatment for gender dysphoria.[97]

Even if one were to accept the Full Court's conclusion in *Re Jamie* as sound – that is, agreeing that ongoing court involvement in stage two treatment for gender dysphoria through an assessment of *Gillick* competence was warranted – a children's rights approach would nonetheless have had an important bearing on the proceedings. Jamie herself would have featured as the focal point of the decision, as a subject with distinct rights and interests that deserved recognition and protection. The *Re Jamie* appeal was more than simply a dispute about the appropriate balance of power between parents and the Family Court in relation to the determination of a child's best interests.

5.3.2 Recognising Jamie as a rights-holder: A 'rhetorical' and 'selective' approach to children's rights

Bryant CJ in *Re Jamie* considered Articles 5 and 12 of the CRC to be 'apposite to the question of *Gillick* competence'.[98] Article 5 requires states to respect the responsibilities, rights and duties of parents to provide 'appropriate direction and guidance' to their child in the child's exercise of their rights, in a manner consistent with the child's 'evolving capacities'. Article 12(1) gives the child who is capable of forming a view the right to express their views freely in all matters affecting the child, with those views being given due weight in accordance with the child's age and maturity. Article 12(2) gives the child the opportunity to be heard in judicial proceedings affecting them, either directly or through a representative or an appropriate body.

The use of the CRC in judicial decision-making, according to Tobin, provides 'a very strong indication' of the extent to which this international convention

95 Ibid [185] (emphasis added).
96 *Re Alex* (2004) (n 45).
97 See Chapter 3 (Section 3.3). See also *Re Sean* (2010) 258 FLR 192, 196 [25]–[26] (Murphy J) (identifying the principle that 'children have rights, including, in specific circumstances, the right to determine for themselves whether a medical procedure can be carried out' as the first restriction on the 'rights and duties' of parents giving authority and consent to medical treatment).
98 *Jamie Appeal* (n 1) [121].

has been 'internalised and brought to life' within a legal system.[99] Bryant CJ in *Re Jamie* discussed at some length the submissions of the AHRC, which argued that a number of rights under the CRC, as well as the *Convention on the Rights of Persons with Disabilities*,[100] were engaged by the proceedings.[101] The AHRC's submissions drew on three key principles emanating from Articles 5 and 12 of the CRC, which are consistent with a children's rights approach to decisional privacy:[102] the importance of children having input into decisions that affect them, including decisions about medical treatment; giving children's views due weight in accordance with their age and maturity; and the special responsibility that parents have to provide direction and guidance to their children in making decisions.[103] The AHRC also cited the 'additional object' of Part VII of the Family Law Act, which is 'to give effect to the Convention on the Rights of the Child'.[104] It submitted that the CRC should be an 'interpretive aid' for the Full Court when considering the meaning of provisions contained in Part VII.[105]

Bryant CJ recognised that Articles 5 and 12 of the CRC were relevant to the question of *Gillick* competence 'in addition to the best interests test'.[106] This observation suggests a conceptual distinction between a child's rights and a child's best interests, which arguably limited her Honour's willingness and ability to engage with children's rights in her reasoning.[107] Indeed, Bryant CJ had previously remarked extra-curially that the best interests test 'is at odds with a child's right to privacy, autonomy, self-determination and freedom of expression'.[108] In *Re Jamie*, Bryant CJ cited Articles 5 and 12 to support the conclusion that, if a child is *Gillick* competent, there is no role for the court in medical treatment for gender dysphoria.[109] However, her Honour did not take the analysis a step further to engage in a substantive discussion of how those rights applied to Jamie or to TGD children more broadly. Bryant CJ held that:

> it would be contrary to the Convention on the Rights of the Child, and to the autonomous decision-making to which a *Gillick* competent child is entitled, to hold that there is a particular class of treatment, namely stage two treatment for childhood gender identity disorder, that disentitles autonomous decision-making by the child, whereas no other medical procedure does.[110]

99 Tobin, 'Judging the Judges' (n 10) 580.
100 *Convention on the Rights of Persons with Disabilities*, opened for signature 13 December 2006, 2515 UNTS 3 (entered into force 3 May 2008).
101 See *Jamie Appeal* (n 1) [46]–[65], [120]–[123].
102 See Chapter 2 (Sections 2.3.2–2.3.4).
103 *Jamie Appeal* (n 1) [48], [64]–[65].
104 *Family Law Act* (n 3) s 60B(4).
105 *Jamie Appeal* (n 1) [48], [64]–[65]. See also Introduction (Section I.4).
106 *Jamie Appeal* (n 1) [121].
107 See Chapter 2 (Section 2.4.2).
108 Bryant, 'It's My Body' (n 67) 199.
109 *Jamie Appeal* (n 1) [129].
110 Ibid [134].

As other scholars have observed, the 'rhetoric of rights' in the application of the *Gillick* competence test can be used to obfuscate paternalistic decisions made about children's medical treatment.[111] Judicial assessments of a child's capacity to consent may embrace the language of rights and include statements that the court will respect the child's autonomy; yet the judge ultimately will apply a welfarist approach,[112] which denies the child decisional privacy. The Full Court's judgment in *Re Jamie* is a sound example of this 'rhetorical rights' approach.[113]

The Full Court's approach in *Re Jamie* also falls within what Tobin has labelled a 'selective rights' approach.[114] Bryant CJ was able to identify some, although not all, articles of the CRC that are relevant to medical treatment for children experiencing gender dysphoria. Notable omissions were the right to preservation of identity under Article 8[115] and the right to enjoy 'the highest attainable standard of health' under Article 24.[116] Bryant CJ informed and justified her resolution of the issues through 'significant rather than incidental' references to children's rights under Articles 5 and 12 of the CRC.[117] In this way, her Honour did make an effort to engage with children's rights, by discussing the AHRC's submissions. However, her Honour's analysis of the rights under Articles 5 and 12 lacked an 'internally coherent' application of the CRC and the children's rights model that it embodies.[118]

Bryant CJ described medical treatment for 'something as personal and essential as the perception of one's gender and sexuality' as 'the very exemplar of when the rights of the *Gillick*-competent child should be given full effect'.[119] Yet the conclusion that the Family Court must remain involved in the decision-making process, by determining the question of *Gillick* competence in relation to stage two treatment,[120] curtailed not only Jamie's decisional privacy rights, but also those of other TGD children seeking to access treatment. This is where, as Stalford and Hollingsworth have noted, one may '[s]cratch beneath the surface' of judges'

111 Tobin, 'Judging the Judges' (n 10) 600, citing Michael Freeman, 'Rethinking *Gillick*' (2005) 13 *International Journal of Children's Rights* 201, 206–8, 211–12; Melinda T Derish and Kathleen Vanden Heuvel, 'Mature Minors Should Have the Right to Refuse Life-Sustaining Medical Treatment' (2000) 28(2) *Journal of Law, Medicine and Ethics* 109, 112–13.

112 See, eg, Jamie Potter, 'Rewriting the Competency Rules for Children: Full Recognition of the Young Person as Rights-Bearer' (2006) 14(1) *Journal of Law and Medicine* 64, 67.

113 Tobin, 'Judging the Judges' (n 10) 599–601.

114 Ibid 597–8.

115 See Chapter 4 (Section 4.4).

116 See Jones (n 59) 388–9; Kirsten Sandberg, 'The Rights of LGBTI Children under the Convention on the Rights of the Child' (2015) 33(4) *Nordic Journal of Human Rights* 337, 343–4; Bryant, 'It's My Body' (n 67) 210.

117 Tobin, 'Judging the Judges' (n 10) 597. By contrast, Finn J and Strickland J, in their separate judgments in the *Jamie* appeal, made no reference to children's rights in general or to the CRC.

118 Tobin, 'Judging the Judges' (n 10) 597.

119 *Jamie Appeal* (n 1) [135].

120 Ibid [140(e)].

explicit reference to children's rights to 'find that it impacts only superficially on the reasoning and outcome'.[121] The Full Court's conclusion in *Re Jamie* impaired Jamie's ability to exercise, consistently with her evolving capacities and with the guidance and direction of her parents, her right to decisional privacy in asserting who she was and who she wanted to become. Respecting children's right to decisional privacy in these circumstances is ultimately 'about letting people be who they were born to be'.[122]

5.3.3 Jamie's right to make decisions about her own body 'taken completely out of my hands'[123]

A children's rights approach to decisional privacy requires that children participate meaningfully in decision-making about matters that affect them, consistently with their evolving capacities.[124] In the context of judicial decision-making, this requires 'child-centric' court processes and procedures to enable that meaningful participation.[125] In *Re Jamie*, Jamie was persistent in her desire to be involved in the proceedings. She sought that her views and preferences in relation to her proposed medical treatment be put before the Family Court. At the first instance hearing, Dessau J took into account Jamie's 'strong and consistent views' that she wanted to commence stage one treatment, finding that Jamie was 'sufficiently mature, intelligent and informed' for 'considerable weight' to be attached to her wishes.[126] However, the judgments in the various *Re Jamie* proceedings demonstrate that Jamie's voice was subject to interpretation by various experts and her views were proffered only through the evidence of adults: her parents; the ICL appointed to represent Jamie's best interests; the family report; and her treating medical practitioners.

It was evident from the judgment in the initial Family Court proceedings that an ICL had been appointed for Jamie.[127] As part of their role, the ICL must 'ensure that any views expressed by the child in relation to the matters to which

121 Helen Stalford and Kathryn Hollingsworth, 'Judging Children's Rights: Tendencies, Tensions, Constraints and Opportunities' in Helen Stalford, Kathryn Hollingsworth and Stephen Gilmore (eds), *Rewriting Children's Rights Judgments: From Academic Vision to New Practice* (Hart Publishing, 2017) 17, 33.

122 Georgie Stone, quoted in Jordy Atkinson, 'Transgender Teen Georgie Stone Lobbying for Fairer Access to Cross-sex Hormone Therapy', *Caulfield Glen Eira Leader* (online, 25 November 2016) <www.heraldsun.com.au/leader/inner-south/transgender-teen-georgie-stone-lobbying-for-fairer-access-to-crosssex-hormone-therapy/news-story/5ae6939f2c734e711994edbaac00663c>.

123 Jamie, letter to the Family Court of Australia, quoted in *Jamie Stage Two* (n 34) [65].

124 See Chapter 2 (Section 2.3.4).

125 See Chapter 3 (Section 3.3).

126 *Jamie Stage One* (n 11) [117].

127 The court can make an order that the child's interests be independently represented by a lawyer in proceedings in which a child's best interests are, or a child's welfare is, the paramount, or a relevant, consideration: *Family Law Act* (n 3) s 68L. The role and duties

the proceedings relate are fully put before the court'.[128] However, the ICL 'is not the child's legal representative' and 'is not obliged to act on the child's instructions'.[129] Rather, the ICL is 'a "best interests" advocate' for the child.[130] At first instance, the ICL supported the desire of Jamie, her parents and her treating medical practitioners for stage one treatment to start immediately.[131] Yet the ICL argued that stage two treatment, which would not occur for another five to six years, should be considered by the Family Court closer to that time, to take into account unanticipated 'prevailing or intervening circumstances'.[132] The divergent stance of Jamie's parents and the ICL on this issue – notably, Jamie's views were not apparent from Dessau J's judgment – reveal a limitation of the ICL as a means of facilitating the expression of the child's voice in Part VII proceedings. The child's wishes and preferences – as expressed by the child and subsequently interpreted and advanced to the court by the ICL – and what the ICL assesses and the judge subsequently determines to be the in child's best interests – might not always align.

A further limitation of the ICL is the conflict between attempting to establish a relationship of trust with the child and encouraging the child to voice their wishes and views, and the ICL's ability to argue against those wishes and views if the ICL considers it to be in the child's best interests. Research has found that this may result in the child feeling disempowered and even betrayed.[133] Children themselves have expressed negative experiences of their interactions with ICLs appointed to represent their best interests, including feeling that they had not been listened to adequately or in a respectful manner[134] and having minimal (and in some cases, no) contact with the ICL.[135]

---

of an ICL are set out in s 68LA. On 6 April 2011, Dessau J made an order discharging the ICL appointed for Jamie: *Jamie Appeal* (n 1) [3] (Bryant CJ).

128 *Family Law Act* (n 3) s 68LA(5)(b).

129 Ibid s 68LA(4)(a)–(b). See eg, *Kingley v Arndale (No 2)* (2010) 255 FLR 326, 332–3 [26]–[28] (O'Reilly J).

130 Rae Kaspiew et al, *Independent Children's Lawyers Study* (Final Report, 2nd ed, Australian Institute of Family Studies, June 2014) ix.

131 *Jamie Stage One* (n 11) [7] (Dessau J).

132 Ibid [10].

133 Rachel Carson et al, *Children and Young People in Separated Families: Family Law System Experiences and Needs* (Final Report, Australian Institute of Family Studies, 2018) 52; Kaspiew et al (n 130) xii, 135–6, 139; Patrick Parkinson and Judy Cashmore, *The Voice of a Child in Family Law Disputes* (Oxford University Press, 2008) 152–4; William J Keough, *Child Representation in Family Law* (LBC Information Services, 2000) 50–3, 61–2.

134 Parkinson and Cashmore (n 133) 152–4; Kaspiew et al (n 130) 132, 135–6, 144; Felicity Bell, 'Barriers to Empowering Children in Private Family Law Proceedings' (2016) 30 *International Journal of Law, Policy and the Family* 225, 226; Carson et al (n 133) 3–4, 47, 51–2; Nicola Ross, 'Independent Children's Lawyers: Relational Approaches to Children's Representation' (2012) 26(3) *Australian Journal of Family Law* 214, 215 ('Independent Children's Lawyers').

135 Kaspiew et al (n 130) xii, 133–4, 142, 144; Carson et al (n 133) viii, 4, 51; Australian Law Reform Commission ('ALRC'), *Family Law for the Future – An Inquiry into the Family*

The use of ICLs in proceedings under Part VII of the Family Law Act is intended to advance children's right to express their views in judicial proceedings that affect them,[136] as provided by Article 12(2) of the CRC. However, the CRC does not specify whether a best interests model or a direct instructions model of representation is required.[137] The extent to which the current ICL model satisfies Australia's obligations under the CRC has been, and continues to be, challenged.[138] A more detailed discussion of the ICL's role in enabling children to express their views and to be heard in Part VII proceedings lies beyond the scope of this book. It suffices to observe that the debate about the purpose and function of independent children's representation – to represent the child's best interests (a concern for the child's welfare) or to advocate the child's own wishes (thereby promoting the child's autonomy) – remains a live one.[139]

On appeal, Bryant CJ in *Re Jamie* agreed with the submission of the AHRC that the CRC 'makes it clear that it is important that children have input into decisions that affect them and that parents have special responsibility for assisting their children in making these decisions'.[140] Article 12 of the CRC highlights a critical distinction between opportunity and obligation; between the rhetoric and

Law System (Final Report No 135, March 2019) 374 [12.59]; Joint Select Committee on Australia's Family Law System, *Improvements in Family Law Proceedings* (Second Interim Report, March 2021) 90–1 [4.52]–[4.54]; Joint Select Committee on Australia's Family Law System, *Improvements in Family Law Proceedings* (Interim Report, October 2020) 183 [8.65].

136 Jennifer McIntosh, Diana Bryant and Kristen Murray, 'Evidence of a Different Nature: The Child-Responsive and Less Adversarial Initiatives of the Family Court of Australia' (2008) 46(1) *Family Court Review* 125, 128; Kaspiew et al (n 130) ix; Laura Lundy, John Tobin and Aisling Parkes, 'Article 12: The Right to Respect for the Views of the Child' in John Tobin (ed), *The UN Convention on the Rights of the Child: A Commentary* (Oxford University Press, 2019) 397, 431.

137 Lundy, Tobin and Parkes (n 136) 426–7. On this issue, see Ross, 'Independent Children's Lawyers' (n 134) 217; Nicola Ross, 'Images of Children: Agency, Article 12 and Models for Legal Representation of Children' (2005) 19(2) *Australian Journal of Family Law* 92; ALRC (n 135) 371–5.

138 See, eg, CRC Committee, 'Concluding Observations on the Combined Fifth and Sixth Periodic Reports of Australia', UN Doc CRC/C/AUS/CO/5–6 (1 November 2019) 5 [22(c)]; Kaspiew et al (n 130) ix; Carson et al (n 133) 3.

139 See, eg, Lundy, Tobin and Parkes (n 136) 428–9; Parkinson and Cashmore (n 133) 49–53; Linda Elrod, 'Client Directed Lawyers for Children: It is the Right Thing to Do' (2007) 27(4) *Pace Law Review* 869; Barbara Atwood, 'Representing Children Who Can't or Won't Direct Counsel: Best Interests Lawyering or No Lawyer At All?' (2011) 53 *Arizona Law Review* 381; Donald Duquette, 'Legal Representation for Children in Protection Proceedings: Two Distinct Lawyer Roles Are Required' (2000) 34(3) *Family Law Quarterly* 441; Geoff Monahan, 'Autonomy vs Beneficence: Ethics and Representation of Children and Young People in Legal Proceedings' (2008) 8(2) *Queensland University of Technology Law and Justice Journal* 392.

140 *Jamie Appeal* (n 1) [122].

reality of children's participation in judicial proceedings.[141] In practice, the right under Article 12(2) does not impose an *obligation* on the court to *seek* a child's views. Rather, it requires that states assure the child the right to freely express their views, by giving the child an *opportunity* to be heard in judicial proceedings affecting them, either directly or through a representative or appropriate body. The Family Law Act explicitly seeks to ensure that the opportunity is not converted into an obligation, providing that '[n]othing in this Part permits the court or any person to require the child to express [their] views in relation to any matter'.[142] The reference to 'the procedural rules of national law' in Article 12(2) gives states a degree of discretion regarding the rules adopted to give effect to this right, subject to the requirement that those rules are effective in enabling the child to enjoy their right to be heard and do not violate any other rights under the CRC.[143]

In *Re Jamie,* Bryant CJ used Article 12 of the CRC to inform her conclusion that a *Gillick* competent child is capable of exercising decision-making autonomy in relation to stage two medical treatment for gender dysphoria. However, her Honour merely quoted verbatim from the AHRC's submissions. She did not examine the nature and content of Jamie's right to express her views and to be heard. The references to Articles 5 and 12 of the CRC, as they were raised in the submissions of the AHRC before the Full Court, remained abstracted. Bryant CJ used those articles of the Convention selectively and rhetorically in her reasoning and conclusions.[144] This approach triggers a concern about the symbolic and normative appeal of participation. The danger is that participatory procedures might play a role that is 'more ideological and symbolic than real'[145] or may become 'a kind of token process, a box that needs to be ticked rather than a genuine consultation' with children in decision-making processes.[146]

The CRC Committee has described children's right under Article 12 of the CRC as 'fundamental' to realising adolescents' right to heath and development.[147] According to the Committee, to enable adolescents to 'safely and properly' exercise this right, 'public authorities, parents and other adults working with or for children need to create an environment based on trust, information-sharing, the capacity to listen and sound guidance that is conducive for adolescents'

141 Liam Cairns, 'Participation with Purpose' in E Kay M Tisdall, John M Davis, Alan Prout and Malcolm Hill (eds), *Children, Young People and Social Inclusion: Participation for What?* (Polity Press, 2006) 217, 217–18.

142 *Family Law Act* (n 3) s 60CE.

143 Lundy, Tobin and Parkes (n 136) 431.

144 See Section 5.3.2 above.

145 Denis J Galligan, *Due Process and Fair Procedures: A Study of Administrative Procedures* (Clarendon Press, 1996) 161.

146 Carol Smart, 'From Children's Shoes to Children's Voices' (2002) 40(3) *Family Court Review* 307, 307.

147 CRC Committee, *General Comment No 4: Adolescent Health and Development in the Context of the Convention on the Rights of the Child*, UN Doc CRC/GC/2003/4 (1 July 2003) [8].

participation equally including in decision-making processes'.[148] The Committee has also recommended that 'wherever possible, the child must be given the opportunity to be *directly* heard in any proceedings'.[149] These observations and recommendations are pertinent to the analysis of Jamie's ability to participate in the court process in the *Re Jamie* proceedings.

At the hearing to determine Jamie's *Gillick* competence to consent to stage two treatment, which was necessitated by the Full Court's conclusion, Thornton J made an order permitting Jamie and her brother to be present in court during the hearing.[150] Her Honour justified this order on the basis of the legislatively mandated need to protect Jamie's rights and to promote her welfare,[151] taking into account, relevantly, Jamie's entitlement to be heard and 'to know what is happening in relation to a very significant aspect of her life'.[152] On the issue of *Gillick* competence, Thornton J noted that Jamie's views had been 'very clearly expressed' through her parents and treating medical practitioners.[153] There was no formal evidence tendered from Jamie herself. Jamie had written a letter to the Family Court in which she expressed her clear desire for stage two treatment. This letter was included as an exhibit to her parents' summary of argument. The letter was not evidence, because there was no application for Jamie to give evidence and Thornton J considered it unnecessary for Jamie to adopt the letter in oral evidence before the Court. However, her Honour recognised that the letter was 'important because it articulates Jamie's views'.[154] Jamie's letter relevantly read:

> I am a normal, cheerful, confident girl and I know who I am. It's just that my exterior, doesn't mirror my interior. I want my body to develop alongside my peers, and I want my body to match who I really am; a girl … It shouldn't be the court's decision. It is my body, and only I have the right to decide what goes into it … However, this right has been taken completely out of my hands … I implore you to let me start stage 2 treatment. Then, I can be who I am, without this worry hanging over me.[155]

Gender identity is a 'dynamic' attribute of a child's identity, which 'has the potential to evolve and develop over time', shaped by the child's own life

148 Ibid.
149 CRC Committee, *General Comment No 12* (n 53) [35] (emphasis added).
150 This order was made following an application by Jamie's parents, pursuant to s 100B(2) of the *Family Law Act*, which provides, relevantly, that a child must not be present during proceedings in the Family Court unless the court makes an order allowing the child to be present.
151 See *Family Law Act* (n 3) s 43(1)(c).
152 *Jamie Stage Two* (n 34) [43]–[44].
153 Ibid [42].
154 Ibid [64].
155 Ibid [65].

experiences.[156] Jamie's ability to make decisions in relation to her identity, consistently with her evolving capacities and with appropriate parental direction and guidance, lay at the core of what Rossler has called the 'freedom to form one's own authentic identity'.[157] Privacy with respect to such decisions serves to promote the child's evolving autonomy: the 'right to be the (part-)author of [their] own biography'.[158] Jamie's letter, in which she expressed her immense frustration at having to 'endure' legal proceedings to 'be who I am', and at having the right to make decisions about her own body 'taken completely out of my hands',[159] exemplifies the extra-curial observation of former Family Court Chief Justice, Alastair Nicholson, that 'many children – and particularly older children – feel disempowered by Court proceedings'.[160] Such disempowerment is also a violation of those children's right to decisional privacy. Without any evidence before the court from Jamie herself,[161] she lost control over how she and her experiences were presented. As a result, the judge's capacity to listen to, hear and reflect in the judgment on Jamie's lived experiences was shaped and coloured by the evidence presented by adults, who were the ultimate definers and articulators of Jamie's best interests.

5.3.4 Communicating and enabling a decision with 'potential relevance for a much wider range of children'[162] than Jamie

i. Jamie's objectification as 'the child concerned'

The *Re Jamie* proceedings, by the time they had reached the Full Court, were less about Jamie as they were about the scope of parental rights versus the state's protective duties in relation to TGD children's medical treatment.[163] The choice of language in the judgment of Bryant CJ appeared to contradict her Honour's agreement with the submission of the AHRC that, under the children's rights model of the CRC, '[c]hildren are rights bearers and not merely objects of protection'.[164] The language and tone of the judgment sustained a construction

156 John Tobin and Jonathan Todres, 'Article 8: The Right to Preservation of a Child's Identity' in John Tobin (ed), *The UN Convention on the Rights of the Child: A Commentary* (Oxford University Press, 2019) 281, 285, 292–3. See also Chapter 4 (Section 4.4).
157 Rossler (n 76) 138.
158 Ibid.
159 *Jamie Stage Two* (n 34) [65].
160 Alastair Nicholson, 'Children and Children's Rights in the Context of Family Law' (Speech, LawAsia Conference, 21 June 2003) 6.
161 It is important to acknowledge that Article 12(2) of the CRC, which provides for the child's right to be heard in judicial and administrative proceedings affecting the child, is not proscriptive as to how the child's views are put before the court. Thus the child's views can be conveyed directly by the child or indirectly 'through a representative or appropriate body', such as an ICL or a family report: see Lundy, Tobin and Parkes (n 136) 402.
162 *Jamie Appeal* (n 1) [5] (Bryant CJ).
163 See Section 5.3.1.iii above.
164 *Jamie Appeal* (n 1) [122].

of Jamie as a passive, vulnerable object of concern. The judgment referred to Jamie as '[t]he child concerned'[165] and 'the child in question'.[166] It conveyed the sentiment that the proceedings were not about what Jamie *herself* should be able to do in the exercise of her rights, but about what should be able to be *done to* Jamie or by others on her behalf. For instance, Bryant CJ noted that Jamie's parents 'were asking the court to authorise them to consent to treatment on behalf of Jamie'.[167] The Full Court's reasons for judgment in an earlier hearing were also framed in terms of Jamie having something done to her: 'Jamie was diagnosed by the medical experts involved in the case with childhood gender identity disorder'.[168]

Characteristic of many judgments in children's cases at the appellate level, Jamie's voice was absent from the judgment, reflecting Rackley's observation that 'the parties can often … disappear from view by the time a case reaches the upper echelons of the legal hierarchy'.[169] Jamie's objectification through language choices in the judgment is consistent with her pathologisation by the Full Court as a child suffering from a mental illness, disorder and disability.[170] This paternalistic approach and its reinforcement through judicial semantic selection are contrary to the features of a children's rights judgment, which centralise and humanise the child and construct a child-focused narrative.[171]

ii. Tension between Jamie's right to share her court experience and informational privacy protection for 'vulnerable' children

In circumstances where Jamie was capable of expressing her tenacious views in a matter that so fundamentally affected her identity and well-being – and indeed where she sought to do so – stringent informational privacy protection for the proceedings further stifled Jamie's right to decisional privacy. Section 121 of the Family Law Act prohibits the publication or dissemination of accounts of family law proceedings that identify a party, witness, or other person associated with the proceedings.[172] In gender dysphoria proceedings, stringent informational privacy norms have been imposed, with the intention of protecting the child from the perceived harms of public identification and the attendant loss of autonomy that would result from a sense of unwelcome exposure. These norms have included

165 Ibid [1] (Bryant CJ).
166 Ibid [149] (Finn J).
167 Ibid [1].
168 *Jamie Application to Intervene* (n 24) 43 [4], quoted in *Jamie Appeal* (n 1) [11] (Bryant CJ).
169 Erika Rackley, 'The Art and Craft of Writing Judgments: Notes on the Feminist Judgment Project' in Rosemary Hunter, Clare McGlynn and Erica Rackley (eds), *Feminist Judgments: From Theory to Practice* (Hart Publishing, 2010) 44, 47.
170 See Section 5.3.1.ii above.
171 See Chapter 3 (Section 3.5.1).
172 *Family Law Act* (n 3) s 121(1).

orders closing the proceedings to the public and the anonymisation of judgments. Orders further suppressing information that could otherwise be published in the judgment, as permitted by section 121, have been 'made almost universally in cases of this type'.[173]

The Family Court's justification for such orders has centred on protecting the TGD child's identity, given that the substance of the proceedings is considered to be 'at the most sensitive end of matters' concerning the child's welfare.[174] In some cases, the issue of the child's gender identity may not have been 'divulged to the world at large'.[175] These judicial statements reflect concerns for 'negative self-presentation'[176] or not giving any, or any particular, impression of the child to a wide audience. The Family Court has sought to ensure that outsiders will not gain any impressions of the child's identity as TGD. However, in doing so, the Court has ignored the importance, for that child, of recognising and affirming their identity through public validation.

The *Re Jamie* proceedings were conducted in camera, having regard to their 'sensitivity'.[177] Additional restrictions, beyond those required by section 121 of the Family Law Act, were imposed on the identification and publication of the proceedings. The reasons for judgment of Dessau J at first instance described the publication restriction and anonymisation orders made as 'deliberately detailed and restrictive, to ensure privacy for Jamie and her family, and protection from these sensitive personal issues being widely circulated'.[178] The potential impacts of media publicity were articulated in terms of categorical harm to Jamie, with Dessau J asserting that '[i]t could only be damaging for Jamie to be identified'.[179]

However, from a decisional privacy perspective, such sweeping publication restrictions 'coerc[e] privacy',[180] as they ignore the element of control that some participants in Family Court proceedings might want to exercise over disclosure of information about their court experience through self-publication.[181] 'Coercing privacy' is a phrase developed by Allen to describe the law's imposition of privacy norms to ensure that individuals live according to a particular understanding of

173 *Re Lucy* (2013) 286 FLR 327, 354 [125] (Murphy J).

174 *Re Rosie* [2011] FamCA 63, [44] (Dessau J) ('*Re Rosie*'). See also *Re O (Special Medical Procedure)* [2010] FamCA 1153, [38] (Dessau J); *Re Sarah* [2014] FamCA 208, [47] (Macmillan J).

175 *Re Rosie* (n 174) [44] (Dessau J).

176 Juha Raikka, 'Privacy and Self-Presentation' (2017) 23(2) *Res Publica* 213, 224.

177 *Jamie Stage Two* (n 34) [45] (Thornton J).

178 *Jamie Stage One* (n 11) [132].

179 Ibid.

180 Anita Allen, 'Coercing Privacy' (1999) 40(3) *William and Mary Law Review* 723 ('Coercing Privacy').

181 Georgina Dimopoulos, '"Divorce with Dignity" as a Justification for Publication Restrictions on Proceedings under the *Family Law Act 1975* (Cth) in an Era of Litigant Self-Publication' (2019) 7(2) *Griffith Journal of Law and Human Dignity* 161, 178.

privacy as a 'foundation' of or 'precondition' to a liberal society.[182] As Inness has explained, 'privacy might not necessarily be opposed to publicity; its function might be to provide the individual with control over certain aspects of her life'.[183] This more nuanced understanding of privacy – which embraces its decisional dimension and understands privacy's value as inhering in autonomy – recognises that information disclosure and publicity might support, rather than undermine, a child's autonomy and identity development.

The notion of control over information as enabling decision-making autonomy is reflected in Article 13(1) of the CRC, which provides for the child's right to freedom of expression. This right includes 'freedom to seek, receive and impart information and ideas of all kinds', through any media of the child's choice, subject to the restrictions in Article 13(2).[184] Article 13 is important not only for its content, but also for its acknowledgement of the child as an autonomous being, capable of participating fully in society.[185] The CRC Committee has identified the child's right to seek, receive and impart information as one of two 'crucial prerequisites for the effective exercise of the right to be heard' in Article 12.[186] In *Re Jamie,* the 'deliberately detailed and restrictive'[187] orders made to purportedly protect Jamie's informational privacy had the effect of curtailing her decisional privacy, by impairing Jamie's ability to selectively share information about her court experience. In a television program that aired several months after the Full Court's decision in *Re Jamie*, but prior to the proceedings to assess Jamie's *Gillick* competence, Jamie said, 'I don't want to be pixelated cause that would kind of be like I'm ashamed and I'm not ashamed … [J]ust my identity is private for the moment'.[188]

In the Family Court proceedings that followed the Full Court's decision, Thornton J made an order enabling Jamie to identify and reveal herself as the young person the subject of the *Re Jamie* proceedings 'as she may choose'.[189] This order was the first of its kind in gender dysphoria proceedings. Given the finding that Jamie was competent to consent to stage two treatment, Thornton

182 Allen, 'Coercing Privacy' (n 180) 728. See also Anita Allen, 'Privacy-as-Data Control: Conceptual, Practical, and Moral Limits of the Paradigm' (2000) 32 *Connecticut Law Review* 861, 871–2.

183 Julie Inness, *Privacy, Intimacy and Isolation* (Oxford University Press, 1992) 6.

184 Article 13(2) of the CRC provides that these restrictions shall only be such as are provided by law and are necessary: (a) for respect of the rights or reputations of others; or (b) for the protection of national security or of public order, or of public health or morals.

185 Freeman, *Moral Status* (n 41) 56. Cf Harry Brighouse, 'What Rights (If Any) Do Children Have?' in David Archard and Colin Macleod (eds), *The Moral and Political Status of Children* (Oxford University Press, 2002) 31, 50.

186 The other being Art 17 (access to information): see CRC Committee, *General Comment No 12* (n 53) [80].

187 *Jamie Stage One* (n 11) [132] (Dessau J).

188 Jamie, quoted in 'Being Me', *Four Corners* (Australian Broadcasting Corporation, 17 November 2014) <www.abc.net.au/4corners/being-me/5899244>.

189 *Jamie Stage Two* (n 34) [46].

J accepted her parents' submission that it was not in Jamie's best interests 'to compel her to maintain secrecy should she wish to reveal her circumstances to people of her choosing'.[190] The order provided a compromise between protecting Jamie's informational privacy in the face of widespread media publicity that such proceedings would likely generate, and enabling Jamie to exercise her rights to freedom of expression and to preserve and forge her own identity. This order also reflected an acceptance that children themselves have the right to play an active role in constructing and discovering their own identities, consistently with their evolving capacities;[191] and that selective, self-controlled information disclosure facilitates social relations of varying degrees of intimacy, which is vital to the experience of decisional privacy.

5.4 Conclusion

The analysis of the Full Court's judgment in *Re Jamie* exposes the fundamental questions of whether, and to what extent, adults are prepared to encourage children to participate meaningfully and actively in decision-making about their medical treatment for a condition that so deeply affects their bodily autonomy and identity. Gerald Dworkin has observed that '[o]ur self-esteem and sense of worth are bound up with the right to determine what shall be done to and with our bodies and minds'.[192] The analysis has served to support the argument that, through its conclusion 'with some reluctance'[193] that the Family Court must remain involved in children's medical treatment for gender dysphoria by determining the issue of *Gillick* competence, coupled with the reasoning to support that conclusion and court procedures that limited Jamie's participation, the Full Court in *Re Jamie* denied the decisional privacy rights of Jamie and other TGD children seeking medical treatment.

The Full Court's decision in *Re Jamie* continued a line of judicial authority in medical treatment cases that displayed 'a confident willingness to intervene in the private world of the family'.[194] The Full Court sustained the assumption of TGD children as vulnerable, incapable of rational decision-making and as members of a 'class of children'[195] who required the Family Court's ongoing protection, even if only in the form of an assessment of their capacity to consent to medical

190 Ibid.

191 Tobin and Todres (n 156) 293–4.

192 Gerald Dworkin, 'Consent, Representation, and Proxy Consent' in Willard Gaylin and Ruth Macklin (eds), *Who Speaks for the Child: The Problems of Proxy Consent* (Plenum Press, 1982) 191, 203.

193 *Jamie Appeal* (n 1) [137] (Bryant CJ).

194 John Seymour, *Children, Parents and the Courts: Legal Intervention in Family Life* (Federation Press, 2016) 138.

195 Sarah Elliston, 'If You Know What's Good For You: Refusal of Consent to Medical Treatment by Children' in Sheila A M McLean (ed), *Contemporary Issues in Law, Medicine and Ethics* (Dartmouth Publishing, 1996) 29, 52.

treatment. The *Re Jamie* judgment also highlights how the ongoing process of identity formation and children's role in creating and preserving their own identities can be judicially muted. The next chapter applies the children's rights approach to decisional privacy to analyse the judgment of the Full Court of the Family Court in *Re Kelvin*. Decided four years after the Full Court's decision in *Re Jamie*, *Re Kelvin* provides a strong point of comparison and contrast of judicial approaches to children's right to decisional privacy in the context of medical treatment for childhood gender dysphoria.

6 The 'greatest advancement in transgender rights' for Australian children?

Re-reading the Full Court's judgment in *Re Kelvin*

6.1 Introduction

This chapter applies the concept of children's right to decisional privacy to analyse the judgment of the Full Court of the Family Court of Australia ('Full Court') in the case of *Re Kelvin*.[1] The *Re Kelvin* proceedings arose from an application by the father of a 16-year-old young person, anonymised in the judgments as 'Kelvin', for Family Court authorisation of stage two treatment (gender-affirming hormones) for Kelvin, who had been diagnosed with gender dysphoria. In a judgment delivered in November 2017, a special bench of the Full Court did not follow its decision in *Re Jamie*.[2] The Full Court held that where a child diagnosed with gender dysphoria consents to stage two treatment, the child's treating medical practitioners agree that the child is competent to give informed consent to that treatment (that is, the child is *Gillick* competent) and the child's parents do not object to the treatment, then the Family Court need not determine the child's *Gillick* competence.[3] However, the Full Court also concluded that there was 'no doubt' that the Family Court had the jurisdiction and power to address questions about the need for court authorisation in circumstances of 'genuine dispute or controversy' between the child's parents and treating medical practitioners about whether treatment should be administered.[4]

To contextualise the *Re Kelvin* decision, this chapter first articulates the growing dissatisfaction with the Full Court's decision in *Re Jamie*. It also provides a brief history of the *Re Kelvin* proceedings. It then applies the children's rights approach to decisional privacy to expose three features of the *Re Kelvin* judgment that it is argued do not demonstrate an appreciation of or respect for TGD children's decisional privacy. The first is the 'invisible' rights approach[5] that the

1 [2017] FamCAFC 258 ('*Re Kelvin*').
2 [2013] FamCAFC 110 ('*Jamie Appeal*'). This judgment is analysed in Chapter 5.
3 *Re Kelvin* (n 1) [177]–[184] (Thackray, Strickland and Murphy JJ), [226] (Ainslie-Wallace and Ryan JJ).
4 Ibid [167] (Thackray, Strickland and Murphy JJ). See also [189] (Ainslie-Wallace and Ryan JJ).
5 See John Tobin, 'Judging the Judges: Are they Adopting the Rights Approach in Matters involving Children?' (2009) 33(2) *Melbourne University Law Review* 579, 593–5 ('Judging the Judges').

DOI: 10.4324/9781003224167-9

Full Court adopted, through its emphasis on parental rights and the noteworthy absence of any consideration of the rights of Kelvin or TGD children more broadly. Secondly, the judgment in *Re Kelvin* was one written by adults, for adults. The Full Court did not embrace the potential to advance the decisional privacy rights of TGD children by writing a judgment *for* them, to explain the significance of the decision. The third feature is the majority's statement regarding the need for court authorisation in circumstances of 'genuine dispute or controversy' about whether medical treatment should be administered.[6]

The decision of the Full Court in *Re Kelvin* was touted, as the title of this chapter indicates, 'the greatest advancement in transgender rights for children and adolescents in Australia'.[7] It 'sw[u]ng the pendulum of decision-making authority for TGD children's medical treatment from the Family Court back to the child, the child's parents and the child's treating doctors'.[8] This chapter argues that, when analysed from a children's rights perspective, the Full Court was not concerned with the rights of TGD children at all. Rather, the *Re Kelvin* decision was about the extent to which the Family Court should encroach on parents' ability and responsibility to make medical treatment decisions for and on behalf of their children, consistently with the latest developments in medical science. It is argued that TGD children benefit only incidentally from the Full Court's decision. Respect for their right to decisional privacy is contingent upon agreement between their parents and treating medical practitioners to the proposed medical treatment. This chapter provides an opportunity to rethink the alleged strides that the Full Court in *Re Kelvin* made in championing the rights of TGD children.

6 *Re Kelvin* (n 1) [167] (Thackray, Strickland and Murphy JJ).

7 See '"Kelvin" Family Court Announcement', *The Royal Children's Hospital Melbourne* (Blog Post, 30 November 2017) <https://blogs.rch.org.au/news/2017/11/30/kelvin-family-court-announcement/>; @RCHMelbourne (Royal Children's Hospital Melbourne) (Twitter, 30 November 2017, 2:38pm AEST) <https://mobile.twitter.com/rchmelbourne/status/936077045376753665>. In support of the view that the Full Court's decision in *Re Kelvin* was a victory for transgender children's rights, see also 'Commission Welcomes *Re Kelvin* Decision', *Australian Human Rights Commission* (Web Page, 30 November 2017) <https://humanrights.gov.au/about/news/commission-welcomes-re-kelvin-decision>; Kym Fraser and Matt Condello, 'Victory for Transgender Children in Recent Family Court Decision', *Clayton Utz* (Web Page, 7 December 2017) <www.claytonutz.com/knowledge/2017/december/victory-for-transgender-children-in-recent-family-court-decision>; Sharon Feldman and Tom Dreyfus, 'Whose Consent Is It Anyway? A Transgender Child's Right to Transition' (2017) 3 *Voices in Bioethics*; Greg McAllister, 'Gender Dysphoria in Australia: The Judicial Response in *Re Kelvin*' (2018) 145 *Precedent* 40, 43. Cf Stuart Lindsay, 'The Family Court Has Failed Gender-Dysphoric Children' (2018) 62(5) *Quadrant* 32.

8 Georgina Dimopoulos, 'Embracing Children's Right to Decisional Privacy in Proceedings under the *Family Law Act 1975* (Cth): In Children's Best Interests or a Source of Conflict?' in Shazia Nasir (ed), *RAIS Conference Proceedings: The 11th International RAIS Conference on Social Sciences* (Research Association for Interdisciplinary Studies, 2018) 129, 134–5.

6.2 Growing dissatisfaction and an 'urgent need ... to undo the consequences'[9] of *Re Jamie*

Former Chief Justice of the Family Court of Australia, Diana Bryant, made the extra-curial observation, notably a few months after *Re Alex* (2004)[10] was decided, that:

> The courts exercising jurisdiction in family law are required to confront social change like it or not, and to make decisions which have far reaching effects on families. It is not surprising therefore that these decisions should be the subject of public debate and divergent views in the community.[11]

The Full Court's judgment in *Re Jamie*,[12] of which Bryant CJ was the lead author, was itself such a decision, subject to much public debate almost a decade after her Honour's remarks. Strickland J, one of the judges who heard and decided both the *Re Jamie* appeal and the *Re Kelvin* appeal (and notably the only judge to do so), made the extra-curial prediction that *Re Jamie* was 'likely to act as a spur for further proceedings ... which challenge the boundaries of the current state of the law governing young people and medical treatment', such that there was 'every reason for confidence that the jurisprudence will develop further, and develop rapidly, following *Re Jamie*'.[13]

Strickland J's prediction of jurisprudential development manifested initially via widespread discontent with the Full Court's decision in *Re Jamie*, including amongst Family Court judges,[14] legal academics[15] and the medical

9 *Re Lucas* [2016] FamCA 1129, [73] (Tree J) ('*Re Lucas*').

10 (2004) 180 FLR 89 ('*Re Alex* (2004)'). See Chapter 4 (Section 4.3.2.ii).

11 Diana Bryant, 'Beyond the Horizon' (Speech, Law Council of Australia Family Law Section National Family Law Conference, 27 September 2004) <www.austlii.edu.au/au/journals/FedJSchol/2004/25.html>.

12 *Jamie Appeal* (n 2).

13 Steven Strickland, 'To Treat or Not to Treat: Legal Responses to Transgender Young People' (Conference Paper, Association of Family and Conciliation Courts Annual Conference, 28–31 May 2014) 72–3.

14 See, eg, *Re Martin* [2015] FamCA 1189, [27], [36], [38] (Bennett J); *Re Harley* [2016] FamCA 334, [42] (Bennett J); *Re Tahlia* [2017] FamCA 715, [4] (Bennett J); *Re Lucas* (n 9) [10], [53], [71], [73] (Tree J).

15 See, eg, Fiona Kelly, 'Treating the Transgendered Child: The Full Court's Decision in *Re Jamie*' (2014) 28(1) *Australian Journal of Family Law* 83, 83–4, 91 ('Treating the Transgendered Child'); Felicity Bell, 'Children with Gender Dysphoria and the Jurisdiction of the Family Court' (2015) 38(2) *University of New South Wales Law Journal* 426, 430; Lisa Young, 'Gender Identity Dysphoria Update and Developments in Property Settlement Law' [2014] *International Survey of Family Law* 1, 5–7; Fiona Kelly, 'Australian Children Living with Gender Dysphoria: Does the Family Court Have a Role to Play?' (2014) 22(1) *Journal of Law and Medicine* 105; Katherine France, 'Let Me Be Me: Parental Responsibility, *Gillick* Competence, and Transgender Minors' Access to Hormone Treatments' (2014) 4(4) *Family Law Review* 227; Malcolm K Smith, 'The Boundaries of Parental Decision-Making

profession.[16] Criticism was directed at two features of the Full Court's reasoning that resulted in children experiencing gender dysphoria continuing to endure 'unnecessary judicial oversight' of their medical treatment.[17] The first, technical legal critique, was the correctness of the Full Court's analysis and application of the distinction made in *Secretary, Department of Health and Community Services v JWB & SMB* ('*Marion's Case*') between 'therapeutic' and 'non-therapeutic' treatment.[18] The second challenge was to the justification for the Family Court's ongoing role in assessing a child's *Gillick* competence, and the attendant financial and psychological burden that the court process imposed on TGD children and their families.[19]

The strong opposition to the Full Court's decision in *Re Jamie* suggests that the dominant '"rescue" ideology'[20] in discourses relating to children's medical treatment, which had since *Marion's Case* justified the Family Court's incursion into what was previously a family decision, had fallen out of favour. Shortly before the Full Court handed down its decision in *Re Kelvin*, the UN Human Rights Committee ('UNHRC') expressed concern about the requirement for Family Court authorisation for stage two treatment for gender dysphoria. It noted that 'the delays and costs associated with obtaining court authorisation may compromise the success of such hormonal treatment ... and cause ... psychological harm'.[21] The UNHRC recommended that Australia consider ways to expedite access to that treatment, including by 'removing the need for court authorisation in cases featuring uncontested agreement among parents or guardians, the child concerned and the medical team'.[22] Despite judicial calls for 'an urgent need for statutory intervention ... to undo the consequences of *Re Jamie*',[23] legislative

and the Requirement to Obtain Court Approval for "Special Medical Procedures": The Recent Decision of *Re Jamie*' (2013) 33 *Queensland Lawyer* 182, 186.

16 See, eg, Michelle Telfer, Michelle Tollit and Debi Feldman, 'Transformation of Health-Care and Legal Systems for the Transgender Population: The Need for Change in Australia' (2015) 51(11) *Journal of Paediatrics and Child Health* 1051, 1052.

17 Kelly, 'Treating the Transgendered Child' (n 15) 94.

18 *Secretary, Department of Health and Community Services v JWB & SMB* (1992) 175 CLR 218, 250 (Mason CJ, Dawson, Toohey and Gaudron JJ) ('*Marion's Case*'). See Chapter 4 (Section 4.3.2.i).

19 See, eg, Fiona Kelly, '"The Court Process is Slow but Biology is Fast": Assessing the Impact of the Family Court Approval Process on Transgender Children and their Families' (2016) 30(2) *Australian Journal of Family Law* 112, 114; Bell (n 15) 451; France (n 15) 245–6; Jacqueline K Hewitt et al, 'Hormone Treatment of Gender Identity Dysphoria in a Cohort of Children and Adolescents' (2012) 196(9) *Medical Journal of Australia* 578, 580; Senthorun Raj, 'Alleviating Anxiety and Cultivating Care: Young Trans People in the Family Court of Australia' (2019) 45(1) *Australian Feminist Law Journal* 111.

20 Michael Freeman, *The Rights and Wrongs of Children* (Frances Pinter, 1983) 249 ('*Rights and Wrongs*').

21 UN Human Rights Committee, *Concluding Observations on the Sixth Periodic Report of Australia*, UN Doc CCPR/C/AUS/CO/6 (9 November 2017) [27].

22 Ibid.

23 *Re Lucas* (n 9) [73] (Tree J).

reform did not ensue. It remained for the Full Court in *Re Kelvin* to consider whether court authorisation was still an essential component of stage two medical treatment for childhood gender dysphoria.

6.3 The *Re Kelvin* proceedings: A brief history

6.3.1 The initial Family Court proceedings

The father of 16-year-old Kelvin applied to the Family Court for authorisation of stage two treatment for Kelvin, who had been diagnosed with gender dysphoria. Kelvin's father sought a declaration or an order that Kelvin was *Gillick* competent to consent to the administration of that treatment; and in the alternative, that the Court authorise the administration of stage two treatment under section 67ZC of the *Family Law Act 1975* (Cth) ('Family Law Act'), on the basis that it was in Kelvin's best interests.[24] Kelvin's treating medical practitioners shared the view that Kelvin was *Gillick* competent. Their evidence was that Kelvin felt that 'his decision-making is clear', he was 'ostensibly free of any pressure, pain or other factors that might influence his decision-making capability' and he was 'able to comprehend the nature of the treatment such that he is able to provide informed consent, according to the *Gillick* standard'.[25] Accepting this evidence, Watts J was satisfied of Kelvin's *Gillick* competence and made a finding to that effect, which enabled Kelvin to commence stage two treatment immediately.[26] While this might have been the end of the matter, Kelvin's father agreed for a special case to be stated for the Full Court's opinion. In light of the case stated, Watts J adjourned the application for a declaration or an order authorising Kelvin's treatment pending determination by the Full Court.[27]

6.3.2 The case stated before the Full Court

Unlike *Re Jamie*, which came before the Full Court following an appeal by Jamie's parents, *Re Kelvin* came before the Full Court by way of a case stated by the trial judge, pursuant to section 94A(1) of the Family Law Act. That section enables the Full Court to hear and determine a question of law arising in proceedings before those proceedings are dealt with further. The six questions stated for the Full Court's opinion, in essence, concerned the effect of the Full Court's decision in *Re Jamie* and the role of the Family Court more generally in relation to stage two treatment for gender dysphoria and the determination of *Gillick* competence.[28] The fundamental issue was whether gender dysphoria should continue to be treated differently from other medical conditions, such

24 *Re Kelvin* [2017] FamCA 78, [3] (Watts J).
25 Ibid [41]–[43].
26 Ibid [57].
27 Ibid.
28 *Re Kelvin* (n 1) [1], [3] (Thackray, Strickland and Murphy JJ).

as to require the ongoing 'filter' of court authorisation for medical treatment to commence.[29]

A special bench of the Full Court departed from its earlier decision in *Re Jamie.* While the majority and minority reached the same conclusion, they diverged on the issue of whether *Re Jamie* was 'plainly wrong' in its application of *Marion's Case.* The majority (Thackray, Strickland and Murphy JJ) justified its departure from *Re Jamie* on the basis of the evolution of the state of medical knowledge and 'the development in the treatment of and the understanding of [g]ender [d]ysphoria'.[30] The minority (Ainslie-Wallace and Ryan JJ) found the decision in *Re Jamie* to be 'plainly wrong' in its application of *Marion's Case.*[31] The minority considered that the Full Court in *Re Jamie*, having determined that stage two treatment was 'therapeutic', should not have applied the principles in *Marion's Case* regarding authorisation of a particularly grave 'non-therapeutic' procedure (sterilisation) for a child who was not, and would never become, *Gillick* competent.[32]

The Full Court in *Re Kelvin* held that in circumstances where a child consents to stage two treatment for gender dysphoria, the child's treating medical practitioners agree that the child is *Gillick* competent to give that consent, and the parents do not object to the treatment, it was no longer mandatory to apply to the Family Court for a determination of the child's *Gillick* competence.[33] The Full Court thus concluded that stage two treatment for gender dysphoria can no longer be considered a 'special medical procedure' for which 'consent lies outside the bounds of parental authority and requires the imprimatur of the [Family] Court'.[34] However, the Full Court left open the possibility of court involvement where there is a 'genuine dispute or controversy' about whether treatment should be administered.[35] In light of the Full Court's answers to the questions in the case stated, Watts J dismissed the initiating application and made orders giving Kelvin the liberty to identify himself as the subject of the proceedings.[36]

6.4 A children's rights analysis of the Full Court's judgment in *Re Kelvin*

On a superficial reading of the Full Court's judgment in *Re Kelvin*, based on the overview just provided, this case is a significant example of the judiciary's activist role in developing the law and so advancing the rights of TGD children,

29 Ibid [119].
30 Ibid [162].
31 Ibid [208]–[209], [225].
32 Ibid [188]–[189]. See also [209].
33 Ibid [177]–[184] (Thackray, Strickland and Murphy JJ), [226] (Ainslie-Wallace and Ryan JJ).
34 Ibid [164] (Thackray, Strickland and Murphy JJ).
35 Ibid [167]. See Section 6.4.3 below.
36 *Re Kelvin [No 2]* [2017] FamCA 1000.

by removing the need for court involvement in the medical treatment decision-making process. The majority in *Re Kelvin* was critical of the legislature's inaction, remarking that it was 'disappointing that the call for legislative intervention following *Re Jamie* went unheeded'.[37] The absence of legislative reform was also surprising, given the extent of vocal opposition to *Re Jamie*[38] and the 'widespread media attention' that gender dysphoria cases tend to attract.[39]

The decision of the Full Court in *Re Kelvin* was lauded as a victory for TGD children's rights.[40] The ensuing analysis exposes three aspects of the Full Court's judgment that it is suggested undermine this conclusion: (i) the invisible rights approach that the Full Court adopted; (ii) the central narrative and writing style of the judgment; and (iii) the requirement for ongoing Family Court involvement in the medical treatment process for childhood gender dysphoria 'where there is a genuine dispute or controversy'.[41] This children's rights analysis supports the argument that the Full Court in *Re Kelvin* was not concerned with advancing the rights of TGD children, but rather, with recalibrating the respective roles and responsibilities of parents and the Family Court in relation to TGD children's medical treatment.

6.4.1 The Full Court's 'invisible rights' approach and a judgment (still) all about parental rights and responsibilities

The judgment of the Full Court in *Re Kelvin* falls squarely within what Tobin has labelled an 'invisible' rights approach, the defining feature of which is 'the failure to identify that the rights of children are relevant to the dispute before the court'.[42] There is not a single reference to the rights of the child in the judgment, yet there are nine references to the rights of parents.[43] This cursory quantitative assessment is supported by a qualitative one. There is an underlying tension in gender dysphoria proceedings between, on the one hand, protecting children, and on the other, affording children autonomy and independence in decision-making.[44] This distinction – between protecting children and protecting children's rights – is, however, false or at least deceptive,[45] because it does not change children's status. Rather, it involves 'substituting one adult decision-maker for

37 *Re Kelvin* (n 1) [104] (Thackray, Strickland and Murphy JJ).

38 See Section 6.2 above.

39 The majority acknowledged this point in its contextual prelude to addressing the questions stated: *Re Kelvin* (n 1) [115] (Thackray, Strickland and Murphy JJ).

40 See n 7 above.

41 *Re Kelvin* (n 1) [167] (Thackray, Strickland and Murphy JJ).

42 Tobin, 'Judging the Judges' (n 5) 594.

43 See *Re Kelvin* (n 1) [73], [123], [124]–[125] (Thackray, Strickland and Murphy JJ), [191] (Ainslie-Wallace and Ryan JJ).

44 Freeman, *Rights and Wrongs* (n 20) 44; Emma Cave, 'Goodbye *Gillick*? Identifying and Resolving Problems with the Concept of Child Competence' (2014) 34(1) *Legal Studies* 103, 110.

45 Freeman, *Rights and Wrongs* (n 20) 60.

another, rather than giving children the choice of deciding whether they like the conditions in which they find themselves'.[46] This 'substitution' of adult decision-makers is illustrated by the emphasis that the Full Court in *Re Kelvin* placed upon the rights of parents to make decisions about their children's medical treatment.

i. The 'right and responsibility' of parents to determine their children's medical treatment

A preliminary issue is whether it can be said that parents have 'rights', as opposed to duties or responsibilities, under the Family Law Act. The definition of 'parental responsibility' in section 61B refers to 'duties' and 'responsibilities', but also to 'authority' and 'powers'; yet the definition does not refer to 'rights'.[47] Whilst a deliberate and 'understandable' omission, the Full Court of the Family Court has noted that the practical effect of having no reference to parental 'rights' is negligible, 'other than to make it clear that there are no possessory rights to children'.[48] The Family Court has observed that the definition of parental responsibility 'deliberately omits any reference to rights in order to discourage any perception the parents own, or have some form of property in, their children'.[49] Parental rights are said to derive from parental duties and 'exist only so long as they are needed for the protection … of the child'.[50]

The majority in *Re Kelvin* observed that: 'The *right* and responsibility of parents to decide upon medical treatment for their non-*Gillick* competent children, *reflected through the prism of the children's best interests*, is the default position, not the exception.'[51] The majority made repeated reference to the 'right and responsibility' of parents,[52] without acknowledging the differences between the two notions, particularly in terms of the dynamics of the parent–child relationship. In discussing the scope of the welfare jurisdiction under section 67ZC of the Family Law Act, the minority noted that '[i]n deciding to control or ignore the parental

46 Michael S Wald, 'Children's Rights: A Framework for Analysis' (1979) 12(2) *University College Dublin Law Review* 255, 263.

47 See *Longford v Byrne* [2017] FCCA 762, [60] n 11 (Judge Harman observing that there is 'no controversy' that the *Family Law Act 1975* (Cth) 'does not contain or provide for the rights of parents', and '[p]arents have duties and responsibilities rather than rights'). Cf *Children Act 1989* (UK) s 3(1) (defining 'parental responsibility' to mean 'all the rights, duties, powers, responsibilities and authority which by law a parent of a child has in relation to the child and his property').

48 *In Marriage of B* (1997) 140 FLR 11, 67–8 (Nicholson CJ, Fogarty and Lindenmayer JJ).

49 *W v G (No 1)* (2004) 35 Fam LR 417, 428 [86] (Carmody J). See also *Pickle v Sackville* [2017] FCCA 1456, [85] (Judge McGuire).

50 *Gillick v West Norfolk and Wisbech Area Health Authority* [1986] AC 112, 183–4 (Lord Scarman). Cf *Dean v Deluca* [2008] FamCA 1193, [25] (Bell J); *Warwick v Warwick* [2008] FamCA 388, [27] (Bell J). See also *Harrow v Eton* [2007] FamCA 812, [6] (Bell J); *Lovine v Connor* [2011] FamCA 432, [35] (Mushin J).

51 *Re Kelvin* (n 1) [123] (Thackray, Strickland and Murphy JJ) (emphasis added). See also *Jamie Appeal* (n 2) [115] (Bryant CJ).

52 *Re Kelvin* (n 1) [123]–[125] (Thackray, Strickland and Murphy JJ).

right the Court should do so only when judicially satisfied that the welfare of the child requires that the parental right should be suspended or superseded'.[53] The Full Court also quoted the High Court in *Marion's Case* regarding the 'parental power' to authorise medical treatment for a child who is not *Gillick* competent. The Full Court's endorsement of this statement, which was said to involve the 'parent speaking for the child',[54] bears remnants of the historical *patria potestas* (parental possession) doctrine.[55] In making these observations, the Full Court in *Re Kelvin* conflated the child's rights and best interests with parental 'rights' and responsibilities. It also conceptualised children as a mere extension of their parents.[56] The Full Court thus failed to identify that children have rights and interests that are distinct from those of their parents and other caregivers.[57]

An aim of a children's rights approach to decisional privacy is to encourage adults to conceive of their role as 'facilitators and advocates rather than controllers' of children.[58] Judicial deference to parental rights and responsibilities must be subject to the child's evolving capacities.[59] Article 5 of the CRC requires that parents provide 'appropriate direction and guidance' to their children in the exercise of their rights, consistently with children's 'evolving capacities'. Importantly, the evolving capacities principle requires that parental rights be exercised 'to *guide and assist* children in the realization of their rights',[60] rather than to uphold or promote the hierarchical (liberal) conception of the family, in which parents

53 Ibid [191] (Ainslie-Wallace and Ryan JJ).

54 *Marion's Case* (n 18) 239–40 (Mason CJ, Dawson, Toohey and Gaudron JJ), quoted in *Re Kelvin* (n 1) [123] (Thackray, Strickland and Murphy JJ).

55 See Tobin, 'Judging the Judges' (n 5) 593; Jill Elaine Hasday, *Family Law Reimagined* (Harvard University Press, 2014) 133; John Eekelaar, 'The Emergence of Children's Rights' (1986) 6(2) *Oxford Journal of Legal Studies* 161, 162; Barbara Bennett Woodhouse, '"Who Owns the Child?": *Meyer* and *Pierce* and the Child as Property' (1992) 33(4) *William and Mary Law Review* 995; David Archard, 'Do Parents Own Their Children?' (1993) 1(1) *International Journal of Children's Rights* 293.

56 Tobin, 'Judging the Judges' (n 5) 594.

57 See Chapter 2 (Section 2.3.1).

58 Barry Percy-Smith and Nigel Thomas, 'Conclusion: Emerging Themes and New Directions' in Barry Percy-Smith and Nigel Thomas (eds), *A Handbook of Children and Young People's Participation: Perspectives From Theory and Practice* (Routledge, 2009) 356, 365. See also John Tobin and Sheila Varadan, 'Article 5: The Right to Parental Direction and Guidance and Consistent with a Child's Evolving Capacities' in John Tobin (ed), *The UN Convention on the Rights of the Child: A Commentary* (Oxford University Press, 2019) 159, 171.

59 See Chapter 2 (Sections 2.3.2 and 2.3.3).

60 John Tobin, 'Fixed Concepts but Changing Conceptions: Understanding the Relationship Between Children and Parents under the CRC' in Martin D Ruck, Michele Peterson-Badali and Michael Freeman (eds), *Handbook of Children's Rights: Global and Multidisciplinary Perspectives* (Taylor & Francis, 2017) 53, 65 (emphasis in original). See also Jonathan Montgomery, 'Children as Property?' (1988) 51(3) *Modern Law Review* 323, 341; John Tobin and Sarah M Field, 'Article 16: The Right to Protection of Privacy, Family, Home, Correspondence, Honour, and Reputation' in John Tobin (ed), *The UN Convention on the Rights of the Child: A Commentary* (Oxford University Press, 2019) 551, 554; Tobin and Varadan (n 58) 167.

exercise exclusive authority and control over that right.[61] To focus on the rights of parents to make decisions for and on behalf of their child, as the Full Court did in *Re Kelvin*, sustained the conceptualisation of the passive, vulnerable, silent child. The Full Court perpetuated this conceptualisation, it is argued, through its failure to acknowledge the child's role in the medical treatment decision-making process for gender dysphoria.

ii. A judgment telling in its omission: The silent and absent child

The Full Court's judgment in *Re Kelvin* is telling for what it does *not* say about children, arguably more than what it does. The Court's construction of the relationship between parents, children and the state in the context of medical treatment for childhood gender dysphoria rendered children all but invisible. This invisibility emerges from the majority's articulation of the stakeholders involved in the decision-making process. The majority emphasised that it was concerned to examine:

> whether there is any role for the Family Court in cases where there is no dispute between *parents* of a child who has been diagnosed with Gender Dysphoria, and where there is also no dispute between the *parents* and the *medical experts* who propose the child undertake treatment for that dysphoria.[62]

The majority referred to special medical procedure cases as requiring court authorisation 'irrespective of unanimity on the part of parents and the medical experts'.[63] The majority said that in these '"special cases", the usual parental right and responsibility for deciding upon their child's care is abrogated in favour of court determination':[64] the child again absent from the picture. The majority also noted that in 'each and every case' in which court authorisation had been sought for a child's treatment for gender dysphoria, the decision had been informed by:

> comprehensive evidence from a miscellany of medical specialists from different disciplines (for example, psychiatry, psychology, paediatrics, and endocrinology) and by evidence from parents, or those otherwise charged directly with the care, welfare and development of the child concerned.[65]

Starkly absent from this list of sources by which Family Court decisions in gender dysphoria cases have been informed, is any reference to the child. On the

61 Tobin and Field (n 60) 554.
62 *Re Kelvin* (n 1) [116] (Thackray, Strickland and Murphy JJ) (emphasis added).
63 Ibid [125].
64 Ibid.
65 Ibid [118].

majority's formulation, the medical treatment decision-making process was one defined and regulated exclusively by adults, namely, parents, treating medical practitioners and Family Court judges. There was no appreciation of the *child's* role in the process or of the child having rights, interests and views that might conflict with those adults.

iii. Why does the Full Court's approach matter?

A question that may germinate from the Full Court's invisible rights approach is that, given that the *Re Kelvin* decision removed the Family Court from the decision-making process for stage two treatment, which many had been advocating for following *Re Jamie*, does it even matter that the Full Court did not engage with children's rights? It could be argued that the outcome would have been the same, regardless. Indeed, the Full Court in *Re Kelvin* was not obliged to take the rights of Kelvin or TGD children into consideration in answering the questions for its determination.[66] As such, it might be argued that the absence of any discussion of children's rights in the Full Court's judgment is understandable. However, had the moral reasoning of the judges in *Re Kelvin* been informed by the values underpinning the CRC, there would have been scope for the Full Court to frame the issues in the case as being about TGD children and their rights. This would have enabled the Full Court to determine the questions for its opinion in a manner consistent with a children's rights approach.[67] The use of 'rights talk' for parents in the *Re Kelvin* judgment, particularly given the omission of any such discourse in relation to children, exemplifies Fortin's observation that judges 'not uncommonly analyse the rights that *adults* have, but fail to articulate those of the children'.[68]

Had the Full Court in *Re Kelvin* adopted a substantive children's rights approach, its attention would have been not on the 'attendant stress and expense' of court proceedings on parents (an argument advanced by some of the parties in *Re Kelvin*),[69] or even on the scope of parental rights in the medical treatment context (the predominant focus of the judgment). Rather, the Full Court's attention would have been on whether removing the requirement for court authorisation, to enable a child experiencing gender dysphoria to commence stage two treatment, and/or removing the Family Court from the assessment of a child's *Gillick* competence, would be in the best interests of the child (Kelvin) or TGD children as a collective, taking into account the child's rights under the CRC. Parental

66 See Introduction (Section I.4.1).

67 See Jeremy Waldron, 'Judges as Moral Reasoners' (2009) 7(1) *International Journal of Constitutional Law* 2, 12; Ronald Dworkin, *Law's Empire* (Belknap Press, 1986) 238–58.

68 Jane Fortin, *Children's Rights and the Developing Law* (Cambridge University Press, 3rd ed, 2009) 96 (emphasis in original). See also Jane Fortin, 'Accommodating Children's Rights in a Post *Human Rights Act* Era' (2006) 69(3) *Modern Law Review* 299, 302–3 ('Accommodating Children's Rights').

69 *Re Kelvin* (n 1) [119] (Thackray, Strickland and Murphy JJ).

interests would have been relevant, but the Full Court's attention would have been directed to parents' primary responsibility for the upbringing and development of their child, having their child's best interests as their basic concern.[70]

6.4.2 *A judgment by adults, for adults: Another missed opportunity to advance children's right to decisional privacy*

While the Full Court's decision was exalted as championing the rights of TGD children,[71] those very children were, it has been argued, largely invisible in the *Re Kelvin* judgment. This is, at least in part, because the matter came before the Full Court in the form of a special case stated, such that the Court's focus was on questions of law for its opinion. Kelvin thus served an instrumental purpose in reforming the law in relation to medical treatment for childhood gender dysphoria. His case was a vehicle for the Full Court to reconsider its decision in *Re Jamie*. By virtue of how the case came before the Full Court, Kelvin himself was not the focus of the Court's judgment; nor, however, were TGD children as a collective. To advance this argument, this section focuses on the central narrative of the Full Court's judgment. It then rewrites the judgment from a children's rights perspective.

i. The central narrative

The 'political potential'[72] of judgments in gender dysphoria proceedings to raise awareness of the perceived unjust incursion into TGD children's rights reached a pinnacle following the Full Court's decision in *Re Jamie*. Activism, academic critique and judicial discontent with the decision and reasoning in *Re Jamie* prompted the Full Court in *Re Kelvin* to 're-shape ... the official "story"'.[73] However, the Full Court omitted any reference to the rights of children in its judgment, instead displaying a predictable preference for the language of children's 'welfare'[74] and parental rights and responsibilities.[75]

What is most telling about the Full Court's judgment, it is argued, is the central narrative that it conveyed: this was not a judgment *about* TGD children or their rights, but about the extent of state incursion into family (parental) decision-making and ensuring that the law kept pace with medical science. According to the majority, the Family Court had 'always recognised ... an appropriate concern

70 *CRC*, art 18(1).

71 See n 7 above.

72 Erika Rackley, 'The Art and Craft of Writing Judgments: Notes on the Feminist Judgment Project' in Rosemary Hunter, Clare McGlynn and Erica Rackley (eds), *Feminist Judgments: From Theory to Practice* (Hart Publishing, 2010) 44, 45.

73 Ibid 46.

74 See Fortin, 'Accommodating Children's Rights' (n 68) 303–4, 306.

75 See Section 6.4.1.i above.

about intruding into the lives of parents' in gender dysphoria cases.[76] The majority added that it was 'readily apparent that the judicial understanding of Gender Dysphoria and its treatment have fallen behind the advances in medical science'.[77] This led the majority to observe that '[i]t would not be heresy to suggest that, in relation to stage 2 treatment, *Re Jamie* would be decided differently today', that case having been decided 'at a particular point in time, and at a particular stage in the development of legal principle, and even more importantly of medical science'.[78]

The minority judgment perhaps showed implicit respect for children's decision-making autonomy, through a clearly stated concern to eliminate the risk that 'in the future *Re Jamie* might be interpreted as providing a basis for court involvement in therapeutic procedures which on a proper application of *Marion's Case* come within the scope of parental authority or the capacity of a legally competent child'.[79] Yet the narrative through which the minority conveyed this sentiment was still one of correct application of legal principle, rather than one of children's rights. The judgment in *Re Kelvin* was thus about the development of the law in line with developments in medical science, rather than about the rights of TGD children.

ii. Rewriting Re Kelvin: A child-friendly version of the Full Court's judgment

The Full Court in *Re Kelvin* also missed the opportunity to advance the rights of TGD children by writing a judgment that was *for* them, to explain the significance of the decision. Given that the Full Court's judgment determined legal questions that directly impacted the rights of TGD children, a children's rights approach to decisional privacy would require that the judgment and reasons be available and accessible to those children. A vital element of communicating a children's rights judgment is ensuring that children, during their childhood, are able to access and understand the court's reasoning and decision.[80] This is a 'child-friendly' judgment: one that has tailored its language, narrative and structure to cater for children as one of its key audiences. A child-friendly judgment also centralises and humanises the child who is the subject of proceedings. It uses narrative to

76 *Re Kelvin* (n 1) [117] (Thackray, Strickland and Murphy JJ).

77 Ibid [152].

78 Ibid [165]. This observation is phrased in almost identical terms to the observation made by Strickland J in a paper presented at a 2014 oration: '*Re Jamie* is … a decision that was made at a particular point in time and at a particular stage in the development of legal principle and medical science': Strickland (n 13) 72.

79 *Re Kelvin* (n 1) [209] (Ainslie-Wallace and Ryan JJ).

80 Kathryn Hollingsworth and Helen Stalford, 'Towards Children's Rights Judgments' in Helen Stalford, Kathryn Hollingsworth and Stephen Gilmore (eds), *Rewriting Children's Rights Judgments: From Academic Vision to New Practice* (Hart Publishing, 2017) 53, 82. See Chapter 3 (Section 3.5.2).

tell the child's story and to highlight the impacts of the decision on the child.[81] Communication of a decision about a child's best interests in this manner is a process integral to children's ability to enjoy and exercise their substantive right to decisional privacy.[82]

In light of the Full Court's 'invisible rights' approach,[83] it is unsurprising that children were not contemplated as an audience of the *Re Kelvin* judgment. The Full Court's inability to conceptualise the issues in the case stated in terms of children's rights meant, as a logical extension, that children's rights would not have been at the fore of the minds of the judges when drafting their judgments. As such, the Full Court did not strive to accommodate and embrace children's rights through a child-friendly version of its judgment. The opportunity nonetheless existed, it is argued, for the Full Court to do so, by articulating in clear, age-appropriate[84] language, what the Court decided and why. This might have been achieved by writing a letter to Kelvin[85] or by producing a short summary of the Full Court's decision,[86] as the author has endeavoured to do below:

> This case is about a young person's right to decide who he is and who he wants to be. That young person's name is Kelvin.
>
> Kelvin was born a girl, but he felt like a boy and wanted to be a boy. He felt like he was trapped in the wrong body. Doctors call this 'gender dysphoria'.
>
> When Kelvin was 16 years old, his father asked the Family Court to allow Kelvin to start medical treatment. This treatment would help Kelvin's body match up with who he was: a boy.
>
> The Family Court asked us to answer an important question: who should decide whether Kelvin can start medical treatment? Should it be the Family Court? Or should Kelvin be able to make the decision, together with his parents and doctors?
>
> Usually, parents can make decisions about their child's medical treatment.

81 Hollingsworth and Stalford (n 80) 80. See Chapter 3 (Section 3.5.1).

82 See Chapter 3 (Section 3.5.2).

83 See Section 6.4.1 above.

84 See Nigel Thomas, *Children, Family and the State: Decision-Making and Child Participation* (Palgrave MacMillan, 2000) 68–9.

85 See, eg, *Gaylard v Cain* [2012] FMCAfam 501; *Re A (Letter to a Young Person)* [2017] EWFC 48.

86 See, eg, the abridged, child-friendly versions of some of the rewritten judgments in Helen Stalford, Kathryn Hollingsworth and Stephen Gilmore (eds), *Rewriting Children's Rights Judgments: From Academic Vision to New Practice* (Hart Publishing, 2017): Michael Freeman, 'House of Lords: *Re T (A Minor) (Wardship: Medical Treatment)*': at 256; Jo Bridgeman, 'Family Division of the High Court (England and Wales): *Re X and Y (Foreign Surrogacy)*': at 104; Anashri Pillay, 'Constitutional Court of South Africa: *The Government of the Republic of South Africa & Ors v Grootboom & Ors*': at 327–8; Laura Lundy, 'European Court of Human Rights: *Valsamis v Greece*': at 344.

> But for the medical treatment that Kelvin wants, the Family Court for a long time has had to make the decision. This is because of the type of treatment, what might happen if a wrong decision is made, and the chance that Kelvin and his parents might not agree.
>
> We have decided that Kelvin and other young people like him should be able to make the decision to start medical treatment themselves, with help from their parents and advice from their doctors. They should not have to go to the Family Court to be who they are.
>
> But if a young person, their parents or their doctors do not agree, then we think that the Family Court should still make the decision.

While Kelvin was 17 years old when the Full Court published its reasons for judgment, the above re-written summary of the *Re Kelvin* judgment is pitched to young people approximately 12 years of age, to make it accessible to a broader range of children experiencing gender dysphoria, who may be contemplating stage two treatment or may have begun that treatment. The primary aim of this rewritten, child-friendly summary of the Full Court's judgment in *Re Kelvin* is to make clear that this is a case about children and their rights: the ability of children experiencing gender dysphoria to make decisions and choices about their bodies and identities. The decision is not justified on the basis of advances in medical science or (in)correct application of legal principle. Nor is the focus upon the recalibration of parental responsibilities and state duties in relation to children's medical treatment. Rather, attention is drawn to the impact of the decision on the decisional privacy rights of Kelvin and other TGD children and young people.

6.4.3 *The need for Family Court authorisation in circumstances of 'genuine dispute or controversy'[87] about a child's medical treatment*

The third feature of the Full Court's judgment in *Re Kelvin* which arguably militates against the conclusion that the decision was a victory for TGD children's rights, is the scope that the Full Court provided for ongoing court involvement in the medical treatment process for gender dysphoria. In concluding that the Full Court did not confirm its decision in *Re Jamie*, the majority in *Re Kelvin* inserted an important caveat:

> we are not saying anything about the need for court authorisation where the child in question is under the care of a State Government Department. Nor, are we saying anything about the need for court authorisation where there is a *genuine dispute or controversy as to whether the treatment should be administered; eg, if the parents, or the medical professionals are unable to agree.* There

87 *Re Kelvin* (n 1) [167] (Thackray, Strickland and Murphy JJ).

> is no doubt that the Court has the jurisdiction and the power to address issues such as those.[88]

This paragraph of the judgment warrants closer scrutiny for how it overlooks the role of the child in circumstances of potential conflict; and its failure to articulate how the 'genuineness' of a dispute or controversy that would justify Family Court intervention is to be assessed.

i. Overlooking the child's role in the decision-making process

In canvassing the possibility of a 'genuine dispute or controversy', the majority in *Re Kelvin* gave no credence to the *child's* role in the decision-making process in relation to their own medical treatment. The majority was silent on the relevance of the child's views and wishes, offering the example of disagreement between the child's parents or the child's treating medical professionals.[89] This judicial silence downplays the impact and importance of children's participation in medical treatment decision-making. The judgment of Bryant CJ in *Re Jamie* provides a neat point of comparison. Her Honour stated:

> If there is a dispute between the parents, *child* and treating medical practitioners, or any of them, regarding the treatment and/or whether or not the child is *Gillick* competent, the court should make an assessment about whether to authorise stage two having regard to the best interests of the child as the paramount consideration.[90]

Bryant CJ explicitly identified *the child* as having distinct rights and interests in the decision-making process, which may very well conflict with those of the child's parents and/or treating medical practitioners. Her Honour appeared to recognise – as a necessary corrective to the perils of family privacy – the real potential for opposing interests, views and wishes within families. The power disparities between and amongst family members add layers of complexity to the analysis of whether proposed medical treatment for a child experiencing gender dysphoria is in that child's best interests in any particular case.[91]

That the majority in *Re Kelvin* omitted the child from its example of circumstances of 'genuine dispute or controversy' might at first blush appear a minor semantic lapse. Yet its implications – both conceptual and practical – for TGD

88 Ibid (emphasis added). See also Ainslie-Wallace and Ryan JJ's statement that 'the principles that emerge from *Marion's Case* when applied to *Re Jamie* should have resulted in the conclusion that in relation to stage 2 treatment for Gender Dysphoria the court has no role to play *unless there is a dispute about consent or treatment*': at [189] (emphasis added).

89 See also Section 6.4.1.ii above.

90 *Jamie Appeal* (n 2) [140(f)] (Bryant CJ) (emphasis added). See also [179], [194], and the submissions of the Australian Human Rights Commission on this point: at [46], [56].

91 See Chapter 1 (Section 1.4.4).

children's decisional privacy rights are more significant. The majority's formulation in *Re Kelvin* suggests that it conceptualised the medical treatment decision-making process for childhood gender dysphoria as, in essence, about adult control over and regulation of TGD children's bodies and identities. It arguably reflects resistance to the notion that children can and should influence decisions that affect their lives,[92] as active participants in the determination of their best interests. It also underpins the problematic assumption that children's views and interests align with those of their parents.[93]

A more redeeming interpretation of the majority's statement in *Re Kelvin* regarding the need for court authorisation – although not accepted here – is that the majority was simply acknowledging that conflicts may more commonly arise between parents and a child's treating medical practitioners about whether a proposed course of action is in the child's best interests.[94] However, potential conflicts also extend to the scope of institutional encroachment into the lives of TGD children and their families. The issue is how to protect and promote children's right to decisional privacy within what Nedelsky has called 'the (many) spheres of state power'.[95] As the majority in *Re Kelvin* (paraphrasing counsel for the Royal Children's Hospital, as an intervener in the proceedings) asked:

> why should the family of a child in one wing of the Hospital be forced to come to court before recommended medical treatment commences when the family of a child in another wing of the Hospital is not required to do so, in circumstances where both forms of treatment carry a significant risk of making the wrong decision as to a child's capacity to consent and with both forms of treatment the consequences of a wrong decision are particularly grave.[96]

ii. Determining the 'genuineness' of a dispute or controversy that would justify court intervention

The statement of the majority in *Re Kelvin*, regarding the Family Court's ongoing role in the medical treatment process for gender dysphoria in circumstances of 'genuine dispute or controversy', also generates unease from a children's rights perspective for the opacity with which it articulates the scope for Family

92 Laura Lundy, John Tobin and Aisling Parkes, 'Article 12 The Right to Respect for the Views of the Child' in John Tobin (ed), *The UN Convention on the Rights of the Child: A Commentary* (Oxford University Press, 2019) 397, 398.

93 See Chapter 1 (Section 1.4.4) and Chapter 2 (Section 2.3.1).

94 See Rob Heywood, 'Parents and Medical Professionals: Conflict, Cooperation, and Best Interests' (2012) 20(1) *Medical Law Review* 29; Margot Brazier, 'An Intractable Dispute: When Parents and Professionals Disagree' (2005) 13(3) *Medical Law Review* 412.

95 Jennifer Nedelsky, *Law's Relations: A Relational Theory of Self, Autonomy and Law* (Oxford University Press, 2011) 118.

96 *Re Kelvin* (n 1) [116] (Thackray, Strickland and Murphy JJ).

Court intervention. The majority considered *who* might generate the dispute or controversy (parents, medical professionals), but was silent on what would make such a dispute or controversy a 'genuine' one that would necessitate Family Court involvement. Writing extra-curially following the Full Court's judgment in *Re Jamie*, Strickland J argued for:

> some discussion of the concept of disagreement in ousting a *Gillick* competent child's right to make decisions about their own medical treatment. Who it is that disagrees, what they disagree about, whether there is a 'reasonableness' requirement surrounding the disagreement, and how much significance should be accorded to a young person's views in the event of disagreement, are some of the issues ripe for judicial contemplation.[97]

Such discussion did not occur in the *Re Kelvin* judgment. A 'grey zone' for assessing the genuineness of a dispute or controversy in this context might arise where a child clearly expresses a view that conflicts with the wishes of their parents, yet the child does not have sufficient maturity and understanding to enable their views to be conclusive on the issue.[98] In these circumstances, a children's rights approach to decisional privacy would require the Family Court to articulate, consider and balance the rights and interests of various parties, including those of the child, the child's parents and the child's treating medical practitioners.[99] This approach, which embraces a relational conception of autonomy,[100] appreciates that 'seeing medical decisions as involving simply the choice of the child is unlikely to reflect reality'.[101] It also accepts, as Gilmore and Herring have argued, that '[t]here is a danger, which is particularly pertinent in the case of children, of viewing the patient in isolation from the context of the relationships within which they (and we all) live'.[102]

The primary interest of the child's treating medical practitioners is not always obvious from the judgments in gender dysphoria proceedings: that interest is to be protected against the possibility of future litigation, through a declaration by the Family Court that the child is *Gillick* competent to consent to the proposed medical treatment. Nicholson CJ in *Re Alex* (2004) described 'a significant onus' placed upon the treating medical practitioner's assessment, because the practitioner 'risks liability unless satisfied that the child or young person has "a sufficient understanding and intelligence to enable [them] to understand fully

97 Strickland (n 13) 78.
98 Tobin, 'Judging the Judges' (n 5) 614.
99 See Chapter 3 (Section 3.4.2).
100 See Chapter 1 (Section 1.4.3) and Chapter 4 (Section 4.2).
101 Stephen Gilmore and Jonathan Herring, '"No" Is the Hardest Word: Consent and Children's Autonomy' (2011) 23(1) *Child and Family Law Quarterly* 3, 23.
102 Ibid.

what is imposed"'.[103] A finding by the Family Court of the child's *Gillick* competence transfers the responsibility for risk from the medical practitioner to the patient, thereby refuting any challenge to the practitioner who administers medical treatment that they had not obtained the child's effective consent.[104] The Family Court has noted that it would be 'sad' and potentially an abuse of court process, if a third party sought a decision from the court regarding proposed medical treatment that was clearly within the bounds of parental responsibility, such as 'where the sole purpose of such an application was as a protection against the prospect of future litigation'.[105]

iii. The practical effect of the 'genuine dispute or controversy' caveat: Further curtailing TGD children's decisional privacy rights

Applications to the Family Court seeking authorisation of medical treatment for gender dysphoria prior to *Re Kelvin* rarely involved a dispute. In one case, the child's treating medical practitioners disagreed on the issue of whether the child was *Gillick* competent.[106] In another, the child's own evidence made it clear that the child's parents were opposed to the course of action that the child sought to follow in seeking treatment.[107] A different conflictual dynamic involved intra-parental conflict: the child's mother brought proceedings for the authorisation of stage one treatment (puberty blockers), while the father opposed the application.[108] As the majority in *Re Kelvin* noted, in no stage two gender dysphoria case had contradictory evidence been forthcoming to challenge the desirability of the relevant medical treatment.[109] Although the majority also acknowledged that the requirement for court involvement might have itself served as a 'filter' for the cases in which stage two treatment was recommended and undertaken.[110]

103 *Re Alex* (2004) (n 10) 116–17 [155] (Nicholson CJ), quoting the High Court in *Marion's Case* (n 18) 237–8 (Mason CJ, Dawson, Toohey and Gaudron JJ).

104 John Seymour, *Children, Parents and the Courts: Legal Intervention in Family Life* (Federation Press, 2016) 160; Priscilla Alderson, 'Younger Children's Individual Participation in "All Matters Affecting the Child"' in Barry Percy-Smith and Nigel Thomas (eds), *A Handbook of Children and Young People's Participation: Perspectives from Theory and Practice* (Routledge, 2010) 88, 94.

105 *Re Sean* (2010) 258 FLR 192, 207 [93] (Murphy J). In *Re a Declaration Regarding Medical Treatment for 'A'* (2020) 6 QR 718, the Supreme Court of Queensland exercised its *parens patriae* jurisdiction to make a declaration authorising stage one treatment for an almost 13-year-old young person diagnosed with gender dysphoria. The Court noted that the medical practitioners were concerned about whether they could commence stage one treatment without the consent of the father, whose whereabouts were unknown: at [36].

106 See *Re Darryl* [2016] FamCA 720, [11]–[20] (Tree J). See also *Re Leo* (2015) 52 Fam LR 533.

107 See *Re Isaac* [2014] FamCA 1134.

108 See *Re Brodie (Special Medical Procedures: Jurisdiction)* [2007] FamCA 776; *Re Brodie (Special Medical Procedures)* [2008] FamCA 334.

109 *Re Kelvin* (n 1) [119] (Thackray, Strickland and Murphy JJ).

110 Ibid.

Following *Re Kelvin*, a number of cases seeking authorisation for gender dysphoria treatment have continued to be heard by the Family Court, as they fall beyond the scope of the Full Court's decision. At the time of writing, three of these cases have involved the issue of *Gillick* competence in relation to stage three treatment (surgical intervention).[111] In *Re Ryan*,[112] there was a controversy between the parents 'over letting Ryan make his own decision'.[113] Cleary J implicitly acknowledged Ryan's evolving capacities and his parents' need to cede their decision-making authority, noting that '[i]n this, Ryan, is like many young people, separating himself from both of his parents in anticipation of an independent life'.[114]

Other cases that have come before the Family Court following *Re Kelvin* have involved a dispute between parents, or between parents and treating medical practitioners, in relation to diagnosis, *Gillick* competence or the proposed treatment itself;[115] one parent's refusal to give consent for treatment to commence;[116] or the inability to obtain one parent's consent.[117] Of these judgments, *Re Max*[118] is noteworthy from the perspective of children's right to decisional privacy, as leave was granted to the young person, Max, to file affidavits in the proceeding.[119] Hartnett J quoted Max's affidavit evidence of a 'powerful desire not to have to wait until my 18th birthday next year before being able to proceed with the next phase of my life'.[120]

A third category of case that has emerged post-*Re Kelvin* – and also following the decision of the High Court of England and Wales in *R (Bell) v The Tavistock and Portman NHS Foundation Trust* ('*Bell*')[121] – has not involved any dispute or controversy. Rather, a declaration of *Gillick* competence has been sought by parents in light of changes to a health service's pathway to stage two treatment.[122] Relevantly, the health service in both judgments in this category submitted that:

> Given the fact of the *Bell* dispute ... the absence of any legislative framework, and the clear position that the question of *Gillick* competency and whether

111 *Re LG* [2017] FCWA 179; *Re Matthew* [2018] FamCA 161; *Re Ryan* [2019] FamCA 112 ('*Re Ryan*'). For a discussion of these judgments, see Steph Jowett and Fiona Kelly, '*Re Imogen*: A Step in the Wrong Direction' (2021) 34(1) *Australian Journal of Family Law* 31, 40–1.
112 *Re Ryan* (n 111).
113 Ibid [31] (Cleary J).
114 Ibid [37].
115 *Re Imogen [No 6]* (2020) 61 Fam LR 344 ('*Re Imogen*'); *Re Ash* [2021] FedCFamC1F 100; *Re Max* [2021] FamCA 290 ('*Re Max*').
116 *Re John* [2021] FedCFamC1F 169; *Re Jesse* [2021] FedCFamC1F 42.
117 *Re G4* [2021] FCWA 102; *Re Addison [No 3]* [2021] FamCA 232.
118 *Re Max* (n 115).
119 Ibid [3].
120 Ibid [47]–[48].
121 [2020] EWHC 3274 (Admin).
122 *Re G2* [2021] FCWA 98 ('*Re G2*'); *Re G3* [2021] FCWA 99 ('*Re G3*').

> there is an adequate understanding of the consequences of the treatment in question are in effect value judgments of the clinicians in question, the [health service's] position is that it considers it appropriate for this Court to exercise its welfare jurisdiction.[123]

The practical effect of the majority's statement in *Re Kelvin* – that the court must remain involved in cases involving a 'genuine dispute or controversy' – is that the ability of children experiencing gender dysphoria to access treatment is contingent upon alignment between the views of their parents and their treating medical practitioners. The decision of the Family Court in *Re Imogen [No 6]*[124] offers a compelling illustration of this result.

In *Re Imogen*, Watts J held that if a child's parent or treating medical practitioner disputes the child's *Gillick* competence, or a diagnosis of, or proposed treatment for, gender dysphoria, then an application to the Family Court is mandatory.[125] Watts J also held that, once an application is made, the Court should make a finding about the child's *Gillick* competence; and that notwithstanding such a finding, if there is a dispute about diagnosis or treatment, the Court should determine the diagnosis and whether treatment is appropriate, and make an order under section 67ZC of the Family Law Act.[126] Most problematic, in terms of its impact on TGD children's decisional privacy rights, is the conclusion in *Re Imogen* that a finding of *Gillick* competence is *not* determinative if parents do not agree about diagnosis or treatment.

The first concern with this conclusion derives from the relational nature of autonomy.[127] Children's decision-making is influenced by the 'scaffolding',[128] support and structure provided by their parents and other caregivers. A relational approach to autonomy in the medical treatment context recognises the significance of the individual's family in the decision-making process, even where that individual is *Gillick* competent.[129] Research has found that TGD children who lack parental and wider familial support are more likely to experience

123 *Re G2* (n 122) [25]; *Re G3* (n 122) [24].
124 *Re Imogen* (n 115).
125 Ibid 351 [35].
126 Ibid. For a detailed analysis of the *Re Imogen* decision, see Georgina Dimopoulos and Michelle Taylor-Sands, '*Re Imogen*: The Role of the Family Court of Australia in Disputes over Gender Dysphoria Treatment' (2021) 39 (Suppl 1) *Monash Bioethics Review* S42; Jowett and Kelly (n 111).
127 See Chapter 1 (Section 1.4.3) and Chapter 8 (Section 8.2).
128 Patrick Parkinson and Judy Cashmore, *The Voice of a Child in Family Law Disputes* (Oxford University Press, 2008) 8.
129 See, eg, Roy Gilbar and Ora Gilbar, 'The Medical Decision-Making Process and the Family: The Case of Breast Cancer Patients and Their Husbands' (2009) 23(3) *Bioethics* 183; Michelle Taylor-Sands, *Saviour Siblings: A Relational Approach to the Welfare of the Child in Selective Reproduction* (Routledge, 2013) 109–23.

gender dysphoria[130] and are at higher risk of suicidality and self-harm.[131] The *Re Imogen* decision arguably 'opens the door for unsupportive, or otherwise disengaged, parents to interfere with their *Gillick*-competent child's access to timely treatment',[132] which may indeed trigger more legal disputes over gender dysphoria treatment than previously.

The conclusion in *Re Imogen* that a finding of *Gillick* competence is not determinative in circumstances of dispute is also troubling for the scepticism that it conveys about young people's capacity. It has been argued elsewhere, including by the author, that to impose such a caveat unjustifiably denies *Gillick* competent young people the ability to exercise decision-making autonomy in relation to their bodies and identities.[133] Indeed, the same limitation upon decision-making capacity would not be imposed upon an adult in like circumstances. If an adult was found to be competent to consent to medical treatment, that consent would not be contingent upon a third party agreeing with the proposed treatment.[134] The author has proposed elsewhere an alternative regulatory framework for the resolution of disputes between a parent and their *Gillick* competent child over gender dysphoria treatment, which removes the Family Court from the decision-making process.[135] The impact of *Re Imogen* on future cases involving a dispute or controversy should be followed with interest, particularly given that legislative reform in this area 'is yet to gain political appetite'.[136]

6.5 Conclusion

Until the decision of the Full Court in *Re Kelvin*, Australia was the only country in the world in which court authorisation was required for the medical treatment

130 See, eg, Annelou L C de Vries et al, 'Young Adult Psychological Outcome after Puberty Suppression and Gender Reassignment' (2014) 134(4) *Pediatrics* 696; Kristina R Olson et al, 'Mental Health of Transgender Children who are Supported in Their Identities' (2016) 137(3) *Pediatrics* e20153223.

131 See, eg, Robb Travers et al, *Impacts of Strong Parental Support for Trans Youth: A Report Prepared for Children's Aid Society of Toronto and Delisle Youth Services* (October 2012) 2.

132 Jowett and Kelly (n 111) 51–2. See also Samuel Dubin et al, 'Medically Assisted Gender Affirmation: When Children and Parents Disagree' (2019) 46(5) *Journal of Medical Ethics* 295.

133 See Dimopoulos and Taylor-Sands (n 126); Jowett and Kelly (n 111).

134 See *Re T (Adult: Refusal of Medical Treatment)* [1992] 4 All ER 649, 652–3 (Lord Donaldson holding that: 'An adult patient who … suffers from no mental incapacity has an absolute right to choose whether to consent to medical treatment, to refuse it or to choose one rather than another of the treatments being offered … This right of choice is not limited to decisions which others might regard as sensible. It exists notwithstanding that the reasons for making the choice are rational, irrational, unknown or even non-existent'). Cf Julian Savulescu and Richard W Momeyer, 'Should Informed Consent Be Based on Rational Beliefs?' (1997) 23 *Journal of Medical Ethics* 282.

135 See Dimopoulos and Taylor-Sands (n 126) S59–S62.

136 Ibid S60. See also Jowett and Kelly (n 111) 55–6; France (n 15) 246–8.

of children experiencing gender dysphoria.[137] The majority in *Re Kelvin* stated that the Full Court's decision was 'not unexpected'.[138] It is also not unexpected that the decision reverberated with positivity throughout Australia's TGD community. This chapter has re-read the *Re Kelvin* judgment from the perspective of children's right to decisional privacy, exposing various problematic features. It has argued that, ultimately, the judgment was not *about* TGD children or their rights; nor was it written *for* them. Rather, the judgment was about the extent to which the Family Court should intervene in parental decision-making about children's medical treatment, consistently with the latest developments in medical science. Children experiencing gender dysphoria benefit only incidentally from the Full Court's decision. Their ability to access stage two treatment without court involvement depends upon agreement between their parents and their treating medical practitioners. The Full Court in *Re Kelvin* was presented with a prime opportunity to unsettle the status quo: not only by deciding that stage two treatment for childhood gender dysphoria was no longer a 'special medical procedure' that justified the exercise of the welfare jurisdiction under section 67ZC of the Family Law Act, but more importantly, by transforming the status of TGD children and young people in Australia. This chapter has sought to show that, through its judgment in *Re Kelvin*, the Full Court did not embrace this opportunity. The next chapter presents an international perspective. It demonstrates that the violation of TGD children's decisional privacy rights through court involvement in the medical treatment process for gender dysphoria is not unique to Australia, but has emerged more recently in England and Wales.

137 Hewitt et al (n 19) 578.
138 *Re Kelvin* (n 1) [165] (Thackray, Strickland and Murphy JJ).

7 Validating treatment that 'goes to the heart of an individual's identity'

Re-reading the Court of Appeal's judgment in *Bell v Tavistock*

7.1 Introduction

The case study of judicial proceedings concerning medical treatment for children experiencing gender dysphoria has thus far focused on Australia. The previous two chapters analysed two judgments of the Full Court of the Family Court of Australia from the perspective of children's right to decisional privacy. This chapter offers an important comparative dimension. It applies the concept of children's right to decisional privacy to examine the decision of the Court of Appeal of England and Wales ('Court of Appeal') in the case of *R (Bell) v The Tavistock and Portman NHS Foundation Trust* ('*Bell*').[1] The initial proceedings before the Administrative Division of the High Court of England and Wales ('High Court') involved an application for judicial review of the practice of The Tavistock and Portman NHS Foundation Trust ('Tavistock'), through its Gender Identity Development Service ('GIDS'), in prescribing puberty blockers to children under 18 years of age who experience gender dysphoria.[2] While the High Court did not find the practice of GIDS unlawful, it made a declaration that specified what 'informed consent' would require in these circumstances, and issued detailed 'guidance' covering children of all ages. The High Court's guidance recommended that court authorisation should be obtained before puberty blockers are prescribed, notwithstanding the absence of a legal requirement to do so.[3] The High Court forged a sequential link between the decision to commence treatment with puberty blockers (stage one treatment for gender dysphoria) and a child proceeding to gender-affirming hormones (stage two treatment).[4] The High Court held that to achieve *Gillick* competence,[5] a child or young person

1 [2021] EWCA Civ 1363 ('*Bell Appeal*').

2 *R (Bell) v The Tavistock and Portman NHS Foundation Trust* [2020] EWHC 3274 (Admin) ('*Bell Judicial Review*').

3 Ibid [138], [145]–[147], [151]–[152] (Sharp P, Lewis LJ and Lieven J).

4 Ibid [136].

5 This is the test to determine a child's capacity to give informed consent to medical treatment. It derives from the decision of the House of Lords in *Gillick v West Norfolk and Wisbech Area Health Authority* [1986] AC 112 ('*Gillick*'). See Chapter 4 (Section 4.3.1) and Section 7.2 below.

DOI: 10.4324/9781003224167-10

would need to understand both the implications of taking puberty blockers and the implications of progressing to gender-affirming hormones;[6] and that 'in many cases, however much information the child is given as to long-term consequences', the child would 'not be able to weigh up the implications of the treatment to a sufficient degree'.[7]

The Court of Appeal overturned the decision of the High Court, setting aside the declaration and holding that it was inappropriate for the High Court to provide the guidance.[8] It held that, as there were no findings of illegality regarding the Tavistock's practices, the High Court had improperly restricted the test of *Gillick* competence, by including age criteria and the requirement to apply to the court for authorisation to commence treatment with puberty blockers.[9] The Court of Appeal's decision has been heralded a 'huge win for trans people and their families'[10] and 'a historic victory for transgender people's rights'.[11] The decision is considered to have restored 'the proper distinction of responsibilities between doctors and the courts'[12] and to signal a 'turning point' for improving TGD children's access to vital healthcare and support services.[13]

This chapter first provides an overview of the legal framework for decision-making regarding children's medical treatment in England and Wales. It then outlines the decisions of the High Court and the Court of Appeal in the *Bell* proceedings. A children's rights analysis of the Court of Appeal's judgment follows, to advance the argument that the judgment is less of a practical 'positive step forwards for trans rights in the UK and around the world'[14] as it is a symbolic one. Three features of the judgment are examined. First, in articulating the issues, the Court of Appeal framed the dispute as being over the appropriate 'gatekeeper' to medical treatment for children experiencing gender dysphoria:

6 Ibid [138].
7 Ibid [144].
8 *Bell Appeal* (n 1) [91] (Lord Burnett of Maldon CJ, Sir Geoffrey Vos MR and King LJ).
9 Ibid [94].
10 'We've Won: Bell v Tavistock Judgment Quashed by Court of Appeal', *Good Law Project* (Web Page, 17 September 2021) <https://goodlawproject.org/update/weve-won-bell-v-tavistock/> ('We've Won, *Good Law Project*'). See also 'Court of Appeal Ruling Step Forwards for Trans Rights', *Liberty* (Web Page, 17 September 2021) <www.libertyhumanrights.org.uk/issue/liberty-court-of-appeal-ruling-step-forwards-for-trans-rights/>.
11 Lucy Morgan, 'In a Historic Victory for Transgender People's Rights, a Ruling which Restricted Under-16s from being Prescribed Puberty Blockers has been Overturned', *Glamour* (online, 17 September 2021) <www.glamourmagazine.co.uk/article/under-16s-puberty-blockers-ruling>.
12 'We've Won', *Good Law Project* (n 10).
13 Emilie Schäfferling, 'UK Court Overturns Ruling Limiting Under-16s Access To Puberty Blockers', *Star Observer* (online, 19 September 2021) <www.starobserver.com.au/news/uk-court-overturns-ruling-limiting-under-16s-access-to-puberty-blockers/205818>.
14 Haroon Siddique, 'Appeal Court Overturns UK Puberty Blockers Ruling for Under-16s', *The Guardian* (online, 18 September 2021) <www.theguardian.com/society/2021/sep/17/appeal-court-overturns-uk-puberty-blockers-ruling-for-under-16s-tavistock-keira-bell>.

medical practitioners[15] or the courts. The problem with this approach is that TGD children were abstracted, relegated to statistics and constructed exclusively by reference to their vulnerability, with no acknowledgement of their evolving capacity and agency. Second, the outcome of the Court of Appeal's judgment could be taken to suggest an implied appreciation of TGD children as rights-bearers with evolving capacities for decision-making. However, the Court's failure to engage with human rights (let alone children's rights) in its judgment, and its stated reluctance to wade into the 'intense professional and public debate' in this 'difficult and controversial area',[16] demand a less reassuring conclusion. Thirdly, the written summary of the Court of Appeal's judgment – one being 'to assist the press and the public'[17] – did not contemplate children as an audience. The judgment thus missed the opportunity to fulfil its 'enormous instructive potential'[18] in articulating the significance of the decision for the bodily autonomy and identity rights of TGD children. However, if a redeeming feature is to be found in the *Bell* judgment from the perspective of children's right to decisional privacy, it is argued that that feature lies in the limited symbolic value of the judgment for the ability of TGD children to exercise choice in developing, discovering and preserving their gender identity without the need for court intervention.[19] This chapter thus argues that the Court of Appeal's judgment represents a partial victory for TGD children and their rights, although its significance should not be overstated.

7.2 Children's capacity to consent to medical treatment in the UK: The legal framework

This section outlines the law regarding children's legal capacity in the UK and their ability to consent to medical treatment. While the age of majority is 18 years,[20] nuances do exist in the law. Children below 18 years of age can, in certain circumstances, give valid consent to medical treatment. The decision of the House of Lords in *Gillick v West Norfolk and Wisbech Area Health Authority* ('*Gillick*')[21] established the principle that a child will be found to be competent to

15 The High Court and the Court of Appeal in the *Bell* proceedings used the term 'clinician'. For consistency with previous chapters, the term 'medical practitioner' is used throughout this chapter.
16 *Bell Appeal* (n 1) [3], [93].
17 *Bell v Tavistock* Judgment Summary, Court of Appeal of England and Wales, 17 September 2021 <www.judiciary.uk/wp-content/uploads/2021/09/Bell-v-Tavistock-summary-170921.pdf> ('*Bell Appeal* Judgment Summary').
18 Helen Stalford and Kathryn Hollingsworth, '"This Case is about You and Your Future": Towards Judgments for Children' (2020) 83(5) *Modern Law Review* 1030, 1052 ('"This Case is about You"').
19 See Chapter 4 (Section 4.4).
20 *Children Act 1989* (UK) s 105(1) ('*Children Act*'); *Family Law Reform Act 1969* (UK) s 1 ('*FLR Act*').
21 *Gillick* (n 5).

consent to medical treatment if the child has achieved 'a sufficient understanding and intelligence to enable [them] to understand fully what is proposed'.[22] The standard of '*Gillick* competence' or '*Gillick* capacity'[23] applies to children under the age of 16 years. Children aged 16 years and over can consent to surgical, medical and dental treatment 'as if [they] were of full age'.[24] What this means, in practical terms, is that children under 16 years are presumed to lack capacity, but can consent to treatment if they are deemed competent; while children aged 16 and 17 years are presumed to have capacity and thus their consent to medical treatment usually suffices.

Most provisions of the *Mental Capacity Act 2005* (UK) ('MCA') and its accompanying Code,[25] also apply to children aged 16 and 17 years.[26] The MCA governs decision-making for adults who lack capacity. Its starting point is a presumption of capacity.[27] Incapacity is determined in two stages: first, whether an individual has 'an impairment of, or a disturbance in the functioning of, the mind or brain';[28] and if so, whether that impairment or disturbance is such that the person lacks capacity to make the relevant decision.[29] Under the MCA, a person is unable to make a decision for themselves if the person is unable to understand the information relevant to the decision, to retain that information, to use or weigh that information as part of the decision-making process, or to communicate their decision.[30]

If a child is not *Gillick* competent to give informed consent to medical treatment, then 'the normal position in law would be that someone with parental responsibility could consent on their behalf'.[31] 'Parental responsibility' is defined to mean 'all the rights, duties, powers, responsibilities and authority which by law a parent of a child has in relation to the child and [their] property'.[32] However, an application can also be made to the Family Division of the High Court by 'any person with a genuine interest in or relation to the child' for an order relating to the exercise of the court's inherent jurisdiction.[33] Such applications most commonly arise in circumstances of dispute between the parents of a child who is not *Gillick* competent and the child's treating medical practitioners over the child's

22 Ibid 188–9 (Lord Scarman).
23 These terms have been used interchangeably: see *Re D (A Child)* [2017] EWCA Civ 1695, [83] (Sir Munby P).
24 *FLR Act* (n 20) s 8(1).
25 Department for Constitutional Affairs, *Mental Capacity Act 2005 Code of Practice* (TSO, 2007).
26 *Mental Capacity Act 2005* (UK) s 2(5).
27 Ibid s 1(2).
28 Ibid s 2(1).
29 Ibid s 3.
30 Ibid s 3(1).
31 *Bell Judicial Review* (n 2) [47].
32 *Children Act* (n 20) s 3(1).
33 *Family Procedure Rules 2010* (UK), SI 2010/2955, Pt 12.

medical treatment;[34] but they may also arise in the context of a *Gillick* competent child refusing life-saving treatment.[35]

The nature of inherent jurisdiction proceedings is framed by the court's duty 'to ensure that a child who is the subject of proceedings is protected and properly taken care of'.[36] In exercising its inherent jurisdiction, the court may 'make any order or determine any issue in respect of a child unless limited by case law or statute',[37] including orders relating to medical treatment.[38] In making such an order, the court must apply the 'best interests' principle – which includes 'every kind of consideration capable of impacting on the decision', such as 'medical, emotional, sensory (pleasure, pain and suffering) and instinctive (the human instinct to survive) considerations'[39] – and must be satisfied that the proposed medical treatment is necessary.[40] Notwithstanding the presumption of capacity for children aged 16 and 17 years,[41] the court can, in the exercise of its inherent jurisdiction, override a child's refusal to consent to treatment, and can override a child's consent if the court considers the treatment not to be in the child's best interests.[42]

7.3 The *Bell* proceedings: An overview

7.3.1 The judicial review application before the High Court

The *Bell* proceedings arose from a claim for judicial review of the practice of the Tavistock, through GIDS and two National Health Service ('NHS') Trusts,[43] of prescribing puberty blockers to children aged under 18 years who experience gender dysphoria.[44] There was no challenge to the lawfulness of the treatment itself. Rather, the claim was that court authorisation should always be obtained before puberty blockers were prescribed.

The regulation of puberty blockers in England is by way of a clinical commissioning policy published by NHS England ('NHS Policy'), which is applied

34 See, eg, *Re JM (A Child)* [2015] EWHC 2832 (Fam); *The NHS Trust v A (A Child)* [2007] EWHC 1696 (Fam) ('*NHS Trust v A*').

35 See, eg, *Re R (A Minor) (Wardship: Consent to Treatment)* [1992] Fam 11; *Re W (A Minor) (Medical Treatment: Court's Jurisdiction)* [1993] Fam 64 ('*Re W*').

36 *Practice Direction 12D – Inherent Jurisdiction (Including Wardship) Proceedings*, [1.1].

37 Ibid.

38 Ibid [1.2(c)].

39 *NHS Trust v A* (n 34) [40] (Holman J).

40 See, eg, *Re TM (Medical Treatment)* [2013] EWHC 4103 (Fam).

41 See *FLR Act* (n 20) s 8(1).

42 See *Re W* (n 35).

43 These were the University College London Hospitals NHS Foundation Trust and the Leeds Teaching Hospitals NHS Trust. These Trusts were the first and second interveners in the proceedings respectively. The third intervener was an organisation known as Transgender Trend Ltd.

44 The administration of puberty blockers is the first stage of medical treatment for gender dysphoria.

by medical practitioners employed by the Tavistock.[45] The NHS Policy is informed by guidelines developed by the World Professional Association for Transgender Health,[46] the Endocrine Society[47] and the Royal College of Psychiatrists.[48] At the time of the initial proceedings in *Bell*, access to gender dysphoria treatment occurred initially via referral of a child to GIDS for assessment. Following that assessment, the child could be referred to a paediatric endocrinologist at one of the two NHS Trusts. The referral only occurred if GIDS assessed that the child would benefit from treatment and was capable of giving informed consent to puberty blockers. The NHS Policy required the informed consent of both the child seeking to commence that treatment, and their parents, at three stages: before GIDS referred the child to the Trusts; before either Trust prescribed puberty blockers to the child; and before the prescription of gender-affirming hormones.[49]

The first claimant, Keira Bell,[50] was referred to GIDS when she was 15 years of age and was first seen by GIDS at age 16. She commenced gender-affirming treatment with testosterone at 17 years of age and was on this treatment for three years, but increasingly began to doubt the transition process.[51] Notwithstanding these doubts, Kiera Bell had a double mastectomy at age 20. The following year, she decided that she wanted to identify as a female and to return to her female identity.[52] The second claimant, Mrs A, was the mother of a 15-year-old girl with a history of mental health and behavioural problems, who was 'desperate to run away from all that made her female'.[53] Mr A was concerned that her daughter

45 See NHS England, 'Clinical Commissioning Policy: Prescribing of Cross-Sex Hormones as part of the Gender Identity Development Service for Children and Adolescents' (16046/P, 2016) <www.england.nhs.uk/wp-content/uploads/2018/07/Prescribing-of-cross-sex-hormones-as-part-of-the-gender-identity-development-service-for-children-and-adolesce.pdf>; NHS England, 'NHS Standard Contract for Gender Identity Development Service for Children and Adolescents: Schedule 2 – The Services' (2017) <www.england.nhs.uk/wp-content/uploads/2017/04/gender-development-service-children-adolescents.pdf> ('NHS Standard Contract').

46 Eli Coleman et al, *Standards of Care for the Health of Transsexual, Transgender, and Gender-Nonconforming People* (World Professional Association for Transgender Health, 7th version, 2012) <www.wpath.org/media/cms/Documents/SOC%20v7/SOC%20V7_English2012.pdf?_t=1613669341>.

47 Wylie C Hembree et al, 'Endocrine Treatment of Gender-Dysphoric/Gender-Incongruent Persons: An Endocrine Society Clinical Practice Guideline' (2017) 102(11) *Journal of Clinical Endocrinology & Metabolism* 3869.

48 Royal College of Psychiatrists, *Good Practice Guidelines for the Assessment and Treatment of Adults with Gender Dysphoria* (CR181, 2013) <www.rcpsych.ac.uk/docs/default-source/improving-care/better-mh-policy/college-reports/cr181-good-practice-guidelines-for-the-assessment-and-treatment-of-adults-with-gender-dysphoria.pdf>.

49 *Bell Appeal* (n 1) [83]. Gender-affirming hormones are referred to in the judgments of the High Court and the Court of Appeal as 'cross-sex hormones'.

50 Referred to in the case title as 'Quincy'.

51 *Bell Judicial Review* (n 2) [79]–[80].

52 Ibid [83].

53 Ibid [89].

would be referred to GIDS and prescribed puberty blockers. However, Mrs A's interest in the proceedings was 'largely theoretical', as her daughter had not yet been so referred and would in any event not meet the criteria for puberty blockers, because her parents would not support the treatment.[54]

The 'sole legal issue' for the High Court (Sharp P, Lewis LJ and Lieven J) was the circumstances in which a child or young person may be competent to give valid consent to treatment with puberty blockers, and the process by which consent to that treatment is obtained.[55] The High Court described the administration of puberty blockers as 'very unusual' and 'experimental' treatment, owing to 'real uncertainty' over the short and long-term consequences, a lack of clarity over the purpose of the treatment, and the 'highly complex and potentially lifelong and life changing' consequences of treatment that 'goes to the heart of an individual's identity'.[56] The Court accepted that stage one and stage two of treatment for gender dysphoria are 'two stages of one clinical pathway and once on that pathway it is extremely rare for a child to get off it'.[57] In light of these findings, the High Court held that to achieve *Gillick* competence, the child or young person would need to understand the implications of both stages of treatment.[58]

The High Court listed eight factors as 'clear guidance as to the application of the *Gillick* tests to the treatment and cohort of children' experiencing gender dysphoria.[59] The 'relevant information' that a child under the age of 16 would need to 'understand, retain and weigh up' to be found *Gillick* competent in relation to puberty blockers was:

(i) the immediate consequences of the treatment in physical and psychological terms;
(ii) the fact that the vast majority of patients taking [puberty blockers] go on to [cross-sex hormones] and therefore that s/he is on a pathway to much greater medical interventions;
(iii) the relationship between taking [cross-sex hormones] and subsequent surgery, with the implications of such surgery;
(iv) the fact that [cross-sex hormones] may well lead to a loss of fertility;
(v) the impact of [cross-sex hormones] on sexual function;
(vi) the impact that taking this step on this treatment pathway may have on future and life-long relationships;
(vii) the unknown physical consequences of taking [puberty blockers]; and
(viii) the fact that the evidence base for this treatment is as yet highly uncertain.[60]

54 Ibid.
55 Ibid [9]. See also [133].
56 Ibid [134].
57 Ibid [136].
58 Ibid [138].
59 Ibid [145].
60 Ibid [138].

The High Court concluded that there would be 'enormous difficulties' in a child under 16 years of age understanding and weighing up this information and deciding whether to consent to the administration of puberty blockers.[61] The Court held that it was 'highly unlikely' that a child aged 13 years or under would be competent to consent to the administration of puberty blockers; and that it was 'doubtful' that a child aged 14 or 15 could do so.[62]

The High Court took a different approach in relation to young people aged 16 and 17 years. It confirmed the legal presumption that they have the capacity to consent to medical treatment,[63] but endorsed the conclusion in *Re W (A Minor) (Medical Treatment: Court's Jurisdiction)*,[64] that a court has inherent jurisdiction to protect a child if it considers treatment not to be in the child's best interests.[65] However, the High Court stressed that the court should not adopt 'an intrusive jurisdiction' that distinguishes one kind of medical treatment without a 'clear legal basis' to do so.[66] The Court held that, if a young person has mental capacity and medical practitioners consider the treatment to be in the young person's best interests, 'then absent a possible dispute with the parents, the court generally has no role'.[67] Yet the High Court also recognised the concerns of medical practitioners over potential liability for failure to obtain valid consent. It held that it would be 'appropriate' to involve the court 'in any case where there may be any doubt as to whether the long-term best interests of a 16 or 17 year old would be served' by the medical treatment for gender dysphoria.[68]

The High Court's decision resulted in public outcry as exerting 'a chilling effect on the rights of young trans people'.[69] The decision was criticised by academics,[70]

61 Ibid [151].
62 Ibid [145].
63 See *FLR Act* (n 20) 8(1).
64 *Re W* (n 35).
65 *Bell Judicial Review* (n 2) [146].
66 Ibid.
67 Ibid.
68 Ibid [147]. See also [152].
69 Libby Brooks, 'Puberty Blockers Ruling: Curbing Trans Rights or a Victory for Common Sense?', *The Guardian* (online, 3 December 2020) <www.theguardian.com/society/2020/dec/03/puberty-blockers-ruling-curbing-trans-rights-or-a-victory-for-common-sense->.
70 See, eg, Simona Giordano, Fae Garland and Søren Holm, 'Gender Dysphoria in Adolescents: Can Adolescents or Parents Give Valid Consent to Puberty Blockers?' (2021) 47(5) *Journal of Medical Ethics* 324; Hannah Hirst, 'The Legal Rights and Wrongs of Puberty Blocking in England' (2021) 33(2) *Child and Family Law Quarterly* 115; Kirsty L Moreton, 'A Backwards-Step for Gillick: Trans Children's Inability to Consent to Treatment for Gender Dysphoria – *Quincy Bell & Mrs A v The Tavistock and Portman NHS Foundation Trust and Ors* [2020] EWHC 3274 (Admin)' (2021) 29(4) *Medical Law Review* 699; Cameron Beattie, 'High Court Should Not Restrict Access to Puberty Blockers for Minors' (2022) 48(1) *Journal of Medical Ethics* 71; Joanna Manning, 'Children, Parents, Courts and Medical Treatment: Now Who Decides?' (2021) 28(4) *Journal of Law and Medicine* 931.

medical professionals[71] and professional associations.[72] Indeed, parallels may be drawn with the condemnation that followed the decision of the Full Court of the Family Court of Australia in *Re Jamie*.[73] A practical consequence of the High Court's decision in *Bell* was an amendment to the NHS Service Specification to require a 'best interests' order from the Family Division of the High Court before patients below 16 years of age were referred to paediatric endocrinologists; and a court order for patients aged 16 and 17 if there was a dispute between parents over treatment or clinical doubt about the patient's best interests.[74] Tavistock appealed the declaration and guidance issued by the High Court to the Court of Appeal.

7.3.2 The Court of Appeal's decision

The only 'real question' for the Court of Appeal (Lord Burnett of Maldon CJ, Sir Geoffrey Vos MR and King LJ) was whether the High Court was right to make the declaration and give the guidance that it did, in light of its conclusion that the policies and practices of the Tavistock were not unlawful.[75]

The Court of Appeal concluded that the declaration should not have been granted. It found that the declaration 'covered areas of disputed fact, expert evidence and medical opinion'[76] and 'implied factual findings that the [High] Court was not equipped to make'.[77] The Court of Appeal also concluded that it was inappropriate for the High Court to issue the guidance regarding when a court application will be appropriate,[78] and to make 'general age-related conclusions about the likelihood or probability of different cohorts of children being capable of giving consent'.[79] The Court of Appeal justified this conclusion on the basis that the High Court was 'not in a position to generalise' about the capacity of children of different ages to consent to puberty blockers;[80] that the practical effect

71 See, eg, Annelou LC de Vries et al, '*Bell v Tavistock and Portman NHS Foundation Trust* [2020] EWHC 3274: Weighing Current Knowledge and Uncertainties in Decisions about Gender-Related Treatment for Transgender Adolescents' (2021) 22(3) *International Journal of Transgender Health* 217.

72 World Professional Association for Transgender Health et al, 'Statement Regarding Medical Affirming Treatment including Puberty Blockers for Transgender Adolescents' (17 December 2020) <www.wpath.org/media/cms/Documents/Public%20Policies/2020/FINAL%20Statement%20Regarding%20Informed%20Consent%20Court%20Case_Dec%2016%202020.docx.pdf?_t=1608225376>.

73 [2013] FamCAFC 110. See Chapter 6 (Section 6.2).

74 NHS England, 'Amendments to Service Specification for Gender Identity Development Service for Children and Adolescents' (December 2020).

75 *Bell Appeal* (n 1) [59].

76 Ibid [72].

77 Ibid [65].

78 Ibid [91].

79 Ibid [89].

80 Ibid [85].

of the guidance was to necessitate a court application in circumstances where the High Court itself acknowledged that there was no legal obligation to do so;[81] that 'it was for clinicians rather than the court' to determine a child's *Gillick* competence;[82] and that the guidance was 'insufficiently sensitive to the role of parents in giving consent'.[83]

The Court of Appeal allowed the Tavistock's appeal, set aside the declaration and dismissed the claim for judicial review.[84] Several weeks after the Court of Appeal's judgment was handed down, Keira Bell indicated her intention – on a 'crowd funding' website for legal fees and costs – to seek permission to appeal the decision to the UK Supreme Court.[85] She expressed disappointment that the Court of Appeal 'did not grapple with the significant risk of harm that children are exposed to by being given powerful experimental drugs'.[86] She asserted that the proceedings had 'shone a light into the dark corners of a medical scandal that is harming children and harmed me'.[87]

The Court of Appeal's decision resulted in another amendment to the NHS Service Specification.[88] This amendment confirmed that children under 16 years of age may be assessed as legally competent to give informed consent to puberty blockers, such that the Tavistock should continue to obtain consent from the child and from one or both parents. Importantly, the amendment introduced an additional layer of institutional review and assurance, to avoid the need for court authorisation, as follows:

> For children under 16 years who are recommended by Tavistock … for referral to a paediatric endocrinology clinic for [puberty blockers], the processes followed by GIDS in reaching the recommendation to commence or continue the intervention in regard to the individual must be assured by an independent Multi-Professional Review Group that has been established by NHS England for that purpose. Where the Multi-Professional Review Group is assured that appropriate process has been followed there is no requirement

81 Ibid [86].
82 Ibid [87].
83 Ibid [88].
84 Ibid [91].
85 Keira Bell, 'Protect Gender Dysphoric Children from Experimental Treatment', *CrowdJustice* (Web Page, 4 October 2021) <www.crowdjustice.com/case/protect-gd-children/>. On 28 April 2022, the UK Supreme Court refused permission to appeal, because the application did not raise an arguable point of law.
86 Ibid.
87 Ibid.
88 NHS England, 'Amendments to Service Specification for Gender Identity Development Service for Children and Adolescents (E13/S(HSS)/e)' (6 October 2021). This amendment replaced the one of December 2020: see n 74 above.

> for the Tavistock … to seek a prior Best Interest order from the Court in regard to an individual.[89]

The amendment requires the Multi-Professional Review Group to review written information supplied by the Tavistock to determine assurance on specified areas,[90] including assessment and diagnosis, the decision to refer a child to the endocrine clinic, parental consent and the child's consent.[91]

7.4 A children's rights analysis of the Court of Appeal's judgment in *Bell*

The decision of the Court of Appeal in *Bell* was welcomed as a 'huge win' and a 'positive step forward' for TGD children and their families.[92] Duffy has gone so far as to frame it as a victory for their decision-making autonomy and rights, arguing that: 'If this is the last that the courts hear of *Bell v Tavistock*, … it can be said that the human rights of trans young people have been vindicated and their decisional autonomy upheld to the same standard as any other young person's.'[93]

While the Court of Appeal's decision may have halted the 'jurisprudential trend towards placing tighter controls on the bodily autonomy of' TGD children,[94] the children's rights analysis of the Court of Appeal's judgment below develops a less sanguine argument: that the decision represents a limited symbolic victory only. Three elements of the judgment are examined from the perspective of children's right to decisional privacy to support this argument: the Court of Appeal's framing of the issues, which focused upon the appropriate gatekeeper to gender dysphoria treatment and emphasised the need to 'protect' a uniquely 'vulnerable' group of children; its failure to engage with rights-based arguments; and a judgment summary that did not contemplate children as an audience.

7.4.1 Determining the appropriate gatekeeper to gender dysphoria treatment … but where are the children?

Insofar as the *Bell* proceedings determined the capacity of children experiencing gender dysphoria to give informed consent to treatment with puberty blockers,

89 Ibid [4].
90 Ibid [5].
91 NHS England, 'Independent Multi-Professional Review Group Decision Document' (2021) <www.england.nhs.uk/wp-content/uploads/2021/10/B1054-independent-multi-professional-review-group-decision-document.pdf>.
92 See nn 10 to 14 above.
93 Sandra Duffy, '*Bell v Tavistock* on Appeal: Court of Appeal Upholds Young Persons' Ability to Consent to Puberty-Blocking Medication', *Oxford Human Rights Hub* (Web Page, 5 October 2021) <https://ohrh.law.ox.ac.uk/bell-v-tavistock-on-appeal-court-of-appeal-upholds-young-persons-ability-to-consent-to-puberty-blocking-medication/>.
94 Steph Jowett and Fiona Kelly, '*Re Imogen*: A Step in the Wrong Direction' (2021) 34(1) *Australian Journal of Family Law* 31, 51.

the proceedings were squarely about the rights of those children. The Tavistock's framing of its submission demonstrates concern with the intrusion that the High Court's declaration and guidance imposed on the decisional privacy rights of TGD children and their families. The Court of Appeal in *Bell* noted that:

> At the heart of Tavistock's appeal is the submission that, in making the declaration, the [High] Court departed from *Gillick*, which had established that children under 16 could make their own decisions if assessed individually as competent to do so by their treating clinician. Tavistock submits that the court '***intruded into the realm of decisions agreed upon by doctors, patients and their parents, where the court had not previously gone***'.[95]

Yet the Court of Appeal framed the dispute as being over the appropriate 'gatekeeper' to gender dysphoria treatment, in terms of who should assess a child's *Gillick* competence to consent to treatment with puberty blockers: medical practitioners or the courts.

i. Gillick competence as a question 'for clinicians rather than the court to decide'[96]

The Court of Appeal identified the focus of the appeal as being 'squarely on *Gillick*', and whether, by making the declaration and giving the guidance that would necessitate '(probably frequent) court intervention', the High Court had imposed 'an improper restriction' on the *Gillick* competence test.[97] However, the Court of Appeal gave no consideration to what such 'restriction' upon *Gillick* competence meant for children experiencing gender dysphoria and their decision-making autonomy. Notwithstanding that the case was, 'and always has been, a case about children [and] their rights',[98] the Court of Appeal framed the case as being about the clinical judgement and practice of medical practitioners, including their interest in avoiding liability, and the need to obtain court sanction before puberty blockers were prescribed.[99]

The Court of Appeal made it clear that it was not – in essence – the court's role to tell medical practitioners how to 'do their job'. The Court held that it was 'a matter of clinical judgement, tailored to the patient in question', of how to explain matters to ensure that consent was properly informed.[100] It held further

95 *Bell Appeal* (n 1) [66] (emphasis added).
96 Ibid [87].
97 Ibid [94].
98 *R (Williamson) v Secretary of State for Education and Employment* [2005] 2 FLR 374, [71] (Baroness Hale). See also Chapter 3 (Section 3.2).
99 In support of this view, see John McMillan and Colin Gavaghan, 'Mature Minors and Gender Dysphoria: A Matter for Clinicians not Courts' (2021) 47(11) *Journal of Medical Ethics* 717, 717.
100 *Bell Appeal* (n 1) [81].

that '[i]t would have been inconsistent with the ratio of the [*Gillick*] case that clinicians must be trusted to make the decisions for the court effectively to give them a manual about how to do so'.[101] The Court of Appeal described the terms of the High Court's declaration as coming 'close to providing a checklist or script that clinicians are required to adopt for the indefinite future in language which is not capable of clear and uniform interpretation …'.[102] It reiterated that 'the principle enunciated in *Gillick* was that it was for clinicians rather than the court to decide on competence'.[103]

The Court of Appeal also made repeated reference to the vulnerability of medical practitioners to liability for failure to obtain informed consent. The Court noted that 'clinicians will be alive to the possibility of regulatory or civil action where, in individual cases, the issue can be tested'.[104] It cautioned that medical practitioners must take 'great care' before recommending treatment with puberty blockers and to ensure that necessary consents from the child and parents are properly obtained.[105] The Court of Appeal endorsed the statement of Lord Scarman in *Gillick* that 'great responsibilities will lie on the medical profession' in determining a child's capacity to consent.[106]

The emphasis remained in the *Bell* judgment upon the appropriate balance between clinical judgement and court intervention, with the Court of Appeal finding that the High Court's declaration 'would require … clinicians to suspend or at least to temper their clinical judgement and defer to what amounts to the clinical judgement of the court on which key features should inform an assessment of *Gillick* competence …'.[107] The Court of Appeal added that:

> it is for the clinicians to exercise their judgement knowing how important it is that consent is properly obtained according to the particular individual circumstances, as envisaged by *Gillick* itself, and by reference to developing

101 Ibid [80].
102 Ibid [70].
103 Ibid [87].
104 Ibid [92]. See also [57], [81], [93]. While it lies beyond the scope of this book to examine the duty to inform and information non-disclosure in the context of children's medical treatment, it should be noted that this remains an underexplored area: see Emma Cave and Craig Purshouse, 'Think of the Children: Liability for Non-Disclosure of Information Post-*Montgomery*' (2020) 28(2) *Medical Law Review* 270.
105 *Bell Appeal* (n 1) [92]. See also Dennis Kavanagh, 'Understanding the Appeal in *Bell v Tavistock*: Legal Analysis by LGN Legal Commentator Dennis Kavanagh', *Lesbian and Gay News* (Online, 19 September 2021) <https://staging.lesbianandgaynews.com/2021/09/understanding-the-appeal-in-bell-v-tavistock-legal-analysis-by-lgn-legal-commentator-dennis-kavanagh/> (observing that 'the significance of [the Court of Appeal's] judgment will not be lost on clinical negligence practitioners who may well see detransitioner claimants seeking to put right wrongs with actions for damages, rather than judicial review').
106 *Bell Appeal* (n 1) quoting *Gillick* (n 5) 191B–C (Lord Scarman).
107 *Bell Appeal* (n 1) [75].

understanding in this difficult and controversial area. The clinicians are subject to professional regulation and oversight.[108]

Not only did the Court of Appeal not conceptualise the dispute as concerning TGD children and their rights; but where the Court did refer to those children in the judgment, it constructed them as uniquely vulnerable and relegated them to statistics and passive objects of medical intervention.

ii. *The need to 'protect' a 'deeply distressed and highly vulnerable'[109] group of 'children'*

The Court of Appeal at the outset noted that '[w]e shall refer to both those aged under 16 and those aged 16 and 17 as "children" in this judgment'.[110] This semantic choice, as has been discussed earlier in this book, reinforces a static conceptualisation of children as binary opposites to adults: vulnerable, dependent and incapable of rational decision-making.[111] The High Court in *Bell*, by contrast, used the composite phrases 'child or young person' and 'children and young persons'.[112] The Court of Appeal noted the High Court's distinction in this regard, referring to its acceptance that 'children under 16 and young people aged between 16 and 18 could, upon a proper interpretation of *Gillick*, consent to embarking on a course of puberty blockers'.[113] Perhaps adopted by the Court of Appeal as convenient shorthand, 'children' was arguably 'a somewhat erroneous term',[114] having regard to the age and maturity of 16- and 17-year-olds,[115] and the evidence before the Court of the age distribution of referrals by GIDS to the Trusts for puberty blockers.[116]

The Court of Appeal in *Bell* constructed children with gender dysphoria as not only vulnerable – consistent with the dominant conception of children in Western liberal societies[117] – but as *uniquely* vulnerable. The Court's choice of descriptors for children experiencing gender dysphoria offers a compelling illustration. There are numerous references in the judgment to 'patients' and 'suffering': the Tavistock operated GIDS 'for patients up to the age of 18 suffering from gender

108 Ibid [93].
109 Ibid [85].
110 Ibid [2].
111 See Chapter 5 (Section 5.3.1.ii).
112 *Bell Judicial Review* (n 2) [5]–[7].
113 *Bell Appeal* (n 1) [58].
114 *Duffy v Gomes (No 2)* (2015) 299 FLR 108, 155 [72] (Judge Harman).
115 See *Re Alex* (2004) 180 FLR 89, 94 [18] (Nicholson CJ).
116 *Bell Appeal* (n 1) [20]. Of the 161 children under 16 who were referred by GIDS to the Trusts for puberty blockers in 2019/2020, 3 were aged 10 or 11, 13 were aged 12, 10 were aged 13, 24 were aged 14, 45 were aged 15, 51 were aged 16, and 15 were aged 17 or 18.
117 See Chapter 1 (Section 1.4.1).

dysphoria';[118] those diagnosed 'suffer associated significant distress or impairment in function'.[119] On one interpretation, the Court of Appeal may be taken to have promoted the 'pathologisation' of TGD children,[120] as the Court's language does not reflect the view of non-cisgender identities as 'part of the normal continuum of human diversity'.[121]

However, in the case of children experiencing gender dysphoria, it is this very 'discomfort or distress' deriving from the discrepancy between their experienced gender and their sex assigned at birth that justifies the need for medical treatment, to help those children 'to explore their gender identity and find a gender role that is comfortable for them'.[122] A preferable interpretation, then, is that the Court of Appeal implicitly recognised the vulnerability of TGD children experiencing gender dysphoria who are left untreated, and the risk that a legal requirement for court authorisation would hinder the timely provision of medical treatment.[123] The Court of Appeal noted the High Court's recognition that 'the cohort of children treated at GIDS suffered from psychological distress by reason of their gender dysphoria and were highly vulnerable'.[124] It added that:

> We recognise that the guidance stemmed from the understandable concern of the [High] Court for the welfare of children suffering from gender dysphoria who, it is common ground, are deeply distressed and highly vulnerable.[125]

The Court of Appeal's appreciation of the vulnerability of children experiencing gender dysphoria and their need to access medical treatment in a timely manner is not misplaced. However, defining those children *exclusively* by their vulnerabilities is liable to result in 'overly protectionist agendas',[126] which bear the potential to harm children's development by cementing assumptions about children's lack of capacity to protect their own interests. This agenda indeed emerged before the High Court in *Bell*, where the Tavistock and the Trusts had argued that 'it would be an intrusion into the child or young person's autonomy if a decision about treatment with [puberty blockers] were to be made by the court not by the patient'.[127] The High Court disagreed. It explained that:

118 *Bell Appeal* (n 1) [1].
119 Ibid [2].
120 This issue is discussed in Chapter 5 (Section 5.3.1.ii). See also, in relation to the High Court's judgment in *Bell*, Moreton (n 70) 704.
121 Melinda Jones, 'Children's Health Rights and Gender Issues' in Jozef HHM Dorscheidt and Jaap E Doek (eds), *Children's Rights in Health Care* (Brill, 2018) 382, 410.
122 See Coleman et al (n 46) 5.
123 The author thanks Simona Giordano for this astute point.
124 *Bell Appeal* (n 1) [44].
125 Ibid [85].
126 John Tobin, 'Understanding Children's Rights: A Vision beyond Vulnerability' (2015) 84 *Nordic Journal of International Law* 155, 167, 169 ('Understanding Children's Rights'). See also Chapter 1 (Section 1.4.1).
127 *Bell Judicial Review* (n 2) [149].

> In principle, a young person's autonomy should be protected and supported; however, it is the role of the court to protect children, and particularly a vulnerable child's best interests. The decisions in respect of [puberty blockers] have lifelong and life-changing consequences for the children. Apart perhaps from life-saving treatment, there will be no more profound medical decisions for children than whether to start on this treatment pathway. In those circumstances we consider that it is appropriate that the court should determine whether it is in the child's best interests to take [puberty blockers]. There is a real benefit in the court, almost certainly with a child's guardian appointed, having oversight over the decision. In any case, under the inherent jurisdiction concerning medical treatment for those under the age of 18, there is likely to be a conflict between the support of autonomy and the protective role of the court ... [W]e consider this treatment to be one where the protective role of the court is appropriate.[128]

The above comments attest to a judicial approach underpinned by a 'paternalistic judgment of welfare',[129] and a perception that promoting and supporting children's autonomy, and 'protecting' children, are mutually exclusive. Such an understanding of the relationship between children's rights and children's best interests or welfare is contrary to a children's rights approach to decisional privacy.[130] On this approach, children's vulnerability is understood as variable or 'episodic', as well as socially constructed and fluid, rather than an 'inevitable and inherent feature of childhood'.[131] Children can be both vulnerable *and* possess evolving autonomy or the capacity for autonomy: these are not binary characteristics.

The Court of Appeal in *Bell* may be taken to have shown some appreciation of this view, in finding that the High Court 'was not in a position to generalise' about the capacity of children and young people of different ages 'to understand what is necessary for them to be competent to consent to the administration of puberty blockers'.[132] However, the Court of Appeal did itself 'generalise' in referring throughout the judgment to the 'cohort'[133] of children which it labelled 'deeply distressed and highly vulnerable'.[134] The Court further abstracted children experiencing gender dysphoria through its discussion of statistics regarding referrals by GIDS to the Trusts for puberty blockers and referrals to GIDS for assessment;[135] and how many GIDS patients proceeded from puberty blockers

128 Ibid.
129 *Mabon v Mabon* [2005] EWCA Civ 634, [28] (Thorpe LJ).
130 See Chapter 2 (Section 2.4.2).
131 Tobin, 'Understanding Children's Rights' (n 126) 169, 182.
132 *Bell Appeal* (n 1) [85].
133 Ibid [19], [44], [46], [89].
134 Ibid [85].
135 Ibid [20].

to gender-affirming hormones.[136] The Court of Appeal observed that '[t]he statements from clinicians and extracts from learned journals are peppered with statistics'.[137] Children experiencing gender dysphoria were thus reduced to 'referrals',[138] 'statistics'[139] and 'random samples'[140] in the judgment.

The Court of Appeal's abstraction in this manner obscured the 'intersectionalities and differences' within the 'group' or 'cohort' of children who would be affected by the decision,[141] contributing to a judgment that 'extinguished the living personality that might otherwise remain associated with it'.[142] The conceptualisation of children experiencing gender dysphoria as uniquely vulnerable, and their relegation in the judgment to statistics or data products of medical intervention, attests to the law's 'generalising impulse'.[143] It simultaneously promotes a judicial narrative of the 'universal' child with gender dysphoria, premised upon a perception of illness and distress, as well as 'innocence, dependence, [and] vulnerability'.[144]

7.4.2 *An evasive approach to children's rights*

The second feature of the Court of Appeal's judgment that arguably justifies the exercise of caution in embracing the decision as an unequivocal victory for children's rights, is the Court's avoidance of rights-based arguments, and its explicit desire to not delve into issues that it considered were more appropriately addressed by the executive and legislative branches of government.

The judgment contains two express references to the 'rights' of children, which take the form of excerpts from the judgment of Lord Scarman in *Gillick*. The first is that 'nor has our law ever treated the child as other than a person with capabilities and rights recognised by law'.[145] The second is that '[t]he truth may well be that the rights of parents and children in this sensitive area are better protected by the professional standards of the medical profession than by "a priori" legal lines of division between capacity and lack of capacity to consent'.[146] The

136 Ibid [26]–[27].
137 Ibid [27].
138 Ibid [20].
139 Ibid [27].
140 Ibid [20], [26]–[27].
141 Kathryn Hollingsworth and Helen Stalford, 'Towards Children's Rights Judgments' in Helen Stalford, Kathryn Hollingsworth and Stephen Gilmore (eds), *Rewriting Children's Rights Judgments: From Academic Vision to New Practice* (Hart Publishing, 2017) 53, 80.
142 Dawn Watkins, 'Recovering the Lost Human Stories of Law: Finding Mrs Burns' (2013) 7(1) *Law and Humanities* 68, 89. See also Chapter 3 (Section 3.5.1).
143 Peter Brooks and Paul Gewirtz, *Law's Stories: Narrative and Rhetoric in the Law* (Yale University Press, 1996) 3. See also Eric Mitnick, *Rights, Groups, and Self-Invention: Group-Differentiated Rights in Liberal Theory* (Ashgate, 2006) 55.
144 Hollingsworth and Stalford (n 141) 80.
145 *Bell Appeal* (n 1) [57], quoting *Gillick* (n 5) 184B (Lord Scarman).
146 *Bell Appeal* (n 1) [57], quoting *Gillick* (n 5) 191B–C (Lord Scarman).

Court of Appeal in *Bell* also quoted Lord Scarman's understanding of children's autonomy as gradual and evolving:

> The law relating to parent and child is concerned with the problems of the growth and maturity of the human personality. If the law should impose on the process of 'growing up' fixed limits where nature knows only a continuous process, the price would be artificiality and a lack of realism in an area where the law must be sensitive to human development and social change.[147]

Although *Gillick* was decided several years before the text of the CRC was finalised, this case has been described as 'a landmark in children's rights jurisprudence'.[148] The values that shaped the House of Lords' decision are considered to be consistent with the conceptualisation of children's rights embraced by the CRC.[149] These excerpts from *Gillick* in the Court of Appeal's judgment in *Bell* judgment may, at first blush, suggest an appreciation that children are rights-bearers with evolving capacities and that they must be recognised as such. However, the analysis below exposes the Court of Appeal's evasive approach to children's rights, through its failure to engage with the rights-based ground of appeal and with broader debates surrounding gender dysphoria treatment.

i. Rights-based arguments as 'unnecessary to consider'[150]

Eight grounds of appeal were advanced by the Tavistock.[151] The eighth ground was rights-based, framed in accordance with Article 14 of the ECHR. It was contended that the High Court's approach discriminated unjustifiably against

147 *Gillick* (n 5) 186. See also 171 (Lord Fraser: '[i]n practice, most wise parents relax their control gradually as the child develops and encourage [them] to become increasingly independent').

148 Michael Freeman, 'Rethinking *Gillick*' (2005) 13 *International Journal of Children's Rights* 201, 201. See also Manning (n 70) 933.

149 John Tobin, 'Judging the Judges: Are they Adopting the Rights Approach in Matters involving Children?' (2009) 33(2) *Melbourne University Law Review* 579, 600 ('Judging the Judges'); Jane Fortin, 'Accommodating Children's Rights in a Post *Human Rights Act* Era' (2006) 69(3) *Modern Law Review* 299, 314.

150 *Bell Appeal* (n 1) [90].

151 Ibid [12]. Grounds one and two were that the High Court misapplied the law in *Gillick*. Ground three was that the High Court's conclusions were inconsistent with the *FLR Act*. Grounds four and five challenged the High Court's factual conclusion that the prescription of puberty blockers for gender dysphoria is 'experimental' and that they have 'lifelong' and 'life-changing' effects. Grounds six and seven challenged the High Court's reliance on expert evidence adduced by the claimants without permission, which contradicted the evidence of Tavistock and the Trusts; and the High Court making findings of fact upon the claimant's expert evidence and relying on it to resolve clinical differences of opinion. Ground eight contended that the High Court's approach breached Article 14 of the ECHR in discriminating against children with gender dysphoria which could not be justified.

children with gender dysphoria and therefore breached Article 14.[152] The Court of Appeal considered that, in light of its conclusions on the declaration and the guidance, it was 'unnecessary to address the arguments made by reference to the *Human Rights Act 1998* (UK)'.[153] The *Human Rights Act 1998* (UK) ('HRA') incorporates most Articles of the ECHR into UK domestic law,[154] such that the 'Convention rights'[155] are enforceable within domestic courts.

It is useful to contrast the Court of Appeal's approach to rights-based arguments with that of the High Court in the initial judicial review proceedings. The claimants had contended that 'the absence of procedural safeguards' and 'the inadequacy of the information provided' to ensure that children and young people under 18 years of age can give informed consent to the administration of puberty blockers, infringed their rights under Article 8 of the ECHR.[156] Article 8 provides for the right to respect for private and family life. It is particularly pertinent to children's right to decisional privacy, given the nexus that the European Court of Human Rights has forged between privacy and identity.[157]

The High Court in *Bell* did not engage directly with this argument based on Article 8 of the ECHR in its judgment. However, it referred to *R (Axon) v Secretary of State for Health (Family Planning Association Intervening)*,[158] in which Silber J considered *Gillick* in the context of Article 8 of the ECHR and the CRC, and 'the increasing emphasis on the autonomy of the child'.[159] The High Court in *Bell* set out principles derived from the case law, including that 'to achieve *Gillick* competence it is important not to set the bar too high', and that '[i]t is not appropriate to equate the matters that a clinician needs to explain ... to the matters that a child needs to understand to achieve *Gillick* competence'.[160] To do otherwise 'would be significantly to raise the bar for competence and capacity', which the High Court considered 'would be contrary both to the common law and to a child's Article 8 rights and the importance of supporting individual autonomy'.[161]

The Joint Committee on Human Rights, in its *Independent Review of the Human Rights Act*, noted that representatives of 'marginalised' groups 'have emphasised the importance of the HRA in enabling those groups to enforce their

152 Ibid. Article 14 of the ECHR provides that: 'The enjoyment of the rights and freedoms set forth in this Convention shall be secured without discrimination on any ground such as sex, race, colour, language, religion, political or other opinion, national or social origin, association with a national minority, property, birth or other status'.

153 *Bell Appeal* (n 1) [90].

154 See *Human Rights Act 1998* (UK) ss 1(1), 1(3), Sch 1. The Act came into force in October 2000.

155 Ibid s 1(1).

156 *Bell Judicial Review* (n 2) [7].

157 See Chapter 4 (Section 4.4).

158 [2006] QB 539.

159 *Bell Judicial Review* (n 2) [108]. See ibid [64], [76]–[79], [118]–[152].

160 *Bell Judicial Review* (n 2) [130].

161 Ibid.

rights', including children's rights.[162] The Joint Committee concluded that 'the HRA has had an enormously positive impact on the enforcement of human rights in the UK'.[163] Without assessing the merits of this conclusion, it is suggested that the approach of the Court of Appeal in *Bell* to human rights – and to children's rights in particular – might appropriately be described as 'evasive'. It is telling that, of the Tavistock's eight grounds of appeal,[164] the only one which the Court of Appeal did *not* consider was the rights-based ground. The Court of Appeal's approach is arguably but another illustration of the 'extraordinarily haphazard' response of the UK domestic courts to the demands of the HRA when dealing with children's cases.[165]

It is significant to expressly articulate why the Court of Appeal's evasive approach matters for TGD children and their rights. What in practice has been lost by the Court declining to address the rights-based ground of appeal? What would have been gained if the Court of Appeal *had* engaged with the rights of TGD children in its judgment? These questions can be addressed briefly, for the response is similar to the argument made in the previous chapter in relation to the Full Court of the Family Court of Australia's 'invisible' rights approach in *Re Kelvin*.[166]

The practical outcome of the Court of Appeal's decision in *Bell* – that it is for clinicians, rather than courts, to determine the question of competence to consent to treatment with puberty blockers – may reinforce an interpretation of the decision as promoting the rights of TGD children.[167] Indeed, it is suggested below that the Court of Appeal's decision bears some symbolic value for TGD children.[168] The outcome of the *Bell* case may not have been any different had the Court of Appeal chosen to address the arguments made by reference to the HRA. However, had the Court of Appeal addressed the final ground of appeal, based on Article 14 of the ECHR, it would have needed to 'actively identify children's claims to independent rights',[169] and by extension, to *expressly* recognise the status of TGD children as rights-bearers, with distinct rights and interests that are worthy of protection and respect.[170] The growing momentum of TGD children's rights in public debate and discourse, coupled with the HRA as a form of express rights protection in the UK, arguably offered the prime 'general

162 House of Lords and House of Commons Joint Committee on Human Rights, *The Government's Independent Review of the Human Rights Act* (HC 89, HL Paper 31, 8 July 2021) 12.
163 Ibid 80.
164 See n 151 above.
165 Fortin (n 149) 300.
166 See Chapter 6 (Section 6.4.1.iii).
167 See nn 10 to 14 above.
168 See Section 7.5.
169 Tobin, 'Judging the Judges' (n 149) 585–6.
170 See Chapter 2 (Section 2.3.1).

intellectual environment'[171] for the Court of Appeal to engage substantively with TGD children's rights in its judgment.

The Court of Appeal in *Bell* articulated the dispute as 'whether an application to the court was always needed before the prescription of puberty blockers because no child under the age of 18 could give valid consent'.[172] Yet the Court focused upon the respective roles of medical practitioners and the courts as potential gatekeepers in assessing a child's *Gillick* competence.[173] The Court of Appeal appeared unable – or perhaps unwilling – to accept the notion of TGD children as rights-bearers. It was also reluctant to embrace explicitly through its reasoning the 'radical change' introduced by the HRA, 'in so far as it apparently gave all children in this country the same [ECHR] rights as adults'.[174] This analysis reinforces the view of Purshouse and Trispiotis, that 'it would be a mistake to think that judges march in lockstep in a progressive direction on the issue of LGBT+ rights'.[175]

ii. Avoiding clinical, moral and ethical issues and debate that 'obscure the role of the courts in deciding discrete legal issues'[176]

The Court of Appeal's evasive approach to children's rights in the *Bell* judgment is also demonstrated, it is argued, by its reluctance to engage with the broader debates surrounding gender dysphoria treatment. The Court of Appeal observed that:

> The question raises not only clinical medical issues but also moral and ethical issues, all of which are the subject of intense professional and public debate. Such debate, when it spills into legal proceedings, is apt to obscure the role of the courts in deciding discrete legal issues. The present proceedings do not require the courts to determine whether the treatment for gender dysphoria is a wise or unwise course or whether it should be available through medical facilities in England and Wales. Such policy decisions are for the National Health Service, the medical profession and its regulators and Government and Parliament.[177]

The Court quoted from the judgment of Lieven J in *AB v CD*,[178] that the use of puberty blockers for gender dysphoria raised 'controversial ethical issues' with

171 Ronald Dworkin, *Law's Empire* (Belknap Press, 1986) 88.
172 *Bell Appeal* (n 1) [69].
173 See Section 7.4.1.i above.
174 Fortin (n 149) 326.
175 Craig Purshouse and Ilias Trispiotis, 'Is "Conversion Therapy" Tortious?' (2021) 42(1) *Legal Studies* 23, 27.
176 *Bell Appeal* (n 1) [3].
177 Ibid.
178 [2021] EWHC 741 (Fam) ('*AB v CD*').

'highly polarised' clinical and ethical views, which were 'precisely the type of matters which are best assessed in a regulatory and academic setting and not through litigation'.[179] Lieven J had expressed wariness about 'the Court becoming too involved in highly complex moral and ethical issues on a generalised, rather than case specific, basis'.[180] The Court of Appeal in *Bell* also endorsed the statement of Lord Phillips in *R (Burke) v General Medical Council*[181] that 'any court should be reluctant to address' 'ethical questions', 'unless driven to do so by the need to resolve a practical problem that requires the court's intervention'.[182] The Court of Appeal added that 'the role of the court is not to draft policy documents. It is to test their lawfulness'.[183]

The Court of Appeal's deference to the legislative and executive branches of government to address 'policy decisions',[184] and its caution 'not to take a position on the debate'[185] about treatment of children with puberty blockers 'in this difficult and controversial area',[186] may be interpreted as a significant 'structural' constraint on the Court's willingness to engage with children's rights in its judgment.[187] As Stalford and Hollingsworth have explained, courts must 'tread a fine line between giving effect to children's rights and respecting the role of the legislature and executive to set appropriate, realistic legal parameters and to allocate resources accordingly'.[188] The Court of Appeal in *Bell* itself acknowledged the practical implications of the guidance issued by the High Court, which 'placed patients, parents and clinicians in a very difficult position' and had the effect of 'denying treatment in many circumstances for want of resources to make such an application coupled with inevitable delay through court involvement'.[189]

By refusing to engage in the debate over the 'wisdom' of gender dysphoria treatment and its availability, the Court of Appeal confined itself to the High Court's approach to the evidence in judicial review proceedings and statements of legal principle regarding *Gillick* competence. The Court of Appeal's caution to not tread upon the decision-making domain of the Government and

179 Ibid [121]–[122], quoted in *Bell Appeal* (n 1) [51].
180 *AB v CD* (n 178) [121], quoted in *Bell Appeal* (n 1) [49].
181 [2005] EWCA Civ 1003.
182 Ibid [21], quoted in *Bell Appeal* (n 1) [77].
183 *Bell Appeal* (n 1) [54].
184 Ibid [3].
185 McMillan and Gavaghan (n 99) 717.
186 *Bell Appeal* (n 1) [93].
187 Helen Stalford and Kathryn Hollingsworth, 'Judging Children's Rights: Tendencies, Tensions, Constraints and Opportunities' in Helen Stalford, Kathryn Hollingsworth and Stephen Gilmore (eds), *Rewriting Children's Rights Judgments: From Academic Vision to New Practice* (Hart Publishing, 2017) 17, 41 ('Judging Children's Rights'). See also Chapter 2 (Section 2.4.4).
188 Stalford and Hollingsworth, 'Judging Children's Rights' (n 187) 43.
189 *Bell Appeal* (n 1) [86].

the Parliament – a manifestation of the 'counter-majoritarian argument'[190] – by extension, it is argued, enabled the Court to 'sidestep' potential children's rights-based claims.[191] Such claims would very likely have emerged from a consideration of any one or more of the 'clinical medical ... moral and ethical issues'[192] that the Court of Appeal identified as emanating from the treatment of children experiencing gender dysphoria. Indeed, it is noteworthy that the Court of Appeal did not list 'human rights' issues as falling along the spectrum of issues that were 'the subject of intense professional and public debate'.[193]

In circumstances where children have minimal political clout to advance their own interests beyond the courts, judges arguably have a duty to protect children and their rights.[194] As Nolan has argued, '[w]hile it is definitely important for judges to understand their relationships with other actors and institutions, such understanding is quite different from ceding responsibility for what ensues on the grounds of judicial deference'.[195] The Court of Appeal in *Bell* was arguably 'too deferential',[196] with the result that the rights of TGD children were not only overlooked, but also devalued.[197]

7.4.3 A judgment summary for the press and the public

The final element of the Court of Appeal's judgment that is examined to support the argument that the decision should not be understood as a practical victory for TGD children's rights, is the written summary of the judgment. The Court of Appeal issued a five-page summary of its judgment, comprising 15 paragraphs, which was prefaced with the '[i]important note' that 'this summary forms no part of the court's decision' and 'is provided so as to assist the press and the public to understand what the court decided'.[198]

In articulating the 'instructive value' of judgments for children – judgments that are accessible to children 'as a group of citizens more widely to whom the rule of law and precedent applies'[199] – Stalford and Hollingsworth provide as an illustrative example the *Gillick* judgment,[200] given the implications of the decision for children's right to access medical advice and treatment without parental consent, and for children's right to decision-making autonomy in other areas of

190 See Aoife Nolan, *Children's Socio-Economic Rights, Democracy and the Courts* (Hart, 2011) ch 3.
191 Stalford and Hollingsworth, 'Judging Children's Rights' (n 187) 44.
192 *Bell Appeal* (n 1) [3].
193 Ibid [3].
194 Stalford and Hollingsworth, 'Judging Children's Rights' (n 187) 44. See also Nolan (n 190) ch 2.
195 Nolan (n 190) 170.
196 Stalford and Hollingsworth, 'Judging Children's Rights' (n 187) 44.
197 Nolan (n 190) 219.
198 *Bell Appeal* Judgment Summary (n 17) 1.
199 Stalford and Hollingsworth, '"This Case is about You"' (n 18) 1052.
200 *Gillick* (n 5).

law.[201] They argue that 'the complexity of the reasoning and the concepts and language used are likely to mean nothing to children'.[202] The same argument may be made in relation to not only the Court of Appeal's judgment in *Bell*, but also the written summary of that judgment.

The written summary of the *Bell* judgment refers to the fundamental legal concepts of 'capacity'[203] and 'competence to consent',[204] the inherently indeterminate and nebulous notion of 'best interests',[205] and 'the broad discretionary power of the court to grant declaratory relief or an advisory declaration'[206] in 'judicial review proceedings'.[207] These are concepts and statements that, without explanation, arguably remain inaccessible to all but those well-versed in the law, and indeed would be 'utterly alien'[208] to children. As would statements that '[t]he Court of Appeal allowed Tavistock's appeal'[209] and that 'the claim for judicial review should have been dismissed'.[210] They would mean nothing to TGD children in terms of their ability, in practical terms, to access treatment with puberty blockers. These examples from the written summary of the Court of Appeal's judgment support the view that children were not conceptualised as one of the audiences of that summary.

To the extent that the Court of Appeal's judgment summary makes the decision and reasoning more accessible to a wider range of individuals than the judgment itself, it goes some way towards promoting the decisional privacy rights of TGD children, by increasing their *visibility* in public discourse and debate. This is particularly important given the scant legal protection available for the identities of TGD children in the UK.[211] However, the *Bell* judgment summary is not written *for* TGD children who may be contemplating treatment with puberty blockers or who may have commenced treatment. The summary explicitly identifies that it is designed to aid 'the press and the public'. The language used is not accessible to children as a sector of that 'public' or as consumers of media.

It is acknowledged that challenges exist in 'translating complex legal decisions into a language, structure and style that children can understand', without

201 Stalford and Hollingsworth, '"This Case is about You"' (n 18) 1052.
202 Ibid 1052–3.
203 *Bell Appeal* Judgment Summary (n 17) [12].
204 Ibid [7]. See also [8], [13], [15].
205 Ibid [5], [8]. See, eg, Michael Freeman, *The Moral Status of Children: Essays on the Rights of the Child* (Kluwer Law International, 1997) 373; Helen Reece, 'The Paramountcy Principle: Consensus or Construct?' (1996) 49(1) *Current Legal Problems* 267.
206 *Bell Appeal* Judgment Summary (n 17) [11].
207 Ibid [11], [12].
208 Stalford and Hollingsworth, '"This Case is about You"' (n 18) 1053.
209 *Bell Appeal* Judgment Summary (n 17) [10].
210 Ibid [14].
211 See Hirst (n 70) 126–7. See also Ana-Maria Bucataru, 'Using the Convention on the Rights of the Child to Project the Rights of the Transgender Children and Adolescents: The Context of Education and Transition' (2016) 3(1) *Queen Mary Human Rights Review* 59.

compromising the integrity of the underpinning law and legal principles.[212] Yet as Stalford and Hollingsworth have argued:

> (especially) in key decisions on children's rights … the obligation for transparency and clarity … is about ensuring, as far as possible, that judgments are comprehensible to children as a wider community of legal citizens affected by the decision. This must include a commitment to developing a 'children's jurisprudence', particularly where the outcome of a decision has long term ramifications for their rights.[213]

The Court of Appeal's failure to produce a summary of the *Bell* judgment that contemplated *children* as its audience means that the judgment has, from a children's rights perspective, failed to fulfil its 'enormous instructive potential'.[214] For a decision of such significance to TGD children, bearing as it does upon their bodily autonomy and identity rights, a child-friendly summary (in addition to the summary written for the press and the public) would have also contributed to upholding the decisional privacy rights of those children, by indicating that the law recognises and respects them as distinct rights-holders.[215]

7.5 The limited 'symbolic value'[216] of the Court of Appeal's judgment for TGD children's rights

The above children's rights analysis of the Court of Appeal's judgment in *Bell* has demonstrated that the Court was not concerned with the rights of TGD children, but with not encroaching upon what it perceived to be a matter for medical practitioners' clinical judgement. Children experiencing gender dysphoria were abstracted in the judgment as a homogeneous, vulnerable 'cohort'. The Court of Appeal was expressly cautious to avoid wading into extra-legal debates 'in this difficult and controversial area'[217] and found it 'unnecessary'[218] to address the rights-based ground of appeal. That this was not a judgment about TGD children and their rights is reinforced by the written summary, which was 'to assist the press and the public' – but not children themselves – to understand the decision. If a redeeming feature is to be found in the Court of Appeal's judgment for the decisional privacy rights of TGD children, that feature arguably lies in the limited symbolic value of the judgment for the ability of those children to exercise choice in developing, discovering and preserv-

212 Stalford and Hollingsworth, '"This Case is about You"' (n 18) 1054.
213 Ibid 1053.
214 Ibid 1052.
215 See Chapter 3 (Section 3.5.2).
216 See Lucy Frith, 'The Concise Argument – Choice, Choices and the Choice Agenda' (2022) 48(1) *Journal of Medical Ethics* 1, 1; Tom Walker, 'Value of Choice' (2022) 48(1) *Journal of Medical Ethics* 61, 61.
217 *Bell Appeal* (n 1) [93].
218 Ibid [90].

ing their gender identity,[219] by commencing treatment with puberty blockers without the need for court authorisation.

7.5.1 The importance of choice for TGD children's evolving identity and autonomy

The Court of Appeal in *Bell* quoted the High Court's description of treatment for gender dysphoria as treatment that 'goes to the heart of an individual's identity'.[220] A children's rights approach to decisional privacy appreciates that children's sense of identity is a work-in-progress: it is evolving and still forming,[221] intertwined as it is with the decisions of parents and other family members.[222] On the relational, gradual and evolving conception of autonomy advanced in this book,[223] children's identity traits provide 'a compass for finding the direction of action' that best aligns with their living an authentic life,[224] and having the ability to make meaningful choices. To be able to exercise autonomy, a child must have the ability to choose between meaningful options. Without options, or without the ability to choose from those options, then the child cannot be autonomous.[225] This action of choosing bears a 'communicative' role.[226] As Walker has explained:

> To be denied a choice that other people would be allowed or expected to make reveals that one is seen as either less competent or less important than them. That is, it marks one out as inferior – at least in the eyes of those determining who gets to choose.[227]

An objective of the NHS Service Specification for GIDS is 'to promote the development of autonomy'.[228] It states that '[t]he Service will … affirm the importance

219 See Chapter 4 (Section 4.4). Article 8(1) of the CRC provides for the child's right 'to preserve [their] identity, including nationality, name and family relations as recognized by law without unlawful interference'.

220 *Bell Appeal* (n 1) [35], quoting *Bell Judicial Review* (n 2) [134]. See also *Bell Judicial Review* (n 2) [148] ('The treatment involved is truly life changing, going as it does to the very heart of an individual's identity').

221 See Chapter 4 (Section 4.4). See also John Tobin and Jonathan Todres, 'Article 8: The Right to Preservation of a Child's Identity' in John Tobin (ed), *The UN Convention on the Rights of the Child: A Commentary* (Oxford University Press, 2019) 281, 292.

222 See Chapter 1 (Section 1.4.4) and Chapter 2 (Section 2.3.3).

223 See Chapter 1 (Section 1.4.3).

224 Marina A L Oshana, 'Autonomy and Self-Identity' in John Christman and Joel Anderson (eds), *Autonomy and the Challenges to Liberalism* (Cambridge University Press, 2005) 77, 85.

225 See Gerald Dworkin, *The Theory and Practice of Autonomy* (Cambridge University Press, 1988) 103–9. See also Chapter 1 (Sections 1.3 and 1.4.4).

226 See Thomas M Scanlon, *What We Owe to Each Other* (Belknap Press, 1998) 251–6; Walker (n 216) 61.

227 Walker (n 216) 61.

228 NHS Standard Contract (n 45) 15.

of each person to develop autonomy in relation to treatment decisions'.[229] An expert witness in the proceedings before the High Court in *Bell* gave evidence that the need to apply to court to obtain consent on behalf of a child was unfavourable, among other reasons, because it would 'increase the distress suffered by the young people themselves, finding that their right to autonomous decision making had been removed from them'.[230] And as Freeman has observed, '[t]o respect a child's autonomy is to treat that child as a person and as a rights-holder'.[231]

Different conceptions of autonomy may produce varied results in terms of what is justifiable interference with an individual.[232] If it is accepted that autonomy embraces an individual's 'freedom to decide what shall and shall not be done with their body',[233] then to return to the words of 'Jamie', the subject of the *Re Jamie* proceedings, '[i]t shouldn't be the court's decision. It is my body, and only I have the right to decide what goes into it'.[234] On a children's rights approach to decisional privacy, the choice whether to commence medical treatment with puberty blockers is a choice that TGD children should be afforded the opportunity to make, consistently with their evolving capacities and with the direction and guidance of their parents and medical practitioners. The High Court's decision in *Bell* deprived TGD children of that choice.

The Court of Appeal reversed that deprivation, to the extent that it found that the High Court had 'placed an improper restriction on the *Gillick* test of competence', including by using 'age criteria' to evaluate *Gillick* competence in relation to puberty blocking treatment and by requiring a court application before such treatment was prescribed.[235] It is in this reversal that the Court of Appeal's judgment, it is suggested, bears some 'symbolic' value for TGD children. The *outcome* signals that those children should be given the choice to exercise their evolving capacity for autonomy in relation to medical treatment that fundamentally affects their bodies, identities and well-being.[236]

It is important to distinguish between an assessment of an individual's ability to *exercise* choice – for example, determining whether a child is *Gillick* competent to consent to treatment – and affording the individual an *opportunity* to choose. The question of whether an individual child has capacity to give informed consent

229 Ibid 24.
230 *Bell Judicial Review* (n 2) [41].
231 Michael Freeman, 'Taking Children's Rights More Seriously' (1992) 6 *International Journal of Law, Policy and the Family* 52, 65. However, Freeman also recognises that, owing to their 'lesser abilities and capacities', and their vulnerability, children require protection: at 65–9. This is discussed in Chapter 1 (Section 1.4.1) and Chapter 4 (Section 4.3.1).
232 See, eg, Cave and Purshouse (n 104) 272; John Coggon, 'Varied and Principled Understandings of Autonomy in English Law: Justifiable Inconsistency or Blinkered Moralism?' (2007) 15(3) *Health Care Analysis* 235.
233 *Montgomery v Lanarkshire Health Board* [2015] UKSC 11, [108] (Lady Hale).
234 Jamie, letter to the Family Court of Australia, quoted in *Re Jamie* [2015] FamCA 455, [65]. See Chapter 5.
235 *Bell Appeal* (n 1) [94].
236 Moreton (n 70) 700–1.

to treatment with puberty blockers – or whether children of different ages as a collective have such capacity (which resulted in the impugned conclusions of the High Court in *Bell)* – are 'beside the point' when assessing whether a child or children 'should have a choice about what happens to them'.[237]

The *context* of choice is also significant. The Court of Appeal in *Bell* noted that the issues raised by the *Gillick* case about contraception for children aged under 16 'were highly controversial in a way that is now hard to imagine',[238] just as treatment with puberty blockers is currently considered (by some) to be 'controversial'.[239] In overturning the High Court's decision, the Court of Appeal thus appeared to be alive to the prevailing social climate surrounding gender dysphoria treatment for children. As Giordano, Garland and Holm have observed, that climate is characterised by 'widespread irrational fears that exaggerate the "threats" posed by increasing trans visibility and the rising number of minors who are seeking treatment'.[240] The societal and institutional frameworks that impede the recognition of TGD children as rights-bearers and 'competent and equal members of society',[241] and impair their opportunity to choose, cannot be overlooked. TGD children and their voices have long been marginalised in legal and policy debates concerning their medical treatment.[242] Further, TGD children experience increased discrimination, social stigma, exclusion and violence owing to their gender identity.[243]

7.5.2 The limitations of the Court of Appeal's judgment for the 'symbolic' value of choice

The symbolic value of the Court of Appeal's judgment, described above, is arguably limited in two significant respects. First, the Court of Appeal did not conceptualise the case as being about TGD children and their rights; nor did it engage with rights-based arguments in its reasoning or endeavour to communicate the decision effectively to children themselves. Indeed, the Court

237 Walker (n 216) 63. This distinction also underscores the difference between the interest theory of rights – upon which a children's rights approach to decisional privacy is based – and the will or choice theory: see Chapter 1 (Section 1.4.2).

238 *Bell Appeal* (n 1) [76].

239 Ibid [3], [48], [93].

240 Giordano, Garland and Holm (n 70) 324.

241 Walker (n 216) 62.

242 See, eg, Sam Winter et al, 'Transgender People: Health at the Margins of Society' (2016) 388(10042) *The Lancet* 390; Giordano, Garland and Holm (n 70).

243 See, eg, Holly V Franson, 'The Rise of the Transgender Child: Overcoming Societal Stigma, Institutional Discrimination, and Individual Bias to Enact and Enforce Nondiscriminatory Dress Code Policies' (2013) 84(2) *University of Colorado Law Review* 497; Amanda Kennedy, 'Because We Say So: The Unfortunate Denial of Rights to Transgender Minors Regarding Transitions' (2008) 19(2) *Hastings Women's Law Journal* 281; Sonja Shield, 'The Doctor Won't See You Now: Rights of Transgender Adolescents to Sex Reassignment Treatment' (2007) 31(2) *New York University Review of Law & Social Change* 361.

found it 'unnecessary' to address the sole rights-based ground of appeal.[244] The Court's evident concern, it has been argued, was with not treading upon the toes of medical practitioners in their assessment of *Gillick* competence. Hirst has argued, in relation to the High Court's judgment in *Bell*:

> In what is one of the most significant decisions relating to young people's capacity to consent to treatment since the landmark ruling in *Gillick*, it is particularly noteworthy that children's rights, and their direct experiences or views, barely feature in the judgment.[245]

This observation applies with even greater force, it is suggested, to the judgment of the Court of Appeal in *Bell*: the rights and direct experiences of TGD children do not feature at all. To read this judgment as advocating the rights of TGD children in any practical way is to read into the judgment an approach that the Court of Appeal expressly avoided: a rights-based approach.

Second, just as the Full Court of the Family Court of Australia did in *Re Kelvin*,[246] the Court of Appeal in *Bell* identified 'disputes between one or more of clinicians, patients and parents' as a circumstance necessitating an application to the court for authorisation of treatment.[247] The Court of Appeal did not identify the nature of the dispute that would require a court application; it merely noted that such disputes were 'difficult to envisage under the service specification and [standard operating procedure] with which this case is concerned'.[248] The Court added that 'applications to the court may well be appropriate in specific difficult cases', but that it was 'not appropriate to give guidance as to when such circumstances might arise'.[249] The vagueness of this qualification suggests that additional jurisprudence on the issue of *Gillick* competence in the context of medical treatment for childhood gender dysphoria is likely to arise in England and Wales.[250] The decisional privacy rights of TGD children seeking access to treatment with puberty blockers remain constrained to the extent that they do not have a 'genuine' opportunity to choose if their choices can be overridden or vetoed by the courts, seemingly in their 'best interests'.[251]

7.6 Conclusion

This chapter has added a comparative dimension to the case study of this book, analysing the judgment of the Court of Appeal of England and Wales in *Bell* from

244 See Section 7.4.2.i above.
245 Hirst (n 70) 116 (citation omitted).
246 [2017] FamCAFC 258 ('*Re Kelvin*'). See Chapter 6 (Section 6.4.3).
247 *Bell Appeal* (n 1) [89].
248 Ibid.
249 Ibid [94].
250 Jowett and Kelly (n 94) 51; Kavanagh (n 105).
251 Walker (n 216) 62.

the perspective of children's right to decisional privacy. The analysis has argued that the decision is not the resounding victory for the rights of TGD children as has been proclaimed. Three features of the Court of Appeal's judgment have been examined to develop this argument: the Court's failure to conceptualise the issues as being clearly about TGD children and their rights, instead focusing on the appropriate gatekeeper to treatment; an evasive judicial approach that found it 'unnecessary' to engage with rights-based arguments and wider debates concerning gender dysphoria treatment for children; and the missed opportunity to communicate the decision to children themselves. In this way, the Court of Appeal's judgment arguably perpetuates the trend – evident in both Australia and the UK – of ignoring the rights of TGD children, driven by paternalistic understandings of their unique vulnerability[252] and perceptions of the 'experimental' and 'innovative' nature of treatment.[253]

Nolan has argued that '[w]here a right cannot be enforced, it is … robbed of any meaningful power and is reduced to being of merely symbolic value to the right-holder'.[254] This chapter has identified a limited symbolic value in the Court of Appeal's judgment for the rights of TGD children. That value derives, it has been argued, from what the outcome of *Bell* conveys about the 'status and vision'[255] of those children in society: a message that they have evolving capacities for decision-making, and should have the opportunity to choose, consistently with those capacities, what to do with their bodies and how to develop and forge their identities, without the need for judicial imprimatur. The judgment may therefore go some way towards recognising the identities of children experiencing gender dysphoria as 'legitimate and worthy of affirmation through puberty blocking'.[256] The symbolic value of the Court of Appeal's judgment is nonetheless limited, it has been argued, by the Court's unwillingness to embrace children's rights in its framing of the issues, reasoning and communication of the decision; and in the scope that the judgment has provided for future court involvement where disputes arise 'between one or more of clinicians, patients and parents'.[257]

The analysis of the Court of Appeal's judgment in *Bell* has attested to the fragility of perceived 'gains' in the area of TGD children's rights.[258] Appellate courts in Australia and the UK have envisaged scope for ongoing court intervention

252 Hirst (n 70) 127.
253 Michelle Taylor-Sands and Georgina Dimopoulos, 'Judicial Discomfort over "Innovative" Treatment for Adolescents with Gender Dysphoria' (2022) *Medical Law Review* fwac018. See also Chapter 4 (Section 4.3.1.ii) and *Bell Judicial Review* (n 2) [28], [74], [129], [134], [143], [148], [152].
254 Nolan (n 190) 219.
255 Tobin, 'Judging the Judges' (n 149) 595.
256 Hirst (n 70) 127.
257 *Bell Appeal* (n 1) [89].
258 Jacqui Thornton, 'Court Upholds *Gillick* Competence in Puberty Blockers Case' (2021) 398(10307) *The Lancet* 1205, 1206.

– such as in circumstances of 'dispute'[259] between parents and medical practitioners – reflecting Freeman's observation that '[t]he law is the cultural and institutional underpinning of autonomy. It gives and it takes away. Families … have as much autonomy as the law allows them'.[260] The next chapter takes the analysis of potential conflicts or disputes further, by responding to concerns about the perceived conflictual consequences of recognising and respecting children's right to decisional privacy. It also articulates the of social value of this right, and suggests two interrelated processes by which the theory of children's right to decisional privacy may be translated into policy and practice.

259 See *Re Kelvin* (n 246) [167]; *Bell Appeal* (n 1) [89].
260 Michael Freeman, *The Rights and Wrongs of Children* (Frances Pinter, 1983) 248.

8 Recognising and respecting children's right to decisional privacy

Conflicts, complexities and opportunities

8.1 Introduction

This chapter addresses the potential for intra-familial conflicts when children's right to decisional privacy is recognised and respected. A children's rights approach to decisional privacy anticipates the potential for such conflicts, given that it acknowledges children as subjects with rights and interests that are distinct from those of their parents and other family members.[1] This chapter first responds to concerns expressed by those uneasy with the notion of children as rights-bearers, that recognising children's right to decisional privacy will incite conflict between children and their parents, fracture family relationships and undermine parental authority, thereby justifying violations of family privacy by the state. The response to these concerns is twofold. The first aspect conceptualises the notion of 'conflict' in the family context using a relational approach to autonomy. It emphasises the influence of children's relationships with their parents and family members in children's ability to exercise and enjoy their right to decisional privacy. In practice, this means that acknowledging children's right to decisional privacy does not necessarily construct an adversarial relationship between children and their parents. However, a rights-based approach does anticipate and accommodate for conflict between children and their parents, through the principle of 'evolving capacities' in Article 5 of the CRC. The second aspect of the response addresses the scope of children's right to decisional privacy. It counters the myth that respecting this right will grant children complete decision-making autonomy in relation to all matters affecting them. It does, however, allow for children's views to be determinative of their best interests in certain circumstances.

The second part of the chapter articulates the of social value of children's right to decisional privacy. This includes the scope for children's meaningful participation in decision-making to challenge existing power structures and institutions, and the opportunity for children's perspectives, views and experiences to shape policy and practice. It proposes two interrelated processes for translating the theory of children's decisional privacy developed in this book into policy and practice. The

1 See Chapter 2 (Section 2.3.1).

DOI: 10.4324/9781003224167-11

first process is conceptual: to challenge and deconstruct the conceptualisation of children as vulnerable objects in need of protection, and to promote greater awareness of the impacts on the rights of children – as distinct from their parents and the family as an entity – of law and policy. The second is institutional: processes and procedures to enable children's more meaningful, active participation in decision-making. This chapter demonstrates that recognising and respecting children's right to decisional privacy has significant implications not only for children themselves, but simultaneously for the dynamics and boundaries of the relationship between children, their parents and the state.

8.2 Child versus parents? Constructing a false dichotomy of interests

A criticism of rights-based approaches is that they tend to 'see familial rights as protections for individual freedom, rather than as rights that create, foster, and protect valued relationships'.[2] Macleod has labelled this the 'discourse anxiety' of 'corrosion', which 'focuses on the threat to family values posed by rights talk'.[3] It is important to reiterate the distinction between theories of rights to appreciate the rebuttal of this 'conflict of rights' argument. The theory of children's decisional privacy developed in this book is premised upon an interest theory of rights, which enables children to have rights irrespective of their capacity to exercise those rights.[4] Under this theory, the child's right to decisional privacy involves the protection of a sufficiently important interest (the child's evolving autonomy) and the imposition of duties on others (usually parents), the performance of which ensures that the child, as rights-holder, can enjoy that interest. The competing theory of rights, the will or choice theory, denies children the status of rights-bearers, as they are perceived to lack the ability to exercise rational choice.[5]

If one ascribes to the will or choice theory of rights, recognising a child's right to decisional privacy would only enliven the conflict of rights argument if the child were able to overcome the hurdle of capacity or competence. The

2 Martha Minow and Mary Lyndon Shanley, 'Revisioning the Family: Relational Rights and Responsibilities' in Mary Lyndon Shanley and Uma Narayan (eds), *Reconstructing Political Theory: Feminist Perspectives* (Polity Press, 1997) 84, 85.

3 Colin Macleod, 'Are Children's Rights Important?' in Elizabeth Brake and Lucinda Ferguson (eds), *Philosophical Foundations of Children's and Family Law* (Oxford University Press, 2018) 191, 204.

4 See Chapter 1 (Section 1.4.2). See, eg, Joseph Raz, 'Legal Rights' (1984) 4(1) *Oxford Journal of Legal Studies* 1; Neil MacCormick, 'Children's Rights: A Test-Case' in Neil MacCormick (ed), *Legal Right and Social Democracy: Essays in Legal and Political Philosophy* (Clarendon Press, 1982) 154.

5 See Chapter 1 (Section 1.4.2). See, eg, Harry Brighouse, 'What Rights (If Any) Do Children Have?' in David Archard and Colin Macleod (eds), *The Moral and Political Status of Children* (Oxford University Press, 2002) 31; HLA Hart, 'Are there Any Natural Rights?' (1955) 64(2) *Philosophical Review* 175.

initial focus would be on whether the child had the capacity to presently assert their right to decisional privacy. By contrast, under the interest theory of rights, the threshold issue of capacity does not arise. Rather, granting a child the right to decisional privacy *does* spark the potential for conflict between the child and their parents, because both are understood as distinct rights-holders. The child's evolving autonomy, as the interest protected by this right, and the performance of parental duties to ensure that the child can enjoy their evolving autonomy, therefore demand closer scrutiny.

8.2.1 Embracing a relational approach to autonomy

This book has advanced the view that the value of privacy inheres in securing the liberal ideal of autonomy.[6] However, as members of a family unit, children do not and cannot enjoy complete autonomy over their lives. Adults and children alike exercise autonomy 'within the shadow of the possibility of conflict' of individual interests.[7] Former Chief Justice of the Family Court of Australia, Diana Bryant, identified a 'tension of rights' inherent in the *Family Law Act 1975* (Cth) ('Family Law Act'), suggesting that 'clashes' between parental rights and children's rights 'should be resolved with principle and transparency'.[8] Silber J in *R (Axon) v Secretary of State for Health (Family Planning Association Intervening)*[9] observed that 'the right of young people to make decisions about their own lives by themselves at the expense of the views of their parents has now become an increasingly important and accepted feature of family life'.[10] Yet it would be 'obviously awkward', as Nedelsky has noted, to conceptualise the parent–child relationship in circumstances of conflict or controversy as '*essentially* one of competing interests to be mediated by rights'.[11] The rights and interests of the child and the rights and interests of their parents will be intermingled, as a child's autonomy and identity are forged and developed through their family relationships.[12]

A theory of children's right to decisional privacy seeks to overcome the objection that rights-based approaches are 'divisive', in that they 'reflect an egoistic,

6 See Chapter 1 (Section 1.3).

7 Jo Bridgeman, *Parental Responsibility, Young Children and Healthcare Law* (Cambridge University Press, 2007) 11.

8 Diana Bryant, 'It's My Body, Isn't It? Children, Medical Treatment and Human Rights' (2009) 35(2) *Monash University Law Review* 193, 207.

9 [2006] QB 539.

10 Ibid [79].

11 Jennifer Nedelsky, 'Reconceiving Rights and Constitutionalism' (2008) 7(2) *Journal of Human Rights* 139, 145 (emphasis in original). See also Mary Ann Glendon, *The Transformation of Family Law* (Chicago University Press, 1989) 308; Martha Minow and Mary Lyndon Shanley, 'Relational Rights and Responsibilities: Revisioning the Family in Liberal Political Theory and Law' (1996) 11 *Hypatia* 4, 6 ('Relational Rights and Responsibilities'); Kirsty L Moreton, '*Gillick* Reinstated: Judging Mid-Childhood Competence in Healthcare Law' (2015) 23(2) *Medical Law Review* 303, 304, 312–13.

12 See Chapter 1 (see Section 1.4.4) and Chapter 4 (Section 4.2).

atomistic situation' and 'teach … us to think of "I" and "I versus you" instead of "we"'.[13] It does so through a relational approach to autonomy.[14] That is, children learn to become, and to be, autonomous in and through their relationships with their parents and other family members. Child is not to be pitted against parents. Focusing on interconnectedness, rather than individualism, reinforces Herring's view that '[p]eople do not understand their personal lives as involving clashes of individual rights or interests, but rather as a working through of relationships'.[15] As Herring has described further:

> The muddled give and take of everyday family life where sacrifices are made and benefits gained, without them being totted up on some giant familial star chart, chimes more with everyday family life than the image of independent interests and rights.[16]

The case study of court involvement in medical treatment for childhood gender dysphoria has reinforced the observation of Gilmore and Herring that 'many children … will wish to make their decisions with their parents and other family members and are unlikely to regard these decisions as simply theirs'.[17] Clinical treatment guidelines in this context emphasise the importance of familial support[18] and of clinicians investing time to support parents to 'assist in creating a shared understanding of the adolescent's experience'.[19] Parental interests and

13 John Hardwig, 'Should Women Think in Terms of Rights?' (1984) 94(3) *Ethics* 441, 448. See also Ferdinand Schoeman, 'Rights of Children, Rights of Parents, and the Moral Basis of the Family' (1980) 91(1) *Ethics* 6, 9; Mary Ann Glendon, *Rights Talk: The Impoverishment of Political Discourse* (The Free Press, 1991) 173.

14 See Chapter 1 (Section 1.4.3). See, eg, Jennifer Nedelsky, 'Reconceiving Autonomy: Sources, Thoughts and Possibilities' (1989) 1(1) *Yale Journal of Law and Feminism* 7; Jennifer Nedelsky, *Law's Relations: A Relational Theory of Self, Autonomy and Law* (Oxford University Press, 2011); Minow and Shanley, 'Relational Rights and Responsibilities' (n 11); Jonathan Herring, *Relational Autonomy and Family Law* (Springer, 2014) ('*Relational Autonomy*').

15 Jonathan Herring, 'Forging a Relational Approach: Best Interests or Human Rights?' (2013) 13(1) *Medical Law International* 32, 35. See also Kathryn Hollingsworth and Helen Stalford, 'Towards Children's Rights Judgments' in Helen Stalford, Kathryn Hollingsworth and Stephen Gilmore (eds), *Rewriting Children's Rights Judgments: From Academic Vision to New Practice* (Hart Publishing, 2017) 53, 69; Virginia Morrow, 'Dilemmas in Children's Participation in England' in Antonella Invernizzi and Jane Williams (eds), *Children and Citizenship* (Sage, 2008) 120, 128.

16 Herring, *Relational Autonomy* (n 14) 20.

17 Stephen Gilmore and Jonathan Herring, '"No" Is the Hardest Word: Consent and Children's Autonomy' (2011) 23(1) *Child and Family Law Quarterly* 3, 23.

18 Michelle Telfer et al, *Australian Standards of Care and Treatment Guidelines for Trans and Gender Diverse Children and Adolescents* (version 1.3, Royal Children's Hospital, 2020) 9 <www.rch.org.au/adolescent-medicine/gender-service/>; Eli Coleman et al, *Standards of Care for the Health of Transsexual, Transgender, and Gender-Nonconforming People* (World Professional Association for Transgender Health, 7th version, 2012) 15 <www.wpath.org/media/cms/Documents/SOC%20v7/SOC%20V7_English2012.pdf?_t=1613669341>.

19 Telfer et al (n 18) 11–12.

views clearly are relevant to a TGD child's medical treatment decision-making, 'insofar as the [child] relies on their parents for ongoing support, care and access to treatment'.[20]

On a relational approach to autonomy, children's rights and interests are integrally interlinked with those of their parents.[21] The onus is on a child's parents to provide 'appropriate direction and guidance' to their child in the child's exercise of their rights, 'in a manner consistent with the evolving capacities of the child'.[22] According to Tobin and Varadan, Article 5 of the CRC 'clearly anticipates that parents must play an intimate and ongoing role in enabling children to enjoy their rights'.[23] However, the focus must remain on the *child's* right to receive parental direction and guidance, rather than on parents' right to state non-interference with their parenting.[24] Given that Article 5 is chiefly a 'scaffolding' provision that aims to protect children's (not parents') rights,[25] it requires parents to provide direction and guidance to their children 'in a child-centred way, through dialogue and example'.[26] The model envisaged is a 'participatory and inclusive' one, premised upon mutual respect between children and their parents.[27]

Children's right to decisional privacy is therefore buttressed by an expectation that children's enjoyment of this right will be interconnected and interdependent with the exercise of parental rights and responsibilities.[28] A children's rights approach does not allow for parenting models that fail to respect children's evolving capacities, or which endorse the outdated mantra that 'children should be seen and not heard' within the family.[29] Such an approach imposes an obligation upon parents to guide and enable their children to gradually exercise and enjoy

20 Georgina Dimopoulos and Michelle Taylor-Sands, '*Re Imogen*: The Role of the Family Court of Australia in Disputes over Gender Dysphoria Treatment (2021) 39 (Suppl 1) *Monash Bioethics Review* S42, S61.

21 See Jonathan Herring, 'The Welfare Principle and the Rights of Parents' in Andrew Bainham, Shelley Day Sclater and Martin Richards (eds), *What is a Parent: A Socio-Legal Analysis* (Hart Publishing, 1999) 89.

22 *CRC*, art 5.

23 John Tobin and Sheila Varadan, 'Article 5: The Right to Parental Direction and Guidance and Consistent with a Child's Evolving Capacities' in John Tobin (ed), *The UN Convention on the Rights of the Child: A Commentary* (Oxford University Press, 2019) 159, 175.

24 Ibid 160. See also Chapter 2 (Section 2.3.3).

25 Tobin and Varadan (n 23) 175; Nicola Taylor, 'Parental Guidance in Support of Children's Participation Rights: The Interplay between Articles 5 and 12 in the Family Justice System' in Brian Sloan and Claire Fenton-Glynn (eds), *Parental Guidance, State Responsibility and Evolving Capacities: Article 5 of the United Nations Convention on the Rights of the Child* (Brill, 2021) 104, 108–9.

26 CRC Committee, *General Comment No 7: Implementing Child Rights in Early Childhood*, UN Doc CRC/C/GC/7/Rev.1 (20 September 2006) [17] ('*General Comment No 7*').

27 Tobin and Varadan (n 23) 175, 183. See also Nigel Thomas, 'Towards a Theory of Children's Participation' (2007) 15(2) *International Journal of Children's Rights* 199, 206–7.

28 John Tobin, 'Justifying Children's Rights' (2013) 21 *International Journal of Children's Rights* 395, 424 ('Justifying Children's Rights').

29 Tobin and Varadan (n 23) 183.

their rights independently. It also requires that parental rights and responsibilities, where exercised appropriately, be respected.[30]

8.2.2 Relationality under the CRC

This relational approach to children's right to decisional privacy is indeed supported by the text of the CRC. The preamble to the CRC provides that 'children should grow up in a family environment' and that 'the family is the fundamental group of society and the natural environment for the growth and well-being of all its members'.[31] To this end, the family is to be 'afforded the necessary protection and assistance so that it can fully assume its responsibilities within the community'.[32] These preambular statements refute the suggestion that granting children a right to decisional privacy will necessarily invite conflict between children and their parents and, taken to its extreme, will undermine the family unit. Rather, these provisions demonstrate a 'normative commitment to the family and parents'.[33]

The significance of a child's family is reinforced by a number of substantive provisions of the CRC. These include the obligation on states to respect the responsibilities, rights and duties of parents to provide appropriate direction and guidance to their children;[34] deference to parents as having primary responsibility for their children's upbringing and development, and the requirement that states assist parents to perform this responsibility;[35] a child's right to preserve their family relations;[36] protection against unlawful or arbitrary interference with a child's privacy, family or home;[37] and a child's right to not be separated from their parents unless separation is necessary for the child's best interests.[38] The conception of rights under the CRC is thus relational, rather than individualistic.[39] The CRC also provides a 'collaborative or cooperative'[40] understanding of the relationship between the state and the family in relation to children's upbringing. That is,

30 Ibid.
31 *CRC*, Preamble.
32 Ibid.
33 Tobin, 'Justifying Children's Rights' (n 28) 423, 425.
34 *CRC*, art 5.
35 Ibid arts 18, 27.
36 Ibid art 8.
37 Ibid art 16.
38 Ibid art 9(1).
39 Katherine Hunt Federle, 'Rights Flow Downhill' in Michael Freeman (ed), *Children's Rights: Progress and Perspectives* (Brill, 2011) 447, 460–2; John Eekelaar and John Tobin, 'Article 3: The Best Interests of the Child' in John Tobin (ed), *The UN Convention on the Rights of the Child: A Commentary* (Oxford University Press, 2019) 73, 105–6.
40 John Tobin, 'Fixed Concepts but Changing Conceptions: Understanding the Relationship Between Children and Parents under the CRC' in Martin D Ruck, Michele Peterson-Badali and Michael Freeman (eds), *Handbook of Children's Rights: Global and Multidisciplinary Perspectives* (Taylor & Francis, 2016) 55, 59 ('Fixed Concepts').

parents bear the primary responsibility for their children's welfare and development, but the state plays an important role in helping parents to fulfil their duties and responsibilities.[41] Children's right to decisional privacy – entailing children's meaningful participation in decision-making about matters that affect them, consistently with their evolving capacities and appropriately guided and assisted by their parents – must be understood within this context. As Tobin has observed: 'Far from seeking to drive a wedge between children and their parents, the CRC makes it clear that children's interests are best served when they enjoy a strong and supportive relationship with their parents.'[42]

A relational approach to autonomy, as reinforced by provisions of the CRC, explains why a perceived 'conflict' between a child and their parents in relation to a decision to be made may not, on a children's rights approach to decisional privacy, amount to a 'genuine' conflict that would justify state intervention. When the concept of 'conflict' in the family is understood through the perspective of relational autonomy, constructing parents and children as being in conflict when children's right to decisional privacy is recognised and respected is both exaggerated and misunderstood.

8.3 Beware a child mutiny! Delimiting the boundaries of children's right to decisional privacy

A concern expressed by some detractors of the notion of children as rights-bearers is that recognising and respecting children's right to decisional privacy will give children a licence to do whatever they choose, in relation to all matters concerning them: children will be 'abandoned' to their autonomy.[43] The result, so the argument goes, is diminished parental authority, conflict between children and their parents, and a chaotic inversion of the parent–child relationship, ultimately justifying violations of family privacy by the state.[44] This argument triggers debate about the scope of children's right to decisional privacy.

41 Tobin and Varadan (n 23) 163–5.

42 Tobin, 'Fixed Concepts' (n 40) 58.

43 See Bruce C Hafen and Jonathan O Hafen, 'Abandoning Children to Their Autonomy: The United Nations Convention on the Rights of the Child' (1996) 37(2) *Harvard International Law Journal* 449.

44 Barbara Bennett Woodhouse, 'Hatching the Egg: A Child-Centered Perspective on Parents' Rights' (1992) 14(6) *Cardozo Law Review* 1747, 1839. See also Michael Freeman, 'Review Essay: What's Right with Rights for Children' (2006) 2 *International Journal of Law in Context* 89, 89–90; Tobin, 'Fixed Concepts' (n 40) 53; Jane Fortin, *Children's Rights and the Developing Law* (Cambridge University Press, 3rd ed, 2009) 5, 8–9; Clare Huntington, 'Rights Myopia in Child Welfare' (2006) 53 *UCLA Law Review* 637, 639–40. For alarmist examples of such a perspective, see Patrick Fagan, William Saunders and Michael Fragoso, 'How UN Conventions on Women's and Children's Rights Undermine Family, Religion and Sovereignty', *Insight* (Family Research Council, 2009) 13; John Rosemond, *A Family of Value* (Andrews McMeel Publishing, 1995) 116; Ingrid J Guzman, *Parent Police: The UN Wants Your Children* (Huntington House, 1995) 3.

The fact that children's right to decisional privacy respects children's evolving capacities for autonomy can 'make practical interpretation … very complex'.[45] It is argued that no fixed boundary should be drawn on *when* children should possess and be able to exercise their right to decisional privacy. However, this does not mean, in a practical sense, that children can and must make all decisions in all matters affecting them.[46] The theory developed in this book contains two important qualifications. The first relates to the practicality of enabling children to meaningfully and actively participate in the making of any decision about or affecting their interests. The second concerns what it means for the child's views to be determinative of the child's best interests.

8.3.1 Consultation with children on all matters affecting them

This book has argued that children's substantive right to decisional privacy requires procedural rights to enable children's meaningful participation in decision-making about their best interests. Children's right to so participate manifests in Article 12(1) of the CRC, which affords the child who is capable of forming a view the opportunity to express their views, with those views being given due weight in accordance with the child's age and maturity. The child's right under Article 12 demands an inclusive understanding of participation and 'a radical reconceptualization of the adult–child decision-making relationship'.[47]

According to Lundy, Tobin and Parkes, the only limitation that the text of Article 12 imposes on the child's right to express their views and to be heard is that the matter 'affect' a child.[48] The CRC Committee has said that the phrase 'in all matters affecting the child' in Article 12(1) should be construed 'broadly'.[49] This means, in practical terms, that the child's right to participate meaningfully in decision-making processes is not limited to matters that affect an individual child. Rather, it captures *all* matters that 'do or will have a real impact on children's lives' – regardless of whether that impact is 'direct, indirect, specific, or incidental'.[50] Importantly, there must be some nexus or connection between the

45 Macleod (n 3) 199.

46 John Eekelaar, 'The Interests of the Child and the Child's Wishes: The Role of Dynamic Self-Determinism' (1994) 8(1) *International Journal of Law, Policy and the Family* 42, 53 ('Dynamic Self-Determinism').

47 Gerison Lansdown, *Promoting Children's Participation in Democratic Decision Making* (UNICEF Innocenti Insight, 2001) 1.

48 Laura Lundy, John Tobin and Aisling Parkes, 'Article 12: The Right to Respect for the Views of the Child' in John Tobin (ed), *The UN Convention on the Rights of the Child: A Commentary* (Oxford University Press, 2019) 397, 401, 406–8.

49 CRC Committee, *General Comment No 12 (2009): The Right of the Child to be Heard*, UN Doc CRC/C/GC/12 (20 July 2009) [26] ('*General Comment No 12*').

50 Lundy, Tobin and Parkes (n 48) 400–1.

matter and the child.[51] Further, children must play an active role in discussions and debates about what these matters 'affecting' them are.[52]

However, children's meaningful and active participation in the making of *any* decision about or affecting their interests would, as Eekelaar and Tobin have suggested, be 'impractical'.[53] While a welfare approach would have adult preferences and assumptions take the place of the child's own views,[54] a children's rights approach to decisional privacy requires that the decision be deferred, if possible, until the child is competent to decide what is in their best interests.[55] Obviously, this will not be possible where a decision is urgent, such as one affecting the child's health, life or well-being. Medical treatment for gender dysphoria is a pertinent example, with potential problems arising for the child's physical and psychological health and well-being where a treatment decision is delayed due to the child's lack of competence to give informed consent.[56] In such cases, where a determination of the child's best interests is urgent, or where consultation with the child is unfeasible due to time constraints, lack of resources or logistical obstacles, adult decision-makers should 'take all reasonable measures, in light of available resources, to ascertain a child's views' when assessing the child's best interests.[57]

8.3.2 Scope for children's views to be determinative of their best interests

A question that remains the subject of debate,[58] and impacts on concerns about children having and exercising a right to decisional privacy, is whether a child's views can ever be determinative of their best interests. Fortin has argued that the

51 Ibid 406–8.

52 Ibid 401.

53 Eekelaar and Tobin (n 39) 85 (offering as an example young children, who will often not have the capacity to express their views about their interests, 'irrespective of the measures taken to enable them to do so').

54 See Introduction (Section I.3.2).

55 Eekelaar, 'Dynamic Self-Determinism' (n 46) 47–8; Eekelaar and Tobin (n 39) 85–6.

56 See, eg, *Re Alex* (2009) 248 FLR 312; *Re Sean* (2010) 258 FLR 192, 206 [86]–[87] (Murphy J); *Re Jamie* [2011] FamCA 248, [5], [53], [111] (Dessau J); Fiona Kelly, '"The Court Process is Slow but Biology is Fast": Assessing the Impact of the Family Court Approval Process on Transgender Children and their Families' (2016) 30(2) *Australian Journal of Family Law* 112, 123–5.

57 Eekelaar and Tobin (n 39) 86.

58 See Lundy, Tobin and Parkes (n 48) 410–12 and references cited therein; Eekelaar and Tobin (n 39) 85–7; Patrick Parkinson and Judy Cashmore, *The Voice of a Child in Family Law Disputes* (Oxford University Press, 2008) 116–17; Tobin, 'Justifying Children's Rights' (n 28) 428–9, 431–2; Harry Brighouse, 'How Should Children be Heard?' (2003) 45(3) *Arizona Law Review* 691; John Tobin and Sarah M Field, 'Article 16: The Right to Protection of Privacy, Family, Home, Correspondence, Honour, and Reputation' in John Tobin (ed), *The UN Convention on the Rights of the Child: A Commentary* (Oxford University Press, 2019) 551, 567.

child's right under Article 12(1) of the CRC 'is about consultation and participation, not about self-determination'.[59] Judicial statements from Australia and the UK echo this sentiment. English courts have noted that the child's right under Article 12 is 'to have the opportunity to express [their] views and to be heard, not a right to self-determination';[60] and that 'taking account' of the child's views 'does not mean that those views are always determinative or even presumptively so'.[61] Similarly, the High Court of Australia has held that children's views 'are but one consideration of a number to be taken into account in the overall assessment of a child's best interests', such that they are not determinative or decisive in and of themselves.[62] However, the High Court has added that 'it may be right, in the exercise of a primary judge's discretion, to accord the views expressed by a child such weight'.[63]

Indeed, Article 12(1) of the CRC does not *necessarily* require that children's views be given 'determinative force'.[64] Respecting a child's right to decisional privacy is not the same as giving the child the ultimate authority to decide, in relation to each and every matter affecting them, what is in their best interests. As Baroness Hale of Richmond observed: 'As any parent who has ever asked a child what he wants for tea knows, there is a large difference between taking account of a child's views and doing what [the child] wants.'[65] The child's right under Article 5 of the CRC to receive appropriate parental direction and guidance, consistent with the child's evolving capacities, anticipates that in practice, given children's lack of capacity to determine their best interests in relation to various matters, parents will regularly make decisions on behalf of their children.

However, to say that 'children have a voice, not a choice'[66] is to misconstrue children's right to decisional privacy. The view advanced here – supported by the text of the CRC[67] and numerous scholars[68] – is that a child's views will, in

59 Fortin (n 44) 236.
60 *Re T (Abduction: Child's Objections to Return)* [2000] EWCA Civ 133 (Ward LJ).
61 *Re M (Children) (Abduction: Rights of Custody)* [2007] UKHL 55, [46] (Baroness Hale).
62 *Bondelmonte v Bondelmonte* (2017) 259 CLR 662, 673 [34] (Kiefel, Bell, Keane, Nettle and Gordon JJ) ('*Bondelmonte*'). 'Any views expressed by the child' are the first of the 'additional considerations' that the court must take into account when determining what is in a child's best interests: see *Family Law Act 1975* (Cth) s 60CC(3)(a).
63 *Bondelmonte* (n 62) 673 [34] (Kiefel, Bell, Keane, Nettle and Gordon JJ).
64 Eekelaar and Tobin (n 39) 86. See also Parkinson and Cashmore (n 58) 199.
65 *Re D (A Child) (Abduction: Rights of Custody)* [2006] UKHL 51, [57].
66 *Duffy v Gomes* (2015) 299 FLR 108, 154–5 [71] (Judge Harman).
67 See *CRC*, arts 5, 12.
68 See John Tobin, 'Understanding Children's Rights: A Vision beyond Vulnerability' (2015) 84 *Nordic Journal of International Law* 155, 180 ('Understanding Children's Rights'); Tobin, 'Justifying Children's Rights' (n 28) 428, 432; Eekelaar, 'Dynamic Self-Determinism' (n 46) 55; Laura Lundy, '"Voice" Is Not Enough: Conceptualising Article 12 of the United Nations Convention on the Rights of the Child' (2007) 33(6) *British Educational Research Journal* 927; Aoife Daly, *Children, Autonomy and the Courts: Beyond the Right to be* Heard (Brill, 2017) ch 6; John Seymour, *Children, Parents and the Courts: Legal Intervention in Family Life* (Federation Press, 2016) 101; Kirsten Sandberg, 'The Rights of LGBTI

circumstances where the child is of sufficient understanding and maturity in relation to a matter affecting them, be determinative of the child's best interests. The child's own views must be respected in these circumstances, even when they conflict with the views of the child's parents. This is because Article 5 of the CRC implies 'a transfer of responsibility for decision-making from responsible adults to children, as the child acquires the competence and … willingness to do so'.[69] The principle of evolving capacities, as the CRC Committee has explained, 'should be seen as a positive and enabling process, not an excuse for authoritarian practices that restrict children's autonomy and self-expression'.[70] Once a child has developed the capacity to effectively claim and enjoy their right to decisional privacy independently of their parents, then the child no longer requires the right to appropriate parental direction and guidance.

In various contexts, including healthcare[71] and child protection,[72] parents, children and practice professionals engage in shared decision-making. The child is provided with the framework or scaffolding to participate in decision-making to the degree that is considered appropriate for the child's maturity and capabilities.[73] Research has identified various concerns with children's participation in this context, related to the dominant perception of children as irrational, dependent and vulnerable.[74] These include adults underestimating children's competence;[75] children feeling that their views are ignored or sidelined by adult

---

Children under the Convention on the Rights of the Child' (2015) 33(4) *Nordic Journal of Human Rights* 337, 344, 347. The alternative argument is that a child's capacity cannot be determinative in relation to matters that are within the scope of parental direction and guidance, because Article 5 of the CRC, when read together with Article 3 (the best interests principle), bestows ultimate responsibility for the determination of a child's best interests upon the child's parent as adult decision-maker: see David Archard, *Children: Rights and Childhood* (Routledge, 3rd ed, 2015) 58.

69 Gerison Lansdown, *The Evolving Capacities of the Child* (UNICEF Innocenti Studies, 2005) 4. See also Gerison Lansdown, 'The Scope and Limitations of the Concept of Evolving Capacities within the CRC' in Brian Sloan and Claire Fenton-Glynn (eds), *Parental Guidance, State Responsibility and Evolving Capacities: Article 5 of the United Nations Convention on the Rights of the Child* (Brill, 2021) 36.

70 CRC Committee, *General Comment No 7* (n 26) [17].

71 See, eg, Anita Franklin and Patricia Sloper, 'Listening and Responding? Children's Participation in Health Care within England' (2005) 13(1) *International Journal of Children's Rights* 11.

72 See, eg, Robert Sanders and Sam Mace, 'Agency Policy and the Participation of Children and Young People in the Child Protection Process' (2006) 15(2) *Child Abuse Review* 89.

73 Laura Lundy, 'In Defence of Tokenism? Implementing Children's Right to Participate in Collective Decision-Making' (2018) 25(3) *Childhood* 340; Jo Moran-Ellis and E Kay M Tisdall, 'The Relevance of "Competence" for Enhancing or Limiting Children's Participation: Unpicking Conceptual Confusion' (2019) 9(3) *Global Studies of Childhood* 212.

74 See Chapter 1 (Section 1.4.1).

75 Moran-Ellis and Tisdall (n 73); Karmen Toros, 'A Systematic Review of Children's Participation in Child Protection Decision-Making: Tokenistic Presence or Not?' (2021) 35(3) *Children & Society* 395.

decision-makers;[76] and a prevalent protectionist instinct, being to shield children from the 'burden' of decision-making and potential exposure to distressing or sensitive information.[77] A children's rights approach to decisional privacy accords with a 'situational' perspective on shared decision-making to the extent that it 'recognises children's right to have a say, without necessarily having full control over decision-making'.[78] However, it proposes that the protective role of the child's parents and practice professionals cannot justify restricting or interfering with a child's autonomy when the child is found to have reached a level of maturity to understand and appreciate the consequences of their decision.[79] For adults to engage in 'best interest-based intervention' and effectively override the child's views of their best interests would be neither legally nor morally justifiable.[80]

The evolving capacities principle under Article 5 of the CRC may therefore challenge parents' perceptions of their 'proper' role. It may even expose parental reluctance to cede their authority on matters where they feel that they know what is 'best' for – and know better than – their child. But as Tobin has observed, '[u]ltimately the principle of evolving capacities demands that parents concede that they are not always the sole arbiters of a child's best interests'.[81] Importantly, however, accepting the child's views as determinative of the child's best interests, in circumstances where the child is competent and capable of making an informed decision, does not automatically make the child's views determinative in relation to what *measures* will be taken to address the matter.[82] In other words, *making* the decision and *implementing* the decision made are two discrete processes. The latter involves a balancing exercise, whereby the impact of the matter on the child must be weighed against the impact on other children and adults involved, and against any other legitimate considerations.[83]

76 Toros (n 75); Mandy Duncan, 'Children's Experiences of Statutory Child Protection Interventions' in Mandy Duncan (ed), *Participation in Child Protection: Theorizing Children's Perspectives* (Palgrave Macmillan, 2018) 13; Jeanette Cossar, Marian Brandon and Peter Jordan, '"You've Got to Trust Her and She's Got to Trust You": Children's Views on Participation in the Child Protection System' (2016) 21(1) *Child & Family Social Work* 103.

77 Imelda Coyne and Maria Harder, 'Children's Participation in Decision-Making: Balancing Protection with Shared Decision-Making Using a Situational Perspective' (2011) 15(4) *Journal of Child Health Care* 312, 313.

78 Ibid 316.

79 Tobin and Field (n 58) 567; Eekelaar and Tobin (n 39) 87; David Archard, 'Philosophical Perspectives on Childhood' in Julia Fionda (ed), *Legal Concepts of Childhood* (Hart Publishing, 2001) 43, 47.

80 Lundy, Tobin and Parkes (n 48) 411; Tobin, 'Justifying Children's Rights' (n 28) 429.

81 Tobin, 'Fixed Concepts' (n 40) 64. See also Tobin and Varadan (n 23) 184; Tobin, 'Justifying Children's Rights' (n 28) 425–6. Cf Matias Cordero Arce, 'Towards an Emancipatory Discourse of Children's Rights' (2012) 20 *International Journal of Children's Rights* 365 (querying the extent to which Article 12 of the CRC recognises children's evolving autonomy).

82 Lundy, Tobin and Parkes (n 48) 411.

83 Ibid.

The model of children's right to decisional privacy appreciates that, in light of children's evolving capacities, there is no 'one-size-fits-all' approach. In some circumstances, parents will be solely responsible for making decisions about their children's best interests; in others, parents and children will collaborate to make such decisions. Perhaps most unnervingly, there will be circumstances where parents must cede decision-making authority to their children.[84] These interactions between children and their parents will be regulated by the range of social norms that operate within families: what Eekelaar has called the 'internal morality' of family life.[85]

8.4 From theory to practice: Reconceptualising children, reconfiguring institutional structures

Moving beyond the family unit, the social value of children's right to decisional privacy arguably lies in engendering respect for children as active beings, and in the rhetorical potency of rights to persuade and trigger change. It also lies in the opportunity for children's perspectives, views and experiences to shape policy and practice. Listening to and respecting children's views can produce more well-informed and relevant decisions,[86] because in Warshak's words, 'children have something important to tell us that may change the decisions we make on their behalf and the way in which we make them'.[87] Lundy, Tobin and Parkes have summarised this broader societal value as 'encouraging more efficient and effective policy making in matters concerning children *and* enabling them to assume more active and effective roles as members of their communities'.[88]

The final section of this chapter proposes two interrelated processes for translating the conceptual model developed in this book into practice. The first process is conceptual: to challenge and deconstruct how children have been conceptualised by and under decision-making frameworks for the determination of their best interests. The second process is the development and implementation

84 Ibid 431–2. See also Parkinson and Cashmore (n 58) 19–20; Harry Shier, 'Pathways to Participation: Opening, Opportunities and Obligations' (2001) 15(2) *Children & Society* 107.

85 John Eekelaar, 'Self-Restraint: Social Norms, Individualism and the Family' (2012) 13(1) *Theoretical Inquiries in Law* 75, 94.

86 Parkinson and Cashmore (n 58) 191–2; Joan B Kelly, 'Children's Living Arrangements Following Separation and Divorce: Insights From Empirical and Clinical Research' (2007) 46(1) *Family Process* 35; Sally Holland and Sean O'Neill, '"We Had to Be There to Make Sure It Was What We Wanted": Enabling Children's Participation in Family Decision-Making Through the Family Group Conference' (2006) 13(1) *Childhood* 91; Richard Chisholm, 'Children's Participation in Family Court Litigation' (1999) 13(3) *Australian Journal of Family Law* 197, 214–15.

87 Richard Warshak, 'Payoffs and Pitfalls of Listening to Children' (2003) 52(4) *Family Relations* 373, 374.

88 Lundy, Tobin and Parkes (n 48) 399 (emphasis in original). See also Jeremy Roche, 'Children: Rights, Participation and Citizenship' (1999) 6(4) *Childhood* 475; Ranjan Poudyal, *Children and Young People as Citizens: Partners for Social Change* (Save the Children, 2003) 6; CRC Committee, *General Comment No 20 (2016) on the Implementation of the Rights of the Child During Adolescence*, UN Doc CRC/C/GC/20 (6 December 2016) [24].

of institutional structures that more effectively enable children's meaningful participation in decision-making.

8.4.1 Reconceptualising children and childhood: The 'democratisation' of decision-making and debate

In reconceptualising the meaning and value of privacy – from its dominant understanding as informational privacy protection for adults[89] – it is worth reciting Parkinson and Cashmore's observation that '[t]he way we see children and construe their competence has considerable implications for the way society, the law and other institutions treat them'.[90] This book has shown that children experience 'structural disadvantage'[91] owing to their status within the family and in society,[92] and that this disadvantage is magnified for TGD children.[93] It has also illustrated how the child's role in the family and in society more broadly is (re) constructed and framed by judicial decision-making.

A children's rights approach to decisional privacy has a 'transformative' nature.[94] It strives to *change* existing power relations; it is a call for children to be viewed as members of society with valuable and legitimate views, perspectives and voices.[95] Participation is the pivotal concept in debates about children's social inclusion and exclusion. 'Exclusion' is used here to denote the various ways in which children are marginalised or omitted from decision-making processes about matters that affect them, such that their views, wishes and preferences are not taken into account, or are not taken seriously, by adults. Social recognition of children's contributions, through respect for their right to decisional privacy, would go some way towards overcoming children's social exclusion.[96]

89 See Introduction (Section I.2.1).

90 Parkinson and Cashmore (n 58) 8.

91 Anniken Sørlie, 'Legal Gender Meets Reality: A Socio-Legal Children's Perspective' (2015) 33(4) *Nordic Journal of Human Rights* 353, 377.

92 See Martha Albertson Fineman, 'Vulnerability, Resilience, and LGBT Youth' (2014) 23 *Temple Political & Civil Rights Law Review* 307. See also Chapter 1 (Section 1.4.4).

93 Sørlie (n 91) 365.

94 Didier Reynaert and Rudi Roose, 'Children's Rights: A Framework to Eliminate Social Exclusion? Critical Discussions and Tensions' in Martin D Ruck, Michele Peterson-Badali and Michael Freeman (eds), *Handbook of Children's Rights: Global and Multidisciplinary Perspectives* (Taylor & Francis, 2016) 36, 47–8; Lundy, Tobin and Parkes (n 48) 408, 417; Arce (n 81) 367; Tobin, 'Understanding Children's Rights' (n 68) 159–60; Anthony Chase, 'Legitimizing Human Rights: Beyond Mythical Foundations into Everyday Resonances' (2012) 11(4) *Journal of Human Rights* 505, 515.

95 See, eg, Brian Gran, *The Sociology of Children's Rights* (Polity Press, 2021); Roche (n 88) 479; Marc Jans, 'Children as Citizens: Towards a Contemporary Notion of Child Participation' (2004) 11(1) *Childhood* 27; Ruth Lister, 'Why Citizenship: Where, When and How Children?' (2007) 8(2) *Theoretical Inquiries in Law* 693.

96 Reynaert and Roose (n 94) 36; John M Davis, 'Analysing Participation and Social Exclusion with Children and Young People: Lessons from Practice' (2007) 15(1) *International Journal of Children's Rights* 121.

To challenge the policies, structures and practices that have excluded children from society has indeed been the thrust of the children's rights movement from its inception.

A purpose of children's participation is to empower children to challenge the status quo,[97] insofar as existing power structures and institutions deny children their rights, or fail to protect and respect those rights. This process enables children to engage in legal and policy development and political activism,[98] which bears an instrumental role in children's development of autonomy.[99] Research has shown that providing children with opportunities to shape decisions that impact them and to make choices improves children's capacity for independent decision-making.[100]

The case study of this book has illuminated the adverse impacts on TGD children's identity, autonomy, self-esteem and self-worth, of imposing a court authorisation requirement to access medical treatment for gender dysphoria. Facilitated by a court order that she be able to identify herself as the young person the subject of the *Re Jamie* proceedings,[101] Georgie Stone became a prominent activist for TGD children and developed a strong media profile. Georgie explained that 'a very important decision about my body'[102] was 'completely out of my hands, I had to ask a complete stranger for permission to take something I know I need'.[103] Georgie's activism occurred outside 'formal' politico-legal processes and governance, seeking to influence law reform 'from the outside, through lobbying, campaigning and mobilising'.[104] In an online petition that gained almost 16,000 signatures, Georgie championed the rights of 'trans teens',

97 Gerison Lansdown, 'International Developments in Children's Participation: Lessons and Challenges' in E Kay M Tisdall et al (eds), *Children, Young People and Social Inclusion: Participation for What?* (The Policy Press, 2006) 139, 144.

98 Lundy, Tobin and Parkes (n 48) 400–1; E Kay M Tisdall and John M Davis, 'Making a Difference? Bringing Children's and Young People's Views into Policy-Making' (2004) 18(2) *Children & Society* 131; Christine Hallett and Alan Prout (eds), *Hearing the Voices of Children: Social Policy for a New Century* (Routledge, 2003).

99 Lundy, Tobin and Parkes (n 48) 397, 399.

100 See, eg, Leon Mann, Ros Harmoni and Colin Power, 'Adolescent Decision-Making: The Development of Competence' (1989) 12(3) *Journal of Adolescence* 265; Parkinson and Cashmore (n 58) 193–4.

101 See *Re Jamie* [2015] FamCA 455, [46] (Thornton J).

102 Georgie Stone, quoted in Gary Nunn, 'The Transgender Teenager who Helped Change Australia', *BBC News* (online, 15 February 2018) <www.bbc.com/news/world-australia-42940411>.

103 Georgie Stone, quoted in Jo Lauder, 'Transgender Young People Won't Need Court Order for Hormone Treatment', *Triple J Hack,* Australian Broadcasting Corporation (online, 30 November 2017) <www.abc.net.au/triplej/programs/hack/transgender-young-people-not-need-court-order-hormone-treatment/9212876>.

104 Joachim Theis, 'Children as Active Citizens: An Agenda for Children's Civil Rights and Civic Engagement' in Barry Percy-Smith and Nigel Thomas (eds), *A Handbook of Children and Young People's Participation: Perspectives from Theory and Practice* (Routledge, 2009) 343, 351.

which she argued were 'not being protected or upheld'.[105] Georgie's ability to tell her story, in her own words, was especially significant given that adults are often 'not very good at identifying those issues that are actually important to children'[106] – particularly children who are members of a marginalised group in society. This example reinforces Smart's suggestion that transforming understandings of children from 'the objects of law's benevolence' to 'the speaking subjects of law' remains a 'quiet, incomplete revolution'.[107]

The process of 'democratisation'[108] of decision-making also necessitates rethinking the role that children themselves can and should play in determining their best interests. As Oswell has remarked, 'it is impossible now when talking about children not also to talk about their stake in the decision-making process and their role in shaping the institutions and organisations that shape them'.[109] This conceptual shift requires a greater awareness of the impacts on the *rights* of children – as distinct from their parents and the family as an entity – of law and policy.[110]

8.4.2 Institutional structures to enable children's meaningful participation in decision-making

A children's rights approach to decisional privacy requires adults to actively seek out children's views and to take those views seriously; listening to children is not enough.[111] As Eekelaar has argued:

> No society will have begun to perceive its children as rights holders until adults' attitudes and social structures are seriously adjusted towards making it possible for children to express views and towards addressing them with respect.[112]

105 'Remove Family Court of Australia from Medical Decisions for Trans Teens. Legislate Now!', *change.org* (Web Page) <www.change.org/p/parliament-of-australia-remove-family-court-of-australia-from-medical-decisions-for-trans-teens-legislate-now>.

106 Martin D Ruck et al, 'Children's Voices about Children's Rights: Thoughts from Developmental Psychology' in Martin D Ruck, Michele Peterson-Badali and Michael Freeman (eds), *Handbook of Children's Rights: Global and Multidisciplinary Perspectives* (Taylor & Francis, 2016) 597, 598.

107 Carol Smart, 'Children and the Transformation of Family Law' in John Dewar and Stephen Parker (eds), *Family Law: Processes, Practices and Pressures* (Hart Publishing, 2003) 223, 224.

108 Minow and Shanley, 'Relational Rights and Responsibilities' (n 11) 6.

109 David Oswell, *The Agency of Children: From Family to Global Human Rights* (Cambridge University Press, 2013) 4.

110 See Chapter 2 (Section 2.3.1).

111 Tobin, 'Understanding Children's Rights' (n 68) 179; CRC Committee, *General Comment No 12* (n 49) [28]; Lundy, Tobin and Parkes (n 48) 430; Parkinson and Cashmore (n 58) 199.

112 John Eekelaar, 'The Importance of Thinking that Children have Rights' (1992) 6(1) *International Journal of Law, Policy and the Family* 221, 228.

In *Karamalis v Karamalis*,[113] Bennett J acknowledged that considering children's views in decision-making under Part VII of the Family Law Act 'imposes certain responsibilities on decision makers' and 'is a two way street'.[114] These responsibilities relate to the respect afforded children as participants in the process, including by notifying them 'in an appropriate manner' of the outcome of proceedings.[115] Bennett J observed that:

> Children should know that such views as they express will be considered and that their perspectives will not be subsumed and lost in the argument between their parents. Children should be accorded the respect which they will be expected to show to others throughout their lives. This includes taking account of their views and opinions in a dynamic sense, not only when convenient and certainly not to just tick the box next to the numerous additional considerations which we are required to take into account.[116]

The 'smorgasbord of ways'[117] that children can participate in decision-making will be influenced heavily by the resources available for this purpose, as well as the amenability of governments and professionals to facilitating the various means of children's meaningful participation. A frustratingly persistent obstacle to embedding children's meaningful, direct participation – obtaining children's views and wishes not merely through the evidence of adults – within the institutional cultures and structures of courts is inadequate resources, infrastructure and support systems for children.[118]

The significance of children's participation as a feature of a wider social inclusion agenda has been recognised by governments at both the federal and state levels in Australia, with the *National Framework for Protecting Australia's Children 2021-2031* underpinned by the guiding principle, amongst others, of '[l]istening and responding to the voices and views of children and young people and the voices and views of those who care for them'.[119] Significantly, this National Framework recognises that '[c]hildren and young people have the right to participate in decisions that affect them'.[120] One of its stated aims is 'to help children express their views in developing and implementing activities', consistently with the CRC.[121]

113 (2018) 57 Fam LR 588.
114 Ibid 591 [16].
115 Ibid.
116 Ibid [17].
117 Parkinson and Cashmore (n 58) 40.
118 See Ruth Sinclair, 'Participation in Practice: Making it Meaningful, Effective and Sustainable' (2004) 18(2) *Children and Society* 106, 116; Daly (n 68) 229–34 and ch 7; Australian Law Reform Commission, *Family Law for the Future – An Inquiry into the Family Law System* (Report No 135, March 2019) 29–30, 32.
119 *Safe and Supported: The National Framework for Protecting Australia's Children 2021–2031* (Commonwealth of Australia, 2021) 36.
120 Ibid.
121 Ibid 14.

Such a policy statement embraces an appreciation of the fundamental features of a children's rights approach to decisional privacy.[122] How it is implemented in practice, however, may be coloured by the protectionist perspective through which the statement has been developed. The National Framework nonetheless offers a useful example of how governments can promote children's participation in decision-making processes relating to their welfare, by recognising and respecting children as rights-bearers.

8.5 Conclusion

This chapter has rebutted the argument that granting children a right to decisional privacy abstracts the child who is seeking to enforce this right from the child's social and family context, thereby encouraging intra-familial conflict.[123] It has articulated the nexus between a child's substantive right to decisional privacy and procedural rights that enable the child to participate in the decision-making process, within an understanding of children's evolving capacities and the parental role to guide and assist children to exercise their rights. The principled approach provided for accommodating a child's right to decisional privacy within the family – guided by Articles 5 and 12 of the CRC, and underpinned by a relational approach to autonomy – has addressed how potential conflicts in the parent–child relationship might be mediated when children's right to decisional privacy is recognised and respected. The resolution of such conflicts, it has been argued, is that the child's views should be determinative of the child's best interests if the child has reached a sufficient level of maturity and understanding in relation to the matter affecting them. There is no longer a role for parents to play in offering appropriate direction and guidance to their child in the exercise of their rights. This does not mean, however, that children's views will always be determinative in relation to how a decision will be implemented.

This chapter has also explained the social value of children's right to decisional privacy, in terms of promoting children's social inclusion, producing more well-informed decisions and shaping policy and practice. It has mapped out two processes – conceptual and institutional – for translating a theory of children's decisional privacy into practice. A children's rights approach to decisional privacy involves moving away from 'protection from participation' to 'protecting [children] in participation'.[124] Recognising and respecting this right for children promotes major moral changes within families: acknowledging that children have a right to participate in decision-making about issues that affect them transforms the hierarchical parent–child relationship to a more egalitarian one. It also transforms children's status under the law, from passive objects of concern and adult intervention to active subjects with distinct rights and interests. Children's par-

122 See Chapters 2 and 3.
123 Smart (n 107) 238.
124 Parkinson and Cashmore (n 58) 219.

ticipation in decision-making about their lives demands that they are actively and meaningfully engaged in the process. It demands that children's views are listened to, heard and given due weight in accordance with their age and maturity. As a conceptual model, children's right to decisional privacy thus reconfigures the relationships between children and their parents, children and the state, and parents and the state. It recognises that children's participation in decision-making is bound up in a web of power dynamics, discourses and relations. Children's expression of their views, whether those views are determinative of children's best interests, and how those best interests are to be implemented, must be understood within this web.

Conclusion

This book concludes with the voice of Georgie Stone, who became a prominent activist for the rights of TGD children following her experience in requiring court authorisation to undergo medical treatment for gender dysphoria:

> I was powerless – I was 15, and there was someone up there making a very important decision about my body. It was out of my hands, but I knew this was really wrong … Through telling our stories, we got this out into the open. It'd been an issue not many knew or cared about, and we changed that … Knowing no kids will have to experience that ever again was massive.[1]

Georgie's quote encapsulates the argument of this book: that court involvement in medical treatment decision-making for TGD children has denied them the ability to ask the 'practical question' and live accordingly: 'how do I want to live, what sort of person do I want to be, and how I should best strive for my own good in my own way?'[2] To have their right to decisional privacy in this context overlooked, rejected, manipulated or politicised rendered these children, in Georgie's words, 'powerless'.

Georgie's quote also illustrates the value of 'telling our stories' to illuminate matters of concern to children and to instigate change. Georgie's advocacy[3] for the rights of TGD children and young people shows that children's rights 'offer a way in: they open doors' for those who have been excluded or marginalised; they also offer 'fora for action'.[4] However, without a 'secure conceptual foundation', Tobin has cautioned that 'children's rights risk becoming invisible to, or rejected

1 Georgie Stone, quoted in Gary Nunn, 'The Transgender Teenager who Helped Change Australia', *BBC News* (online, 15 February 2018) <www.bbc.com/news/world-australia-42940411>.

2 Beate Rossler, *The Value of Privacy* (Polity, 2005) 43, 50–51.

3 See Michelle Telfer et al, 'Transgender Adolescents and Legal Reform: How Improved Access to Healthcare was Achieved through Medical, Legal and Community Collaboration' (2018) 54(10) *Journal of Paediatrics and Child Health* 1096.

4 Michael Freeman, 'The Human Rights of Children' (2010) 63(1) *Current Legal Problems* 1, 18 ('Human Rights of Children'). See also Chapter 8 (Section 8.4).

DOI: 10.4324/9781003224167-12

by, those for whom they are not self-evident', and vulnerable to manipulation as a 'rhetorical device' for 'subjective preferences or political agendas'.[5]

By developing a sound conceptual framework within which children's rights are located, this book has sought to enhance children's voices in decision-making processes about matters that affect them, and to improve the willingness and ability of adult decision-makers to listen to and hear those voices. It has done so by reconceptualising the meaning and value of privacy from a children's rights perspective. The theory of children's right to decisional privacy presented is a right which enables children to 'make their own lives, rather than having their lives made for them'.[6]

Decisional privacy, as it has been defined in this book, protects an individual's ability to make decisions which contribute to defining their identity, free from the unjustifiable interference of other individuals or the state.[7] It creates an area for choices and the development of 'plans of life'[8] and a sense of self. The value of privacy has been justified as inhering in the value placed on autonomy in liberal societies. That is, privacy is a necessary condition for enabling individuals to live autonomously. Autonomy has been conceptualised as embracing both negative freedom (the absence of intervention by the state and others) and positive freedom (personal self-determination and reflection about how an individual wishes to live their life).[9]

The notion of autonomy in relation to children and their lives has never sat comfortably, driven by the dominant conception of children in Western liberal societies as vulnerable, dependent on adults and incapable of rational decision-making.[10] To counter this discomfort, a relational, gradual and evolving understanding of autonomy, rather than a static and individualistic one, has been advanced.[11] Such an understanding enables children to be conceptualised as having the capacity for autonomy, and in some circumstances, in fact possessing autonomy. It also recognises that a child's autonomy is both enabled and constrained by their social context, including the role of the family in society and the complex nature of a child's family relationships.[12]

The children's rights approach to decisional privacy developed in this book consists of four fundamental principles:[13] (i) children are subjects with distinct rights and interests; (ii) children exercise autonomy consistent with their evolving capacities; (iii) children require appropriate direction and guidance in the exercise

5 John Tobin, 'Justifying Children's Rights' (2013) 21 *International Journal of Children's Rights* 395, 398.
6 Freeman, 'Human Rights of Children' (n 4) 17.
7 See Chapter 1 (Section 1.2.3).
8 John Rawls, *A Theory of Justice* (Harvard University Press, 1971) 407–15, §63.
9 See Chapter 1 (Section 1.3).
10 See Chapter 1 (Section 1.4.1).
11 See Chapter 1 (Section 1.4.3).
12 See Chapter 1 (Section 1.4.4).
13 See Chapter 2 (Section 2.3).

of their rights; and (iv) children must meaningfully participate in decision-making about their lives. It has been argued that this fourth principle is the most critical, as children require procedural rights to be able to exercise their substantive right to decisional privacy effectively. Meaningful participation is essential to children's experience of autonomy and for offering children the independence to forge their identities and to make choices that help to define them and their values. Emphasis has been placed upon the unique and significant role of parents in supporting and enabling children to enjoy their right to decisional privacy.[14] The nature of parental direction and guidance shifts and its degree diminishes as children mature and develop, thereby enabling children to experience increasing agency, autonomy and responsibility in the enjoyment and exercise of their rights.[15]

This book has also highlighted a deep-seated anxiety about the notion of children's rights, including how those rights might undermine parental rights and authority and the institution of the family.[16] A children's rights approach balances the child's rights and best interests (which are not necessarily opposed) against the rights and interests of other individuals and groups affected by the decision, through an 'inclusive and nuanced'[17] process that moves beyond the shallow rhetoric that 'we are all doing what we think is best for the child'.[18] This conceptual model can thus respond to criticisms that recognising and respecting children's right to decisional privacy when determining children's best interests would threaten 'parental control rights'[19] or would be unworkable in practice. Put simply, 'children's rights' rhetoric is not a trump card in all matters requiring the determination of a child's best interests.

The theory of children's decisional privacy has been applied, for illustrative purposes, to the context of judicial proceedings concerning medical treatment for children experiencing gender dysphoria. This case study has shown that the role of courts in moderating the relationship between children's rights, identity and autonomy remains fraught in both Australia and the UK. There are significant tensions in this area of healthcare between recognising and upholding children's rights, respecting parental responsibilities and maintaining the court's duty to 'protect the rights of children and to promote their welfare'.[20] In both conceptual and practical terms, TGD children have been excluded from the decision-making

14 See Chapter 2 (Section 2.3.3) and Chapter 8 (Section 8.2.1).
15 See Chapter 2 (Section 2.3.3) and Chapter 8 (Section 8.3.2).
16 See Chapter 8 (Sections 8.2 and 8.3).
17 John Tobin, 'Judging the Judges: Are they Adopting the Rights Approach in Matters involving Children?' (2009) 33(2) *Melbourne University Law Review* 579, 589.
18 John Eekelaar, 'Deciding for Children' (2006) 7(2) *Australian Journal of Professional and Applied Ethics* 66, 77.
19 Scott Altman, 'Parental Control Rights' in Elizabeth Brake and Lucinda Ferguson (eds), *Philosophical Foundations of Children's and Family Law* (Oxford University Press, 2018) 209.
20 *Family Law Act 1975* (Cth) s 43(1)(c).

process for their medical treatment and 'denied the agency to autonomously determine and express their gender identity'.[21]

For children experiencing gender dysphoria, the need for court authorisation of medical treatment that so fundamentally affects their current desires and identity, as well as their future values and long-term choices, curtails those children's ability to choose. Having a court determine whether they can commence treatment, or whether they have the capacity to consent to treatment, takes their right to decisional privacy 'completely out of [their] hands'.[22] The common thread that binds the three appellate judgments analysed in this book – those of the Full Court of the Family Court of Australia in *Re Jamie*[23] and *Re Kelvin*,[24] and that of the Court of Appeal of England and Wales in *R (Bell) v The Tavistock and Portman NHS Foundation Trust*[25] – is that the decisions raise the uncomfortable spectre of ongoing judicial validation of TGD children's gender identity. The case study has reinforced the observation of Berg and Cave that:

> as involvement in medical decision-making is designed both to recognize and facilitate a child's developing autonomy, questions about treatments that go to fundamental issues of identity, such as ... treatment for gender dysphoria, highlight the difficulties with our current frameworks and indicate how much more work needs to be done in this area.[26]

The case study has also shown that the issue of *who* decides what medical treatment is appropriate for a child evokes society's normative beliefs about children's capacity and autonomy. Acknowledging that *how* such decisions are made – according to what criteria and in what manner – differs as between the 'public' and 'private' regulation of children's lives, and raises the challenge of how the law can and should protect children's rights.[27] This book has exposed that challenge in the context of medical treatment for children experiencing gender dysphoria. It would be an equally valid concern in relation to a plethora of other issues concerning children. The aim is to make children not only present and visible in decision-making processes about matters that affect them (where

21 Sara Frödén and Ann Quennerstedt, 'The Child as a Gendered Rights Holder' (2020) 27(2) *Childhood* 143, 150. See also Shannon Price Minter, 'Supporting Transgender Children: New Legal, Social, and Medical Approaches' (2012) 59(3) *Journal of Homosexuality* 422; Kasia Szczerbinski, 'I Am Whoever You Say I Am: How the Custodial Decisions of Parents Can Affect and Limit a Transgender Child's Freedom and State of Mind' (2016) 36(3) *Children's Legal Rights Journal* 177.

22 Jamie, quoted in *Re Jamie* [2015] FamCA 455, [65].

23 [2013] FamCAFC 110. See Chapter 5.

24 [2017] FamCAFC 258. See Chapter 6.

25 [2021] EWCA Civ 1363. See Chapter 7.

26 Jessica Berg and Emma Cave, 'Patient Autonomy, Capacity and Consent: Children' in David Orentlicher and Tamara K Hervey (eds), *The Oxford Handbook of Comparative Health Law* (Oxford University Press, 2021) 459, 473–4.

27 Graeme Austin, *Children: Stories the Law Tells* (Victoria University Press, 1994) 147.

they have previously been absent and invisible), but most importantly, to make children's own, unfiltered voices audible to adults.

The theory of children's right to decisional privacy developed in this book challenges the existing power dynamics between children, their parents and the state, with a view to enhancing children's ability to participate effectively in decision-making processes. At a policy level, the task is to progress children's status under the law – most critically, by ensuring that children have a meaningful opportunity to express their views and to be heard – in such a way that the notion of 'children's rights' does not become a rhetorical proxy for 'parental interests'.[28] According to the CRC Committee, this requires 'dismantling the legal, political, economic, social and cultural barriers that currently impede children's opportunity to be heard and their access to participation in all matters that affect them'.[29] Dismantling these barriers may prove a formidable task, requiring as it will countering the prevailing assumptions about children's incapacity, vulnerability and dependence.

Most vitally, the CRC Committee has said that 'making reality of the human rights of children … needs to engage all sectors of society and, of course, children themselves'.[30] If this is so, then ultimately, translating a theory of children's decisional privacy into practice will require engendering a stronger commitment from adults, who are key to upholding and giving effect to children's rights. This need becomes more pressing if it is accepted that children are a 'segment of the community who in the main have little political clout and rely on the moral integrity of adults for respect of their rights and protection of their interests'.[31]

In a judgment delivered in 2004, the Family Court of Australia asserted that:

> The law relating to children in this country now unequivocally and unapologetically treats children as active shapers of their own lives and able to make decisions independently of adults.[32]

It would be optimistic, even naïve, to claim that this currently is, or has ever been, the case in Australia or elsewhere. But the author's humble hope is that it might be one day – and that this book is embraced by adult decision-makers as an opportunity to reflect on *how* they make decisions for and about children, and how children can become more 'active shapers of their own lives' by playing a meaningful role in those decision-making processes.

28 See Katherine Hunt Federle, 'Review Essay: Rights, Not Wrongs' (2009) 17 *International Journal of Children's Rights* 321, 324; John Tobin, 'Understanding Children's Rights: A Vision beyond Vulnerability' (2015) 84 *Nordic Journal of International Law* 155, 177.

29 CRC Committee, *General Comment No 12 (2009): The Right of the Child to be Heard*, UN Doc CRC/C/GC/12 (20 July 2009) [135].

30 CRC Committee, *General Comment No 5: General Measures of Implementation for the Convention on the Rights of the Child*, UN Doc CRC/GC/2003/5 (27 November 2003) [1].

31 Alastair Nicholson, 'Advancing Children's Rights and Interests: The Need for Better Inter-Governmental Collaboration' (1996) 26(2) *Western Australian Law Review* 249, 249–50.

32 *W v G (No 1)* (2004) 35 Fam LR 417, 430 [108] (Carmody J).

Index

For Product Safety Concerns and Information please contact our EU representative GPSR@taylorandfrancis.com Taylor & Francis Verlag GmbH, Kaufingerstraße 24, 80331 München, Germany